THE PROBLEM OF
THE CHRISTIAN MASTER

THE PROBLEM OF THE CHRISTIAN MASTER

Augustine in the Afterlife of Slavery

MATTHEW ELIA

Yale
UNIVERSITY PRESS
NEW HAVEN & LONDON

Published with assistance from the Louis Stern Memorial Fund.

Yale University Press books may be purchased in quantity
for educational, business, or promotional use. For information, please
email sales.press@yale.edu (U.S. office) or sales@yaleup.co.uk (U.K. office).

Set in Spectral type by IDS Infotech, Ltd.
Printed in the United States of America.

Library of Congress Control Number: 2023952234
ISBN 978-0-300-26659-7 (hardcover : alk. paper)

A catalogue record for this book is available from the British Library.

This paper meets the requirements of
ANSI/NISO Z39.48-1992 (Permanence of Paper).

10 9 8 7 6 5 4 3 2 1

A slave, caught in a sin which is such that he is held worthy of cleaning the sewer, adorns the sewer even in his disgrace. Both these things, the slave's disgrace and the cleaning of the sewer, are joined together and brought into a certain kind of unity, adapted to and woven into an orderly household . . . a whole with the most orderly beauty.
—Augustine, *On Free Choice of the Will* (c. 390)

The master sees the horrors of slavery with unseeing eyes.
—W. E. B. Du Bois, *John Brown* (1909)

Contents

LIST OF ABBREVIATIONS   ix

INTRODUCTION. Dusk   1

ONE. The Master's House   16

TWO. The Road and the Woods   41

THREE. The Form of the Slave   83

FOUR. Abolition's Time   120

FIVE. The Table and the Sea   159

EPILOGUE. Tenebrae   175

ACKNOWLEDGMENTS   207

NOTES   211

INDEX   273

Abbreviations

For the sake of readability, I have restricted the Latin titles of Augustine's works to the endnotes and parenthetical citations in the text. In the body of the text, I use the title of the English translation which, except where noted, belongs to the Works of Saint Augustine series published by New City Press.

civ.	*De civitate Dei (The City of God)*
conf.	*Confessiones (Confessions)*
lib. arb.	*De libero arbitrio (On Free Choice of the Will)*
doct. Chr.	*De doctrina christiana (Teaching Christianity)*
en. Ps.	*Enarrationes in Psalmos (Expositions of the Psalms)*
ep.	*Epistulae (Letters)*
Gn. adv. Man.	*De Genesi adversus Manichaeos (On Genesis: A Refutation of the Manichees)*
Gn. litt.	*De Genesi ad litteram (The Literal Meaning of Genesis)*
Jo. ev. tr.	*In Johannis evangelium tractatus (Homilies on the Gospel of John)*
qu. Hept.	*Quaestiones in Heptateuchum (Questions on the Heptateuch)*
s.	*Sermons*
Trin.	*De Trinitate (On the Trinity)*
vera rel.	*De vera religione (True Religion)*
WSA	*Works of Saint Augustine: A Translation for the 21st Century*, ed. John E. Rotelle (Hyde Park, NY: New City Press, c. 1990-)

THE PROBLEM OF
THE CHRISTIAN MASTER

Dusk

In the midst of these dark shadows of the social life . . .
—Augustine, *The City of God*

It has been dusk for four hundred years.
—Saidiya Hartman, "The Time of Slavery"

Ask an undergraduate what they recall of the *Confessions* of Augustine and—if it isn't his anguish over sex, or the restlessness of his heart until it rests in God—it's sure to be the pears. Pears he doesn't want, stolen to impress friends he doesn't like—who can't relate? Narrating the human condition at the site of this theft, Augustine merges two of his favorite images: slavery and the shadows. "Here is a runaway slave," he laments, "fleeing his master and pursuing a shadow. What rottenness!"[1] Just twelve words in Latin, the lines seized my attention when I first encountered them, then never quite let go. Years passed, and now there is this book—my attempt to unfold all that lies compressed within them. I want to pull apart, gently and with care, their fragile threads of meaning, woven here so tightly that they have come to appear seamless, as though there were no threads at all. More than seamless—inescapable. A picture Augustine offers us of God, and of human life away from God, that would prove so enthralling that even those ambivalent or indifferent or hostile toward Augustine himself cannot seem to do without the terms of the scene: God as master fled, man the sinner fleeing, a world drained of light and thrown into the terror of shadow.

The picture certainly did not originate with the fifth-century bishop of Hippo.[2] But he improvised within its terms more brilliantly than those around him, I will suggest, and so came to take up the imaginative possibilities afforded him by a slave society, transforming them inside an emerging conception of Christian political order—at precisely the moment that society found itself hurtling toward collapse.[3] This is not a book that tars Augustine for his qualified, theologically serious defense of slavery, but nor does it absolve him of it. Rather, I am interested in what the enduring picture woven by these three threads—the master, the slave, the shadows—aims to capture, and especially in what eludes that capture, what slips off silently into the night. The book is not about the "ethics" of slavery. It is about a *break* that emerges within the kind of moral worlds slavery makes—a fracture we will discover in a moment as we follow the path Augustine carves for us into what he calls famously, in *The City of God*, "these dark shadows of the social life." Only inside that break can we glimpse what I will term, in this book, *the enduring problem of the Christian master*, then probe why it matters for our political crises today.

Matters for whom? For scholars and Christians who have recently made a striking return to the Augustinian tradition for help in reimagining a contemporary ethic of democratic citizenship (about whom, much more in what follows), as well as for their critics, who sometimes remain tempted to imagine that by dismissing Augustine as predecessor, we will have left his troubling inheritance behind. (I'll suggest we can't be rid of him so easily.)[4] But the book is also for anyone who—perhaps especially in a post-Trump moment of democratic crisis—has grown dissatisfied with the state of the "religion and the public square" conversation.[5] For those who have noticed that conversation's inability to reckon with what stood in public squares not so long ago: auction blocks where, church steeples looking on, human commodities were bought and sold.[6] For those who notice that the enormity of this violence has not ceased so much as taken new forms. And for those who notice that despite its enormity the violence nevertheless failed to suppress the worldmaking practices of those bought and sold throughout the modern Atlantic world—that is, failed to erase Black people's thinking and living, diasporic innovations in social life under immense duress.[7] The book shows how race still matters for religion and vice versa. But more, it asks: How has the Christian imagination which *produced* those steeples been disrupted, unmade, and transformed by the creativity and critique emanating from life at and beyond the auction block? What might the rigors and complexity of an ongoing task of unmaking and transforming

Introduction

Christian political thinking demand of us in the present? (And of course: who is the *us*?)

This book is the first to bring the Augustinian tradition of political thought into extended conversation with Black Studies.[8] It belongs neither to specialist literature on Augustine (though it is informed by such literature) nor to a narrow "confessional" theology—its purpose neither to impugn Augustine nor absolve him. Rather, it finds in Augustinianism an opening—a window inside which to glimpse a deeper crisis at the heart of the western philosophical-theological tradition itself. This crisis is the enduring problem of the Christian master: the alignment in late antiquity of Christian thought with the standpoint of the master class, its withering effects upon the transformative social possibilities implicit in the Christian story, and its afterlife as an ongoing, if undertheorized, dimension of our democratic crisis today—amid enduring racial violence, mass incarceration, and a troubling global resurgence of white nationalist politics. My purpose is to understand how *this* public square—haunted by the auction block, the plantation, and the ghosts of slaves and masters and those who looked on—yet shapes the conditions for religious participation in democratic struggles toward justice today.

In the last two decades, scholars of religion and politics made a striking return to Augustine's texts, not just as objects of historical interest, but as constructive resources for reimagining citizenship, virtue, and religion's role in public life.[9] But while Augustine-inspired engagements with various aspects of contemporary politics proliferate—its secularism, liberalism, pluralism, and more—no Augustinian project has directly confronted the *racialized* character of political modernity: how white supremacy structures its institutions, how colonial legacies haunt the category of the citizen, and especially, how the racial hierarchies entrenched by slavery did not disappear, but still pervade the conditions for democratic life and thought today. Nor have Augustinians reckoned with how this underside of modernity, when faced, would reconfigure what sort of questions we bring to Augustine in the first place, while providing a previously unexplored vantage from which to assess the legacies of Augustinian thought. At once timely and long overdue, this reckoning is the aim of *The Problem of the Christian Master: Augustine in the Afterlife of Slavery.* Centered upon the enduring problem of the Christian master, the surprising connections (and sharp disjunctures) between Augustinian politics and Black Studies are neither arbitrary nor obvious. To see more, we return to Augustine's seamless picture and begin there as the shadows grow longer at dusk.

·

Here is a fugitive slave, fleeing his master, pursuing a shadow. What rottenness. Translators name two allusions Augustine has in mind: Henry Chadwick notes Job 7:2; Maria Boulding points to Genesis 3:8–10.[10] In this merging of Job and Genesis, the significance of the link between slavery and shadows begins to emerge. The line from Job reads: "Like a slave who longs for the shadow / and like laborers who look for their wages." The passage from Genesis yields the man and the woman, hiding from God beneath the trees "at the time of the evening breeze." Both scenes unfold at dusk. In Augustine's scriptural imagination, Job's figure of the slave—desiring an end to the day's toil—echoes and recalls the primordial parents, crouching in the shade as the sun falls. In context, the line marks Job's poetic image of human existence itself as a kind of slavery: "hard service on the earth."[11] If life is like an enslaved person's long day of work, Job reasons, then naturally human beings look forward to its end—an end figured symbolically in the Hebrew word *sēl*, "shadow." A double entendre, *sēl* invokes "shadows" as an image of the transience of human life (as used also in 8:9 and 14:2), even as, commentators note, "for the oppressed slave . . . the shadow which marks the end of life is in reality a refreshing 'shade.' "[12]

On this reading, Job's metaphor depends for its coherence upon imagining what shadows could signify "for the oppressed slave," that is, from the imagined vantage of the enslaved person. Its unsettling power and ambiguity hang on being able to imagine how an enslaved person might long for day's end, cool winds after heat, relief from the master's gaze. In 3:18–19, Job imagines the realm of the dead as a place finally beyond unfreedom: "There the prisoners are at ease together / they hear not the voice of the taskmaster. / The small and the great are there, / and the slave is free from his master." *Hear not.* Death as blessed silence. A place emptied at last of the voices of masters, droning on and on.

Augustine reads the passage differently.[13] In *Notes on Job,* a series of sparse and scattered remarks dated to 399 (nearly contemporaneous with the composition of *Confessions),* Augustine makes explicit the connection of Job to Genesis which both translators of *Confessions* imply. He quotes the

Introduction

line from Job in Latin translation (in italics here), then provides his own gloss by way of Genesis 3: *"like a slave who fears his master and pursues a shadow* (7:2), which signifies Adam's concealment from the face of the Lord, and the covering of leaves, from which a shadow is cast, which the man pursued when he deserted God."[14]

With the "shadow" transplanted and recontextualized, the enslaved person's longing for relief becomes the sinner's abandoning his God. For Augustine, writes Paul Griffiths, "sinners are like those who exchange God for a shadow . . . they abandon substance for its insubstantial counterfeits, an act for which Augustine's paradigm is Adam's futile attempt to hide himself from God in the shade of Eden's trees after eating the forbidden fruit (Gen. 3:8–10)."[15] Augustine's reading works seamlessly with his emerging metaphysics of evil as *privatio*—evil as only a shadow of the real, defection from being itself, flight from the Lord's created order.

Are the shadows of fugitive flight Augustine's "rottenness" or Job's "refreshing shade"? It seems to depend on who you are, on where you find yourself in relation to order. At issue for us is not determining which reading is "right" (or what rightness would mean), but displaying how the divergence itself brings into view the central conflict of using slavery symbolically—a disjuncture the slavery metaphors inscribe into the two readings introduced here, Job's and Augustine's.[16] This gap introduces the *break* mentioned above and the question of what that break implies about how slavery functions symbolically in Augustine's, and perhaps Augustinian, thought. For Augustine, the shadows to which the fugitive slave flees can function as coherent symbols of evil and nothingness *precisely insofar as the master being fled is an unequivocally good master*—God—rendering the act of flight itself evil.[17] This symbolic procedure—as I will argue in what follows, but can only hint toward now—indicates something about the deep, ambivalent Augustinian interest *in* and alignment *with* the position of the master. For him, the position of the master, when critiqued and recalibrated inside an emerging Christian conception of political order during this fallen age, opens profound moral, theological, and political possibilities. Indeed, this book is about the challenges posed to politics by how we remain, in complex ways, inside these possibilities, and so ensnared by the enduring problem of the Christian master.

But the other way of reading Job—the one sketched above—does not seem similarly interested in preserving the figure of the good master. (Read the rest of Job to find out why, but that isn't quite the point here.) It places

— 5 —

the emphasis elsewhere, such that the passage gains sense only if one reads with attention not simply to "the slave"—for Augustine too is interested in, indeed *identifies* himself with that position—but rather with a delicate and precise sense for what an enslaved human being under duress might *want*. Which is to say, a sense for the way the time of the shadows, the moment of approaching dusk in twilight and darkness, might be "longed for." Desired for how "lengthening evening shadows" open up a life conceived *elsewhere*— beyond the master's reach.[18] Dusk is the scene of a fracture opening up: a chasm between what the master wants and a set of prospects and plans inscrutable to the eyes of those yet to learn that a person is not a thing.[19]

•

Here is a fugitive slave, fleeing her master, pursuing a shadow. It is this notion of dusk as prospect—possibility, not privation—which later fugitive interpretive traditions in Black thought would seize upon. Dwight N. Hopkins calls it "sundown to sunup time," an evocative and poetic term for the nighttime insurgency of plantation life. Shadow time reclaimed by enslaved people for themselves is contrasted against "sunup to sundown time invented by the slave master."[20] The master's sunup to sundown time included, centrally, the "architecture of slavery churches"—the white steeples looking on, the master's religion in the public square. Against and beyond this conception, alternative "religious means, theological myths, and regularized rituals" would emerge after the sun went down, presenting forms of life otherwise and elsewhere, inside "a dimension often hidden from plantation owners, though it might be displayed before their unseeing eyes."[21]

At dusk "slaveholding men . . . looked with suspicion on the landscape they created," write architectural historians Clifton Ellis and Rebecca Ginsburg:

Each day when the sun set, a new landscape emerged in which slaves moved more freely and not always with benign intent. Male slaveholders acknowledged a loss of control when they instituted and maintained nightly slave patrols. This nightly ritual was so ubiquitous and emphatic that historian John Hope Franklin likened the nighttime South to "an armed camp." Slaveholders often found themselves constricted by the very environments they so diligently arranged and commanded.[22]

Dusk as doctrine of creation: *a new landscape emerged.* As ecological ethic: *the very environments* invite a verb. They *constrict* the slaveholders who ordered them. Dusk as liminal time, a time lived at the edges of the master's *loss of control.* Revealing and concealing, bordering known and unknown, dusk is also danger. It is *entre chien et loup,* in an old French expression, the time "between dog and wolf," as the light dims and you risk mistaking one for the other—a figure of threat in the guise of a friend. The phrase has Latin roots, one linguist says, from "ancient times [when] villages were often located in a clearing on the edge of the forest. The Latin word *foris* (which is the root of 'forest' and 'foreign' in English) means 'outside.' The forest was the outside, the territory of the wolf—the dark, the night and fear from prehistoric times through the Middle Ages."[23] These memories, their subtle traces preserved silently across languages, are among the threads woven into Augustine's scene as we receive it today. Dusk as seam—joining forest to village, outside to in, bordering night and day, wild and safe, animal and human. *Here is a fugitive slave, fleeing her master, pursuing a shadow.* No wonder dusk for masters is fraught.

But for precisely this reason, as Hopkins has pointed out, dusk for others is an opening. Dusk opens a light of flight and a dimension of freedom, as suggested in lines from "Sundown" by the poet Elma Stuckey, drawn from songs she heard growing up amid formerly enslaved people in her north Memphis neighborhood in the early twentieth century:

> The sun's goin' down, heavenly Lord,
> And I go right behind it.
> Cover my track, heavenly Lord,
> And Ole Marse never find it.[24]

As shadows stretch across the plantation landscape at dusk, a fugitive invocation of "heavenly Lord" in lines 1 and 3 plays off "Ole Marse" in line 4. The plantation master tended to posit an analogy between the two, whereby his own position of benevolent mastery over the slave is sanctioned as imperfect echo of God, who is the true master of both.[25] Where masters posited an analogy, the fugitive song posits a break—a divergence at sundown between the plantation master's desire to recapture the fugitive and the heavenly Lord's desire to cover her tracks, conceal flight, and confound what earthly masters want. Theologically and practically, Ole Marse and the Lord aren't on the same side.[26]

What comes into view, then, is the possibility of recognizing a fracture between sunup-to-sundown and sundown-to-sunup approaches to reading, moral reasoning, and theologizing—a break which opens in the shadows, in the twilight space between variant uses of slavery's symbolic resources for imagining life with God and one another. For a variety of complex reasons to be explored in what follows, Augustine does not generally attend to the theological and ethical possibilities implicit in an enslaved person's "longing for" something beyond and otherwise than being properly mastered. This inattention operates not despite, but precisely in and through what will emerge as a defining habit of the intellectual labors of masters: rhetorically identifying themselves *with* the position of "the slave," as Augustine so often does.[27]

The shadows then, might be imaginatively reworked as the scene of this break: the twilight moment of the day, in which unfolds a diverging of paths for those invested in the position of the master and those in flight from such investments—both financial and psychic—a parting of ways which is also a contestation (Hopkins calls it a "battle") between opposed ethical modes of faith, forms of life. These contestations, I will argue, are not limited to holding competing positions on the institution of slavery itself. We are far beyond something like the "ethics" of slavery. Rather, the break I have suggested here extends subtly but decisively into other matters too. As historian Vincent Brown writes, "the farther slaveholders moved toward the goal of complete mastery, the more they found that struggles with their human property would continue, *even into the most elemental realms: birth, hunger, health, fellowship, sex, death, and time.*"[28]

•

If the way Augustine employs slavery as a symbolic and conceptual resource tends to align him with the vantage of the master, then this alignment calls us not simply to attend to his position on slavery in the oft-discussed Book 19 of *The City of God,* as many have done, but rather to track the underlying problem of mastery across a deeper and wider and more *elemental* range of ethical concerns: *fellowship, sex, death, time,* and more. Indeed, as we will see, it takes us deep inside the very sites of his ethical thought which prominent Christian thinkers in the political Augustinian conversation have most wanted to repurpose for contemporary democratic life. In Chapter 1,

I develop a rationale for bringing these two modes of inquiry together—Augustinian politics and Black Studies—and an approach for doing so, one which centers not upon "applying" Augustinian concepts to previously neglected "race issues," but upon drawing from Black political and religious thought to explore the deeper question of why and how this neglect occurs in the first place, how it shapes Augustinian engagements with these most elemental realms of Christian political thought, and what might be done moving forward. (I also address certain methodological problems and anticipate key objections to the method.) Put schematically, this approach consists in taking up one key theme of Augustinian political thought at a time in order to explore (a) how Augustine uses slavery to clarify, amplify, or make concrete his treatment of it; (b) how this use of slavery metaphors presumes alignment with the standpoint of the master; and (c) how the problems generated thereby present us with parallel moral dynamics in the present, which can be addressed by thinking with modern Black thought on the afterlife of slavery, including key reception histories of Augustinian thought within it.[29] Each of the next three chapters examines an Augustinian theme in its relation to this previously neglected dimension, namely, how entanglement with the master's position shapes the way Augustine and the Augustinian tradition have deployed that theme within Christian political thought.

Chapter 2, "The Road and the Woods," applies this approach to the signature Augustinian theme of "pilgrimage" (*peregrinatio*) as an image of Christian citizenship: the notion that Christians are like exiles on the move through this world, toward their true homeland in heaven.[30] Tracking this image through *Confessions* and key sermons, I show how the pilgrim works in tandem with a second figure—the fugitive slave. In both, the symbol of bodies in motion, exposed to terror and without home in this world, gives rise to thought. But whereas, for modern readers, the image of fugitive slaves evokes the Underground Railroad, the courage of Tubman, and the resistance of Douglass, Augustine's symbolic system invests the fugitive with wholly negative moral valence, indeed, with the precise opposite moral evaluation of the pilgrim: the latter signifies the heavenly city's humble citizens, the former the false freedom of the disobedient. The latter sticks faithfully to the road, the former strays from it, finding life in the woods.[31] Drawing from treatments of fugitivity in Black thought—Douglass, Saidiya Hartman, Neil Roberts—I show how Augustine's moral-symbolic contrast between pilgrim and fugitive presents a problem for contemporary

Augustinian redeployments, insofar as it attains coherence only from the master's side of the master–slave relation and thus risks aligning would-be pilgrims with the interests of the master class. To reanimate its power to foster democratic belonging, Christian thought must reorient itself around the forms of collective life taking place in the woods—the hidden and unthought spaces of political life today, still moving in flight from the official, the regulatory, the normative—and explore how Christian pilgrims might reimagine their journey through the world as solidarity with those in fugitive motion.

The third chapter, "The Form of the Slave," begins from Lewis Ayres's perceptive observation that, in the text of Philippians 2, and especially in "the form of the slave," Augustine finds not only an exegetical tool, but "a comprehensive conception of what it means to read scriptural accounts of Christ at this moment in the life of faith." Ayres calls this Augustine's "Panzer text"—a "tank" he trundles onto the doctrinal battlefield, mowing down all heterodox positions in its path.[32] I examine how Augustine uses slavery to interpret Christ's identity, which unfolds as a complex negotiation between two figures of the Roman household: first, the *filius* of the *Dominus,* the son of the Master, which Christ is "by nature"; second, the *servus,* the "form of the slave," which Christ assumes in the incarnation. Tracking these symbolic forms, son and slave, through *On the Trinity* 1–2 and key sermons, I demonstrate the ways Augustine imagines the political significance of Christ's central virtue—*humilitas*—by appealing to obedient slaves and humble masters, tropes which are not morally neutral, but reflect an evaluative regime bound to the master's self-interest. Bringing this tradition into clearer view by way of one reception history of Augustine's thought in the famed "Augustinian piety" of Cotton Mather—illumined by critical tools from W. E. B. Du Bois and James Cone—I then contest recent treatments of humility as virtue formation by reframing their treatment of these topics in the racialized context of the afterlife of slavery.

Chapter 4, "Abolition's Time," begins at one of the few extended comments on Augustine's thought in Black Studies, as David Scott invokes Augustine's searing meditations on temporality. It is not merely that political life takes place *in* time, but that something about doing politics *temporalizes*: it makes and unmakes our experience of time's passage, alters how we remember the past (or how and why we forget it), and conditions what we anticipate as possible and impossible in the future. The chapter examines how for Augustine, as Scott writes, "fictive models of time shape our experience," that is, not simply how we imagine time, but how imagined temporalities inhabit us, foreclose or open lines of theological and ethical inquiry, and thus constrain or enable forms of life. At issue specifically is how the Augustinian "fictive model" of the present time—*saeculum,* and especially what he calls *in hoc saeculo,* "in this age"—shapes his narration of where slavery comes from, what it's for, and how it structures agency, human and divine. His strongest argument in defense of slavery is the *inevitability* of slavery or slaverylike forms of domination under the present conditions of fallenness. Yet John Rist rightly points out that the same is true of concupiscence (our disordered desires)—these cannot, on Augustine's own account, be eliminated in this life; yet here, unlike slavery, Augustine insists the struggle against it must be undertaken anyway.[33] This chapter suggests that the most promising avenue forward is to reanimate this Augustinian mode of enduring struggle in the present by highlighting how its power to foster belonging has been hampered by its alignment with the position of the master. Overcoming the enduring position of the master would mean placing Augustinian patience in conversation with that specific sensibility of contemporary Black abolitionist thinking which believes—to invoke Angela Davis's oft-cited dictum—that "freedom is a constant struggle." Contemporary abolitionist struggles against the racialized carceral state's threat to democratic life provide a fruitful site for seeing how the critique and transformation of Augustinian political theology works in a concrete moment of struggle in the Black Lives Matter era.

Chapter 5, "The Table and the Sea," recapitulates the argument, then asks: What then do we do with Christian language and practices involving longstanding imagery drawn from mastery and slavery? Now that the signifying system of slavery clings to the historic western Christian theological grammar we've inherited, how might it be used otherwise, turned in a new direction? Here I make clear that Augustine's thought is not jettisoned, but constructively brought into encounter with Black and womanist thought. While rejecting that moral approach Katie Grimes has rightly criticized as "sacramental optimism"—and *"depristinating"* the category of practice itself as Lauren Winner has done—I take as my starting point a suggestive rereading of the founding practices of Christian signification, the Lord's Supper and baptism. This rereading is informed by both Augustine's theory of signs and Black Studies' interventions into theories of signification, grounded in the Black Christology inaugurated by James Cone, animated by the possibility introduced at the end of Chapter 2: solidarity between the pilgrim and the fugitive, solidarity at the shadow point linking the road to the woods. In the Epilogue, "Tenebrae," I explore a return to the shadows opened by "Dusk," now drawn within a wider narration of twilight and reconfigured by the liturgical practice of tenebrae, and in this way note some implications for wider questions of contemporary theological method. As a final introductory note here, it may be appropriate to locate myself briefly but carefully within the inquiry to follow, returning once more to a scene at dusk.[34]

•

In a remarkable two-page essay entitled "Near a Church at Dusk," Saidiya Hartman walks along a gravel path behind the writer James Agee and photographer Walker Evans as they approach a country church in Alabama—beautiful, plain—redescribing an unforgettably tense and ambiguous passage from their 1941 book *Let Us Now Praise Famous Men*.[35] The two white artists want to get inside to take a picture while the light is just right. As they stand contemplating how to pry a lock or force a window, they notice "a Negro couple has observed [them] lurking near the church, determined to trap and possess," leaving them "ashamed and insecure . . . thwarting, at least momentarily, the intrusion." They decide to seek permission. Still, the sun is going down fast and "in the end, permission granted or not, they will do what they want." Agee begins walking briskly toward the couple, but just as he opens his mouth to speak, "*at the sound of the twist of my shoe in the gravel, the young woman's whole body was jerked down tight as a fist into a crouch*," then she explodes into flight, then she stops, and now the couple turns to face him, knowing that despite his collapse into an "indulgence of apology and self-flagellation"—"*I'm sorry. I'm sorry. I didn't mean to scare you. I wouldn't have done any such thing for anything*"—the encounter cannot outrun what both parties know: "*no Negro safely walks away from a white man.*" Agee does not allow himself to lie to himself about this, Hartman notes. He does not "disavow what he has done," and this, she continues, invites us to "consider whether this refusal to disavow the violence that is whiteness (here revealed in its guilt and benevolence) is a moment when whiteness itself trembles." (No answer, no closure—just *consider*.) In either case, there is no escaping that he represents the power of the law and the force of violence and he has de-manded yet one more thing from them . . . everything else—the beauty of a white church at dusk, his good intentions, his shame, the answer needed to a simple question, the will to abasement—pale in comparison to all that the Negro couple is forced to bear on that road. . . . The violence that animates this encounter . . . is not the consequence of anything terrible that he has done or has failed to do; rather the violence is inescapable, it is the weather, it is everywhere. One small step anchors the world, and he, they, are bound to it.

"It has been dusk," Hartman writes elsewhere, "for four hundred years."[36] Layering senses of dusk drawn from W. E. B. Du Bois and Jamaica Kin-caid upon this ambiguous scene of a church between night and day, light and darkness, Hartman finds in dusk an image of the "*enduring* moment of injury," of the sense of loss, of grief—engendered from the founding moments of capture, conquest, stolen life—which yet suffuses the present, forms the ground beneath Agee's shoe, sets loose a scene of terror. It's the 1930s, not the 1850s. Agee is a liberal white reformer, not a Southern white slaveholder. Yet the ghost of the master haunts the scene. To say it has been dusk for four hundred years, to dare to speak of slavery's afterlife not just in the 1930s but in the twenty-first century, is not to "gainsay the small tri-umphs of Jubilee," Hartman notes, but to grapple for a language which might help us "contend with the enormity of emancipation as both a breach within slavery and a point of transition to what looks more like *the reorganization of the plantation system*" than its sheer disappearance.[37] There is something vaguely Augustinian in the recognition of this unyielding "ambivalence," its absence of a "definite partition between slavery and freedom," its ambiguity both a refusal of clean Manichaean categories of justice and injustice and a claim to a "transient and fleeting expression of possibility."[38]

In the meantime, what is obliquely present in the notion of dusk is what Dwight Hopkins speaks of as "a dimension often hidden," a hiddenness in Black thought and life as it moved beneath the gaze of the plantation masters. It is hidden, in part, because the scene through which it moves, the scene whose afterlife we inhabit today, remains a scene of threat, unspeak-able violence, and irreparable loss—even as uncapturable joy and beautiful experiments persist in its midst—a scene sustaining, across historical ruptures, a continuity of racial enclosure: from the slave ship, to the plantation complex, to the prison, to the segregated ghetto, and beyond.[39] What survives beneath and amid that violence survives in constant risk. What survives, what makes and resists and nourishes and acts, what slips off into the night, is a form of fugitive social life which—at least on some accounts—comprises both the object and the practice of what has come to be called the Black radical tradition.[40] What follows here, the work of a non-Black person whose life is not "imperiled and devalued by a racial calculus" in the manner in which Hartman writes, "I too am the afterlife of slavery,"[41] must struggle to avoid twin dangers, without any guarantee of closure or success. On one hand, I must try to avoid a false impulse toward claiming a place internal to that tradition which is not mine to claim, and so to avoid partaking in a longstanding practice, persisting up to present-day academic life, of treating Black life and thought as property to be claimed.[42] On the other, I must avoid the no less illusory notion that I could make sense of the conditions of my thought and life—to whatever small extent I have begun to do so— without the view of the world which Black intellectual tradition(s) make possible. Indeed, it is an aspect of that very world that major quarters of Christian intellectual life, including the political Augustinian conversation, have largely attempted to do just that: to make sense of themselves within interpretive frames unhaunted, without looking down at the gravel of the plantation afterlives which yet mark ethical life under the imprecise heading of *race*. There is no separate ground, no cleanly isolable "context" inside which Black thought happens, to which its relevance may be then safely contained.[43] Its scope is not limited to the narrow purview of "identity." Its analytic and imaginative power builds directly from, but is not reducible to, the "experiences" of one group of people. Instead, as Cedric Robinson has written, referencing the eminent C. L. R. James, Black Studies is nothing less than "a critique of Western civilization."[44]

We still inhabit this shifting light at dusk. It is still not quite clear when a white man follows after Black life in the shadows of a church what his intentions might be, and in any case, his intentions cannot overcome the threat. There is no resolving the problem, Hartman points out. There is only facing the violence tacit in the scene and working toward other forms of life: "Anything short of the ardent desire for something else, other social arrangements, and the breaking of this world only reproduces the violence. This world must be broken."[45] This demands reckoning with the grounds of contemporary thought as the enduring ground of the plantation.[46] Black thought has often emerged from and in turn reflected upon this scene of the fugitive. But to attempt to reckon with these histories as a non-Black person is to be pressed to confront whiteness as the counterpart to that fugitive motion: the master left behind. The figure who, unknowing, catches a glimpse of the human as it slips from view, vanishes from the control he imagined he held, and so experiences a threat not only to his property, but to what mastery of that property enabled—a sense of himself *as* master. "The scholarship that looks into the mind, imagination, and behavior of slaves is valuable," Toni Morrison writes, "but equally valuable is a serious intellectual effort to see what racial ideology does to the mind, imagination, and behavior of masters."[47] Following the lead of Black Studies' excavations of slavery's shadows, aiming not to speak primarily about (and certainly not for) lives emerging from the position of the enslaved,[48] I bend the analytic instead toward the afterlives of mastery, their deep roots in Christian thought, and the enduring legacies of the Christian master.[49]

ONE

The Master's House

There is only one slave in this house: the master.
—Libanius, Oration 25

But in the household of the just man ... those who give
orders are the slaves of those whom they appear to
command.
—Augustine, *The City of God*

Masters always pretend that they are not masters,
insisting that they are only doing what is best for society
as a whole.
—James Cone, *A Black Theology of Liberation*

In a 2017 issue of the *New York Review of Books,* Peter Brown credits a
new translation of Augustine's *Confessions* with a startling feat. While most
translations give us "an ever-so-human Augustine," Brown notes, they often
leave his God "an immense Baroque canvas ... suitably grand, of course
... but flat as the wall."[1] So in the eyes of the preeminent scholar of late
antiquity, what does this translator, Sarah Ruden, do differently? How does
she bring Augustine's God back to life? "She renames Him," writes Brown.
"He is not a 'Lord.' That is too grand a word. ... Augustine's God was a
dominus—a master. And a Roman *dominus* was a master of slaves." Augustine calls God *dominus* dozens of times in *Confessions,* and each one Ruden
renders "Master," breaking with the long-standard "Lord." "Unlike 'Lord,' "
writes Brown, "the Latin word *dominus* implied, in Augustine's time, no
distant majesty, muffled in fur and velvet. It conjured up life in the raw—life
lived face to face in a Roman household, lived to the sound of the crack of

the whip and punctuated by bursts of rage." The image is a "rude shock," Brown continues, but it shouldn't surprise us, given the "brilliant recent studies" by historians like Kyle Harper which establish that the system of "slavery was alive and well in Roman Africa and elsewhere," shaping the social imaginary in Augustine's time. Of slavery's central place in that world, Brown writes, there can be "no doubt."[2]

Nevertheless, a few days after Brown's review appeared online, one scholar objected to the "Master" language and Brown's praise of it. Philosopher James K. A. Smith took to his blog to make an apt if familiar point: translation dilemmas like this one cannot always be settled lexically, nor by reference to the translated culture alone. "Words in either language are not static," Smith writes, "they have a life of their own."[3] His point is that movement from the translated culture to the translator's is a journey, "an adventure in sailing from one language to another, and often from one time to another." Sometimes passengers jump ship: upon reading "Master" in the first line, Smith recalls, "I quite literally closed up the Ruden translation in a kind of literary disgust."

What matters for us is that Smith goes on to make explicit what usually remains unsaid: his disgust had everything to do with his having just read Colson Whitehead's novel *The Underground Railroad,* where he encountered white Christian plantation owners called "Master."[4] Smith makes explicit that the way we read *Augustine's* slave language today has everything to do with *our own* slave-haunted imagination—everything to do with inhabiting a social world that is, as Saidiya Hartman writes, "the afterlife of slavery."[5] *That's* what made the Ruden translation "jarring and offensive" to Smith, and that's what made Brown's praise for it feel like "willfully ignor[ing] all the connotations that have attached themselves to the word 'Master.' "[6] Smith does not mention that Ruden herself notes she had to "govern her distaste" toward the imagery with "its reminders of American plantation slavery."[7] The "disgust" Smith feels toward these connotations of New World racial slavery drives him (and us) to the critical point: "In some ways," he writes, "this is a question of who 'owns' Augustine . . . which *afterlife* of words is most germane to the project that Augustine himself is engaged in? Which history of connotation overlaps with Augustine's endeavor?"[8] Based on this searing and lucid set of questions, one might expect the connotations of "master" language would press Smith to examine Augustine's slavery talk more closely, to explore its moral significance in view of both the differences and the continuities between ancient Roman slavery and modern New World slavery. Instead, turned away by "disgust" for the connotation itself, Smith proposes "digging in and sticking with" the "Lord" translation of *dominus* in the name of "Christian piety," and in this way, he finds himself not only turning away from Brown's point about the social realities of Augustine's day, but also turning away from the helpful, if disturbing, questions he himself has raised: What does it mean to read Augustine's slavery discourse within the modern world as we have it, haunted as it is by slavery's tenacious after-lives in the present? How might the figure of the Christian master, glimpsed through an encounter with Augustine, open up surprising new ways to see and respond to our own racialized crises of democracy—in the era of Black Lives Matter, Trumpist resentments, mass incarceration, renewed racist voting laws, militarized borders against Black and brown migrants, and a warming world where more and more racialized peoples will be on the move?[9]

This book lingers inside these questions a little longer. In this chapter, I develop an approach to reading the moral and theological significance of Augustine's slavery discourse for contemporary Augustinian thought, while opening out into the wider question of how the problem of the Christian master endures, shaping the conditions inside which the racial world emerged, and with which western democracies in their present crises yet contend. The task comes into view more clearly when we locate Smith's question—about how to properly translate Augustine's slave master God—within this larger context of political Augustinianism, itself a translation project in the following broader sense.

In the last two decades, scholars of religion and politics made a striking return to Augustine's writings not as "pure" historical study, but rather in search of constructive, normative resources to theorize citizenship, virtue, and the place of religion in contemporary public life.[10] Distinctive to the current moment in political Augustinianism is a particular kind of interpretive task which Eric Gregory and Joseph Clair recently called "democratic translation": the thorny problem of "translating" Augustine's counsel to the elite statesmen of antiquity into guidance for the citizens of modern liberal democracies.[11]

In Part 1 of this chapter, I contend that this modern Augustinian translation project has not yet reckoned with the challenges posed by the central place of slavery in Augustine's thought. Instead, Augustine's slavery discourse often generates an affective response—Smith's "disgust," Brown's "rude shock," Ruden's "distaste"—which results in the gesture Smith here performs: the recognition of a problem, then a turning away from it toward other concerns—a simultaneous acknowledgment and denial. I show how several key modern Augustinian texts display this double-movement of disavowal in concert with a general assumption that Augustine's legitimation of slavery, however unfortunate, may be easily excised from those political insights to be "translated" into modern democratic life.[12] Parts 2 and 3 identify two challenges to this assumption which, I suggest, must be examined together if Augustinians wish to enrich their capacity to bear faithful witness amid ongoing racial injustice in the era of Black Lives Matter. Part 4 clarifies how these first three parts provide a kind of template for the reading strategy which will then be applied to specific topics in Augustinian political thought in the following three chapters.

It should be noted at the outset that the difficulties raised by positing parallels between slave systems ancient and modern are considerable, but not unique to this project.[13] Moving from one context to another demands intense labors of translation, but translation itself is not anachronism.[14] Internal to all constructive political thought in particular is the challenge of letting an ancient figure be not only an object to scrutinize, but a voice to translate and thus a subject to converse with, speak for or against.[15] If political Augustinians are right to insist Augustine's resources are "translatable" *mutatis mutandis* into modernity, so too are the distinct moral challenges which arise from inhabiting the master's position—or inheriting its legacies in the present.[16] The point is not to vilify Augustine's ambivalent entanglements with the position of the master. Rather, in reading him with care, we learn better to confront our own.[17]

Black religious and political thought provides a privileged "conceptual precipice" for this task—to borrow Alexander Weheliye's term—from which to recognize the problem with these Christian slavery metaphors: the problem of the master, that is, that these metaphors index nothing about the slave so much as the master's own self-deceptions.[18] If the concepts of citizen or city or public/private can travel, so too do the moral risks of entanglements in the master's position. From this reckoning, a stronger picture emerges of how one might build a constructive vision of religious ethics for moral agency and political citizenship in our world—marked by the afterlife of slavery. By eschewing neither "traditionalist" nor "liberationist" strands of Christian thought, I aim instead to pose an encounter, at once timely and long overdue, between the wisdom of an ancient figure of Christian tradition and the distinct moral challenges of ongoing racial violence in the era of Black Lives

Matter. In this way, I hope the work will interest not only specialists of either Augustine or Black religious thought, but anyone concerned with imagining generative strategies of encounter between so-called traditionalist and liberationist modes of ethical reflection.

The work is also for those dissatisfied with treatments of the relation between race and religious ethics. Dissatisfied, that is, with the fact that religiously grounded accounts of ethical life often treat race, at best, as an important "issue" on which to test out various conceptions of justice, rights, norms, and so on, *or*, at worst, as a side show—a minority matter of special interest. More recent attempts to press beyond these options still almost inevitably collapse race into the problem of "racial diversity," which is a species of the broader problem of "the fact of pluralism," such that race emerges alongside a host of other modifiers in a sequence of "racial," "ethnic," "cultural," and "religious" "differences."[19] Such accounts are important, but only superficially related to the conditions on view in what follows, haunted as they are—and as the theories are not—by slavery's afterlife in the present, where the *after-* is a placeholder for a specific temporal sensibility, one which eludes easy assimilation into most critical discourses tracing slavery's "legacies" or "effects" in the postemancipation world. Inside the center of that word, *after,* is a haunted voice, a lingering and unsatisfied demand. To hear differently would be to find modern ethical life playing out in a specific kind of silence: what Hartman identifies as the "absence of a consummate breach," the lack of a "durable temporal marker" providing a "definitive partition between slavery and freedom."[20] This absence provides the basis for a less superficial account of the racialized conditions in which modern ethical life occurs. This project takes up the dilemma of the Christian master as one key position to be theorized within these ongoing racialized conditions, the Christian master being an ideal-type, a figure whose position some of us have inherited, whose power many of us have been subjected to, and inside whose still unfinished story all of us—in ways to be worked out in what follows—yet remain.

Part 1. Augustinian Disavowals: On Morrison, Gilroy, O'Donovan

In this section, I want to set the scene of the present political conversation in Augustinianism as it pertains to the concerns of the book. The argument is simple: Augustinians have not simply been "silent" about modern racial slavery *or* ignored the slavery in Augustine's own thought. Rather, there has been a "disavowal" of both, a term I use in a technical sense borrowed from political theorist Neil Roberts and will clarify in a moment. To sketch how that works, I begin with a story.

In a 1988 interview with Paul Gilroy, Toni Morrison gave us an adage that now appears everywhere: "Modern life begins with slavery."[21] This adage first gained prominence in 1993 when Gilroy himself quoted it in the final chapter of his now-classic work *The Black Atlantic: Modernity and Double Consciousness.*[22] For Gilroy, Morrison's adage offers a dense restatement of a founding argument of Black thought, found in canonical works like W. E. B. Du Bois's *Black Reconstruction* and C. L. R. James's *The Black Jacobins.* Put simply, this argument contends that western modernity is unintelligible apart from grasping slavery as a phenomenon of worldmaking significance—not only for enslaved persons, but for everyone else too. More than thirty years later, it seems that every week a new book confirms that argument, showing slavery's key role in the making of capitalist economy, or property law, or the insurance industry, or the university, or medical science.[23] With each new example, Morrison's adage gets weightier: modern life begins with slavery.

In the year after Gilroy's book emerged, just up the road from where Gilroy was teaching in London, Oliver O'Donovan delivered the prestigious Hulsean Lectures at Cambridge. Those lectures became *The Desire of the Nations,* in which O'Donovan writes the following: " 'Slavery' has existed, for most of the last millennium, only on the fringes of civilization, as a colonial indulgence or as a sub-political pathology. To the ancient world, on the other hand, it was central to any imaginable economic organization."[24] *The Desire of the Nations* is a major work of Christian ethics, and O'Donovan is an especially crucial figure in the political Augustinian renaissance of the last few decades.[25] It's been almost twenty years since the book was published, and it's been met with many pages of scholarly engagement, but as best I can tell, this take on the "fringe" importance of modern racial slavery has not yet elicited a single line of criticism. No trace of Morrison's adage emerges, nor the founding texts of African American thought, and this absence invites us to consider another line from the same Toni Morrison interview: of the centrality of slavery to modern life, Morrison says, there is a "struggle to forget which was important in order to survive."[26] In this section, I am interested not simply in pointing out that O'Donovan's claim reflects a serious neglect of available historical evidence, but in asking, what might this wider struggle to forget the centrality of slavery to modern life, a forgetting implicit in the absence of scholarly interest in contesting O'Donovan's claim, imply about the broader relation of the Augustinian conversation to matters of race?

It may be objected that O'Donovan's claim occurs in a context in which he is not primarily talking about modern racial slavery at all. Or at least, he is *trying* not to talk about it, but finds that he cannot avoid doing so while discussing what he *wants* to discuss, namely, slavery in the ancient household codes of the early churches. Our own slave-haunted imagination intervenes. O'Donovan finds he cannot discuss one context without dealing with the other. And so, quite reasonably, he wants to ensure ancient Christianity's entanglements with slavery are not dealt with in an anachronistic, presentist manner. There are good reasons for avoiding using the word *slavery* in too univocal a way.[27] But for that very reason, it's all the more striking that O'Donovan's desire to avoid conflating ancient slavery with modern slavery winds up distorting both. Consider the full quote:

> The misunderstanding arises in part from the word "slave" itself, which to us denotes a social institution altogether apart from the normal structures of economic organization and exceptionally oppressive in the terms on which it governs the exchange of labor for livelihood. "Slavery" has existed, for most of the last millennium, only on the fringes of civilization, as a colonial indulgence or as a sub-political pathology. To the ancient world, on the other hand, it was central to any imaginable economic organization, providing the only skilled labor-market for the chief unit of production, which was the household business. So the word *douleia* appears in contexts where we might speak not of "slavery" but of "domestic service," or quite simply of "employment."[28]

O'Donovan's worries about anachronism lead him to overcorrect for and thus reinscribe the problem of anachronism, as he presses a series of contrasts between what "slavery" indexes in modernity versus antiquity which is far sharper than what evidence can support. To us, he says, slavery is an institution "altogether apart from the normal structures of economic organization."[29] But to them, slavery was so normal we should "speak not of 'slavery' but of 'domestic service,' or quite simply of 'employment.' "[30] This claim raises questions: If I were to mention an "employee," would that bring to your mind a person whose body is her employer's legal property? A person whose children are her employer's legal property? If I speak of an "employee," do we picture a person subject to being whipped by her manager, tortured with no legal recourse, regarded with shame and dishonor, and made available as a sexual outlet with no right to say no? As numerous historical studies show, these conditions of life were utterly normal for most enslaved persons in antiquity, *and* they are precisely those connoted to modern ears by the word *slave* itself, precisely because that word conjures disturbing images from New World plantations.[31] "Employment," then, is the misplaced, anachronistic term, not "slavery."

As I stated already, though, my purpose is not simply to try to supplement historical facts that have been neglected, but to consider how the neglect occurred in the first place, explore why it matters for how political Augustinians do their work, and probe its wider significance for Christian engagements with political life.[32] To understand that, we need to recognize that the simplistic contrast O'Donovan draws in the claim above—between the "fringe" importance of slavery in modernity and its "central" importance in antiquity—does not emerge from nowhere, but rather serves a specific aim within O'Donovan's argument: namely, to shield Christianity from what he variously refers to as "discomfort," "disappointment," and the "quarrels" which emerge for moderns upon encountering early Christian acceptance of slavery.[33]

This affective register, leading to a double movement of acknowledgment and denial, recalls the gesture we saw in Smith above. In this way, O'Donovan's extended engagement with slavery suggests that what Morrison termed "the struggle to forget" not only takes the form of "silence" about slavery. Nor is the problem simply that Augustinians have been silent, or that they have ignored or failed to mention the history of slavery and issues of race more broadly. Instead, the problem we see in O'Donovan's statement marks an instance of what Black political theorist Neil Roberts calls *disavowal*: "Disavowal," he writes, "centrally requires what I take to be a simultaneous *double movement*: an acknowledgment *and* a denial. By simultaneously acknowledging and denying an event, one does not silence its existence. Rather, one strategically locates an event and then rejects its relevance, knowing full well that it occurred."[34] Strategically locating something in order to reject its relevance. *Forgetting in order to survive.* In the case of this Augustinian disavowal, who and what is meant to survive?

Where Smith's denial looked like simply turning away from the questions raised, O'Donovan aims to confront the discomfort directly and reveal it as a "misunderstanding" resulting from what the word *slave* denotes "to us." Given my stated aims in this section, I am interested in the composition of that "us." Who is included in it? What questions matters to this "us" and what questions does this "us" preclude? The "us" O'Donovan invokes is evidently a group of people who consider slavery "*exceptionally* oppressive," that is, those who consider slavery to be an exception to, or a departure from, the normal course of European modernity.[35] O'Donovan's "us" is a group in whose grammar the words "colonial indulgence" suggest a matter of marginal rather than central importance. But as we have already seen, the founding works of Black thought saw things rather differently: modern life begins with slavery. It is central. And again, by now mainstream scholarship has begun to catch up with what the Black intellectual tradition, arising from the experience of capture, enslavement, and flight, saw from the beginning. What this suggests, perhaps somewhat uncomfortably, is that O'Donovan's "us" is unintentionally, but inescapably, an unmarked *white* "us," one with liability to certain blind spots. And if there is an unnamed whiteness to the political Augustinian conversation itself, it is perhaps best seen as not merely about the skin color of the bodies in the room, but as involving deep epistemic commitments which govern what counts as "central" and what counts as "fringe," guiding our sense of what "we" wish to discover and what some are willing not to know—even as we inhabit mastery's afterlife in the present.[36] For others who, in Audre Lorde's words, "were never meant to survive," forgetting has never been an option.[37]

The disavowals of slavery, then, serve to protect both the moral priorities of an implied white readership and their investment in the authority of ancient texts in which slavery appears. Through this juxtaposition of ancient and modern settings, O'Donovan believes he has fended off any critique of Christianity's entanglements with *both*: in antiquity, slavery was so central that its embrace by Christians cannot be faulted; in modernity, it was so minor that its perpetuation by Christians may be safely left aside. Any seeming challenge slavery might pose to Christian self-understanding is misplaced, since, it seems, its existence in society was always either *too* central or not central enough. "One strategically locates an event and then rejects its relevance, knowing full well that it occurred." Forgetting to survive. The disavowals necessary to secure this survival risk creating distortions not only of modern racial slavery, but also of the conditions of ancient slavery, which in turn leads to impoverished understandings of ancient thinkers, including the writings of Augustine himself.

The limited nature of this "us" can resurface in much subtler ways than O'Donovan's here, often when issues around slavery appear among political Augustinian writers who, elsewhere in their work, show serious interest in the differences internal to any claim to "we." In his influential work of Augustinian ethics, *Politics and the Order of Love*, Eric Gregory writes, "It would be ironically prideful to blame Augustine or any other premodern author for limited historical horizons of social and economic reform, most especially in relation to his often neglected moral criticisms of slavery. Augustine was no abolitionist."[38] Here Gregory rightly cautions us as modern readers to avoid placing ourselves in a superior moral position to premodern authors like Augustine on slavery. He also models a response to the discomfort generated by Augustine's acceptance of slavery which has become something of a standard formulation: Augustine was no abolitionist, the line goes, but facts x, y, and z complicate any portrayal of him as a villain. Robin Lane Fox, in his excellent new biography, writes, "Augustine was not an abolitionist, but he was not blind to the individual suffering which slavery could cause."[39] Rowan Williams writes, "[Augustine] may not give the answer we would like (he is never a straightforward abolitionist), but he concludes that slavery is a sign of something fundamentally wrong in human relations."[40] This formulation does not at all imply that Gregory is mitigating the sinfulness of ancient slaveholders, so much as reveal that he—and "we," or some of "us"—find ourselves already aligned with, identifying with, *their* position in society and the questions it poses. His statement juxtaposes our modern response to that of Augustine, slaveholders, and those who failed to criticize ancient slavery. But the silence of the statement is our position vis-à-vis the ancient slaves. Did they also fail to resist ancient slavery? This question never arises. There is no slave agency to contend with.[41] So it is the moral vantage of the masters that we find ourselves contending with, whether we criticize it or empathize with it, and this unstated condition—our shared moral horizon with the master class—is a deeper aspect of the unmarked "us," a condition of moral reflection which we may wish to bring more clearly into view. What brings it into view most powerfully, as the subtitle "Dusk" hinted at in my Introduction and as I'll argue more fully below, is the fugitive flight of the enslaved person, ancient and modern, which confounds the way "slavery" is posed as a moral dilemma.

The enslaved person's flight suggests that the structuring feature when it comes to examining slavery as a moral problem is not whether one identifies with ancient "moral sensibilities" or modern ones, but whether one identifies with the ethical dilemmas faced by the master or the slave.[42]

Another aspect of the unmarked "us" as a question occurs in the work of Charles Mathewes. "In the Middle Ages," writes Mathewes in *Republic of Grace: Augustinian Thoughts for Dark Times*, "scholars wrote guidebooks for kings, known generically as 'mirrors for Christian princes,' wherein the contours of a virtuous ruler were displayed. . . . Today we may use the virtues analogously, to detail a mirror of Christian citizenship . . . where there is no king, where 'the sovereign' is *us*—you and I and our neighbors, those we like and those we cannot stand."[43] As with O'Donovan, some readers may not find it straightforward to locate themselves within that "us" of sovereign citizens, due to intersecting histories of violence, subjugation, and exclusion, and therefore may not share Mathewes's confidence that "we need not be victims of the rulers anymore. We are not subjects of kings, we are citizens of republics, sharing in our common sovereignty; genuine participation in the governance of our world is possible. Because of this, we have reason for hope."[44] Who is the we? The histories of racial slavery and its afterlives have made this hope uncertain for many,[45] but these histories surface nowhere in the account of the present Mathewes here offers, the present into which Augustinians wish to translate Augustine's best insights through "democratic translation."[46]

A kind of selective ahistoricism results, whereby ancient concepts like "citizens," "city," or "republic" are presumed translatable, *mutatis mutandis,* into modern political life, while the moral problems of mastery and slavery are left safely in the ancient past, an unfortunate relic of a different age.[47] In this way, by reinscribing patterns of disavowal, even the strongest accounts of Augustinian politics risk standing at a remove from the social world revealed in Morrison's adage—modern life begins with slavery. The way forward begins with reconsidering the specific ways slavery animates Augustine's own texts.

Part 2. On the Master's House: Augustine's Slave Metaphors

[Paul] set houses in good order with clear doctrine, preaching
and teaching what wives owed their husbands, husbands their wives,

children their parents, parents their children, slaves their masters, masters
their slaves—for how could these be done without a *domus*?
—Augustine, Letter 157.30[48]

In the previous section, I highlighted the habit of disavowal present in
the political Augustinian conversation toward the significance of slavery in
Augustine's thought and in the modern social world to which Augustinians
apply it. The next two sections develop two arguments for why the objects
disavowed must instead be addressed. The first key fact challenging this
disavowal is that "slavery" is best understood not as simply one, isolable
moral "issue" in Augustine's texts. Rather, slavery forms an abiding presence in Augustine's writings, not only as a social institution he occasionally
defends, but as a pervasive series of interrelated metaphors animating his
treatment of God, sin, Christology, desire, order, virtue, and freedom. And
indeed, it is one of my central contentions that literal and metaphorical slavery are not as easy to separate in Augustine's thought as is often assumed.
Instead, we find that both work intimately together, comprising what I call
"the master's house," a symbolic space in which Augustine both uses slavery
metaphorically to clarify theological matters *and* speaks theologically about
"actual" masters and slaves in tightly interconnected ways.[49]

Stipulating this term, "the master's house," is thus intended to do three
things throughout the book: (1) to call the reader's attention back to a key
argument, viz., that these two registers of Augustine's slavery discourse—
slavery-as-institution and slavery-as-metaphor—work in intimate union
together, as Augustine routinely moves across any would-be border between
them; as such, it is important to view both registers as encompassed within
this expansive symbolic structure: a *domus* (household) headed by a *dominus*;[50] (2) to underscore the fact that the master–slave relation unfolds not as
the one-on-one dialectical struggle between two individuals—as moderns
are prone to imagine, often from the residue left by Hegel's Lord–Bondsman
image—but rather as one node within a network of relations which together
comprise the symbolic space of the *domus*.[51] As such, it is important to track
Augustine's symbolic use of master (*dominus*) and slave (*servus*) imagery in
its relation to adjacent figures within the household (i.e., the master's son
[*filius*], which I examine in Chapter 3) and to the specifically *gendered* dimensions of how slavery functions in Roman household relations, especially in
sexual relations (which will reappear especially in Chapter 4's discussion
of the *partus sequitur ventrem*, by which the enslaved status of the mother

legally transfers to the child, thus ensuring the reproduction of the enslaved "supply," even as the descriptions of this supply on the part of the master class, including Augustine, tend to pass over this source in silence); and (3) to pose the question of how the function of the *domus* in Roman life as a building block of social order presents us with parallel moral dynamics in our context, with modern slavery and its racial afterlives. For those familiar with the literature of New World slavery, my use of "the master's house" should call to mind a parallel not just with "the big house"—which tends to function, problematically, as the center of popular memory of slavery[52]—but with the wider analytic importance of the plantation household as a window into slavery and the arrangements of gender, race, and land it birthed in the wake of its juridical abolition.[53] For all the differences between the Roman *domus* and the plantation household as conditions of moral life inviting critical reflection, the parallel moral dynamics between them—when necessary adjustments and qualifications are made—are no less plausible as a topos for constructive ethical thought than those which are so often made between "citizenship," "public life," "cities," and so on among modern political thinkers, especially those who "retrieve" and "translate" ancient sources for liberal democratic societies.

With this in mind, I refer to the master's house throughout to call the reader's attention back to the way slavery functions not only as a particular moral "issue," nor as an isolated metaphor, but as an expansive symbolic structure. For Augustine, to make a claim work within the terms of reference set by that structure—whether a claim about the proper conduct of enslaved persons or a claim about God, Christ, or selfhood through metaphors of slavery—is to draw upon the stability and coherence afforded by the self-evident character of social order as it presently exists.

Take the Ruden controversy I introduced at the start, in which Peter Brown reminds us that whenever Augustine calls upon God as his slave master, he is "conjuring up the life of the Roman household." Throughout *Confessions,* this household image, Brown notes, "brings Augustine to life. In relation to God, Augustine experiences all the ups and downs of a household slave in relation to his master. He jumps to the whip. He tries out the life of a runaway. He attempts to argue back."[54] It is as though Augustine looks upon the body of the fugitive slave and finds his own restless soul staring back. Reflecting his aimless wandering and his stubborn pride, his illusory freedom and his will to flight, the fugitive also signified for him the final impossibility of escape. In Book 2, he renarrates his famous theft as a "perverse imitation of my Lord [*dominum*]," one which, like all sin, turned out to be self-defeating: "you are the creator of all nature and so . . . there is no place where one can entirely escape from you. . . . Here is a runaway slave fleeing his master [*dominum*] and pursuing a shadow [Job 7:2]. . . . What rottenness! What a monstrous life and what an abyss of death!"[55]

This image of the fugitive amid shadows forms only one subset of Augustine's larger metaphorical use of slavery, which plays flexibly with the appearance of actual enslaved persons in Augustine's account.[56] In a memorable passage of *Confessions,* Book 9, Augustine displays Monica's virtue by her teaching other women that, in marriage, wives "become slaves" to their husbands; they must not, she says, "proudly withstand their masters." The very next paragraph finds her virtuous reputation threatened by the "interfering tongues of the slavegirls," then restored by her husband "subjecting the girls to a whipping." The wife-as-slave bit is straightforwardly "metaphorical," but the "actual" slaves of the second event serve as a kind of metaphor as well—the enslaved body's radical vulnerability to violence—in order to illustrate a larger point about the restoration of "domestic harmony."[57] Monica's "patience and gentleness" work in tandem with her husband's whip to restore "peace in the household" and a "memorably gentle benevolence" (*conf.* 9.9.19–20).

Indeed, the image of the bad slave punished—for gossip, for theft, for running away—does especially wide-ranging conceptual and symbolic work across Augustine's corpus. In *On Free Choice of the Will,* the slave "caught in a sin" is forced to clean the sewer: by this "detestable" punishment, "the slave's disgrace" and the cleaning of the sewer are "woven into an orderly household . . . with the most orderly beauty" (*lib. arb.* 3.9.27.96–97).[58] In Letter 185, Augustine frames the Donatists as a band of runaway thieves who must be "recalled to their [Master] by the stripes of temporal scourging, like evil slaves, and in some degree like good-for-nothing fugitives" (*ep.* 185.21). In *Homilies on the Gospel of John,* Augustine likens schismatic groups to Hagar, the fugitive slave who gave Sarah and Abraham the slip: when authorities punish them, "this is God stirring up Sarah to give Hagar a beating." Therefore, "Let Hagar . . . yield her neck" for punishment; after all, the angel sends the slave girl back to her masters (*Jo. ev. tr.* 11.13).[59] And again, in these anti-Donatist examples, the line between metaphorical and literal slaves is blurred by the discursive context, his well-known complaint about the actual practices of the Donatists, recorded in his letter to Boniface: "What master was not forced to live in fear of his slave, if the slave fled to the patronage of the Donatists?"[60]

Indeed part of the difficulty of interpreting the slave images in Augustine is that Augustine himself routinely moves across what would seem to be a boundary between slavery as metaphor and slavery as social institution. Yet for Augustine, as for many Stoic writers before him, the latter is by no means more "real" than the former.[61] Indeed, slavery to sin, particularly to the *libido dominandi* (lust for domination), is itself the truest slavery of all.[62] As historian Susanna Elm argues, "Augustine . . . in nearly all his writings, moves seamlessly between actual and metaphorical slavery because these are the metaphors he and his audience *lived by.*"[63] In forms both "metaphorical" and "literal," the slave's body appears at key junctures in the major works following Augustine's ordination in 391, treatises like *The Advantage of Believing* (*De utilitate credendi*, c. 391), *Teaching Christianity* (*De doctrina Christiana*, c. 395), and *The Excellence of Marriage* (*De bono conjugali*, c. 401).[64] In Augustine's last work, cut short by death, *Against Julian* (*Contra Iulianum*), the soul–body relation is conceived as a master–slave relation: the soul rules the body's lusts "as a master commands a slave, since it coerces it and breaks it."[65] Perhaps most famously, in *The City of God*, Augustine confronts the slave logic of civilization itself: "human society is generally divided against itself," such that "the conquered part" chooses "peace and survival at any price—so much so that it has always provoked astonishment when men have preferred death to slavery." Existing relations among various empires and peoples obtain, Augustine suggests, when guided by the "voice of nature" the conquered choose enslavement over death.[66] Blurring the line between literal and metaphorical slaveries yet again, here Augustine sees in the slave's body civilization writ small—the secret truth of the body politic, made visible in her chains.[67]

Those lines occur in Book 18 of *The City of God*, but when slavery in Augustine's thought has received attention in modern political Augustinianism at all, it has overwhelmingly been in the form of debates over Book 19's treatment of the nature of political authority in relation to sin. That book has been rightly considered a "microcosm of Augustine's social thought," to use O'Donovan's phrase, and yet, in the last ten years especially, Augustinians have helpfully expanded our sense of Augustine's politics beyond it.[68] It's worth mentioning in this context that it is sometimes presumed that whatever qualms one may have about Augustine's acceptance of slavery can be mitigated, if not resolved, by pointing to Book 19's explanation of slavery as caused by sin rather than nature: "By nature," Augustine writes, "as God first created man, no one is a slave either to man or to sin [*servus est hominis aut peccati*]."[69] For example, the lines from Rowan Williams quoted above (about Augustine concluding that "slavery is a sign of something fundamental wrong in human relations") are preceded by this: "[Augustine] wants to understand, for example, why such a strange and unnatural institution as slavery exists: not a question his contemporaries worried much about . . . [he] refuses to accept that this or that way of doing things and distributing power is just 'natural.' . . . We can imagine societies, not just inherit them."[70]

This is a complex claim, and I return at length to Book 19 in my fourth chapter, but we can say for now that if it is taken to foreclose upon a deeper look into the question of slavery in Augustine, such an attempted resolution is premature on three counts. For one, it is misleading to frame as radically countercultural Augustine's notion that slavery does not belong properly to "nature." One finds in legal texts of the period statements like that of Florentinus—"Slavery is an institution of the law of nations [*ius gentium*], whereby someone, against nature, is made subject to the ownership of another"—alongside a wider array of "expressions of anxiety, doubt and criticism over both the justice of the institution and the way its victims were treated," of which Peter Garnsey provides a helpful overview.[71] Second, it is premature just to the extent that Augustine then immediately clarifies: "But it is also true that the punishment of slavery is ordained by precisely the same law which commands that the natural order is to be preserved and forbids it to be disturbed."[72] Thus, although slavery is punishment for sin, it is indeed *divinely ordained* punishment, blessed by God not as an original purpose but as a secondary solution, directed to that end of preserving the order of limited temporal peace which is itself among the most important shared goods which the heavenly city shares with the earthly during the *saeculum*. In light of that, it should not surprise us that when it comes to slavery matters of daily life, Augustine's basic concern is most often the containment of disorder, both social and moral. Practically speaking, that looks like denouncing the fugitive option to enslaved persons and encouraging a "loving spirit" among masters, while acknowledging that if a master were to ask him, "Shall discipline sleep?," he would have to clarify: "That's not what I'm saying . . . if you see your slave living badly, what other punishment will you curb him with, if not the lash? Use it: do. God allows it. In fact he is angered if you don't."[73] And third, the resolution is premature in light of the reception histories by which these texts now come to us. Or in other words, if it is true that calling slavery "unnatural" necessarily implies some sort of destabilizing critique of or challenge to actually existing slave regimes, then it becomes difficult to explain why there is little evidence to suggest that the legacy of the Augustinian position was seen as some sort of obstacle to overcome when his texts were being read as authoritative at the turn from the medieval period to the dawn of New World colonization or in various contexts throughout the slaveholding societies of the Americas.[74] It seems nearer the mark to note that Thomas Aquinas, in question 52 of the *Summa Theologiae* ("Of the Impediment of the Condition of Slavery") is being quite a careful Augustinian defender of slaveholding when he notes that "slavery is contrary to the first intention of nature. Yet it is not contrary to the second, because natural reason has this inclination, and nature has this desire— that everyone should be good; but from the fact that a person sins, nature has an inclination that he should be punished for his sin, and thus slavery was brought in as a punishment of sin."[75] It lies beyond my scope to offer a full historical treatment here, but there is a coherent lineage to be traced from Augustine through Thomas to Francisco de Vitoria to European intellectuals of the sixteenth-century colonization project like Alberico Gentili, who writes that he "agree[s] with Thomas Aquinas that slavery is really in harmony with nature; not indeed according to her first intent, by which we were all created free, but according to a second desire of hers, that sinners should be punished."[76]

It's perhaps best to say that Augustine, while genuinely troubled over the presence of slavery, seeks not to challenge the institution, but rather to Christianize it, which is to say, to recalibrate it within the terms of an emerging Christian conception of political order, and thus, to stabilize it. Interpretations which wish to find in him the contrary, while intending to be "charitable" toward intellectuals of a different time, are often themselves anachronistic, imputing to Augustine or other ancient Christians subversive inclinations which available evidence cannot support. Instead, we find that Augustine explicitly defends the justice of slavery because he believes it provides a modicum of order to a fallen world, denounces slaves who run away from or resist their masters, supports the use of the whip to prevent this, and marshals theological reasons for all of it.

My primary concern is not to use the assessment I've just outlined as a reason to stop reading Augustine, but on the contrary, to shift the terms of the debate to see how Augustine's inhabiting a world organized by the slave system inflects his proper theological and ethical thought, especially those areas of his thought that are often taken to have little to do with slavery. In that way the hope is that we might become *better* readers of Augustine in these areas which Augustinians wish to recover—the notion of pilgrimage, his account of the virtues (especially *humilitas*), his Christology, his eschatology—which are so often articulated precisely through the metaphorical resources of slavery.

The point is certainly not to propose one more reductive caricature of Augustine's politics as mere slaveholding "ideology," or worse, to make an easy critique of Augustine in the form of either moral anachronism or an uncritical valorization of modern liberal sensibilities (which, after all, often went hand in hand with modern racial slavery).[77] Nor still can we afford to resort to a gut-level affective offense at Augustine's slavery discourse—shock, discomfort, distaste—which, as I've argued above, often leads to disavowal rather than reckoning with the ancient thought-world of Augustine and the connotations of slave language in the present. To move beyond that, it's important to note that up to this point in this chapter, I have advanced no argument to suggest why the slavery metaphors themselves are problematic, only shown, in Part 1, how they have not yet attracted significant attention among political Augustinians, and in Part 2, that they provide an organizing structure to Augustine's thought, inside which the theological metaphor of slavery cannot be neatly separated from Augustine's more practical statements about life under slavery.

Part 3. How Black Thought Discloses the Problem of the Master

Now, as I begin the third part of my argument, I turn to several resources from Black thought's analysis of slavery and its afterlives in order to illumine the nature of slavery metaphors further and specify with precision what sort of problem they present to Augustinian moral and theological thought. The problem cannot be simply *that* Augustine liberally uses slavery metaphors. In the world he inhabited, how could he not? Rather, the problem which requires further analysis for those of us who apply his social and political vision to the present, especially those of us who hope that an encounter with Augustine's thought has something to offer in the era of Black Lives Matter, lies with examining *how* these slave metaphors do their work.

Returning one more time to the Ruden translation controversy, it's worth noting that neither Brown nor Ruden believes that Augustine is reflecting the experiences of enslaved persons with his slave metaphors. Instead, as Ruden writes, "Augustine's humorously self-deprecating, submissive, but boldly hopeful portrait of himself in relation to God echoes the rogue slaves of the Roman stage."[78] Similarly, Brown likens the slave images which Augustine invokes to "Zero Mostel as the plump and bouncy Pseudolus in *A Funny Thing Happened on the Way to the Forum*."[79] The point is: Augustine's slave metaphors reflect not the perspective of enslaved persons—about which the sources tell us very little—but rather the vantage of the masters themselves. In noting this, Ruden and Brown have their fingers on something more significant than either acknowledges, given what the Black intellectual tradition, especially womanist and Black feminist scholarship, has repeatedly taught us about the dynamics in play when the captive body functions as a "playground for the imagination," as Toni Morrison says.[80]

Just as "the subject of the dream is the dreamer," Morrison argues, so too does the literary and philosophical use of the figure of the enslaved open up, in the mind of the master, a space for "extraordinary meditation on the self," for "powerful exploration of fears and desires."[81] In this way, "the slave population, it could be and was assumed, offered itself up as surrogate selves for meditation on problems of human freedom, its lure and its elusiveness . . . for meditations on terror . . . internal aggression, evil, sin, greed."[82] Similarly, Hortense Spillers notes that when the dominant culture proposes to elaborate the figure of the slave, these elaborations, metaphors, symbols, and signs "tell us little or nothing about the subject buried beneath the epithets, but *quite a great deal more concerning the psychic and cultural reflexes that invent and invoke them.*"[83] These reflexes interest me, which come into view when, as Saidiya Hartman writes, the symbolic activity of the dominant "[makes] the captive body speak the master's truth."[84] Hartman in particular has tracked in archivally exacting detail how it is precisely those scenes in which masters orchestrated the appearance of enslaved persons' enjoyment, contentment, and harmony—and *not* more familiar scenes of overt brutality—which underscore the violence inherent in the enslaved person's body being "deploy[ed] as a vehicle for exploring the human condition," deployed as a symbolic resource for the master's own intellectual and cultural expression.[85]

This is not to too quickly assimilate the arguments of Morrison, Spillers, and Hartman to one another, but to underscore a specific point of convergence among a key strand of Black feminist criticism at the site of the enslaved body's *use* as a metaphor for the master, and especially in the way each of them, while attending to a wide range of culturally and archivally specific variations of the phenomenon, links this metaphorical use to the structure of the master–slave relation itself. Hartman deploys the analytic concept of *fungibility* to name this crucial link between the figurative and signifying capacities of the enslaved body and its status as an exchangeable commodity within a slave society.[86] In the *Cambridge World History of Slavery,* historian Sandra Joshel identifies this dynamic in ancient Roman intellectual culture, in which "the fungibility of the slave takes two directions: in the economic sense, as a thing, property item or tool, and in an ideological sense, as a vessel or site of projection for masterly meanings."[87] To acknowledge this, put simply, is to acknowledge that the figure of "the slave" here is fundamentally an index of the mind of the master. Its referent is to the master's own desires, wishes, reflections, meditations, *not to that of the enslaved person.* The chapters to follow explore this neglected dynamic of the fungibility of the slave in Augustine again and again, from multiple angles, attending to the myriad, complex, and sometimes conflicting ways in which the figure of the enslaved functions, for Augustine, as a symbolic register in which to raise, make concrete, and resolve contradictions in his treatment of what I above called, following Vincent Brown, the most "elemental realms": death, sin, humility, temporality, sex, and freedom. What is the moral significance of the master's significations—the master's symbolic use of the slave's body—being built into the grammar of Christian thought and practice at each of these sites?

The answer lies, in part, in recognizing that because the relation between an enslaved person and his or her master is always premised upon force, domination, and antagonism, to accept such metaphors on their own terms is, subtly but unmistakably, to adopt the perspective of the master and thus *to take the master's side against the slave.* Here I want to be careful to avoid misunderstanding: I am not exporting the problem of race back to the fifth century, where there is no modern conception of race. What I am tracking is a set of parallel moral dynamics which race indexes in the present—the dynamics produced by the structure of master–slave relations. The method of "democratic translation" discussed above obscures these dynamics by positing a univocal "transferability" between the ancient elite man and the liberal democratic citizen, thus erasing the ethically salient fact of domination from the picture and generating unseen problems which we must now make visible again, foremost by returning to slave imagery in Augustine himself.

From the instances surveyed in Part 2, with numerous metaphors based on disobedient slaves punished and restored into good order, one might get the impression that the body of the slave works as a signifier of evil or disorder for Augustine. But that's misleading. For Augustine, it is not that *slaves* are univocally bad, only that *bad* slaves are bad. The fugitive slaves punished in the images above are contrasted not only against the figure of the faithful pilgrim throughout Augustine's writings (e.g., *conf.* 7.27), but against the figure of the *good* slave. And "good slave" images also appear throughout Augustine's work, whether in his use of the apostolic self-designation "slaves of God," or in his articulation of Christ himself as one who took the form of the slave—a crucial term in *Confessions* 7.9 and in his mature Christology of *On the Trinity* 1–2. This slave Christology, as we should expect, also traverses any neat border between actual slavery and figurative slavery, as seen in the guidance given to masters and slaves in his sermons. To the Christian who finds herself enslaved, Augustine writes, "That is as it should be. . . . [Christ] has not made slaves free, but turned bad slaves into good slaves."[88] (I return to treat this passage in some detail in Chapter 2 and to examine the "form of the slave" at length in Chapter 3.)

As we try to assess the moral significance of the master's house in Augustine's thought, then, here is the crucial point: Augustine's slave metaphors function as a moral-symbolic contrast between "good" slaves and "bad" slaves, which is not a neutral description of facts, but a particular way of encoding social reality, one which serves to perpetuate that reality and preserve its stability.[89] In this way, it displays what Willie Jennings calls a "fabricated moral universe," in which "good" and "evil" are calibrated to the aims of masters regarding their slaves' conduct. This evaluative measure is one in which "evil," in the context of slave behavior, means fugitivity and disobedience, and "goodness" means humility and obedience.[90] In short, then, the problem with these slavery metaphors is that they presume a moral-symbolic contrast that becomes coherent only from the vantage of the master's side of the master–slave conflict—not the vantage of the enslaved. In an arresting footnote, Augustinian philosopher James Wetzel hints at this dynamic in Augustine, who, he writes, tends to "measure the success of different definitions at least partly in terms of their facility to identify as evil what the consensus of his society identified as evil (for example, slaves killing their masters) and to leave as permissible what the consensus left as permissible."[91] So when what's permissible includes the master's lash but not the slave's resistance to it, it's evident enough that the public consensus of that society, on the matter of moral "goodness" in master–slave relations, was, quite naturally, built to reflect the vantage not of the enslaved but of their masters.[92] A good slave is a useful, obedient, humble slave who enables the smooth functioning of household order. A bad slave is one who makes such order more difficult or, in the case of running away, impossible. A bad master resorts to excesses of desire and cruelty. A good master is benevolent in his total control of the slave's life, inspiring unquestioning devotion and loyalty.

That this set of moral-symbolic contrasts so clearly reflects the vantage of the master class suggests that the responsible historian of antiquity must remain skeptical as to whether enslaved persons ever internalized this evaluative view of the moral life as their own.[93] We do know slaves resisted: fled, stole, lied, stopped work, and occasionally physically confronted their masters, sometimes to the point of revolt.[94] We can never know whether or how enslaved persons in antiquity may have described the moral significance of such actions, insofar as the historical evidence provides only the most fleeting, indirect, and opaque points of access to the viewpoints of enslaved persons. For that reason, even scholars whose interests are purely "historical," in the narrowly descriptive sense, now increasingly turn to comparisons from the literature of New World slavery in order to illumine ancient enslaved life.[95] How much more does such comparative work make sense for those of us who want to think constructively and normatively in conversation with ancient thinkers like Augustine?

Part 4. Sketch of What Lies Ahead

In Part 1, I showed how certain strategies of disavowal have prevented sustained engagement with Augustine's slavery discourse and the question of how to read its moral significance amid the afterlife of modern racial slavery. Part 2 sketched the contours of that discourse while demonstrating that it provides for Augustine's thought an organizing *structure*—a conceptual space I term "the master's house"—inside which the theological metaphor of slavery cannot be neatly separated from Augustine's more practical treatment of life under "actual" slavery. In Part 3, I showed how some of the intellectual tools of Black thought can help us assess the moral and theological problems these slave metaphors pose to normative and constructive ethical thought, chiefly, that they reproduce what I call "the problem of the Christian master." This problem consists in Christian theological discourse invisibly reproducing the vantage of the masters, and thus a moral universe in which virtue and vice are calibrated to the interests and self-deceptions of the masters themselves. In this final section, I offer a brief methodological remark and clarify how this opening chapter has provided a reading strategy to guide the next three chapters.

Methodologically, this book is a work of constructive Christian theological ethics. It brings into contact two distinct traditions of inquiry: modern Augustinianism and Black religious and political thought. Put somewhat reductively (for now), its method aims to reread the constructive possibilities of the first tradition in light of the critical interventions of the second. (The Epilogue subtitled "Tenebrae" returns to the scene of dusk to reflect more precisely on how to name this method in relation to several wider theological questions.) The second tradition—Black Studies—does not drive me to dismiss Augustine's thought for its association with slavery, but rather to press conversations among Augustinians deeper into the conceptual problems which result from the master's structural position necessitating certain strategic self-deceptions. Insofar as the book tracks *conceptual* problems which come into view through certain *historical* examinations, its methodology is broadly similar to a turn in recent political theory on race which aims to carefully bridge the traditional gap between the conceptual-normative and historical-descriptive camps.[96] For this reason, throughout the book I often attend to forgotten chapters in the modern reception history of Augustinian thought, finding in these a kind of laboratory in which to examine, analyze, and clarify the inner workings of Augustinian concepts.

This methodology works together with what I have shown in this opening chapter, namely that tracking the two neglected problems of Augustinianism—Augustine's slavery metaphors and the racial afterlife of slavery—provides the reading strategy which will guide the next three chapters. This strategy consists in taking up one key theme of Augustinian political thought at a time in order to explore (a) how Augustine uses slavery to clarify, amplify, or make concrete his treatment of it, (b) how this use of slavery metaphors presumes the master's vantage, and (c) how the problems generated thereby present us with parallel moral dynamics in the present, which can be addressed by thinking with modern Black thought on the afterlife of slavery.

The contributions of this approach are fourfold. First, it enriches Augustinian politics by showing how *race* constitutes a crucial, heretofore neglected aspect of the American scene into which Augustinians wish to "translate" Augustine's enduring political wisdom. This contribution will be of interest to modern Augustinian political thinkers, who have, up to this point, viewed as essential neither the problem of race to modernity, nor the resources of Black thought to their intellectual task. Second, the book contributes to the field of Black Studies by showing how its critical and constructive resources extend in surprising directions, far beyond the narrow constraints sometimes imposed upon it. In arguing that Black Studies opens up new pathways in reading an ancient figure like Augustine and his modern "political Augustinian" inheritors, I think of the great C. L. R. James who, in a 1970 interview, framed the task of the field as "the intervention of a neglected area of studies that are essential to the understanding of *ancient and modern* society."[97]

Third, this approach experiments with bringing together two powerful approaches to the problem of revitalizing religious life and thought under the ambiguous conditions of "modernity"—however defined. These two camps too often remain in binary isolation from one another: tradition and critique, or "traditionalists" and "liberationists"; or again, those who retrieve premodern Christian tradition to tackle modern dilemmas and those who proclaim God's action in and as the liberation of the oppressed.[98] I take modern Augustinianism as an especially important species of the former, and Black theology of the latter. These two frameworks meet in my approach neither by mere "critique" of tradition by liberation, nor by simply "applying" tradition to a particular "context." Instead, my hope is for something like a constructive *encounter* between them, one explored not for its own sake, but for the sake of yielding a theologically rich intervention into a perennial and timely dilemma, especially visible in this moment of American politics: the longing of human creatures for dominance sanctioned by the divine, for Godlike power, that is, for claiming the position of the master and sacralizing that claim as the work of God. Fourth, just to the extent that this intervention is found persuasive in its account of contemporary life, the book demonstrates the ongoing relevance of what we might call unlikely humanities encounters, that is, dialogues between texts which broadly belong to the curriculum of humanistic inquiry, but have not yet been found relevant to each other. The point is not to mash up any random two traditions of thought, but rather to let a particular problem—in this case what I have designated the problem of the Christian master—elicit whatever tools fit the task.

TWO

The Road and the Woods

The heavenly city, while on its earthly pilgrimage, calls forth its citizens
from every nation, and assembles a multilingual band of pilgrims; not
caring about any diversity in the customs, laws and institutions whereby they
severally make provision for the achievement and the maintenance of earthly
peace. . . . *The heavenly city does not repeal or abolish any of them,* provided
that they do not impede the religion whereby the one supreme and true
God is taught to be worshipped.
—Augustine, *The City of God*

As itinerancy, nomadism, migration, roving, or simply walking, moving
about occurred below the threshold of formal equality and rights and
articulated the limits of emancipation and the constrained terms of
agency. . . . The freedom experienced was in the search and not the destination.
—Saidiya Hartman, *Scenes of Subjection*

In a sermon delivered at Carthage in 412, Augustine offered a characteristic invocation of one of his most enduring themes: "everyone is on the
move in this life."[1] The figure of the *peregrinus* remains the central image of
Augustinian political thought.[2] Its wide and contested lexical range—exile,
pilgrim, wanderer, sojourner—indicates a certain density of meaning, a
saturation point of intimately related, but nonidentical signifying possibilities. Aliens are not quite the same as exiles, nor are pilgrims interchangeable
with travelers.[3] *Peregrinatio* emerges in English translation not as a single
thing, but a cluster of overlapping concepts which elicit close attention and
careful untangling.[4] This is especially the case insofar as their moral and
political significance consists in the way they enable Augustine and Augustinians to conceptualize the role of the City of God on pilgrimage in the

world, the shape of human life during its journey toward eternity through the present age, and the position of moral agents in relation to the existing political order through which they sojourn.[5] These three issues—the role of the City of God, the temporality of human life, and moral agency in relation to political order—are neither identical nor easily separable in Augustine's thought.

The semiotically dense cluster of *peregrinatio* concepts signals Augustine's immersion in scripture—echoing Israel's exodus, the prodigal son's wanderings, Jerusalem as heavenly home—even as it connects him, in complex ways, to Plotinus, "the Platonists," and similar imagery in other major religious traditions.[6] If a glimmer of truth appears, however partial, in the tendentious claim of one modern philosopher, it connects Augustine to "the core of all religions, of any genuine religious experience . . . the fundamental message [of which] is: our home is elsewhere."[7] And finally, it also connects Augustine's thought to a series of strikingly contemporary issues concerning the centrality of migration, refugees, and statelessness to questions of social and political order in twentieth- and twenty-first-century political thought.[8] A family of *peregrinatio* concepts, then, lies at the heart of late ancient religion and modern politics alike, and noting the parallels and disjunctures between the two matters greatly for understanding Augustine on his own terms, and thus matters in a special way for constructive thinkers who resource his writings for contemporary moral and political questions.

In Sarah Stewart-Kroeker's incisive treatment of *peregrinatio* in Augustine, she locates "its most iconic iteration" near the end of *Confessions* 7, a passage she quotes as follows: "It is one thing from a wooded summit to catch a glimpse of the homeland (*patriam*) of peace and not to find the way (*iter*) to it. . . . It is another thing to hold on to the way (*uiam*) that leads there, defended by the protection of the heavenly emperor."[9] The ellipsis Stewart-Kroeker inserts between these two sentences appears in just the same place when the passage is quoted in recent works by Matthew Levering (2013), Michael Barnes (2008), and Annemaré Kotzé (2004).[10] Buried inside the ellipsis we discover a second, neglected figure of Augustinian thought: the fugitive slave.

The "iconic" road Augustine depicts, the elided material reveals, is "surrounded by the ambushes and assaults of fugitive deserters." As translator Henry Chadwick clarifies in a footnote (*conf.* 3.8.16n32), this *fugitivis desertoribus* image draws on the well-known danger in antiquity of traveling on side-roads, where the pilgrim's safe passage was ever threatened, where thieving bands of runaway slaves and army deserters lay in wait in the woods. The simultaneous appearance and disappearance of the slave in the scene—the integral role of fugitives to Augustine's purpose, their erasure by the Augustinians' insertion of ellipses—displays again the interpretive habit of disavowal introduced in the previous chapter, prompting again the need for a closer look.[11]

This chapter examines constructive and critical ethical dimensions of this "iconic" Augustinian scene. It is iconic insofar as it provides a window into the disavowed relation between these two figures and the spaces where Augustine imagines them: the pilgrim and the fugitive, the road and the woods.[12] In modern Augustinian political thought, the notion of the *civitas peregrina*—the heavenly city on pilgrimage, in exile, sojourning through the world—has long provided a framework for faithful Christian citizenship (if a highly contested one),[13] especially in the context of widespread perceived diminishment of Christian influence in western public life.[14] In such accounts, western Christians are said to be like exiles in a strange land, with the condition of modernity—especially in its secularity and religious pluralism, however theorized—imagined as the "desert" or "wilderness" through which modern pilgrims must sojourn on their way home. I follow Willie James Jennings in finding such assessments, for the most part, "painfully superficial," as they "bypass the deeper realities of Western Christian sensibilities, identities, and habits of mind which continue to channel patterns of colonialist dominance."[15] Meanwhile, if political Augustinianism is distinctive in its focus upon the figure of the *peregrinus,* it is fully at home in most western political thought insofar as this second figure—the fugitive slave—attracts little attention at all.[16]

Yet both figures saturate Augustine's political and theological writings. In both, the symbol of the body in motion, exposed to terror and without home in this world, gives rise to thought.[17] And both, as I show in this chapter, provide Augustine with sites for conceptualizing forms of moral agency in relation to political order, as both conceive moral and political action as ways of "moving" through the world.[18] But whereas, in the Black radical tradition, the image of fugitive slaves evokes marronage throughout the Americas, the Underground Railroad, the courage of Harriet Tubman, or the resistance of Frederick Douglass, Augustine's symbolic system invests the fugitive slave with a wholly negative valence, indeed, as the above passage shows, with the precise opposite moral evaluation of the pilgrim. The pilgrim signifies the heavenly city's humble citizens, the former the false freedom of the disobedient, including demons in the *Confessions* passage above, and elsewhere the wretchedness of Augustine himself: "I loved my own ways, not yours. The liberty I loved was merely that of a runaway [*fugitivam*]" (*conf.* 3.3.5). If Augustinian politics has been largely negotiated through competing conceptions of (and resistance to) the image of *peregrinatio*, and especially the *civitas peregrina*, how might attending to the fugitive as the pilgrim's other—the sign of an alternative mode of movement through the world, as theorized and enacted in the Black radical tradition—clarify the limits and possibilities of Augustinian pilgrimage politics, particularly by disclosing its entanglements in the enduring position of the master?

With this question as my driving concern, I do not advance an exhaustive or systematic treatment of all instances of these two images in Augustine's thought, nor do I contend Augustine himself used them together in a unified or systematic way. Indeed, to the contrary, what interests me are the implications of the fact that he doesn't; that is, what interests me is the fact that both figures, pilgrim and fugitive, appear fluidly across wide-ranging contexts, while retaining the basic moral orientation glimpsed in the iconic scene above: pilgrims are nearly always broadly "positive"; fugitive slaves nearly always "negative." At issue is the orientation itself, the antifugitive valorization of the pilgrim, as one key site for displaying the problem of the Christian master. Thus, the sharp disjuncture which emerges at the site of the fugitive and the pilgrim provides a window into what it means to theorize issues of contemporary moral concern within the world race built—issues like agency, order, and the virtues—while connecting them to the problem of the master. Doing so presents us with both a problem and an opportunity.

The problem is this: If modern Augustinians, unlike Augustine himself, reject the notion that enslavement is a divinely ordained, if tragic, post-fall necessity,[19] then they must also reconsider the *moral-symbolic universe* that accompanies Augustine's justification of slavery—that is, the moral orientation in which fugitive slaves are fitting emblems of evil, disorder, and disobedience.[20] This chapter clarifies the specific contours of this problem by analyzing the moral-symbolic contrast between the wandering pilgrim and the fugitive slave, between the road and the woods. While both pilgrim and fugitive signify homelessness within the *Confessions* and beyond, their metaphorical uses presume different forms of the agent's relation to the political order of the surrounding world, and thus offer us different models for conceiving social and political agency. In short, paying attention to the appearance of "bad" slaves, especially fugitives, in Augustine's thought clarifies an abiding problem with his pilgrimage politics—namely, the problem of the master: the alignment of "pilgrims" with the moral and intellectual vantage of the master class, along with the conceptual and moral self-deceptions that this vantage entails. The alignment of pilgrims with masters emerges most clearly when the framework of analysis centers upon what previous Augustinian political thought has neglected: the image of disobedient and unruly slaves in Augustine's texts, the fugitive actors who disturb order and inhabit the woods as outlaw spaces of political life. In Augustine's assessments of good and bad slave behavior, we see how readily the moral framework of "pilgrims"—those in the "pilgrim" position of society, which I specify further below—can be captured by the masters' narrations of ethical life, by what I will call, following Willie Jennings, "the fabricated moral universe" of master–slave relations in which fugitivity is encoded as evil, obedience lauded as virtuous, and the household's peace protected as the central, if fragmentary, temporal good.[21]

But this problem also presents an opportunity: it opens a path for Augustinians into a more serious engagement with the present moment of western political and social life, in which the ongoing salience of race as the afterlife of slavery has attained a certain mainstream visibility in the Trumpist era—dispelling whatever misguided fantasies of postracialism might have lingered from the Obama years. Augustinians have tended to have little to say of race directly, instead preferring to place it within a catalogue of serial "differences"—usually a list that reads something like, "cultural, ethnic, racial, national, and religious differences"—as part of an overarching multiculturalist framework in which "pluralism" is the central problem of modern politics, providing a neutral description of the conditions of secularity and modernity which Augustine's pilgrimage politics will then help us address.[22] A richer, more serious Augustinian engagement with modern political life as an irreducibly racialized landscape—that is, with the afterlives of Atlantic slavery, settler colonialism, and Indigenous genocide in the present—is both necessary and possible. It is possible, I suggest, by finding in the concept of slavery, and especially in the fugitive slave, a category *internal* to Augustine's own thought and thus a promising point of contact for constructive encounter with the present.[23]

This in turn opens a way toward a rich, long-overdue dialogue with the tradition of Black Studies, which has long reflected on the meaning of being fugitive in the world, finding in fugitivity a profound sign of what Robin D. G. Kelley calls "freedom dreams" amid the radical precarity of human life under death-dealing structures of mastery.[24] This encounter of Augustinianism with Black accounts of fugitivity can enrich and clarify, even as it elaborates the limitations of, Augustinian models of citizenship premised upon pilgrimage. What might an account of the moral agency of the City of God on pilgrimage look like when analyzed in relation to the fugitive spaces of modern life, the woods, the maroons in the swamps or up on the hillside, or in the ecologies J. Kameron Carter and Sarah Jane Cervenak recently theorized as "the black outdoors"?[25]

This chapter argues that the *problem* consists in the figurative role the fugitive plays in the pilgrim imagination, which is rife with self-deception insofar as the latter is captured by the moral vantage of masters—as displayed in Augustine's own texts, and as these have been taken up and mined for a contemporary Augustinian politics. The *opportunity* consists in the pressure exacted upon Augustinianism by encountering fugitive enactments of ethical life as being-at-home-elsewhere—as displayed in Black political and religious thought which emerged, in key part, *from* the position of the fugitive, while not being reducible to "the particular context of its genesis."[26]

After sketching the present state of *peregrinatio* in Augustinian political discourse by mapping its three key coordinates in Part 1, Part 2 stipulates basic definitions for pilgrim and fugitive as they appear in Augustine and Augustinian thought, providing a basic account of the social positions they index within a given political order, and drawing out the contrast between the forms of moral agency available to these two positions. Part 3 turns to examine one text in particular, Augustine's exposition of Psalm 124, as a window into the issues raised in Part 2. With an eye toward how this text indexes certain key debates in the history of Augustinian reception, I not only argue that Augustine's uses of pilgrim and fugitive slave operate through the master's house (the point of section 2), but that these uses put on display what I have called "the problem of the master," that is, the specific self-deceptions, moral antinomies, and theological missteps which emerge from doing ethical reasoning from the position of the master. To do this, I draw upon the work of Hortense Spillers, Saidiya Hartman, and Orlando Patterson. Finally, having displayed the *problems* presented by the fugitive/pilgrim contrast, the fourth part takes up a constructive encounter with the notion of fugitivity, specifically marronage, in modern Black thought, raising prospects for rethinking an Augustinian model of the *civitas peregrina* as an alternative form of movement through the world in relation to its projects of mastery.

Part 1. Mapping *Peregrinatio* Politics:
Three Coordinates

Historically, the *peregrinatio* image—particularly the notion of the heavenly city on pilgrimage (*peregrinator in mundo, civ.* 1.35)—has both tended to provoke and been used to correct a series of flat, reductive accounts of Augustine's political views: as otherworldly and spiritualizing; or as solely grim and pessimistic; or as instrumentalizing the finite, the material, and the neighbor for the sake of (respectively) the infinite, the immaterial, and God; or, finally, as generating a teleological structure (a "home" unavailable to us now, but toward which we journey) which leads either to paternalistic coercion in the world or to quietist retreat from it. Whether condemned or praised, *peregrinatio*—and its related vocabulary of exile, pilgrimage, wandering, and so forth—still sets the terms for debate. And in each of these debates, the political significance of *peregrinatio* as a framework in Augustinian thought has proved inseparable from the question of the present time as *saeculum*, and thus in contemporary thought, inseparable also from debates concerning modern conceptions of the secular.[27]

More than fifty years after the publication of Robert Markus's seminal work *Saeculum: History and Society in the Theology of St. Augustine*, most of the book's critics have come "to accept his emphasis on eschatology but veer from his insistence on the historical invisibility of the two cities," James Wetzel notes, with many taking issue especially with the *neutrality* and *autonomy* Markus's Augustine imputed to the secular sphere.[28] In more recent work Markus himself has largely accepted the validity of the latter criticism, while defending his view that the heart of "Augustine's distinctive view of the secular is his persistent eschatologism."[29] The debates rage on.[30] Yet Eric Gregory and Joseph Clair contend that, for all the ink spilled across the twentieth century and beyond on Augustine and politics, the wide-ranging attempts to "construct institutional renderings" predicated on Augustine's *peregrinatio* framework of temporal and eternal goods have, in the end, "run their course and climaxed in the stalemate of a liberal and antiliberal debate over secularity."[31] I concur with that assessment of the state of the question as a stalemate and therefore restrict myself here to identifying what I see as the three key coordinates which help us map the present moment in political Augustinianism moving forward, that is, the three aspects of a *peregrinatio* politics which are closest to commanding some measure of agreement among diverse Augustinians in the wake of this (anti)liberal stalemate.

The purpose here is not to provide an exhaustive review of the literature, nor to move too quickly to lump together thinkers with profound disagreements, but rather to chart the coordinates of the shared terrain, the common ground on which various skirmishes among contemporary political Augustinians play out. By highlighting three salient aspects of that shared terrain, I advance my sense of where the conversation is heading and set the stage for introducing, in the next section, how this conversation might shift when viewed in relation to the master's house—Augustine's symbolic and material uses of slavery.

The three coordinates are: (1) temporality against totalization, (2) earthly peace amid pluralism, and (3) virtue ethics against theories of state and individual. Significantly, each of these reflects the broad method of "democratic translation" discussed in Chapter 1, that is, the political Augustinian approach of "translating" a specific theme in Augustine's writings into transferable wisdom for modern political thought. Or more precisely, we should note with Eric Gregory that among political Augustinians, "differences may arise not simply from interpreting the historical Augustine, but from assessing the needs of our age."[32] Each of the three elements of *peregrinatio* politics glimpsed here describes *both* an interpretation of some feature in the writings of "the historical Augustine" *and* an assessment of how that feature can address the perceived "needs of our age." With each of these three elements, my intervention unfolds at both levels—interpretation and assessment. I challenge political Augustinians' assessment of the needs of our age, insofar as the dilemmas posed by the ongoing racial afterlives of slavery—its effects across multiple domains of social and political life—have not yet formed an object of inquiry in modern Augustinianism, that is, have not yet been recognized as belonging to the "needs of our age."[33] And thus, my strongly divergent reading of the character of these needs does not prompt me to impute foreign concerns to Augustine, but rather *attunes* me to features of his thought left underexplored, namely, his treatment of slavery, and in particular the fugitive slave as a contrast to the figure of the pilgrim.

My intervention thus contends that it is the use of mastery, slavery, and fugitive slaves by "the historical Augustine" that invites further consideration, as it is these core themes which most powerfully reveal "a different Augustine for our time," to use Gregory's helpful language again, one bearing the "Augustinian lessons" we need for this particular moment in the discourse of pilgrimage politics.[34] Neither the "pessimist Augustine," nor the "historicist Augustine," nor the "civic Augustine" has yet given us the Augustine we need to confront this particular moment. The Augustine which emerges in this chapter as an alternative to these does not form an easy target for anachronistic judgment for his subtle alignment with the position of the master; to the contrary, it is this Augustine and his alignment with mastery which best shows us—or some of us—to ourselves as masters, and thus opens a path toward rethinking our agency in relation to the structures of mastery we have inherited. In this way, it is also worth noting that all three of these elements—temporality, peace, virtue—are fundamental enough to the study of race, religion, and the public square to be of interest beyond the Augustinian conversation.

Temporality Against Totalization: Preserving Ambivalence

The first element of *peregrinatio* politics is a distinctly Augustinian sensibility toward temporality characterized by *ambivalence,* which is enlisted to help modern Augustinians counter both totalizing utopian and totalizing pessimistic tendencies in modern political thought.[35] I choose the word *sensibility* carefully, to indicate not a wholesale agreement among Augustine's interpreters regarding either Augustine's conceptions of temporality, or how such conceptions might inform a contemporary politics. Both are notoriously contested and complex. Rather, I suggest that just to the extent an account of political life is genuinely Augustinian, it will be marked by a deep and abiding sensitivity toward the way temporality (in contrast to eternality) shapes what politics is and can be "during the world."[36] By "ambivalence," I mean that for Augustinians, all political projects during the temporality of the *saeculum* are marked, irreducibly, by the conflict between two dimensions of human life on earth: (a) the inescapable *absence* of any finality, purity, or ultimacy in the capacity of political life to secure the ultimate goods of human life; and (b) the inescapable *presence*, nonetheless, of a crucial set of real, limited temporal goods which politics makes available. Dimension (a) means that higher, eternal goods are to be *preferred* to lower, temporal goods. Dimension (b) means that such lower goods may be used properly in the meantime so long as they are *referred* toward the higher.[37]

This inescapability of both presence and absence, preferring and referring, positive and negative dimensions taken together, marks the temporal condition of politics, ensuring that all genuinely Augustinian political projects are marked by a sensibility which manifests in a kind of lexicon of ambivalence, a recurring set of Augustinian terms of art: for the disposition of pilgrims, those terms are verbs like *longing, yearning, enduring, hoping;* for the status of political life, those terms are nouns like *ambiguity* and *tension, mixture* and *fragment, contingency* and *indeterminacy.* The lexicon of ambivalence opens a middle road between extremes.[38] As Luke Bretherton writes, it "constitutes a response to both Constantinian triumphalism (marked by an expectation of progress until the church would overcome the world and universally display heaven's glory in history) and Donatist separatism from the world (wherein history is oriented toward regress or a movement away from God)."[39] For this preservation of tension, holding at bay the calcification of either the total "presence" or total "absence" of humankind's final ends during the *saeculum,* I stipulate as a shorthand the term *ambivalence.*[40]

And it is precisely the *peregrinatio* framework and the figure of the *peregrinus* which enable Augustinians to display this temporal sensibility of ambivalence, as when Charles Mathewes writes, "to understand our life in its full ambivalence" is to "[recognize] our real joys while also acknowledging the distance we have yet to travel to the kingdom."[41] Much earlier Peter Brown recognized that, for all the angst it generates in modern moral thought, the genius of the *peregrinatio* image has always been precisely its ability to hold together, in ambivalent and tragic mixture, these positive and negative aspects of a pilgrim politics—exile away *and* journey toward, absence *and* presence, grief as well as longing:

> For the *peregrinus* is also a temporary resident. He must accept an intimate dependence on the life around him: he must realize that it was created by men like himself, to achieve some "good" that he is glad to share with them, to improve some situation, to avoid some greater evil; he must be genuinely grateful for the favorable conditions that it provides.[42]

Given that *peregrinatio* as an "image-system" is "both pervasive and diffuse . . . [i]ts boundaries . . . porous,"[43] as Stewart-Kroeker's recent work has shown, I thus limit my scope in what follows to the social and ethical dimensions which Brown's description glimpses: *peregrinatio,* for my purposes, names a form of movement through the world which, as a framework for conceiving moral agency in the world, emphasizes not only the "negative" aspect of exile from the heavenly city but also the "positive" aspect of what he calls "temporary residence," "shared goods," "favorable conditions," and "intimate dependence on the life around" the pilgrim.[44]

Earthly Peace amid Pluralism: Engaging Difference

This brings us to the second element of contemporary Augustinian *peregrinatio* politics: the focus upon *partial, but crucially important earthly peace*—especially as a response to the modern challenges of pluralism and difference. As suggested by Brown, the *peregrinus* provides a model of Christian life in this world that emphasizes the limited, but real temporal goods which the pilgrim holds in common with the surrounding world—chiefly an "earthly peace," partial and fragmentary, never to be confused with the lasting peace of the eternal city, but a genuine good nonetheless. Here as above, the point is not to grasp for wholesale agreement among contemporary Augustinians where there is none. Rather, it is to identify the specific, shared connection among multiple Augustinian accounts between the interpretation of a feature of Augustine's thought—his concern with the capacity of political life to provide a modicum of "earthly peace" amid intractable conflict[45]—and an assessment of the particular needs of our time. That perceived need is for those on pilgrimage to respond to the dilemmas posed to modern political life by pluralism and difference, most often viewed in relation either to the economic and political transformations gathered under the heading "globalization," to the cultural and religious transformations associated with the erosion of "Christendom," or to both.[46]

Variations upon what I have termed here the second theme of *peregrinatio* politics abound in contemporary Augustinianism, but I mention briefly three influential accounts—one ethicist, one political theorist, one historian.[47] In Eric Gregory's article "Strange Fruit: Augustine, Liberalism, and the Good Samaritan," the concept of earthly peace emerges at a crucial pivot in the argument: between Gregory's acknowledgment of Augustine's deep skepticism of political life and Gregory's contention, nonetheless, that there exists an Augustine whose deep civic engagement can inform our own.[48]

Kristin Deede Johnson's book-length engagement with the politics of pluralism, *Theology, Political Theory, and Pluralism: Beyond Tolerance and Difference,* finds the upshot of her engagement with Augustine at precisely the intersection of ambivalence (the preservation in time of tension between two extremes), earthly peace, and their capacity to respond to modern pluralism:

> The answer to what all of this means for the relationship of citizens of the Heavenly City to the earthly city lies somewhere in between the two extremes of completely abandoning the earthly city and looking to the earthly city to achieve utopian-like harmony and peace. Augustine is clear that citizens of the Heavenly City share in the goods of the earthly city, making use of its earthly peace and helping to defend and sustain the limited harmony that is possible in the earthly city, "a kind of compromise between human wills about things relevant to mortal life." . . . Citizens of the Heavenly City can help foster those goods in the many different earthly cities in which they find themselves.
>
> As these citizens contribute to the goods of their earthly cities, they need not try to force their different earthly cities into one supposedly God-prescribed political arrangement.[49]

And in Deede's account, it should not surprise us that it is precisely the figure of the pilgrim, and the framework of *peregrinatio,* which holds together temporal ambivalence and earthly peace as response to pluralism.[50]

Similarly, when historian R. A. Markus returned, in the last sustained treatment of Augustine of his illustrious career, to the question of "what kind of a political theory in present-day terms an Augustinian model of society might point to," he immediately looks to the seventeenth chapter of *The City of God* 19: "[Augustine's] keynote is consensus: 'The heavenly City during its pilgrimage here on earth makes use of the earthly peace and of a certain cohesion of human wills concerning the things pertaining to men's mortal nature.' " The "cohesion of human wills"—or the consensus—of which he is speaking here is central to his conception of what the earthly and the heavenly Cities share: he insists on it twice in the same chapter.[51] Markus then elaborates the significance of this interpretation in light of his assessment of the needs of our political age, offering what he calls a "*retractio*" of his previous, widely contested (though still influential) embrace of an Augustinian sanction for modern secular liberalism,[52] while developing a thoughtful engagement with major figures in the liberal-communitarian debates like Alasdair MacIntyre, Michael Walzer, and Charles Taylor. At issue in this engagement, in key part, are "questions about the nature and scale of the community in which moral value can be embodied, promoted, and taught."[52] Markus acknowledges that Augustine's sensitivity to sin's deforming effects "would incline him to be suspicious of claims on behalf of the political community's capacity to promote the moral life." But with that key reservation stated, Markus's Augustine conceives the scale of seeking "earthly peace" in a form broadly translatable, in modern liberal democratic terms, neither to defending personal liberty at the level of the individual, nor merely to promoting security and order at the level of the state,[54] but rather to an intermediate level of "maximizing the moral and cultural consensus which make it the society it is." This is so, Markus continues, even or perhaps especially given that "his earthly City was inevitably what we would nowadays call 'pluralistic' in its nature, composed of diverse cultures . . . committed to different and conflicting value systems."[55] Read carefully within the complexities and tensions of Augustine's mature thought, then, earthly peace is never to be confused, on the one hand, with the final and lasting peace to which totalizing empires (or states) pretend, nor on the other is it a private matter for the self (fragmented by sin, distended in time); rather, it is a shared good of which pilgrims may and must avail themselves with their neighbors amid the differences, tensions, and conflicts interminable during this temporal sojourn. This intermediate level brings us to the third coordinate.

Virtue Ethics: Recovering the "Middle Distance" View Against Theories of Individual and Institution

Here, again, I follow the lead of Eric Gregory and Joseph Clair's 2015 assessment of the state of Augustinian (and Thomist) political thought. They contend that the stalemate over secularity between Christian liberals and antiliberals results from the attempt to specify the Augustinian relation between temporal goods and eternal goods (or the Thomist relation of natural and supernatural) "*at the institutional level*," that is at the level of questions of church and political community.[56] The way beyond the stalemate, then, is "to focus not simply on institutions but on individuals; not on raw individuals, but socially coded individuals in their distinctive roles, as members of all levels of society and as tenders of particular common goods who are in need of specific virtues."[57] That is, the focus ought to be on an intermediate level of virtue formation for citizens-in-relation, not on the deracinated individual or the institutional arrangement of church and political community.

This proposal is not novel,[58] but rather reflects a helpfully concise restatement of the broad movement of Augustinianism beyond postwar, midcentury debates, which focused on how to apply the two cities framework to the emerging western consensus of liberal democratic orders, toward the late-twentieth-century turn to the virtue ethics of citizenship.[59] The latter shifted the terms of the debate away from Christian "realists" and their opponents trying to determine which institutional arrangement between church and state Augustine might have favored (a debate that centered, textually, upon interpreting Book 19 of *The City of God*). It moved toward the question of "translating" Augustine's concern with "the public official's soul" into counsel for the virtues needed in the souls of democratic citizens, with the concomitant shift of the "textual center of gravity" toward letters, sermons, scriptural commentaries, and overtly "doctrinal" works like *On the Trinity*.[60]

On this too, Peter Brown's work proved prescient. In 1972, his *Religion and Society in the Age of St. Augustine* recognized that, even within *The City of God*, Augustine's account of political life "deliberately focuses attention upon that 'middle distance' of human habits, values and instincts, which, far more than its structure, remains the greatest mystery of political society."[61] This focus upon the "middle distance," Brown continues, offers a striking contribution to modern political theory, which has tended to analyze politics as a "matter of structure" with "component parts," namely, the "isolate[d] individual on the one hand, and the state, on the other." Augustine's middle distance helps us recognize this as a "self-limiting myth." A middle-distance focus redirects our attention to the loves, desires, values, and habits of citizens, and with it the central matter of the cultivation of the virtues needed to seek earthly peace together, the sort of cohesion amid difference which provides a "far more tenacious bond of obligation" than the abstractions of state, market, or individual.[62] Certainly, not all scholars of Augustine will concur entirely with this application of his thought to modern political theory.[63] But most significant for my purposes, as I conclude my mapping of the current terrain of *peregrinatio* politics, is the fact that even someone like Robert Markus—thirty-five years after becoming (in)famous for advancing an Augustinian basis for a minimalist conception of the secular liberal state—has moved his account of the focus of Augustine's political wisdom to something very close to Brown's middle distance, and Gregory and Clair's social individuals-in-relation: "For Augustine, the nexus of the objects of its members' 'cohesion of wills,' or what Oliver O'Donovan has called its 'common objects of love,' is what constitutes the society's value system, which defines it as this particular society and sustains it as such."[64] It is upon that intermediate level of a society's loves, values, habits, and virtues that the insights of Markus's Augustine most directly come to bear.

To summarize, then, when we look upon Augustine's "iconic" roadside scene, Augustinians find folded into the figure of the *peregrinus* an image of political life marked by a temporal sensibility of ambivalence which rejects the closures of totalizing pessimism or totalizing optimism. This ambivalence emphasizes the limited but real goods pilgrims share with the earthly city, chiefly a partial and fragmentary peace amid plurality, conflict, and difference. This in turn draws our attention beyond the institutional level to the "middle distance," where selves-in-relation undergo formation into the virtues necessary for public life, whether as an elite statesman (in Augustine's time) or as a democratic citizen (in the Augustinians' translation to the present).

And it is precisely this turn among the current generation of political Augustinians to the middle distance, as distinct from the previous one's preoccupation with the institutional and the structural, which provides the opening for my approach in the next section. There I turn to examine the significance, for *peregrinatio* politics, not simply of the existence of slavery as an institution, but of the presence of the other figure of the iconic roadside scene, her fugitive movement inside, against, and beyond the master's household throughout Augustine's corpus. It is that movement which, I will claim, confounds a neat conceptual distinction of the move to "the middle distance," that is, the clean distinction between the structural and the social. How then do the preceding three coordinates of *peregrinatio* politics play out when viewed in relation to the master's house, the symbolic space of slavery—at a scale calibrated between "raw individuals" and "the institutional level"—in which the figure of the bad slave has closely entangled "metaphorical" and "literal" implications in Augustine's thought? Chapter 3 will develop an extensive engagement with the third coordinate, virtue, by discussing Augustine's central virtue of *humilitas*. Chapter 4 will focus on what I have here called the first coordinate—temporality, ambivalence, and Augustine's conception of providence. The remainder of this chapter implicates all three coordinates, but primarily focuses on the second: earthly peace.

Part 2. Earthly Peace and the Master's House: Fugitive Disruptions of Order

As I noted in the previous chapter, when slavery is not being disavowed in the pilgrimage politics of Augustinianism, its discussion most often centers upon the vexed question of political authority in Book 19 of *The City of God*, whether and how such authority is "natural" or unnatural, how civic authority relates to ecclesial authority, and what this implies about how the institutions of church and state relate to one another in the *saeculum*.[65] This focus is understandable, and Chapter 4 will return to these issues, but what makes that discussion possible is first to clarify what this way of posing the issue of slavery often conceals from view. By framing the interpretation of slavery in Augustine solely at the macro-institutional level, the pattern of reasoning which tends to follow can only concern whether Augustine could have reasonably been expected to "disapprove" of or call to abolish an institution which, as the historical record attests, was taken to be fundamentally woven into the fabric of life in Roman late antiquity.[66] As Ilaria L. E. Ramelli notes in the opening paragraph of her ambitious study of slavery in ancient Jewish and Christian thought, "One major problem in this kind of study is, of course, that ancient authors, and ancient people in general, could hardly envisage or imagine slavery as a stand-alone institution, separate from the socio-economic, political, cultural and religious milieu in which they lived on a day-to-day basis."[67] And yet, the remainder of her study proceeds precisely to demonstrate, as one perceptive reader noted, that it does not follow that "ancient authors were . . . simply compelled to accept or reject slavery; rather, they negotiated with aspects of the institution, often from positions of uneasiness."[68]

The specific dynamics of this uneasy negotiation—of ancient authors with the institution, and of masters with enslaved persons themselves—are typically absent when mentions of slavery appear in political Augustinianism, preoccupied as the conversation has been with understanding Augustine's views on the origins of political authority. In the historiography of slave systems ancient and modern alike, scholarly debate in the last fifty years centered upon developing appropriate analytic tools for "recovering the agency" of enslaved persons—a self-conscious attempt to correct longstanding habits of treating "slaves" as inert and unthinking objects to whom various things happen.[69] In a slightly strange contrast, the Augustinian conversation, both in its focus on other questions and in its attempt to avoid "anachronistic" moral judgments, functionally erases the agency of *masters*.[70] The question of the shape of the masters' agency, of the complex social and political formations by which that agency is conditioned, and of its implications for how masters construct ethical and theological arguments, remains not unanswered but unasked.

The shift in Augustinianism to the middle distance of "socially coded individuals in their distinctive roles" has not yet generated a corresponding shift toward considering how the relations of mastery and slavery shaped the dynamics of the key social unit—the *domus*, the household. This despite (as I show below) the crucial role the household continues to play in Augustinian conceptions of pilgrimage politics, earthly peace, and the specific character of the virtues that subtend both during this temporal condition of ambivalence.[71] Nor have Augustinians, in their democratic translation project's neglect of race, begun to ask how that question (how master–slave relations shape the sociality of the household), to the extent it can be addressed as a matter of interpreting the historical Augustine, might then alter what a contemporary Augustinian vision looks like in our own parallel context. That is: in a context in which the moral dynamics of American slave society, as Black radical thought from its inception has insisted, *did not disappear* after abolition, but rather—by way of the persistent racialized inequalities of social, legal, economic, and political life—assumed new forms. What follows addresses both questions: interpreting Augustine, assessing implications for the present. In so doing it troubles the stability of the conceptual distinction above, that of the structural from the social, of the "institutional level" of politics from the values, virtues, and habits of moral agents. The institution of slavery, its wide-ranging and haunting afterlives, and crucially, one's position with reference to them disrupt claims to an unmarked univocal "we" of citizenship and thus shape what virtue looks like, what values one holds, and what specific possibilities of agency are available in one's movements on pilgrimage during the world.

One way to begin that work is to note how frequently, in modern Augustinian thought, the household constitutes a key instance of that "intermediate" level of social life between individual and state, focus upon which enables pilgrims to imagine and share in earthly peace. In staging a comparative dialogue with contemporary critics of liberal individualism, Markus proposes that the analogous "category" in Augustine for the intermediate level that communitarian thinkers call us to focus upon—that in which social bonds of filiation are cultivated—is "the household, or extended family, [as] the community in which domination has no place; the hierarchy of command and obedience exists for the mutual good. Here rule is truly service, and obedience exists for the mutual good."[72] In similarly sanguine terms, Rowan Williams's pathbreaking 1987 essay "Politics and the Soul" described the order of the household's hierarchy as a crucial, underacknowledged dimension of Augustinian politics. But where Markus subtly removes the question of slaves in the household from view, suggesting that the household "contrasted radically with slavery,"[73] Williams recognizes that in Augustine's account of the household's role in contributing to earthly peace, "the natural order of family life" *includes* "the not-quite-so-natural appendage of the household slaves."[74]

This explicit acknowledgment from Williams that the *paterfamilias* is also, for Augustine, a *dominus* makes it all the more striking that Williams then proposes that, just to the extent that a Christian master possesses "a lively apprehension of the true meaning of *ordo* and of the indivisibility of peace (as [*civ.*] XIX, 14 explains at length)," his mastery over slaves "does not run the risk of slipping over into *libido dominandi.*"[75] To the contrary, Williams continues, "so far from being the sphere of bondage and necessity, the household has become a 'laboratory of spirit,' a place for the maturation of souls (the soul of the ruler as well as the ruled)."[76] The relation between masters and slaves, then, belongs to that "*pax* of the household [which] is to be 'referred' *ad pacem civicam,*" writes Williams. What this entails is that a key aspect of the *peregrinatio* politics we have been tracking, earthly peace, encompasses multiple levels of what Augustine calls "properly ordered concord, with respect to command and obedience": body submits to soul, wives to husbands, children to parents, slaves to masters, and citizens to the "law of the city" (*lege civitatis*).[77] It is precisely on this basis that Williams arrives at the insight that helped launch a thousand civic Augustinian ships: *pace* Hannah Arendt's famous critique, Augustine's critique of Roman politics does not lead to a withdrawal from public life; to the contrary, "the member of the city of God is committed *ex professo* to exercising power when called upon to do so ... [by] continuing in a practice of nurturing souls already learned in more limited settings."[78] Those more limited settings, unmistakably, include, first, the soul's "nurturing" sovereignty over his body, and second, the master's "nurturing" sovereignty over his house. Thus, it should be stated explicitly here: in the "iconic" roadside scene above, it is not simply that "pilgrims" can turn out to be masters. It is that pilgrim politics, as a framework for the Christian use of temporal goods, centrally *requires* the work of what Williams calls "nurturing" mastery, and it is this aspect—the nurturing, teaching, caring element of being a master—which begins to distinguish the Christian master from other masters, and so brings the object of my inquiry into view.[79]

What surfaces nowhere in Markus or Williams is what the available historical scholarship on late antiquity *and* Augustine himself in the very same passage bear witness to, namely, the central problem confronting this glowing picture of the Christian household's contribution to earthly peace: enslaved persons, in each historical instance in which we find them, retained agency in the midst of the conditions of domination, and that agency surfaces in the historical record primarily in myriad forms of resistance, disobedience, flight, and criminality. Or in short, it surfaces in the form of their *performing*—if not articulating—a rejection, in ways small or large, mundane or dramatic, of the position assigned to them for the sake of earthly peace. And in so doing, they threaten, for Augustine, "the tranquility of order," since "order is the arrangement of things equal and unequal that assigns to each its due place."[80] Evidently declining what Williams described as a proposal for the "maturation" of their souls, withholding the contribution of their obedience to the building of earthly peace, enslaved persons of Augustine's day—as in our own more recent past—instead shirked, stole, fought, and fled.[81]

Augustine was well aware of this.[82] After offering the intriguing notion that it is a "greater obligation" for fathers to "put up with being masters," than for slaves to "put up with being slaves," he indicates a key problem of slavery which has not yet penetrated modern Augustinianism's discussion of the household: "If anyone in the household disrupts domestic peace by his disobedience, he is corrected by word or blow or some other just and legitimate kind of punishment."[83] Likewise, "it is entirely just that a slave should pay the penalty of years in shackles when he has provoked his master with no more than a passing word or struck him with a blow that is over in a second."[84] And in the more practical context of a sermon, as we saw above, Augustine insists, "if you see your slave living badly, what other punishment will you curb him with, if not the lash? Use it: do. God allows it. In fact he is angered if you don't."[85] Indeed, "the whip was the icon of mastery," according to historian Kyle Harper,[86] but within the master's house, writes Augustine, this lashing is "for the benefit" of the enslaved persons themselves, to bring them "back into line with the peace from which [they] had broken away."[87] Notwithstanding this instance of what Peter Garnsey calls "the beneficial thesis"—a common trope in the discourse of masters across various contexts: proper mastery benefits the slave—we know enslaved persons continued to "break away" from their owners, whether pagan or Christian, from the abundant presence in the historical record of fugitive flight.[88] Part of how we know this is the existence of widely discussed slave collars dating to the fourth century, thick iron rings locked onto the neck, often bearing Christian iconography and inscriptions such as "I am the slave of the archdeacon Felix. Hold me so that I do not flee."[89]

Two related points must be inserted here. First, fugitive flight was not a single thing, but a range of disobedient actions, a range of ways of being *not at home,* being elsewhere, indeed, being, as Augustine termed it, "out of alignment" with the peace of the household. Flight "came in different styles," as Kyle Harper writes, "along a full spectrum from true escape to temporary asylum."[90] What is especially pertinent for our purposes is a suggestive detail of Roman juridical thought. According to W. W. Buckland's still-classic study of Roman slave law, the definition of *fugitivus* is straightforward enough: "He is one who has run away from his master, intending not to return."[91] What is ordinarily meant by *servus fugitivus* is that the person in question is "in flight at the present moment." But an ambiguity is introduced by the fact that, at the point of sale, one of the regular warranties exacted is a pledge on the part of the seller, not only that the person is not currently a *fugitivus* (obviously, for how then would the sale take place?), but further, that he or she is not *fugax*. What is *fugax*? To be *fugax* is to be "given to running away—which is itself a punishable offense." That is, to be *fugax* is to bear the "tendency to flight," to be "in the habit of running away," or to be "inclined to run away." It is closely related, Buckland further notes, to being deemed an *erro,* one who is "given to wandering about."[92] In other words, to be a fugitive was not simply a matter of committing an individual crime—the theft of self. Instead, it was a matter of *being* fugacious, of *being* errant. It was a "habit," a "tendency," an "inclination," and in this sense fugitivity surfaces—even in the problematic archive of the masters' own law—as something rather like a counterformation in waywardness, an alternative "middle-distance" set of habits, values, and desires, a social life calibrated to other aims, to an elsewhere and otherwise in the woods beyond the master's house.[93]

Second, although there are many significant points of discontinuity between the slavery of Augustine's day and the slavery whose afterlife we inhabit today, it is this omnipresence of fugitivity as an option for the enslaved and as an ever-present threat to the master class that forms, according to major contemporary historians of both antiquity and modernity, one of the strongest and most promising points of comparative view with New World slavery.[94] For our purposes, this means that tracing the parallel moral dynamics of the present is especially important at this juncture for my project (while noting relevant discontinuities), just as conceptions of "citizenship," "the city," and the public/private distinction are deemed to "travel" in Augustinian democratic translation. As Neil Roberts argues persuasively in his study of modern slavery, "the analytical juxtaposition of slavery ancient and modern . . . is not a formula for conflating the historical circumstance of eras. . . . [Rather,] peering deeper into ancient and modern slave societies, thinkers, and revolutions discloses experiences of flight that excavate common submerged discursive knowledges."[95] The encounter between those shared discursive knowledges, together with their implications not just for Augustinianism, but for the critical study of race, theology, and religion in the present, forms the central purpose of this study.

And so the ubiquity of flight, or flight as being *fugax*—an alternative practice of elsewhere—presents itself as an implicit question in Augustinian thought which demands encounter with Black fugitive ethical imaginaries, like the following from James Cone: "The prevalence of flight, theft, arson, and other forms of resistance meant that the slave and master did not share the same ethical perspective."[96] Indeed, as though speaking directly of Augustine's reliance upon the moral evaluative regime of the good-slave-versus-bad-slave framework (see Chapter 1), Cone continues: "Owners thought that 'good' slaves were those who were obedient and diligent in the masters' interest, while the 'bad' ones stole, malingered, or ran away."[97] Yet as Cone makes clear, to say this is not to suggest Black people rejected the moral life. "Rather they formulated a *new* law and a *new* morality that reflected the requirements of *black* existence. . . . To make ethical judgments in this context required that slaves 'take the law into their own hands.' "[98] To note that fugitive ethical lives emerge from the spaces of mastery is not to propose too quickly that pilgrim politics attempt to align its "movement" with the fugitive. Rather, in glimpsing fugitive movement, I am suggesting it becomes possible for pilgrims who inherit the afterlife of mastery to more adequately recognize themselves *as* masters, and thus to ask what this—we might call it the white racialization of *peregrinatio*—means for their pilgrimage imaginings.

This reckoning with the racialization of pilgrimage presents a direct point of conflict with the contemporary Augustinian model of earthly peace as a response to "cultural difference," a model which presumes that life during these times demands living in accord with "the laws of the city," rather than taking "law into their own hands." It complicates—and as I will argue at length in Chapter 4, *transforms*—what it means to be made *ambivalent* by temporality. Among contemporary Augustinians, ambivalence means for Mathewes refusing the "anxious grasping after control" for the sake of "a relaxed playfulness."[99] This may be the sort of ethical injunction which makes sense, or even is needed for those inclined to positions of dominance, but it is hard not to notice the contrast emerging at the site of the hands: between "taking the law into their own hands" in Cone, and having the privilege to playfully let go of "grasping" in Mathewes. This does not on the front end settle the issue, but only begins to suggest the extent to which many Augustinian projects have not yet recognized themselves as contextual theologies, constrained by their limited relevance. Similarly, Paul Griffiths's proposal for ambivalence as generating an elegant and world-weary "quietism" seems only a possibility for some.[100]

Others sought out—and indeed, are yet seeking out—"a new style of earthly freedom."[101] To view that style of fugitive imaginings as not restricted to specific acts of "resistance," in the way that term has historically been used (with its often masculinist trappings), but rather as encompassing the full middle-distance range of being *fugax*—*inclined to flight*—is to open our conceptions of agency to the forms of care which "nourish the latent text of the fugitive," to invoke Saidiya Hartman, highlighting a broader range of possibilities for what life with God looks like during the world.[102] What I am attempting to bring into view for Augustinian politics, by shifting focus from the road to the woods, from the pilgrim to the fugitive, is a whole range of possibilities which Hartman calls "politics without a proper locus." It would be to reopen, as sites for ethical and political reflection, the everyday sort of "interventions and challenges of the dominated [which] have been obscured when measured against traditional notions of the political and its central features: the unencumbered self, the citizen." Bringing them into view as a kind of being *fugax*, an everyday orientation to resistance and refusal, underscores both "the capacity to act . . . *and* the limited and transient nature of that agency." Highlighting this kind of fugitive action shifts and expands, beyond the citizen and beyond the state, what sort of practices invite political and theological attention, as well as what counts as "action" in the first place.[103]

And so with these modern reckonings in mind, we might now be attuned differently to this: appearing alongside the band of pilgrims in the iconic roadside scene of *Confessions* 7 above, and throughout Augustine's writings, is another mode of movement through the world. This way of moving doesn't symbolize faithful Christian life for Augustine, but precisely its refusal. When fugitives appear in Augustine's text, they bring into view a different kind of social subject, and with it a set of concerns which may help us see certain implications of the Augustinian model of citizenship-as-pilgrimage more clearly. My hope is to attend to the contrast between pilgrim and fugitive slave in a way that recalibrates the significance of the three coordinates above—temporality, earthly peace, virtue—displays their being entangled in the formation process of the master, and presses them into a critical and constructive encounter with fugitive possibilities.

The *peregrinus* faced real danger and misery—risk, hunger, thirst. And yet, when we picture this iconic scene—pilgrims on the road, fugitives hidden in the woods—it clarifies that the model of pilgrimage still presumes relatively free, uncontested movement through the world empire built. As Stewart-Kroeker points out, in Augustine's image system, the road the pilgrim travels is explicitly an imperial road.[104] This movement along the road is a fitting symbol of the way Christians do not enjoy the goods of temporal order for their own sake, but rather use them in a new way, referring them to their higher good. And yet, what does it mean when a different social subject emerges in the text, the fugitive who *cannot* walk the road in the same way, who cannot "use" the limited goods which the imperial road represents—earthly peace, political stability, a modicum of order? One whose movement, instead, is by its very nature deemed *antithetical* to that peace, a threat to that stability, an emblem of disorder to be captured?

At issue in this question is whether, in relying upon what Peter Brown above called the "favorable conditions" empire provides, pilgrims also thereby rely upon the pursuit, capture, and punishment of that other social subject to make their journey. Normative challenges emerge, I suggest, when the pilgrim's use of earthly peace rests upon the subjugation of these other social subjects, those external to the category of the citizen. Put simply, it matters that for those "other" subjects, their social position complicates the very possibility of a "common good" shared with the political order as it currently exists, since that order is premised upon their own subjugation, their willingness to consent to "alignment" with the position assigned to them by the peace of the household and the city.

The strength of the *peregrinatio* image, as I have argued above, is that it models a relation of Christians to a political order in which *their* eternal good and *its* temporal goods are neither identical to one another *nor fundamentally opposed.* This ambivalence opens the possibility of a common good, of limited but real virtue ethics, and of citizenship itself. But what about those who find the temporal goods of that order fundamentally *opposed* to their eternal good? This antagonism is what the position of the fugitive slave indexes. If, in Augustine's account, the *peregrinus* is threatened by those below or outside the social world, the bands of fugitive deserters, what limits does this framework place upon speaking to or about those agents in motion who are threatened by the structures of the social world itself? How does this framework speak in the present to previously colonized African migrants trying to cross into Europe across the Mediterranean, often left to drown, or of Black and brown peoples living life amid the violence of policing and prisons in American cities? Does their existence more closely resemble the model of the *peregrinus* or of the fugitive slave? These subjects are confronted not with the general problem of cultural pluralism, but with the need to imagine other modes of ethical life amid and against specific ghosts of a logic of organizing political and social life—race—distinctive in its global histories of racial enclosure: the slave ship, the plantation, the prison, the ghetto, and beyond. In the spaces of Augustine's fugitive slaves, we see the closest thing to a parallel to this contemporary situation, our situation. If race is not to be subjected, once again, to strategic acts of disavowal, then what it presents to Augustinian thought cannot be treated merely as an issue of different cultures or religious communities existing in pluralism, but rather grasped as the ongoing antagonism between agents who are rejecting their subordinate place in the "household" of racial capitalism and those agents who placed them there for the sake of "earthly peace" in the first place. Fugitivity indexes, but is not exhausted by, the disorder generated by that rejection and refusal.[105] I will return to the specific contours of these fugitive modes of ethical life in Part 4 below, but first I need to clarify that the purpose of doing so is not solely to posit an additional perspective as an alternative to be tacked onto the Augustinian one. Rather, it is to show how the problems I have been tracking here thus far, the problems of doing Augustinian ethics without attention to the master's house, generate problems *internal* to Augustine's own thought. Moreover, we must resist the temptation to move too quickly toward fugitive possibilities, rather than tarrying inside the problem of the master.

In the passage we have returned to throughout, from *The City of God* 19.17, Augustine posits "a multilingual band of pilgrims" who move through the world "not caring about any diversity in the customs, laws and institutions whereby they severally make provision for the achievement and the maintenance of earthly peace." It indeed would be anachronistic if the purpose of this chapter were simply to fault Augustine for failing to recognize slavery as presenting a set of "customs, laws, and institutions" which "should" be rejected, or at least of which one ought not to say, "the heavenly city does not repeal or abolish any of them." But more to the point, to cast moral judgment on Augustine for getting an isolated moral issue "wrong" would be simply uninteresting. What *is* interesting, in my view, is to trace the implications of the fact that precisely because of how ubiquitous slavery was in Augustine's day, the range of relevant inquiries buried beneath the heading "slavery" is in fact *not* an isolated issue. And therefore they inevitably shape how he developed the very concepts which Augustinians wish to retrieve.

In the next section, I want to trace the root of those implications to their source, namely, the problem of the master, that is, the specific position of moral reasoning from which one is compelled to accept, that is, to recognize the legitimacy of, the central premise of the "law" of earthly peace as it is constituted in a slave society. What is this central premise? It is not an accidental property of a given slavery system, but rather what makes slavery, definitionally, slavery:

> The essential characteristic of slavery, distinguishing it from all other human
> relationships, is the commodification of the human being, the reduction
> of the human body to a piece of property. In late antiquity the experience

of slavery was diverse, because circumstances and masters and slaves were diverse. But the essential core of the slave experience, shared by slaves of all stripes, was the fact that the slave was human property. The slave was the one whose body had a price, who might someday know what it was like to sit on the auction block and watch "the bidder lifting his finger."[106]

What does it mean when one of the central features of that law and society "which the heavenly city does not repeal or abolish" is the necessary legal fiction of a human person who is also a thing, a chattel?[107] The issue of how to frame, address, and resolve the conflicts and contradictions which arise when a person is classified, ambiguously, as both subject and object, agent and thing, person and property—*that* is the juridical, moral, and practical issue which the master's intellectual resources must address.[108] The problem of the Christian master entails the question of what specific theological modes of reasoning were called upon to stabilize the contradictions of that fiction. "In its potent ability to decree that what is is not," writes poet and lawyer M. NourbeSe Philip, "as in a human ceasing to be and becoming an object, a thing or chattel, *the law approaches the realm of magic and religion.*"[109] The vision of "nurturing" sovereignty referred to above, with its rightly ordered desire, as distinct from the *libido dominandi*, may be considered one example of theological reasoning being brought inside this legal-religious-magical realm which is called upon to transform a human into a thing. It is for that reason that the next section undertakes something of a journey in rereading Augustine's exposition of Psalm 124, showing how it does this sort of work by displaying its role in a certain neglected reception history of Augustine in American slavery. This reception history prompts an occasion for probing the limits of the standard Augustinian modes of interpretation, and exploring how alternative tools drawn from the resources of Black thought help us drill deeper into the structures of reasoning which the position of the master performs.

Part 3. A Reception History of Augustine's Exposition of Psalm 124

In 1864, John Henry Hopkins, Episcopal bishop of Vermont,[110] published a widely read defense of the southern slave system entitled *A Scriptural, Ecclesiastical and Historical View of Slavery, from the Days of the Patriarch*

Abraham to the Nineteenth Century. At a key moment in this sweeping narrative, Hopkins finds in Augustine, whom he calls "prince of the fathers," ample support for his proslavery position. He reproduces familiar passages from *The City of God,* then concludes with what he calls "one interesting extract more" to complete Augustine's "testimony": "Behold," reads Augustine's exposition of Psalm 124, "he [Christ] *does not make free men* [out] of servants, but he makes *good* servants [out] of *bad* servants."[111] In this moment of profound political and cultural upheaval, Hopkins finds comfort in Augustine's reassurance that one can indeed be at once a pilgrim and a master.

There remain untold reception histories of texts like this one, and with them unexamined problems. As I noted in Chapter 1, two neglected problems confront the Augustinian translation project, and revisiting Augustine's exposition of Psalm 124 provides one especially clear way of bringing those problems into view in the context of the moral contrast between the pilgrim and the fugitive I've been discussing here. The first problem, we recall, is the abiding presence of slavery in Augustine's writings—not only as a social institution he defends, but as an extended organizing metaphor in Augustine's thought. Here I'll show again how the line between "actual" and "symbolic" slavery is not as easy to draw as has been previously assumed. Instead, both show Augustine's subtle alignment with the moral and intellectual standpoint of the master class, even as he criticizes, reworks, and Christianizes that standpoint. The second problem is the fact that this alignment—the problem of the Christian master—has certain parallels with the present, given that the contemporary scene into which Augustinians "translate" his insights *is itself the afterlife of a slave society,* the afterlife of the political order John Henry Hopkins defends here with Augustine's Psalm 124 sermon.

"As things are at present," Augustine says in this homiletical exposition of Psalm 124, "the just are rather hard pressed, and the unjust sometimes have dominion over them." It won't be that way forever, he says, but it "holds under the present dispensation." As though he hears his congregants wondering silently *quibus modis?*—"*In what ways* do we find this [dominion] happening?"—he continues: "I will give one example of this situation, from which you can extend the principle to every case. The most obvious example of the authority of one human being over another is one we encounter every day: that of a master's power over his slave."[112] In other words: Do you want to know what politics in these times is like?, Augustine asks. Look at the body in chains. Look at its owner, bearing lawful authority over a chattel that lives and thinks.

For modern readers, the statement is striking for the way it seems to consider utterly normal an institution now condemned. Here Augustine neither argues "for" slavery nor defends it from attack. He simply presumes it as a fundamental part of the world. But if that presumption stops the modern reader in her tracks, no less arresting is the apparent humanism of the statement which immediately follows: "There are masters, and there are also slaves," Augustine continues, "these are two different names; but if you remember that both are human beings, there is a name common to both." In a lexical appeal to the shared category of the human, this second statement advances a theological point concerning the image of God as present in both master and slave.

In terms of the interpretations they seem to invite, these two statements on slavery may be read, with only a little simplification, as representative of two broad sensibilities in modern Augustinian reception. Take the first statement—binding politics to slavery—as representing a familiar portrait of Augustine: he is grim and pessimistic, we're told, he is "otherworldly" about the significance of politics. This surely is the sort of text that prompts David Bentley Hart to bemoan Augustine's "darker, colder, more brutal vision of the fallen world," John Rawls to call him "one of the two dark minds in Western thought," and Hannah Arendt to charge him with making "a desert out of the world," draining force and energy and meaning from public life. It's a reputation so durable that some argue it originated with Julian—Augustine's own contemporary.[113]

Take the second statement—the one linking master and slave to the shared name "human" or the shared identification with the image of God—to stand in for the type of surprising, complex insights in Augustine's thought which allow a more recent wave of his modern interpreters to insist that "pessimism" and "otherworldliness" hardly exhaust what Augustine has to say about politics. Indeed, though the last twenty years have witnessed a particularly striking Augustinian renaissance, as suggested in the terrain mapped out in Part 1, earlier writers challenged the dour and dreary caricature of Augustine, too.

Eight years before Arendt's doctoral dissertation on Augustine, the apparent "humanism" implied in statements like the second one above captured the wartime imagination of English political thinker J. N. Figgis. His still-cited 1921 book *Political Aspects of S. Augustine's City of God* was seminal in the twentieth-century recovery of Augustine for modern politics, and in it he advances a bold claim: "No one before or since [Augustine] taught more plainly the solidarity of man."[114] By "solidarity of man," Figgis means Augustine's frequent assertion that *proximus homini est omnis homo* (every man is a neighbor), an assertion which displays, according to Figgis, the seeds of a "humane, social, cultured ideal," a latent "humanism" grounded in what Figgis calls "the fundamental likeness between man and man."[115] Christianity's rise to moral and intellectual authority in the western world, seen most decisively in Augustine, led to the emergence in world history of what Figgis alternately calls "a notion," "a belief," and "a sentiment": humanism. "All people are neighbors to one another," writes Augustine. "Ask nature. Is a person unknown to you? He is a human being. Is he an enemy? He is a human being. Is he a foe? He is a human being."[116] Figgis chalks up for this "notion" momentous triumphs indeed: "Despite many inconsistencies, that sentiment remained unchanged. It helped to produce the French Revolution; it ended the slave-trade, and ultimately slavery."[117]

Figgis's rhetoric is notably ambitious. But he is far from alone in proposing that moral values in Augustine, like early Christianity itself, denaturalized the slave system, softened relations between master and slave over time, and in this way, despite the absence of "outward" resistance, ultimately *undermined* the basis of the pagan Roman slave system "from within." Contemporary Augustinian Eric Gregory stands broadly in this tradition when he finds in Augustine a "deeply humanitarian ethic," "a cultural and intellectual watershed."[118] In another text, as we have seen, he acknowledges what he calls Augustine's "often neglected moral criticisms of slavery," further concedes "Augustine was no abolitionist," but then appeals to Augustine's rejection of natural slavery, among other things, in order to relativize the force of that concession.[119] "It is not hyperbole to think," Gregory writes, "that if Augustine had not begun this reevaluation of classical philosophy and its world, we would live in a very different moral and political universe."[120]

As variations upon the classic "amelioration thesis," such claims are as ubiquitous as they are difficult to prove. That thesis—according to which Christianity's moral culture softens master–slave relations—is now widely rejected among historians, notes Kyle Harper, who has written extensively about slavery in late Roman antiquity, but it was, he says, "the basis for a long-lived if superficial optimism about slavery in the Christian era, among ancient Christians and modern historians alike."[121] Indeed, Augustine himself had written: "You teach slaves to be faithful to their masters from a love of duty rather than from the necessity imposed on them by their status. You make masters more benign toward their slaves out of regard for the one God who is Master of both, and you dispose them to look after their interests rather than keep them down by force."[122]

Harper points out that the amelioration thesis has now "quietly faded from respectability" among historians while, perhaps more important, noting that it was never even clear what sort of evidence *could* prove such a thesis.[123] After all, Augustine's appeal to the shared category of the human, so celebrated by Figgis, appears just as easily in another sermon discussing the beating of slaves: if you are a Christian, Augustine suggests, then when you beat your slave, you do so not out of hatred but mercy: "you show pity precisely at the moment when you appear to be inflicting punishment."[124] Whether this adjustment of the master's heart was celebrated by the person *being* whipped as "improving" the relationship is, of course, not possible to determine. The pervasiveness of flight surveyed above injects doubt.

Here I want to suggest that when it comes to grappling with the significance of slavery in Augustine's thought for today, we are best served neither by dismissing him as a pessimist, nor by resisting those dismissals by highlighting competing, surprisingly "humanist" or liberal strands of his thought and life (always with disclaimers to fend off charges of anachronism), nor still by a historicist debunking of theological naïveté. Each of these three approaches has enriched the conversation. But as valuable as each is, they have not yet enabled us to dig deeper into the problem of the master—the deep structural issue of reasoning while accepting the central legal fiction of slavery. This is the challenge which meets us in the lines which come next in Augustine's sermon.

These lines are worth quoting at some length, not only because they provide the context for what John Henry Hopkins found so useful in Augustine amid the U.S. Civil War, but because they show how literal and symbolic slavery in Augustine's thought cannot be neatly disentangled. In this passage, both are drawn together inside the master's house as, at once, a material arrangement of social life *and* a conceptual space for naming who God is, what politics is, what this present age is like. After citing Paul's words to enslaved persons in Ephesians 6, Augustine expounds them as follows:

[God] is the true and eternal slave master [*dominus*], whereas those others are masters only for a time. While you are walking in the way, living in this present life, Christ does not want to make you proud. Perhaps it happened that you, having become a Christian, found yourself subject to a human master. That is as it should be . . . he has not made slaves free, but turned bad slaves into good slaves.

What a debt of gratitude rich people owe to Christ for bringing peace to their households! If in such a house there were an unbelieving slave and Christ were to convert him, he would not say to him, "Leave your master, for now you have come to know him who is your true master. . . ." No, that is not what Christ has said; rather he commands, "Do your duty as his slave."[125]

A passage like this complicates the common suggestion that certain theological insights in Augustine "might have" pressed him to reconsider his stance on slavery in a different era, since here, to the contrary, his discourse on slavery works quite seamlessly with precisely those insights—the model of pilgrimage, the *totus Christus,* the theme of pride and humility. In other words, the slavery discourse seems to work well with the very resources political Augustinians aim to recover, the same conceptual terrain we surveyed in Part 1. And so, what the previous three reading strategies—the pessimist Augustine, the civic Augustine, the historicist Augustine—haven't quite brought into view is the constructive ethical questions which emerge at this site, as the very voice of Jesus is brought inside and echoes through the walls of the master's house. Most inquiries have tended to ask whether Christian sensibilities challenged Roman slavery; but whether the answer is yes or no, the inverse question is often left unasked: how did *slaveholder sensibilities*—more precisely, the position of the master—shape the grammar of Christian political thought? What effects emerge when the voice of Christ comes to pilgrims through the grammar of masters and slaves?

I am less interested, then, in identifying the possible "social consequences" of Augustine's thought upon the slave system, whether good or bad,[126] still less in anachronistic moral judgments of Augustine's character. I am more interested in unfolding the moral significance of what emerges in this sermon, that is, in how life in the master's household has shaped Augustine's Christology, and thus, the significance of his political theology for readers who inhabit the afterlife of slavery and confront its racialized legacies in the present. To get at that, I think we need subtler, stronger analytic tools for grasping the logic of slavery itself, and for that in turn, I suggest we look to the immense resources of the African American intellectual tradition, particularly womanism and Black feminism, which arose from fugitive spaces and have long excavated the position of the master.

As one step in that direction, we might notice that when Christ's voice emerges in Augustine's sermon, it emerges in *the subjunctive mood*—the grammatical mood expressing wishes, doubts, possibilities. *If* there were an unbelieving slave in the master's house, Augustine says, and *if* Christ were to convert him, and *if* that person wanted to leave, Christ *would not* tell him to become a fugitive; Christ instead *would* tell him, do your duty as his slave.[127] This subjunctive mood implies something about the logic of mastery itself, I suggest, something Hortense Spillers examines in her classic essay "Mama's Baby, Papa's Maybe: An American Grammar Book." What Spillers notices from reading the legal codes of U.S. slavery is that in order to sustain slavery's underlying and fundamental contradiction—the "transforming [of] *personality* into *property*," of person into thing—the legal code itself *has to make recourse to the subjunctive mood*. In a sentence from the law like "Slaves shall be *reputed* and *considered* real estate," Spillers notices that "*reputed* and *considered* [function] as predicate adjectives that invite attention because they denote a *contrivance*, not an intransitive 'is.' . . . The mood here—the 'shall be'—is pointedly subjunctive, or the situation devoutly to be wished."[128]

What this insight from Spillers helps us see in the present context is twofold: First, if the subjunctive expresses wishes, doubts, possibilities, then when the subjunctive Christ of Augustine's sermon appears, we should ask: *whose* wishes are being expressed here? Whose anxieties, whose desires? Given that this Jesus denounces fugitive resistance as sinful, given that the explicit aim is to secure earthly peace for the master's house, the answer to that question is clear enough—it is the master's desires shaping who Christ is and what his voice sounds like. Second, what Spillers suggests is that the master's subjunctive—his wishes and doubts, his desires and anxieties—is linked to a prior, underlying linguistic act: the transformation of person into property, that is, the enslaving logic of slavery itself. And so it is not only that the master's Christ is a fantasy, but that it is a fantasy *in response to slavery's own wobbly construct—the regarding of person as property*.[129] It is the very unresolved antinomy of the chattel fiction, its unresolved and unresolvable act of self-deception, which calls into being the master's illusory Christ. We might say, building from Saidiya Hartman's term "scenes of subjection," that the master's house is a scene of *subjunction,* in which even the voice of God must be filtered through the self-deceptions the master needs to sustain his position *as* master. And this means, to the extent that a way of living has been built up around this position, the master is fundamentally unable to recognize, or at least unable to truthfully acknowledge, the very conditions of his own life. His own house is to him opaque. And thus, it is worth considering the deep structures underlying how, in Augustine's thought, the master's house—with its distinctive desires and anxieties and self-deceptions—gets built into the very grammar of Christian thought and the pilgrim's politics.

Thus, as Chapter 1 has already argued, Augustine's slave "metaphors" reflect not the perspective of enslaved persons—about which the sources tell us very little, but which we can only infer based on various acts of everyday resistance and occasional revolts—but rather the culture of the masters themselves. To acknowledge this is to acknowledge that the "slave" here is fundamentally an index of the mind of the master. Its referent is to the master's own desires, wishes, reflections, meditations, *not to that of the slave.* And because the relation between the two is always premised upon force, domination, antagonism, these metaphors built from the perspective of the master *are a way of taking the master's side against the slave.* These are best understood as fictions in the master's imagination, not unrelated to social reality, but a deceptive re-encoding and masking of social reality. What does it mean that Augustine's slave discourse does something similar in valorizing the ideal of the good slave and denouncing the fugitive slave?

This question points to the reality that at the heart of the intellectual life in a slave society lies a vexing dilemma: The body of the enslaved person at once *clarifies* and *confounds* the categories of the master's thought. Or put differently: The culture of the master cannot afford to stop talking about what the slave's body means, on the stages of its theaters, in its philosophy and theology, in its political and social life, and at the same time, the master cannot afford to know the slave at all. On one hand, the body of the enslaved facilitates reflection upon various classic theological dilemmas: the nature of the passions, the intractability of the will, or, notably, the sort of relation humanity bears to God or the gods—a relation of total authority on the part of the master, total dependence on the part of the slave, and total devotion flowing from the latter to the former. Here the figure of the slave's body lends clarity, making notoriously obscure relations—God to self, the body to the soul—a little more transparent. These "figurative" slave bodies, as we have seen, are ubiquitous in Augustine, but are also ubiquitous throughout western thought, highly variegated in purpose and meaning, and truly ancient—at least as old as Plato's *Phaedo*: "we men are one of the chattels [*ktemata*] of the gods."[130]

On the other hand, the slave's body also *confounds*—mixes up, scrambles, confuses, threatens the coherence of—the categories of the master's thought. "As to most chattels," writes Plato in *Laws*, "it is easy enough both to see what they should be and to acquire them; but slaves present all kinds of difficulties. The reason is that our language about them is partly right and partly wrong; for the language we use *both contradicts and agrees* with our practical experience of them."[131] Some of "our" language builds from the axiomatic truth that "one ought to own slaves that are as docile and good as possible," indeed, that sometimes slaves have "proved themselves better in every form of excellence [*arête*, virtue] than brothers or sons" in protecting their masters' interest. The ideal slave forms a very model of virtue. But "the opposite kind of language," which Plato finds in no less a figure than Homer, considers virtue contrary to the very "soul of a slave," which must instead be dealt with "like brute beasts," marked by fundamental untrustworthiness. That kind of language, it seems to Plato, accords better with our "actual" or "practical" experience of slaves, which teaches us "the slave is no easy chattel." How many "evils" result from slavery, Plato writes, from revolts in Messenia, to "crimes of all sorts" by the Corsairs, to the intriguing fact that evils seem to occur inevitably whenever slaves are kept "who speak the same tongue." Call these, then, "actual" slave bodies—the sort which can appear on the surface of the master's speech only as bad slaves, stubborn and intransigent and revolting slaves, criminal slaves, slaves who band together in groups in the woods. These too are ubiquitous throughout the texts of Augustine and of western political thought, but they provide problems, not solutions. These are not a prism or a window through which to look at other problems. These resist reason. They are opaque.[132]

What's striking here, in comparison to Augustine, is what Plato tacitly admits: the actual actions of enslaved bodies exert a kind of pressure back upon the master's language, upon his ability to find in them a model *either* of goodness or dissolution, of virtue or vice. An unspoken break opens up, between the transparent slave and the opaque slave, the slave of the master's imagination and the slave of his experience. At issue, then, is this instability of the master's thought at dusk, the site of this disjuncture, this break. It runs aground on the slave's fugitive motion. The figurative slave body, idealized for whatever conceptual purpose, exists inside the space of the master's thought. This slave tells us more about how the master thinks than it does about the slave as an "actual" agent acting in the world. This disjuncture, the aporia between the figurative body of the slave and the "actual" body of the slave, is best seen as merely the surfacing at the level of text what Hortense Spillers already pointed to in highlighting the subjunctive mood: the underlying structural contradiction inherent in slavery itself—the transmutation of human into chattel, person into property, what Aimé Césaire calls "thingification," what Bill Brown calls slavery's "ontological scandal."[133]

At the heart of intellectual life in any genuine slave society—Augustine's late antiquity, or slave-haunted Atlantic modernity—lies this underlying irresolution.[134] Its existence does not arise from contingent features of a particular time or place. It is not, in this sense, a "historical" problem, but a conceptual one. This irresolution is slavery's logical center, the structure of thought which makes slavery slavery and around which all else turns: the collapse of the distinction between person and property—human and thing. This collapse and its effects form the titular "problem of slavery" in the eminent historian David Brion Davis's series of works. The notion of human property, or what Americans at the time called "property in man," was theorized in James W. C. Pennington's fugitive slave narrative *The Fugitive Blacksmith* (1850) as "the chattel principle": "the being of slavery, its soul and body, lives and moves in the chattel principle, the property principle, the bill of sale principle; the cart-whip, starvation, and nakedness, are its inevitable consequences." In what could be taken as a condensed version of the critical portion of my entire argument, he writes:

> This case [his own narrative] presents the legitimate working of the great chattel principle. It is no accidental result—it is the fruit of the tree. You cannot constitute slavery without the chattel principle—and with the chattel principle you cannot save it from these results. Talk not then about kind and Christian masters. They are not masters of the system. The system is master of them.[135]

In short, the chattel principle means that the act of *enslavement*, that is, the symbolic and legal and material act of regard in which the master *regards* the slave as chattel, unleashes a set of contradictory demands: the master needs the person to be a thing (and so, not a person in the way that *he,* the master, is a person) *and* the master needs the person to be a person, with the unique faculties thereof—memory, speech, intelligence, and so on. (Otherwise, why not simply have an animal or a machine do it? It is no coincidence that slaves are so often likened to animals and machines.) This is to make no claim about the subjective inner state of the individual slaveholder. As Pennington says, it does not matter whether the masters are "kind and Christian." It is a claim about the logical structure of the chattel relation itself. The chattel principle, in this way, unleashes a cleavage between "the slave" as regarded chattel by the master, and the enslaved person as she actually exists. (This is not identical, but isomorphic with the factors which generate W. E. B. Du Bois's famous double consciousness.)[136] The slaveholder cannot afford to acknowledge the latter. He nevertheless may—indeed, at some level surely does—*believe* in the existence of the latter. But the structural position of the master binds him from *acknowledging* it, that is, from formally recognizing the non-thinghood, the personhood of the slave.[137]

At issue is the very center of the dilemma of doing ethics in the afterlife of slavery: "In a post-slave society where the historical victory of the enslaved stratum was incomplete," writes the late Cedric Robinson, "the question of the humanity of the enslaved people would linger."[138] In other words, the chattel principle with its traumatic effects *lingers.* He identifies two consequences from this lingering, this haunting question, both of which hold together to animate my project as a whole. First is the fact of the slaveholder's bind, the problem of the master: "We now 'know' what the master class certainly knew but for so long publicly denied only to be confronted with the truth in its nightmares, its sexual fantasies, and rotting social consciousness: the enslaved were human beings."[139] In the racialized aftermath of a slave society, the slaveholder's bind lingers too—his disavowals rooted in an affective distaste, his subjunctive Christ in various guises, his silences, his turning away from the questions posed by racial capitalism, and thus his self-imposed blindness concerned the conditions of his own life. But second, Robinson underscores that the effort of historians to restore the human status of enslaved actors is not satisfactory. The point is not simply to "include" the enslaved in a preexisting framework of "the human."[140] Rather, "the more authentic question was not whether the slaves (and the ex-slaves and their descendants) were human. It was, rather, just what *sort* of people they were . . . and could be."[141] It is this open question which Black radical thought pursues, negotiates, explores: not the inclusion of Black "subjects" within preexisting categories of thought, but the destabilizing, unmaking, and remaking of the very conceptual frameworks within which they appear—citizenship, democracy, civic virtue, and more—through the specificities of Black intellectual traditions.

In complex and interesting ways, then, the texts from Black religious and political thought surveyed in Part 4 below are premised on a different act than inclusion or recognition: the slave in flight, the fugitive, the one who is indifferent to, or at least not invested in, the master's recognition. With this act, "the slave" and the agent moving beneath that term are separated. A break opens up. And the space that opens means that "the slave" who has formed the object of the master's desire, the scene and screen in which the master thinks about himself, is revealed to be a phantom, a ghost. The chattel principle means the master is structurally positioned inside his own opaque position, inside his own forgetting, his own unknowing, his own scene of subjunction.[142] To imagine oneself a master means nothing more than this: to embrace a social position which is finally inscrutable to itself. A position which has routed its own identity through the slave's, and the slave's through the fiction of the chattel principle, and for this structural reason, *rather than through any particular moral deficiency,* cannot afford to see itself clearly. And this means that just to the extent that a household has been built up around this position, the master is fundamentally unable to recognize, or at least unable to truthfully acknowledge, the very conditions of his own life. At some level, the master knows this, and has always known this, and thus is prone to alternating bouts of anxiety and melancholy: anxiety when the slave is here, melancholy when the slave is gone. These psychological dynamics are complex and diffuse, but in part they bring into view the way that the enduring legacies of mastery, as Anne Cheng's work has explored, tend neither to entail "a clear rejection of the other" nor "to fully expel the racial other," as is often assumed, but rather "to *maintain* that other within existing structures." "Segregation and colonialism," she continues, "are internally fraught institutions not because they have eliminated the other but because they *need* the very thing they hate or fear."[143]

It is this fraught need within the master's thought, its internally ensured instability, foundering on its own incoherence, which, Cedric Robinson notes, "inevitably generate[s] fugitive, unaccounted-for elements of reality."[144] This "unaccounted-for" is a precise articulation of what Plato admits above and what I am suggesting must be unfolded within Augustine. It is the Black intellectual tradition which has analyzed this instability most effectively, in key part because it has always known—unlike, for instance, Foucault's circular theory of power—that the "object" on which the master's power operates *precedes* the capture of power, and in fact, calls that project of capture into being, and so does not resist it so much as *is resisted by it.*[145]

Part 4. Fugitive Possibilities in the Afterlife of Slavery

The work worth doing, I have suggested, is not to condemn or vilify Augustine, but to encounter his conceptual world in a way that pushes pilgrims who are masters toward confrontations with our own houses, so to speak, to reckon with our forms of thought and life as legacies of mastery, particularly those of us who—by way of intersecting vectors of power: whiteness, class, education, and so on—inhabit the afterlife of the master's position in the present. What would it mean for us to find in Augustine, illumined by Black thought, an occasion for confronting our own self-deceptions about the conditions and contradictions of our lives?

It is tempting, I think, for a theological ethics sensitive to the concerns thus raised, to try to make a striking move in the wake of the master's Christ: from the subjunctive to the indicative. To say something like: *that* Christianity was entangled with the master's fantasy, but *real* Christianity is on the side of the enslaved person's reality, and thus we can save Christianity from itself. But it is, in a sense, too early and too late for that. Too early in that, really, we do not yet know what a political order fully beyond the one John Henry Hopkins defended might look like. Black thinkers long before Afropessimism excavated the way the racial order of slavery survives its abolition, haunting the present scene.[146] And it is too late in that there is too much blood already on the ground, too many silences and lost traumas in the archive, too many drowned in the sea, too many violated wombs, too many families torn apart. It will not work simply to claim, from the privilege of the present, that "true" Christianity *is* on the side of the slave, with the certainty of the indicative mood.

Perhaps the move to make is to acknowledge a quieter, more impossible task. Here something like a countersubjunctive might emerge, the one

Saidiya Hartman signals when she writes of her own work: "Is it possible to exceed or negotiate the constitutive limits of the archive? By advancing a series of speculative arguments and *exploiting the capacities of the subjunctive . . . in fashioning a narrative . . .* I intended both to tell an impossible story and to amplify the impossibility of its telling."[147] The notion of modes of belonging otherwise, to borrow language from Ashon Crawley, even of forms of faith and practice otherwise: perhaps these call us not to abandon the archives we've inherited, but rather to take them up toward these impossibilities, in fugitive flight toward a world that does not yet exist.[148] What if the move is not from subjunctive to indicative, but from subjunctive to countersubjunctive mode, learning to fantasize differently, what Moten calls "fantasy in the hold," what Robin D. G. Kelley calls "freedom dreams"?[149] Dreams and fantasies, alternative enactments of *as if* take shape as a concrete ethical demand when, as Angela Y. Davis, says, "You have to act *as if* it were possible to radically transform the world. And you have to do it all the time."[150] Hence, the would-be pilgrim citizen must discern which subjunctively expressed set of possibilities—which middle-distance values, wishes, doubts, desires—will form her movement through this world: the longing to restore order, to retain the slave within the proper alignment of the household and city? Or the longing to imagine alternatives, to take flight, to reconceive intimacies beneath the master's gaze?

I have not argued that Augustine is simply "baptizing" the Roman household with a Christian seal of endorsement; to the contrary, my point is that this household is neither resisted nor repeated, but rather *recalibrated* in the terms of an emerging Christian vision of political order. But this recalibration has retained the project of mastery. We know this because it hasn't bothered to ask about, and indeed couldn't bear to know, the perspective of the enslaved about what the master's house is and is about, and how it relates to the new social space of God in Christ. The master's house is a shorthand for the symbolic structure, the old symbolic architecture, which Augustine goes on inhabiting but in a new way, thus coming to enjoy it for its own sake, rather than setting off, restlessly, in search of a homeland that does not yet exist. The master's house is indeed a *house:* a dwelling place, a scene of restored comfort and safety. For Augustinian thought, the house continues to play this role, as I suggested in the discussion of Rowan Williams's classic essay above. What Augustinians want out of Augustine is built into the concrete foundation, the door jambs, the framing, the sheet rock, of this house of the master.[151] What Charles Long calls "theologies opaque" have fled this house.[152] These enact a fugitive Christ, rather than the subjunctive Christ who is the master's good son now in the "form of the slave," as I turn to examine in the next chapter. The question is whether white Augustinians will preserve this house, make it ever kinder, ever gentler, ever more self-deceived. Or whether they will open it to acts of Black reconstruction, fundamental transformation.

In an extended way, I am interested in the problems which this symbolic form, the master's house—and with it, the subjunctive Christ of the master—generates for those who would look to Augustine for normative resources. And yet, my inquiry, and the critical tools it brings to the analysis, is in a certain sense subjunctive too. If James Cone is right, if God is Black, what would this mean for the Christ of the Augustinians? That is, if God has fundamentally revealed Godself in the Exodus event of liberating the slaves of Israel from the masters of Egypt, and in the Christ event of "taking the form of the slave," and in Mary's proclamation that the messiah would "set the captives free," and in that messiah's execution in the paradigmatic manner of the rebellious slave, if all that is the case, then what would this mean for the symbolic space of the master's house? (I return to this possibility in Chapter 5.) Of course, Augustinians may simply wish to say God is not Black. God is not on the side of the slaves, but beyond such sides altogether. This option is available, indeed, it is the default position. But if Augustinians wish to contend with the world as we have it, haunted by slavery's afterlife, then they may wish to explore alternatives.

I have argued that, when accepted by the pilgrim, the evaluative regime of "good" slaves and "bad" slaves—even as an ambivalent frame for pursuing earthly peace in the city—places the pilgrim at odds with other kinds of social subjects, those whose very position in society constrains their ability to share in any of its goods and, wittingly or not, aligns the pilgrim with the interests of the masters. The responsible historian must remain skeptical as to whether enslaved persons ever internalized this evaluative view of the moral life as their own. We can never know this for sure, insofar as the historical evidence provides only the most fleeting, indirect, and opaque points of access to the viewpoint of enslaved persons. But we do know enslaved people resisted: fled, stole, lied, stopped work, and occasionally, physically confronted their masters, sometimes to the point of revolt.[153] This drives us back to the "iconic" *Confessions* scene of the road leading from summit to homeland through the woods, but this time, in whatever limited ways we can, with attention to the woods, not the road.

Accessing any sense of that vantage is no easy task. And yet given the near-total absence of enslaved perspectives preserved from antiquity, late ancient historians increasingly turn to do comparative work with New World slavery, carefully marking its disjunctures as well as its often striking continuities.[154] This comparative sensibility is already familiar to political Augustinians, who have long contended that Augustine's best insights can be translated, *mutatis mutandis,* into parallel dilemmas of modern political life. In this chapter, I have argued that if pilgrimage and citizenship are Augustinian concepts which travel, so too are the unresolved dilemmas of the iconic roadside scene, posed by the unheard vantage of the fugitive. In conclusion, then, I want to make brief suggestive comments in this direction, first by building from one of the most lucid theorizations of Black fugitivity, Neil Roberts's *Freedom as Marronage,* then by proposing two avenues for further Augustinian inquiry.

Bringing together historical and normative camps of political theory, Roberts builds political concepts from the maroon communities which sprang up from Brazil to Haiti to Venezuela to the United States: marronage names the phenomenon of fugitive slaves in flight from the plantation system into the surrounding woods, hills, and mountains, who from there, in the shadows of colonial empire, reconstructed political and ecological life otherwise. Once in a discussion of *The City of God,* I listened as a senior Augustine scholar suggested one simply *cannot* think politically from the vantage of the subjugated, since precisely as the subjugated, they do not construct political order. This apparent impossibility is precisely what Roberts enacts, bringing his theoretical elaborations on marronage into wide-ranging constructive dialogue with theorists from Rousseau to Hannah Arendt to Philip Pettit. Significantly, the history of marronage remains a crucial imaginative horizon for the present moment, as when Barbara Ransby, in *Making All Black Lives Matter,* describes movement spaces of contemporary Black organizing as "modern maroon spaces," where "marronage, in the era of slavery, was not simply about escape . . . they also often confronted and fought against slave empires."[155] In thinking about such confrontation and struggle, one especially promising insight worth flagging is the technical distinction Roberts draws between what he terms "sovereign marronage" and "sociogenic marronage." Simplifying for our purposes here, sovereign marronage names freedom struggles which culminate in *a reproduction of* the very order of sovereignty from which maroons took flight.

By contrast, sociogenic marronage is an enactment of freed social life which does not simply mimic the sovereign world, nor make a bid for inclusion within it, nor merely stand in a "negative" or deconstructive relation to politics. Rather, sociogenic marronage has been poetically conjured by Caribbean thinkers in the image of the sea: the space of the Middle Passage and the slave trade reemerges as the source of life, where a new sociality, a new ecology of relation is born. And this image of the sea converges, surprisingly, with one of Augustine's own images, indeed, the only "positive" image of fugitivity in his texts I've yet found: when Augustine reads Exodus, as Israel crosses the sea in flight from her masters, Augustine sees a moving image of baptism: a new community emerges from the waters (Sermon 4.9).[156] Yet unlike the examples above, here he doesn't blur the lines between the metaphorical and literal: he doesn't tell slaves to take flight and do likewise. Pressing Augustine's logic beyond himself, what would it mean to rethink baptism in this way, as initiation into the ancient and fugitive movements of God's people? Second, Sarah Stewart-Kroeker highlights the fact that the beauty of Christ looks to the world like ugliness and deformity.[157] This key Augustinian insight prompts a question by analogy at the roadside scene: What if Christ's obedience to the God of Exodus can only look to the world like disobedience to masters, only sound like a rustling in the woods?

In the iconic roadside scene I have been examining in this chapter, as Stewart-Kroeker points out, in addition to the figures of pilgrims and fugitives, it is significant that the scene "evokes the imperial Roman road system," and thus *is* "a kind of imperial discourse." And yet, because ultimately Christ himself is figured *as* this royal road, "Augustine also subverts the very terms of imperial dominance, for Christ's is the way of humility."[158] The next chapter takes up the limits and possibilities of this enduring Augustinian hope—that the humility of Christ is subversive, that it enables pilgrims to walk the old road in a new way.

THREE

The Form of the Slave

The way is first humility, second humility, third humility. . . . If you ask and as often as you ask about the rules of the Christian religion, I would answer only, "Humility."
—Augustine, Letter 118

In that order of peace which prevails among men when some are placed under others, humility is as profitable to those who serve as pride is harmful to those who rule.
—Augustine, *The City of God*

In Book 7 of *Confessions*, Augustine states that the Platonic books gave him a great deal of knowledge—about time, materiality, and knowledge itself—but there is one thing they did not give him: "the form of the slave." "In reading the Platonic books," he writes, "I found expressed in different words, and in a variety of ways, that the Son, 'being in the form of the Father did not think it theft to be equal with God.' . . . But that 'he took on himself the form of a slave' . . . that these books do not have."[1] The *forma Dei* of Philippians 2:6, they gave him; the *forma servi* of verse 7, they lacked. Why is the form of the slave so crucial for Augustine, such that he finds in it a synecdoche for all that was missing from Platonic wisdom? In short, the slave form of Christ is where God has most decisively "shown humanity the way of humility" (*conf.* 7.9.13). For Augustine, the *via humilitatis* sets us free from bondage to *superbia* (pride), the supreme and supremely self-defeating vice of humankind.

According to the *Augustinus-Lexikon*, the words *humilitas* and *humilis* appear more than 2,400 times in Augustine's writings.[2] Humility is central to *Confessions'* treatment of the limits of Neoplatonic wisdom, *On the*

Trinity's account of the incarnate mission of the Son, and *The City of God*'s critique of the Roman desire for domination. Calls for humility pervade his sermons as ubiquitously as its antonym, *superbia*, appears in polemical descriptions of foes in each major controversy. Little surprise, then, that humility also plays such a central role in the ongoing revival of political Augustinianism as a virtue that enables a distinctly Christian form of participation in public life.

In the previous pages, I've examined how this political Augustinian project has neglected to grapple with the central place of *slavery* in Augustine's thought, not only as a social institution he occasionally defends, but as a wide-ranging symbolic resource, as a set of metaphors that animates his articulation of sin, virtue, desire, God—the very conceptual resources Augustinians wish to recover for the present. The previous chapter mapped out three rough coordinates of *peregrinatio* politics, with one of them being the shift in twentieth-century thought from the institutional-structural level of postwar Augustinian debates to what Peter Brown calls the "middle-distance" level of more recent civic Augustinian debates—a focus upon the virtues, habits, and values of citizens in pluralist societies. There I began to show how attending to the presence of slavery in Augustine's world and the afterlife of slavery in our own confounds a neat distinction between these two levels. The structural level of slavery and one's social position within the "earthly peace" the institution provides cannot but shape precisely how one conceives goodness and badness, virtues and vices. In this chapter, I am interested in the concept of humility as one such virtue—indeed the central one for Augustine, without which the others are impossible—and in particular, in Augustine's preoccupation with the *forma servi*, the form of the slave concept he draws from Philippians 2:5–11.[3] The form of the slave is a crucial site of Augustine's articulation of humility and its closely related theme, obedience.[4] In Lewis Ayres's *Augustine and the Trinity*, he notes that in the text of Philippians 2, and especially in the words "the form of the slave," Augustine has found not only an exegetical tool, but "a comprehensive conception of what it means to read scriptural accounts of Christ at this moment in the life of faith."[5] Ayres calls this Augustine's "Panzer text," a kind of "tank" he trundles onto the battlefield of doctrinal struggle, mowing down all heterodox positions in its path.[6]

My purpose in this chapter is neither to give an overview of Augustinian humility in general, nor to provide a "pure" intellectual reconstruction of how this Panzer text functions throughout Augustine's thought. Instead, I am interested in what we may call *the politics of humility,* and so also in how Augustine's Panzer text finds a symbolic home for humility in the figure of the enslaved body—a figure that takes on particular significance in Augustine's Christology. Although humility plays a key role in modern political Augustinianism, it functions there with little reference to the way Augustine himself talked about it: namely, in and through the symbolic resources of a slave system that remained utterly central to Roman life in Augustine's time.[7] How should modern Augustinians—who themselves inhabit a racialized *afterlife* of slavery in the present—assess the normative significance of this slave Christology which lies at the heart of Augustine's vision of humility as both a religious and civic virtue? Based on the preceding, one might expect this project to advance a broadly "Nietzschean" critique of Augustinian humility as mere "slave morality," but for at least three reasons, this is not the case.

First and most basically, I follow Jennifer Glancy in casting doubt upon whether the virtues associated with so-called slave morality—humility, industry, patience, and so on—should not rather be treated as "slaveholder morality," that is, as the "moral values that slaveholders extolled for slaves."[8] This indicates the overarching orientation of this project to the problem of the master. Second, granting the first point, it is easy enough to find places where Augustine, like all those broadly aligned with the slaveholder-generated Roman codes of acceptable moral behavior, exhorts slaves to be humble. In the previous chapter's extended discussion of the master's Christ in *Expositions of the Psalms* 124.7, for instance, Augustine reminds enslaved persons, "Christ does not want to make you proud." But to focus on this alone—the exhortation to enslaved persons to be humble—would be to risk reducing Augustine's thought to mere ideological utility, as though his theological and political innovations are, in the end, simply epiphenomenal to an underlying commitment to preserving a certain social arrangement. R. W. Dyson's account comes rather close to this approach when he explains Augustine's views on slavery by appealing to Augustine's supposed "conservative habit of mind," the purpose of which is simply "to defend and justify the arrangements that we find in this world, notwithstanding the flawed and unworthy character of those arrangements."[9]

But this is not my argument, nor do I find much explanatory power in a quasipsychologizing appeal to "moderation and conservatism [as] typical of his general attitude to the arrangements by which earthly life is regulated."[10] While I have demonstrated that indeed the position of the master shapes Augustine's moral and political thought, it is not my argument that Augustine is simply "baptizing" or "sacralizing" the Roman ethic of mastery. To the contrary, my argument is that in his rigorous theological work, he is *transforming* it, recalibrating it within the terms of an emerging conception of Christian political order, at a particularly unstable moment in which it is far from clear that such a conception will win the day.[11]

And so, third, my argument in what follows does not focus on the humility which is proper to enslaved persons, as that sort of humility reflects, in a fairly straightforward and therefore not particularly interesting way, the standard framework of slaveholder morality. Put in the terms of the epigraph from *The City of God* 19 above, I focus not on the first clause but on the second: not on the fact that, within the order of earthly peace which pilgrims value, "humility is . . . profitable to those who serve," but on the fact that "pride is harmful to those who rule."[12] My argument thus concerns exclusively the significance and the character of the humility Augustine proposes for *masters*—and by extension, of that humility which gets transferred, in the Augustinian "democratic translation" project, into virtue for Christian citizens in democratic orders, whose humility is enlisted to foster earthly peace amid pluralism and subvert the "pride" of modern liberalism. More specifically: my argument is (a) that the *humilitas* of Christ in "the form of the slave" must be grasped as the central site of the Augustinian transformation of the project of Roman mastery, and (b) that contrary to much Christian hope for the "subversive" possibilities of Augustine's critique of *superbia,* the humble Christian master is best understood as offering a critique, but *not* an overcoming of, or a moving beyond the project of mastery. Counterintuitively, humility is better understood as itself *providing* the distinctly Christian mode of exercising mastery. In this way, I aim to respond to what I anticipate as one of the strongest overall objections to the project: How can Augustinianism display "the problem of the Christian master" when Augustine railed incessantly against pride, extolled humility, and decried the *libido dominandi* which "enslaves" those who long to be masters of others?[13]

This chapter advances my extended response to this question in four parts. Part 1 surveys the central role of Augustine's account of humility in modern political Augustinianism, with particular focus on the way humility is thought to undermine, subvert, or offer an alternative to the "pride" of modern secular liberalism. Part 2 tracks the slave Christology of Augustine's "Panzer text" (Philippians 2), looking first at *On the Trinity*, Books 1 and 2, and proposing that this symbolic use of slavery—and its moral significance—is clarified when read alongside a key passage in *Homilies on the Gospel of John*. I then examine how this slave Christology functions in two of the "new" Dolbeau sermons which display a feature of Augustine's slavery discourse that has received little scholarly attention, namely, the image of the master's house as a *domus* with a three-layered hierarchy: at level one is the *dominus* (the master), level two the *servus* (the slave), and level three a *servus vicarius*, a slave owned by the slave in position two. I'll suggest that humility for Augustine has much to do with inhabiting position two in that hierarchy—the one who, precisely insofar as he is a good and faithful slave to his *Dominus*, is now fit to be a master of others. Tracking these symbolic forms, while drawing from a neglected passage of Orlando Patterson's *Slavery and Social Death*, enables us to allow that Augustinian humility is a critique and "subversion" of masculinist Roman ideals of mastery, as modern Augustinians often claim (and celebrate).[14] But it also presses us to consider that precisely in this critique Augustine risks reproducing humility itself as a new, distinctly *Christian* style of mastery over the bodies of slaves and others. Part 3 explores the significance of that claim by displaying the problem of the Christian master in several key reception histories from the modern racial world. Part 4 makes a case that the underlying issue in proposing humility for masters is that it is an attempted "reconciliation" project: it tries to reconcile the splitting of human flesh into master and slave, and its failure to do so instead prompts a return to the vulnerability of human flesh itself in Black ethical thought.

Part 1. Humility in Contemporary Augustinian Political Thought

It is not surprising that appeals to humility pervade contemporary Augustinian thought, in view of how indisputably common the words *humilitas* and *humilis* are within Augustine's writings and the central role humility as a concept plays in his epistemological, theological, moral, and political thought. My aim here is to sketch three basic ways this humility discourse most often functions in political Augustinianism's response to the ethical conditions of liberal modernity: (a) with respect to liberal modernity's *secularity*, Augustinians invoke humility as a check to the "pride" of western societies' attempt to organize social and political life around the human and humanism without reference to God; (b) with respect to liberal modernity's *plurality*, Augustinians invoke humility as a resource for heavenly citizens to live peaceably among their neighbors; and (c) with respect to modern critiques of Augustine, Augustine's invocation of humility and his critique of the *libido dominandi* often serve to fend off various reductive moral judgments against Augustine himself. Here, as in earlier chapters, we will note certain instances of "disavowal" of the conditions of racial modernity.

Augustinian Humility Against Secular Pride

At the heart of this strand of Augustinian humility discourse is a framework according to which the contrast between Christian belief and its absence just *is* the distinction between humility and pride.[15] We see this framework expressed concisely in Charles Norris Cochrane's famous Yale lectures titled "Augustine and the Problem of Power": "To acknowledge God in this sense is ... the first demand of Christian faith; the point of divergence between Christian humility and secular pride."[16] Thus, the absence of belief glimpsed in Augustine's polemics against paganism transfers neatly to the absence of institutionally legitimated belief at the heart of modern secularity. In a striking and elegant revisionist history of modern pride, Julia E. Cooper begins by noting the likeliest source of the enduring Christian value of humility: "Augustine offers what is arguably the canonical account of humility's meaning and value."[17] This canonical account did not remain locked in antiquity. Rather, Cooper is interested in showing that by "the seventeenth and eighteenth centuries, many thinkers adopted Augustine's Christian humility / pagan pride antithesis as the authoritative framework for understanding humility. ... As Augustine establishes the terms of the debate, humility provides the litmus test separating Christianity from paganism."[18] This line of demarcation would prove not only crucial to "the continued prestige of Augustinian ethics in the seventeenth century,"[19] but also useful for the renaissance of Augustinian ethics at the end of the twentieth. Indeed, Augustine's radical critique of Roman pride and concomitant valorization of Christian humility have proved an irresistible resource for modern Christian critiques of secular pride under liberalism.

A particularly striking iteration of both the appeal to Augustinian humil-ity against secular pride *and* the implicit disavowal of race is in Oliver O'Donovan's *Desire of Nations*, which we've discussed above. O'Donovan not only claims that it is the role of the church to teach the state how to be humble—"to instruct it in the ways of the humble state"[20]—but also pro-poses that it is the loss of distinctly religious humility that is to blame for our collective hesitancy about the detection and punishment of crime, a loss of trust in the God who will have mercy on whom he will have mercy:

> Christian liberalism taught judges to look over their shoulders when they
> pronounced on fellow-sinners' crimes. . . . Ex-Christian liberalism inherited
> all the hesitancy; but, no longer grounded in religious humility, it became
> moral insecurity. From this springs the haunted unease with which the West
> views its own agents of law, an unease which cries out unmistakably from the
> incessant flow of police dramas that flicker across our television screens. We
> have made the detection and punishment of major crime more efficient than
> any other society, yet we believe in it less. When we punish we feel we have
> betrayed somebody.[21]

For O'Donovan, the "haunted unease" western society feels toward its pun-ishment of crime has nothing much to do either with the European histo-ries of producing criminality through regimes of reason and unreason, as in Foucault's famous genealogy, or with the specifically anti-Black continuity of slave ship, plantation, and prison.[22] Rather, it is the loss of "religious humil-ity" which leads us to "feel we have betrayed somebody," though O'Donovan leaves unaddressed the issue of whom in particular "we" might have betrayed. Here it should be mentioned too that this is not, as is so often suggested in certain quarters, a simple matter of United States versus United King-dom difference, where the latter's social differences supposedly center only upon class, not race. To the contrary, to take just one measure, according to a recent study of the punishment of crime in the U.K., "black people were five times more likely to be stopped and searched than their white counterparts. . . . Black men and women are incarcerated in the British prison system at five and nearly nine times, respectively, over the proportion of blacks in the British population."[23] Perhaps this condition, a ghostly afterlife of Atlantic slavery, at once acknowledged and erased, a double movement of disavowal, lingers inside what O'Donovan has called the west's "haunted unease."[24]

The Form of the Slave

Augustinian Humility for Liberal Democratic Engagement with Pluralism

A second and more recent strand of Augustinian humility avers that a pluralistic society calls for a deeper awareness of our epistemic and moral limits. Scholars in this strand claim that Augustine's rich sensitivity to our time-bound embodied existence provides important resources for meeting this crucial liberal need. Charles Mathewes stands in this tradition in suggesting that Augustine provides in humility "a provisional tolerance of difference."[25] Similarly, in *The Republic of Grace,* Mathewes makes the case for humility's role in the democratic order:

> Citizens wield sovereignty and grant the right to exercise it to certain elected officials (and their authorized deputies), but in doing so that granting should carry with it the citizens' own humility, their wariness of their own presumption in the exercise of power; and it should also communicate the citizens' earnest desire that sovereignty be exercised always with an eye to human fallibility, with a will to allow humans to correct their mistakes, and with a hesitancy to pronounce absolute judgments and execute complete justice— in short, with mercy.[26]

Here too we see the focus mentioned above, not upon a humility designed to help the disempowered accept their lowly station, but to the contrary, upon humility as a check on "presumption in the exercise of power," particularly in a setting in which mistakes are inevitable amid cultural difference. "In the humility of hope," Mathewes writes elsewhere, "we know our place as the common human place of finite and fallible understanding." Yet this does not lead to a false modesty toward one's own claims. Rather, it opens the possibility of genuine cross-cultural and cross-religious dialogue insofar as "confidence and humility go hand in hand, as one has both confidence in the truth of one's claims, and humility about one's understanding of those same claims, even as one is making them."[27] Similarly, Gerald W. Schlabach argues that Augustinian humility provides a middle path for Christians to engage in robust debate in the public square, navigating between the Charybdis of moral relativism and the Scylla of moral imperialism.[28] Deborah Wallace Ruddy moves in a similar direction in highlighting the fact that, although humility "goes against deeply imbedded impulse[s] in our culture," which often finds in it "a fawning deference to those in power," Augustinian humility can instead "enrich democratic education and public discourse," and indeed "is crucial to the renewal and revitalization of education and public discourse which will advance a true democracy."[29]

Paul Weitham's important essay "Toward an Augustinian Liberalism" develops a dialogue with political theorist Judith Shklar's notion of "ordinary vices," proposing that pride constitutes precisely one such vice for secular liberalism, and accordingly, an Augustinian perspective can—despite Augustinian detractors of liberalism and liberal detractors of Augustinianism—in fact *enhance* liberal citizenship.[30] It should not surprise us, based on the preceding, that Weitham also frames this Augustinian-enhanced liberalism through an appeal to John Rawls's "fact of pluralism" and explicitly limits the relevance of his arguments to "*maturely pluralistic* democratic societies." He warns that "Augustinians in societies with histories of minority repression . . . may have good reason to be liberals, but they do not have the reasons to which I shall appeal."[31] In other words, he will not be saying anything of relevance to such societies. It is unclear by what analytic criteria Weitham has determined which societies in the modern west qualify as being free of "histories of minority repression," but evidently these not only exist (!), but exist in sufficient numbers to merit Weitham's exclusive attention.[32] If modern life begins with slavery, to harken back to Toni Morrison's axiom and the founding arguments of Black radical thought, then it would seem Weitham's claim addresses itself to a near-empty set. It displays too, as I have argued in the previous chapter, that the haunting afterlife of mastery has helped render to him opaque the conditions of his own life and thought.

Augustinian Humility as Defense of Augustine Himself

Finally, we can identify the implicit appeal to Augustinian humility in statements defending Augustine against his modern detractors, as for instance with the defense offered by Eric Gregory discussed at length above: "It would be ironically prideful to blame Augustine or any other premodern author for limited historical horizons of social and economic reform, most especially in relation to his often neglected moral criticisms of slavery."[33] The "irony" of such a critique of Augustine presumably derives from the fact that one accuses Augustine of being prideful for his failures on slavery, when it is in fact one's *own* lack of humility which comes to the fore in one's anachronistic judgment, resulting from one's failure to grasp Augustine within his own rich theological and political context. I have already noted how my approach differs insofar as it highlights as a neglected problem for ethical thought our tacit alignment with the moral vantage of masters, foregrounds the unresolved question of how we position ourselves vis-à-vis enslaved peoples in their silenced archival presence, and presses up against the tenuous nature of the "we" itself. But I also move broadly with the grain of Gregory's point here insofar as I attempt throughout to read Augustine's thought in the present without being presentist, to enter into its full theological specificity (as I do in the section below) rather than treat it reductively through ideology critique, and to advance a case for finding in an encounter with Augustine—illumined in a transdisciplinary conversation with Black Studies—a clearer critical view of *ourselves*.[34]

Moving along broadly similar lines of critique, Robert Dodaro defends Augustine against the charges brought by William Connolly's *The Augustinian Imperative* by proposing that Augustine's disparagement of alternative (non-Christian) sources of civic virtue is no mere "religious chauvinism" or self-centered pride, but to the contrary, is itself a critique of "a hidden, insidious form of pride."[35] If it does not appear this way initially, this is due not to Augustine but to "modern ears."[36] Augustinian reversals of this sort are at their best when they lead modern readers into a deeper encounter with Augustine's theological brilliance on its own terms (and not just for how it can be translated into the terms of political theory), and few have done this as successfully as Dodaro's *Christ and the Just Society in the Thought of Saint Augustine,* which likewise finds in the Christian humility–pagan pride contrast a central feature of Augustine's political thought:

> Cicero thus regards glory both as the source of personal motivation for Rome's "best citizens" and as the key element in the political discourse which urges Romans to virtuous public service. Augustine, instead, holds that humility, not glory, is the foundation of statesmanship and political discourse in a truly just society. Augustine's preference for humility . . . is rooted in the example of Christ, the divine Word who assumed human nature in the incarnation.[37]

Here Dodaro underscores the way that, in Augustine's thought, the contrastive device of pagan pride and Christian humility maps precisely onto Augustine's contrast of Rome's "best citizens" and Augustine's own ideal "statesman," Christ himself. But more, Dodaro here and throughout his illumining study consistently drives us to connect the virtue of humility explicitly to "the example of Christ" and the theological question of the incarnation. Hence, as I turn to Part 2's examination of how the master's house—the symbolic and material space of slavery—shapes the Augustinian humility discourse, I begin with the proper Christological grammar Augustine develops in *On the Trinity* through "the form of the slave." Because it is an important aspect of my overall argument that slavery is not merely present in Augustine as an isolable ethical "issue," but rather shapes his treatment of more elemental questions insofar as he thinks about them through the master's house, it makes sense to grasp here Augustine's *slave Christology* in some detail and with care, before moving on to consider how humility and the form of the slave are woven together in his homiletical, moral, and political writings.

Part 2. Augustine's Slave Christology

In Augustine we witness a key moment in the development of a strand of the western theological tradition I will call *slave Christologies*—a term which neither appears in standard introductions to Christian doctrine, nor is directly employed by Augustine himself. Rather, it is a term stipulated, a term for bringing something into view. For my purposes, *slave Christologies* isolates that strand of the tradition—from ancient to medieval to modern— which develops a theological account of the person and work of Jesus Christ through the figural identification of his body with the body of the enslaved. In so doing, it weaves the *symbolic* order of slaveholding into the texture of Christian thought, while operating in the context of practical reasoning about the *social* order of slavery. Augustine did not invent slave Christology, nor is it self-evident that slave Christologies are inherently virtuous or vicious, and so Augustine will not be treated here, as he so often is, as a tragic figure of declension—the corrupter of an emancipatory faith into a repressive religion.[38] He is preceded by and forms part of a rich tradition in the Latin west of theological reflection upon the Philippians hymn, from which he emerged, as Jaroslav Pelikan's magisterial history of doctrine notes, "its most creative interpreter."[39] It is difficult to convey how massively influential this hermeneutical creativity would prove.[40] How Augustine thinks about the political and ethical significance of humility cannot be separated from the strand of slave Christologies which emerged in Christian thought principally as reflection upon "the form of a slave" (Phil. 2:5–11), and so I develop here a partial, selective account of Augustine's theological reception of the Philippians hymn as a window into the politics of humility.[41]

If slave Christology is, on my terms, a key "strand" of the western tradition, then I wish to isolate three major "threads" of that strand which emerge in Augustine's slave Christology, three organizing themes for his theological use of the Philippians hymn: *intimacy, ascent,* and *obedience.* These three would travel together in the tradition again and again. Inside the humility of "the form of the slave," a powerful Christian longing would come into view, a project which would look upon the body of the subjected and build from it a model for speaking of human life with God: of the *intimacy* which existed in the person of Jesus Christ between two natures, human and divine, which in turn makes intimacy possible between fallen humankind and the God of Israel; *ascent,* in that the vision laid out in the Philippians hymn was not a static picture of the state of creation; rather, it would come to offer a program of education, the transformation of our attention and desire, and from this formation would emerge a profound *habitus* of being in the world; and *obedience,* in that the relation of Jesus to his Father would involve his acceding to divine demand, yes, but most crucially, in that this obedience would come to stand in an utterly fraught relation to the world Jesus entered, a world *already* structured by "command and obedience,"[42] to use Augustine's terms. It was this world inside which the vision of humility found in the Philippians hymn would have to make sense of itself.

Intimacy: God in Human Flesh

At the heart of Augustine's Christology, like that of the Council of Chalcedon (451) it anticipated, was the drive to preserve, rather than resolve, the central mystery of the incarnation—in Christ, God the creator is joined in unthinkably intimate union with the humankind God created. "Jesus is not," Linn Tonstad writes, "a hybrid of divine and human that would be neither divine nor human. Jesus is *both* divine and human. For most Christian theologians, this surprising, unimaginably intimate union between divinity and humanity is possible because *God is intimate.*"[43]

In *On the Trinity,* Books 1 and 2, Augustine's central concern is to preserve the theological and scriptural basis for this intimate union by arguing—against the Homoians and various anti-Nicene traditions—for the fittingness of speaking of Christ as one subject in two natures, divine and human, inseparable and yet without confusion. He wants to do this while maintaining the absolute equality of Father and Son (against any impulses of ontological subordinationism) and preserving the *immutability* of the Word in taking on flesh. To these opponents' credit, Augustine acknowledges, "many things are said in the holy books to suggest, or even state openly that the Father is greater than the Son."[44] Based in a nontrivial reading of scripture, his opponents' position was a serious argument, meriting serious response. In particular Augustine's *On the Trinity*—like similar treatments in Ambrose's *Exposition of the Christian Faith (De fide)*, and Hilary of Poitiers's *On the Trinity (De Trinitate)*—needs to stave off the apparent subordinationist force of 1 Corinthians 15:28, which speaks of Christ being "subjected to God the Father." Augustine learns much from both, even while much of what he does here is, as Lewis Ayres says, "peculiarly his."[45]

Augustine grounded his intervention into the Christological controversies in the Philippians hymn, finding there an exegetical and theological *regula*, a rule for interpreting such passages as upholding Nicene orthodoxy, whereby Christ is absolutely equal to the Father according to his divine nature, less than the Father according to his human nature—and indeed, "in the form of a slave he is less than himself" (*Trin.* 1.3.14). This is precisely the genius of the terms *forma Dei* and *forma servi*, form of God and form of a slave: they provide a conceptual distinction *internal to the scriptural witness itself* which enables Augustine now to refer all passages that seem to imply Christ's inferiority to the Father to the form of the slave. "Provided then that we know this rule for understanding the scriptures," Augustine writes, we "can thus distinguish the two resonances in them, one tuned to the form of God in which he is, and is equal to the Father, the other tuned to the form of a slave which he took and is less than the Father" (1.4.22). So when Christ says in John 14:28, "the Father is greater than I," Augustine argues, Christ is speaking in *forma servi*—according to his human nature. When Christ says in John 10:30, "the Father and I are one," he is speaking in *forma Dei*—according to his divine nature. Augustine offers a litany of scriptural examples in chapter 4 of *On the Trinity* 1, underscoring the *equality* of Father and Son: for to be in *forma servi* is to take on "the likeness of men" (*similitudinem hominum*), while yet *being* in full equality with the Father in *forma Dei*. The distinction between *assuming* the form of the slave and *being* in the form of God is likewise crucial. This is what enables Augustine to preserve a way of speaking not only of the Son's equality with the Father, but also his *immutability*. In this way, the form of the slave provides the *regula* for harmonizing the scriptural witness with the emerging grammar of orthodox Christology.

Ascent: The Three-Layered Hierarchy of the Master's House

And yet the Philippians hymn is also more than this, to stay with Ayers's account—more than merely a rule for sorting out various kinds of text: "It is a rule which Augustine presents as implying and revealing a comprehensive conception of what it means to read Scripture at this point in the life of faith." What is this moment? "A point when we should seek to see what is said and done in *forma servi* as a drawing of our desires and intellects towards the *forma Dei* that will remain hidden until the eschaton."[46] This drawing of our desires, the movement of our attention toward God, is "ascent" in the Augustinian sense: the Incarnation of the Word is not static, but involves transformation, the education of our inner life as it is formed, ordered, and trained upon the mystery of God. As Ayers shows, the early Augustine inherits "ascent" from ancient Platonist educational theory, but by his mature period has shifted its significance "towards a conception of ascent that is always a building on faith in humility."[47] To understand how the *regula* above, what Augustine calls "the form-of-a-slave rule,"[48] relates to ascent through humility, we must first grasp *descent*—how humankind has fallen. And that requires clarifying how the symbolic order of slavery works for Augustine, how it lends intelligibility and force to his slave Christology, by way of two remarks.

First, at the general level, we return again to the familiar point—here following Christopher L. de Wet—that when we find Augustine using slavery as a "metaphor," we must pause over the distinction between "actual" and "metaphorical" slavery, or literal and figurative slavery. This distinction is vital, for reasons that become clearer below, but, depending on how we understand it, risks being slightly anachronistic to how Augustine thinks. As de Wet points out, for Augustine, as for most writers in Roman antiquity, slavery is not so much a "metaphor," for which other language could just as easily substitute the same underlying content, as much as it is a *cosmology*. De Wet calls this "the doulological [from *doulos*, Greek for slave] structuring of the cosmos—that is, placing God exclusively in the position of master, and creation in a subordinated position."[49] Or as Thomas Aquinas might put it, writing centuries later: "God is master [*dominus*] not in idea only, but in reality."[50]

Second, more specifically, when approaching master–slave relations in Augustine, I have suggested above that we avoid imagining a Hegelian personal struggle between lord and bondsman, two individuals abstracted from any wider organization of social life. Instead Augustine thinks about master–slave relations within the structure of a *domus* (household) headed by a *dominus* (master or owner), a lived social reality—the master's house.[51] At this point in the argument, it becomes crucial to add further historical depth and texture to this aspect by highlighting the special importance for slave Christology of Augustine's use of a *three-layered hierarchy* within this house. This tripartite structure recurs all over his corpus, but we see it come into view in an especially explicit way in Sermon 159B, dated 404, around the time Augustine likely began composing *On the Trinity*.

Here Augustine begins from Psalm 118: "It is good for me that you have humbled me, so that I may learn your justifications."[52] In elaborating what this means, Augustine invites hearers to "take a look at this point in everyday life" by introducing the image of a master beating his slave not in anger, but as an act of mercy.[53] Imagine a household, Augustine says, in which there is "one man who has a slave and also has a master, as it frequently happens that property-owning slaves have slaves themselves. Pay careful attention; he has a slave, he has a master; he's subject to one, in command of the other; he is over his slave, under his master . . . he is secure in his possession of his slave, provided he doesn't offend his master."[54] We see a three-layered hierarchy: position 1 is the absolute master (*dominus* who is also a *paterfamilias*), ruling over position 2, the slave (*servi peculiosi*, often a *vilicus*, a managerial slave), who in turn rules over position 3, his own slave (*servus vicarius*, the slave of a slave).[55] Augustine seizes upon this configuration of the master's house and then weaves it seamlessly into a picture of the cosmos itself:

> So if three men, though they are all equally human, are related by some
> social arrangement of this life in such a way that one of them is lord and
> master only, another is slave only, while the third is both slave of the master
> and master of the slave, don't you think the whole creation would be both
> more readily and more distinctively arranged on those lines—the nature

and substance of mind placed under God, the nature of material bodies as a whole placed under mind?[56]

In the context of this argument in Sermon 159B, Augustine uses the structure of this "social arrangement" to conceptualize humility as man's proper recognition of his own "middle" position within the order of the cosmos: in being made in the image of God, with faculties of mind, he stands *under* God as slave; in bearing this image as a rational creature within the material world, he stands *over* all the rest of material creation as its master.[57] It is difficult to overstate the extent to which this threefold structure, the master's house with its three levels of hierarchical authority, permeates Augustine's thought as a *cosmology,* a framework encompassing reality itself, whereby "the whole creation [is] distinctively arranged on those lines," and nowhere is this clearer than when we see how his account of sin and slavery fits into the picture.

"The first sin of man was pride," Augustine continues, "that's what we read in Genesis," where in paradise man was placed "under a certain commandment . . . which was imposed upon him [to] show him this: . . . humility was always to be held onto [because] all things were under him, but over him was the one who made all things."[58] Once solidly at position 2 in innocence, man in sin is punished by falling under the wrath of the slave of position 3, that is, by becoming under the power of bodily creation, which now "flogs" him at the command of God in position 1, just as a *dominus* would order the elite slave to be beaten by a lower slave for disobedience. How does Genesis display this? There Adam's pride issued in "wishing to be its own authority,"[59] or as Augustine puts it elsewhere, returning us to the grammar of the Philippians hymn, Adam sought to "make himself equal to God," following the devil who told him: "Seize illegally what you are not according to your creation because I too fell by stealing what was not mine."[60] In other words, both man and the devil reach up to "grasp" (*rapinam*) position 1 in the hierarchy, but in grasping *fail*, falling to position 3—"cast down to the level of the beasts."[61]

In *Confessions,* we see how this same tripartite structure can function subtly without being explicitly named as such:

> I was superior to these external objects but inferior to you, and you are my true joy if I submit to you, and you have made subject to me what you created to be lower than me. This was the correct mean, the middle ground in which

I would find health, that I should remain "in your image," and in serving you be master of my body [*et tibi serviens dominarer corpori*]. But when in my arrogance [*superbe*] I rose against you and ran up against the master [*dominum*] . . . even those inferior things came on top of me and pressed me down. . . . This grew out of my wound, for "you have humbled the proud like a wounded man" (Ps. 88:11).[62]

This is precisely the logic of the *servus vicarius* being used by the *dominus* to punish the *servus,* the one in the "middle ground" who is both master and slave.

In Orlando Patterson's massive global comparative study of slavery, he finds "the *servus vicarius* (slave of a slave) was a universal occurrence. I know of no slave society in which slaves who could afford them were denied the purchase of other slaves."[63] This universality becomes less astonishing when we recognize the tripartite hierarchy as no Roman cultural peculiarity, but as a twofold consequence of the logic of slavery itself. First, "slaves were the extension of a man's person and honor," and so "there could be few greater testimonies to a man's power than the fact that even his slaves possessed slaves."[64] But more important, if slavery is always an internally unstable site of struggle, in which the will of the enslaved must ever be contained within the structure of master–slave relations, then "nothing more confirmed the loyal slaves' acceptance of the condition of slavery and their own enslavement to the master than their willingness to own slaves themselves. The servus vicarius was the best way of making it clear to all that slavery was part of the natural order of things."[65] When the naturalness of this threefold hierarchy becomes written for Augustine into the very fabric of creation, and when this shape of the created order decisively animates how Augustine envisions key aspects of the moral life, as I will show below, it becomes less plausible to suggest, as so many Augustinians have done, that Augustine "denaturalized" the slave system, rendering it merely "a contingent and unnecessary form of relation."[66]

With this framework established, Augustine will again and again envision humility *not* as a position of unqualified lowliness,[67] but rather as precisely the only way of ascent, the virtue proper to being ordered and restored to position 2, the middle point and center—the one who both rules and is ruled, one who, as we'll see in more detail in a moment, is *a master who can command others precisely insofar as he is also a slave who obeys.* Augustine now reminds his hearers that "the first sin of man was pride"—where pride means

Adam's grasping after equal status with God, or in other words, attempted robbery in trying to lay hold of position 1, of unqualified mastery. But in paradise man was placed "under a certain commandment . . . imposed upon him [to] show him this: . . . humility was always to be held onto [because] all things were under him, but over him was the one who made all things."[68] Positioned with the creator alone above him, the human creature has "all things under him," and in this dual position of masterly authority and servile submission lies the meaning of humility for the Christian master.[69] "Surprisingly, then," Augustine writes in *The City of God*, "there is in humility something that lifts up the heart, and there is in exaltation something that brings down the heart."[70] To clarify this, I now turn toward what has already been implied here: the question of obedience, and in particular, the relation of the obedience of Christ in the form of the slave to the obedience of human beings inhabiting a social order premised on domination.

Obedience: Christ Brings Order to the Household

"The form of the slave" is not the only part of the Panzer text which draws upon slavery imagery. A subtler use lies in the phrase *non rapinam*—as in, for Christ, equality with God was "not a thing to be grasped." This will form a massively influential strand not only of theological reflection, but of a certain intertextual strategy of reading. In Augustine's *On the Trinity* 1–2, and most explicitly in *Homilies on the Gospel of John* 17.16, Augustine reads Philippians 2's *non rapinam* in relation to Isaiah 14 and Genesis 3. There, in a manner that will be picked up by many later theologians, Augustine connects the fact that Christ does not "grasp" at equality with God in an act of "robbery" with the fact that Satan tries to do exactly that: in Isaiah 14, he says he will be like the Most High, and this for Augustine is his attempted theft, his prideful attempt to *illegally seize* equality with God.[71] Likewise, in Genesis 3, by reaching out and grabbing the fruit of the tree, a prideful Adam and Eve attempt to "rob," to steal for themselves this same equal status with God. Augustine thus expands the grammar of the Philippians 2 slave Christology into a *comprehensive account of salvation history*, reaching from angelic fall to human fall to incarnation and beyond. With this, Augustine goes further than Ambrose, Hilary, and Pope Leo, who each developed influential slave Christologies.[72] And with this, Augustine reads Christ's *non rapinam* as precisely the *overcoming* of the robbery attempted by man and

Satan, while also looking forward to the Eucharistic table, in which now, we who are gathered do not reach out and "grasp" the fruit of paradise. Rather it is handed to us, by Christ. We receive it in humility and obedience.

It is a crucial part of the household drama of slavery, Kyle Harper points out, that enslaved people were imagined as constantly trying to steal things, "to assert control over the fruits of their labor," and especially to steal themselves by running away. Pilfering slaves were trope figures in popular plays and literary works, but they were also the subject of sermons. Harper references one sermon by John Chrysostom that exhorts the virtues of asceticism by proclaiming that the one who rids himself of possessions rids himself also of the fear of the thieving slave.[73] Indeed Augustine himself tells the wealthy members of his congregation: "What sort of riches are they that have you in dread of a robber, that have you in dread of your slave, in case he should kill you, grab them all, and run away?"[74] The implicit work of Augustine's use of the Philippians hymn's *non rapinam*—equality with God as "not a thing to be grasped"—slowly emerges into view: both humankind and the devil are like thieving slaves, who are ungratefully reaching and grasping to take what belongs, *by right,* to the Son of God, namely, equality with God.[75] Christ in the form of the slave will present humankind with an example, "by Wisdom itself becoming visible in the flesh and laying down for us an *exemplum vivendi,* an example or pattern of living."[76] Hence, the rightful Son, who *naturally* is equal with God, must take on the form of the slave, *in order to show what a "good slave" looks like*—a Christological recalibration of the longstanding trope in Roman law and literature of good slaves versus bad slaves, a moral calculus which, I have been suggesting, reflects what Willie Jennings calls the "fabricated moral universe" of masters, in which "good" and "evil" are calibrated to the aims of masters regarding their slaves' conduct.[77]

Consider how this ethical vision works in the context of ecclesial life. In Sermon 359B, also preached in 404, Augustine employs the tripartite hierarchy of the master's house again, while making explicit appeal to the slave Christology of Philippians 2. The context is a particular "disturbance" that occurred the day before among the laity, some kind of rumpus forcing Augustine to abandon the pulpit before returning to provide them a remedial lesson in obedience. To that end Augustine brings his hearers back into the Genesis scene of the garden, where he again invokes slavery imagery to clarify the purpose of the divine prohibition: "because among all the good things put in paradise," Augustine says, "obedience was better still, God slapped a prohibition order on one of them, or else by not forbidding any-thing he might have ceased to be master."[78] In this way, Adam's sin is again framed as a prideful act of disobedience, as a bad slave lacking the humility to submit to his master's commands: *that,* Augustine says, was "the first ruin of mankind." Into that scene of ruin, Augustine rolls out the Panzer text once more: "Adam was for us the author and model of disobedience," he says, "Christ of obedience. And how is Christ the model of obedience? Though he is equal to the Father, he says he is the slave of the Father. . . . *Since he was in the form of God, he did not think it robbery to be equal to God* (Phil. 2:6). For Christ . . . equality is not robbery, but nature. The one for whom it was rob-bery stood up and fell; the one for whom it was nature stayed on his feet even as he stooped down."[79] Augustine goes on to repeat the climax of the Panzer text: Christ "humbled himself, becoming obedient to the death." If Christ himself is willing to take the form of the slave, to be humble and obedient, Augustine reasons, such that the *Dominus* and the one who took the form of the *servus* are joined—in intimate concord of positions 1 and 2—how dare you disobey the bishops of his church? "Listen, slave, if your bishop were not one who obeys as a slave, he would not be fit to command you as slaves."[80] The bishop is precisely the one restored to position 2, one who is fit to mas-ter other slaves because of his humility—because he has become obedient to the master. In such texts we begin to glimpse how slave Christology was no mere "metaphor," but instead authorized particular political and social practices, arrangements of bodies, space, and power.

Yet not only was this obedience demanded of laity to bishops on the basis of Christ's obedience. More to the point, we can now turn to see how the master's house, working in tandem with the slave Christology of Philip-pians 2, emerges into view in a tightly interdependent relation between the *symbolic* order of slavery and the *social* order of slavery. Or more precisely, we can raise the question: What is the relation between the obedience of Christ in the form of a slave given to his Father and the obedience demanded of enslaved people to the people who enslaved them? At the heart of this question, we might begin to unfold the normative implications of a profound ambiguity at the heart of Christ's identification with the form of the slave. Augustine emphasizes, polemically, that "the Jews" saw that Christ was *claiming* to be equal with God, and in this way were closer to the truth than the Arians, but their problem was this: they could not recognize Christ's equality with God because they "despised the slave form."[81] If humble, faithful Christians, then, are willing *not* to despise the slave form, but to recognize Christ there, what does this recognition mean for enslaved peoples—for the oppressed and the dispossessed, for the incarcerated and unfree? Does his identification intensify the salience of their voices, or cement their status as an obstacle to be overcome? Are they to be looked to as partners in discerning the good, or "looked through" as a window into the path of ascent? Does Christ in the form of a slave make their presence visible, or take its place and so erase it from view? Is the whole point to get beyond the embarrassment of the slave form to the God form, such that the degradation of the enslaved person is reified, or does the slave form a place from which, against all cultural expectations, the Creator of the world is governing creation?

The clearest way into these questions is to return to a text we have encountered already, but which now can be read more carefully as bringing together Augustine's Christological vision of intimacy, ascent, and obedience with its wider implications in a world ordered by domination, indeed read as the coherent social and political outworking of the mature Christology explored throughout this section. After citing Paul's words to enslaved persons in Ephesians 6, "obey those who are your masters according to the flesh . . . like slaves of Christ," Augustine expounds them:

> [Christ] is the true and eternal slave master [*dominus*], whereas those others are masters only for a time. While you are walking in the way, living in this present life, Christ does not want to make you proud. Perhaps it happened that you, having become a Christian, found yourself subject to a human master. That is as it should be . . . he has not made slaves free, but turned bad slaves into good slaves.
>
> What a debt of gratitude rich people owe to Christ for bringing peace to their households! If in such a house there were an unbelieving slave and Christ were to convert him, he would not say to him, "Leave your master, for now you have come to know him who is your true master. . . ." No, that is not what Christ has said; rather he commands, "Do your duty as his slave."[82]

Augustine insists God's entrance into human life in Christ does not liberate enslaved peoples. It binds them even more tightly to the will of their enslavers, shedding light on the ethical upshot of his slave Christology. The apparent coherence of this ethical vision with other core themes of his thought might give pause to Augustinian thinkers who continue to invoke them as resources for the present. In the lines that follow, Augustine appeals explicitly to the slave Christology he has developed so profoundly: "And then, to strengthen the slave, [Christ] tells him, 'Follow my example in being a slave, for I went before you in submitting to evil men.' . . . If the Master of heaven and earth . . . bore himself like a slave to the unworthy . . . how much less should an ordinary man or woman disdain to serve a master with sincerity, total good will, and love—even if the master is bad?"[83] Christ appears here both in the form of the slave modeling obedience and in the form of the master to whom all obedience is owed, both in intimate union, without division or separation or confusion. The path for people who find themselves enslaved is to search the face of the one who enslaved them—even if they are "bad"—for glimmers of their true *Dominus,* and on these grounds, obey, stay humble, and continue in the journey of inward ascent. No trace emerges here of what is hinted at in the dusk, within the spiritual life of the enslaved—the interminable conflict between the Lord and Ole Marse.

If Christ himself is willing to take the form of the slave, to be humble and obedient, Augustine reasons, how can you be disobedient to the bishops of his church or the masters of your household? It is this sort of exhortation that has occasionally led modern critics to accuse Augustine of "slave morality," that is, of trying to make virtue out of mere subservience.[84] But in sum, what's more interesting for my purposes is how Augustine makes it clear that humility is not for slaves alone, but *is itself the surest basis of mastery.* He anticipates that someone from the crowd will try to turn the logic of humility against him: " 'But look here,' someone will say; 'my bishop should follow my Lord's example, and serve me as my slave.' I'm telling [you]—let those get the point who can—*if* [your bishop] *wasn't serving you as your slave, he wouldn't be giving you orders.* You see, the one who gives useful orders is serving you, serving you by watching over you . . . even the one who in that text made himself a [slave] . . . certainly gave orders to his disciples."[85] The point is: In discussing the theme of humility and obedience here, and in invoking Christ in the form of the slave, Augustine is interested in articulating the authority of being located at the center, in position 2: the figure who is, at once, fit to obey *and* command, to stand in the position of ruler *and* ruled. Or more precisely: one who has submitted to the ultimate *Dominus* in humility, and therefore, by that humility is fit to be the master of others.

This in turn helps us make better sense then of the precision with which Augustine famously excoriates the *libido dominandi* of the earthly city. The problem is certainly not simply the fact that earthly cities like the Roman Empire practice slavery, as Augustine regarded this divinely ordained and inevitable. Nor is it strictly that they are interested in occupying the position of the master rather than the slave—who wouldn't? The problem is that in their own prideful rebellion against God, their own true master, they fall down, in a deeper sense, to position 3 of the hierarchy: "even though whole peoples are its slaves, [the earthly city] is itself under the dominion of its very lust for domination."[86] The problem with the *libido dominandi,* in short, is that by disordering the soul's relation to its *Dominus,* by instead desiring badly, especially desiring material power for its own sake, the lust for mastery ensures that one will *fail in the task of being a master.* Humility, in key part, is precisely the answer to this dilemma.

As Augustine writes in *True Religion* (*De vera religione*), this disordered love is how the human heart "is made restless and wretched, as it longs to lay hold of the things it is held by." But when one is drawn into God's rest, and only then, the heart "masters" such things: "it will not be held by them but will hold them down." The yoke of Christ is light, Augustine reminds us, and the payoff for accepting it is extraordinary: "Those then who are subjected to this yoke have everything else subjected to them." This *everything* is immediately expounded as follows: "if they are willing to be sons of God, seeing that he gave them the right to become sons of God," then "they will be the masters of . . . the friends of the world."[87] Within the master's house that is the whole creation, those who embrace their role in subjection to their *dominus,* those who thereby become "good" slaves after the pattern of the master's son who took the "form of the slave" to show them how, these become fit to be the masters of the level below, the *servi vicarii,* the bad slaves who remain malformed and prideful and disobedient.

This tripartite structure, the master's house as a cosmological structure, thus also helps make sense of why and how this image *would be so beautiful—so compelling* for a late Roman audience. There is a master, and there is an elite slave who became "elite" because he was the "good slave" who obeys, and there are slaves at the bottom (who are there often because of disobedience, because they are "wicked slaves"). Christ is the one who is, by nature, the Son of the *Paterfamilias,* the one who is therefore a child of the master. He does not *grasp* at his father's authority (*auctoritas*) because he already has it, by virtue of his *being* Son by nature (*esse se aequalem Deo*). But because mankind has tried to seize equality with God by robbery, we are the *wicked slaves,* the slaves who in reaching up to the top of the hierarchy in pride have now fallen all the way to the bottom, to position 3. Christ thus takes on the form of the slave, in order to show us how to be good slaves in humility and obedience. But more crucially: insofar as we come to learn this humility from him, insofar as we learn to *be* slaves or be adopted as sons, we also join him in the second position of the tripartite hierarchy, so that "we"—or at least some of us—are now fit to master others.[88]

Of course, there are many other symbol systems in Augustine, and this one, like all others, is elastic, polymorphic, and complex. But at least in this strand of texts, in the cosmological structure of the master's house, Christians are *not* imaged as freed slaves—perhaps unsurprisingly, as manumission was at times an ambiguous, not always attractive option.[89] Rather, Christians take on the status of the *vilicus,* the elite slave in the *domus* of God, the managerial slave in the cosmos of the master's house, and thus are those whose obedience qualifies them to be the masters of others. This is not an arrogant mastery, not the *libido dominandi,* but mastery as a mode of love, mastery as benevolent care—what Rowan Williams called "nurturing" sovereignty. For modern Augustinians who wish to claim that Augustine challenges, undermines, or subverts Roman mastery, it is worth considering whether these texts in Augustine, somewhat troublingly, instead suggest the *reproduction* of the slave master's position in a new form, suggest that humility itself—subjection to God—is the mode of a new and distinctly Christian mode of mastery. The humility of the slave form of Christ must be grasped in connection to the slave form of order. The true human and the true order go hand in hand. This becomes especially visible by turning to a particular Augustinian reception history in modernity.

Part 3. Cotton Mather's Dream

Tucked away in a footnote of Eric Gregory's *Politics and the Order of Love,* with which we have been in dialogue throughout this book, we find the following point of contact with the history of Christian mastery: "Some scholars, adapting Perry Miller's famous description of 'the Augustinian strain of piety' in colonial New England, have argued that Augustinian theology was a formative background for the emergence of American liberal democracy."[90] A key exemplar of Miller's "Augustinian strain of piety" emerges in the form of Cotton Mather—famed Puritan minister and theologian of the early eighteenth century. Rick Kennedy's biography does not merely find in Mather the "Augustinian piety" Perry identified a generation earlier—one focused on divine sovereignty and human sinfulness, reflecting a familiar, relatively uncomplicated "Augustine" toward which many Augustine scholars today would no doubt feel ambivalent.[91] Instead, Kennedy identifies a deeper form of Augustinianism in Mather's sense of "entanglement" in the messiness and complexity of earthly political life, one which underscores the mixed nature of the two cities during this temporal dispensation, and thus harkens back to the first coordinate of *peregrinatio* politics I identified in Chapter 2. It is on this basis that I find in Cotton Mather an illuminating site of Augustinian reception, all the more given how Mather's life as a Christian slaveholder came to be remembered by his religious biographers as an icon of religious humility.[92]

One key episode in Mather's life provides a window into the relation of humility to the enduring problem of the Christian master in racial modernity. On the evening of Friday, December 13, 1706, Mather retired to his study on Hanover Street, pen in hand, to reflect on the day's chief event—an unexpected gift from his Boston congregation. "Some Gentlemen of our Church," he writes in his diary, "purchased for me, a very likely *Slave*; a young Man, who is of a promising Aspect and Temper." At once Mather christens him "Onesimus." The old name disappears into the silence of the archive. The new one evokes the Apostle Paul's letter to Philemon. It locates the enslaved man's life, as well as Mather's own, within the contours of an ancient Augustinian hope: the distinctly Christian possibilities of intimacy between master and slave, of a rightly ordered love between them, rooted in care rather than command, in humility rather than domination. Onesimus ancient and Onesimus modern—for all their many and important differences—are alike transformed by the speech of the Christian master, welcomed anew as "beloved brother" into the space of two social realities merging carefully together: the master's house and the household of God. Neither reducible to the other, the two nevertheless join—the former a partial and imperfect echo of the latter—in a single and lasting theological vision of immense power and clarity. "It seems to be," Mather writes, "a mighty Smile of Heaven upon my Family."[93]

The voice and actions of the first-century Onesimus are mostly lost. No historical evidence has been found that would inform us whether or not this ancient Onesimus accepted Paul or his master's view of him and his situation, or their conception of an emerging Christian faith. In the case of the modern Onesimus, the record suggests he did not. In charting what happened to the modern Onesimus, I aim to draw Augustine's ethic of humility into a confrontation with the figure of the white Christian master—introduced here in the person of Cotton Mather—as an overlooked theological problem. I contend that the relevance of this figure as a problem for Christian ethics has not abated, despite the formal abolition of slavery throughout the Atlantic world, but rather, in subtler and more intractable forms, *persists.*

In the diary entry discussed above, Mather articulates two desires which subtly correspond to two social realities: first, "I wanted a *good Servant* at the expence of between forty and fifty Pounds,"[94] and second, a few lines later, "I resolved with the Help of the Lord that I would ... make him a Servant of Christ." Servitude here is not univocal: the first slavery is "literal," the second "metaphorical." The first displays Mather's desire for a particular way of organizing a life together: the well-ordered household, possible only through the labor of "good" servants; the second, Mather's longing to find in that configuration of community—the master's house—a space of Christian education as well, of training in virtue, of formation into the Christian way of life. "There are several Points," he writes, "relating to the Instruction and Management of my Servant Onesimus, which I would now more than ever prosecute. He shall be sure to read every Day. From thence I will have him go on to Writing. He shall be frequently Catechised."[95] In that ingenious phrasing—"Instruction *and* Management"—the master's pedagogy comes into view. The master's "and" subtly weaves together his two tasks: catechizing the convert into faith *and* educating the slave into profitable and orderly servitude.

What sort of moral agent is fit to accomplish this dual work of mastery and teaching, who can suture home to school, belonging to becoming? Standing at the juncture is the figure whose neglected significance—whose conflicting desires and latent afterlives—occupies my attention throughout this project: the figure of the Christian master. The master's meaning and identity, as Orlando Patterson notes, marks a point of contact between two definitions of "master" in the Oxford dictionary: "a man having control" and "one qualified to teach."[96] What interests me in Mather's diary—for the purposes of this chapter—is not so much a "shift" from one meaning to the other, nor only its accompanying concealment: slavery's brutality hidden beneath benevolent household order.[97] That way of framing the issues at stake is important. But what I hope Mather's diary can illustrate for my purposes is neither a disjunctive shift in meaning, nor a contradiction between reality and falsehood, but to the contrary, the disturbing *coherence* of an ancient and lingering Christian theological vision centered on the master's humility: his willingness to learn, be formed, be subjected to Christ, and *on these grounds,* his fitness to teach, form, and subject others. I am interested precisely in its *absence* of contradiction or disjuncture, and its presence—in clarity, power, lucidity—as a social imaginary: the master's house as imperfect echo of the household of God, providing a conceptual and symbolic space in which Mather's—that is, the master's—two desires may coincide: (a) his desire to stand in the position of mastery, securing social and political order by relations of sovereign control over what surrounds him, human and animal bodies, trees and fields, the built environment of an emerging household-cum-plantation structure; and (b) his desire to occupy this position not by mere force, not by willful self-assertion, but through a subtler and therefore stronger set of attachments, those bonds of legitimacy and indeed affection possible only to the position of the pastor-teacher, that one whose humble obedience before the "true" Master alone qualifies him to impose order elsewhere. Given the convergence of these two desires, as Orlando Patterson says, "Who . . . would not want to be a master?"[98]

Mather's desire for a "good Servant" rests inescapably on the *material* reality of slavery—the logic of personhood reduced to the status of commodity, to forty or fifty pounds' "expence"—while his desire for "a Servant of Christ" rests on slavery as *figurative* reality, its capacity to signify Christian communion as a spiritual household of teaching and learning, in which all of us, our distinct social roles notwithstanding, become formed into the humble and obedient slaves of a faithful master, God.

This dream, the careful, seamless theological convergence of the master's house and the household of God, of two desires, of two slaveries and two masteries, this Mather would develop most powerfully in *The Negro Christianized* (1706), a treatise he distributed throughout New England, with plans to send copies to the Caribbean just months before the gift of Onesimus.[99] Unlike later southern sensibilities, Mather actively sought to educate the new, enslaved member of his household and further to promote this education as an expanding hemispheric project. Even, or especially, in the space of Onesimus's grief upon the death of his son, Mather finds an opportunity to teach: "My Servant has newly buried his Son; (*Onesimus* his

Onesimulus). Lett me make this an Occasion of inculcating the Admonitions of Piety upon him."[100]

In the wake of these soaring hopes of Christian intimacy, perhaps unsurprisingly, the reader of Mather's diaries finds only the slow unraveling of both desires. The life of Onesimus, or rather, its fragments filtered through the master's eyes, displays the failure of Mather's dream. The first trace of this failure appears in the entry dated December 9, 1711: "I must keep a strict Eye on my Servant *Onesimus;* especially with regard unto his Company. But I must particularly endeavor to bring him unto Repentance, for some Actions of a thievish Aspect. Herein I must endeavor that there be no old Theft of his unrepented of, and left without Restitution." No entry implies Onesimus would come to repentance. To the contrary, matters grew worse. "My Servant *Onesimus,* proves wicked, and grows useless, Froward, Immorigerous [disobedient, rebellious]. My Disposing of him, and my Supplying of my Family with a better Servant in his Room, requires much Caution, much Prayer, much Humiliation before the Lord. Repenting of what may have offended Him, in, the Case of my Servants, I would wait on Him, for his Mercy." Again, Mather appeals to his own need to be humbled before his Master, to occupy level 2 in the order of the master's house, in hopes that his servant might gain obedience as well.

Instead, Onesimus sought only to get away, purchasing his freedom shortly thereafter, with Mather conditionally and somewhat begrudgingly granting it. (The editors of Mather's diaries relegate this freedom to a footnote.)[101] Not by fugitive flight, but in legal manumission, Onesimus goes elsewhere, seeks out the woods, and abandons Mather's humble dreams of household formation in virtue. Later, it would emerge that Onesimus's medical knowledge, gleaned from African sources, provided the basis for Mather's push for smallpox inoculation, saving thousands of Bostonian lives.[102] But the absence of Onesimus in the household would remain present to Mather as both melancholia and warning, indeed would come to *haunt* Mather's writings: "The uninstructed *Negroes* about your houses, appear like so many *Ghosts* and *Spectres.* You may, without being Fanciful, imagine that like so many Murdered *Ghosts,* they look very Ghastly upon you, and summon you to answer before the Tribunal of God. . . ."[103] It is the dream of the master, it is Mather's dream—in a real sense: an *Augustinian* dream— that the promise of social intimacy which is implicit in Christian social life, implicit in the vision of Christ's body with its many members, can be compatible with master–slave relations. If only the education of desire by the humility of Christ, the well-ordered desire which just *is* virtue comes to pass, the contours of peace can emerge at the seams of each level of the threefold hierarchy. Onesimus abandons the master's house, leaves behind this ancient Augustinian hope.[104]

Part 4. Humility, Vulnerability, and the Splitting of the Flesh

What to do, then, with humility amid slavery's afterlife? Can it be recovered, retrieved, or transformed? I have advanced a somewhat counterintuitive argument that the virtue of humility in Augustine, not despite, but precisely *as* a thoroughgoing critique of Roman lust for domination, presents a transformed, distinctly Christian mode of mastery. This builds from the previous chapter's discussion of the way the "middle distance" of Augustinian ethical life—attention to the virtues, habits, values—cannot be neatly separated from the structural and the institutional, insofar as the master's house so clearly shapes both. I am not invested in arguing that humility in the abstract can be recovered or must be discarded.[105] Instead I am interested in what set of issues, within a conjuncture of social arrangements organized by racial domination, lies inside of or beneath the question of humility. What is the master's humility for? What does it do, and what does it foreclose? For this, again, my approach will be to take apart and reread a neglected text from Augustine through conversation with modern Black Studies.

In a sermon preached in 403, Augustine takes up themes of wealth and poverty, humility and pride, and having noted that he did not choose the reading for the day, eventually he finds himself discussing the words Jesus speaks to a rich man in Luke 18:22: "If you wish to be perfect, go, sell everything you have, give to the poor, and you shall have treasures in heaven." After a lengthy discussion of various questions around riches, Augustine addresses the realities of the Christian master in relation to slavery, and commends to the rich man who commands a household a particular kind of humility:

> Let him consider, if he were stripped of all those exterior trappings, what sort of rich man he could be, because he's flesh and blood, because he belongs equally with his slave to that mass which derives from Adam and Eve. But

as a rich man he cannot engage in such reflections; you will have difficulty in stripping him of all his trappings. Nor is it desirable that he should be stripped of them; what's desired is that he should throw them away. So it's difficult to persuade him of what he really is in himself, surrounded by all these things. Let him turn his thoughts to what he was like in his mother's womb, naked once upon a time and helpless, just like that poor man. A different lot awaited him when he was born, and the lot that awaited him will remain his here, just as he didn't bring it with him. When the rich man lets his thoughts run on those lines, he is inwardly *poor in spirit* (Mt. 5:3), *that is, he blows pride out of his system, he takes himself down a few pegs. And if he presents a stern and frightening face to those who must be subject to his control, his heart is still humble under the eye of God,* and he knows with what kind of conscience he beats his breast.[106]

Here, Augustine encourages the rich man not to sell everything he has, but to "turn his thoughts"—to *imagine* a world in which he has disposed himself of all his wealth, stripped himself "of all his trappings" so that he can visualize himself "naked" and "helpless," "just like that poor man." By way of these imaginative labors, the rich man might bring his pride into subjection so that he might rule over his slaves while remaining humble before God. Augustine continues:

It's all too easy for the rich man to say, "You bad slave!" It sounds as if he has haughty ideas about himself, and yet if he didn't say it, perhaps he would be failing to keep control of his household. Frequently, I mean to say, he controls it more by harsh and frightening words than by savage beatings. He says this, compelled to say it, no doubt, by the need to be in control of his household; don't let him say it inwardly, don't let him say it in his heart, don't let him say it in the eyes and ears of God. He mustn't think he's better, just because he's rich; let him reflect on the frailty of his flesh, once he has put off his clothes.[107]

In other words, the call to humility centers upon an inward reality, even as outwardly it must not be allowed to inhibit the master's grasp on his household. He is "compelled" to be harsh in his words and with his hands. But "in his heart," he can be humble.

But Augustine is not naïve. In the next two paragraphs, he keenly acknowledges the danger with this being an inward reality, since "every rich man" would be quick to answer, "God knows I don't have haughty ideas about myself; and if I happen to shout, and say something harsh, God knows my conscience, that I say that sort of thing from my need to exercise control, not because I consider myself a cut above other people, as though being richer automatically made me more important." Still, Augustine reasons that the rich man is at "liberty to say this," adding, "only God can observe whether he's telling the truth." He does not ask whether it is possible for the master to be humble—or what the value of humility is—while existing in a relationship explicitly predicated on "control." The structure of the relation itself is not thought to pose any *necessary* barrier to the master's humility. Nor is the possibility raised of a form of sociality *not predicated on sovereign control.* Unimaginable here is that possibility which marronage raised and raises throughout the Americas in Neil Roberts's theorization of a strand of modern Black thought. Unimaginable is the possibility that humility, by stabilizing the unstable relation between the outward demands and inward dynamics of mastery, blocks the path to imagining worlds of relation otherwise, and instead locks ethical life inside the dictates of the position of the master.

Most important, this sermon clearly illustrates the *break* that occurs in the master's self-understanding as a result of the fiction of the chattel principle. Here, Augustine explicitly acknowledges that "the rich man" (the slave master) finds himself *split* between two conceptions of himself which cannot sit easily with one another: his understanding of himself as the master who *must* control his household through fear, and his sense of himself as "flesh and blood," as "belong[ing] equally with his slave to that mass which derives from Adam and Eve."[108] The break I explored in the image of dusk is strikingly no longer only a break between enslaved and masters, but a split running *internal* to masters themselves. Notice the work that humility must do in such a context. Augustine acknowledges this decisive split between the master qua master and the master qua human being, then aims to resolve it by way of humility. Humility, on this account, is thus a sort of *reconciliation* project: a reconciliation of the outward demands of Christian mastery (control, fear, violence) with the inward demands of Christian mastery (humility, peace, salvation). This reconciliation project proves perennially attractive for Christian masters, as it later proved attractive to readers like Alonso de Sandoval—a Jesuit missionary to Colombia who incorporates the teachings of Augustine as he advises his fellow missionaries in their efforts to govern and evangelize African slaves. As though invoking the sermon above, Sandoval writes: "masters should not take pleasure in ordering others but should try to improve themselves first and then rule over others, *without losing either their humility or their authority.* They can have a commanding outward appearance but still stay humble inside.... Everyone must carry out God's laws by treating their fellow human beings with respect."[109]

This hope for retaining both humility and control, of course, is the master's dream, Cotton Mather's dream, which the fugitive leaves behind. As James Cone argues, "There can be no reconciliation for masters, as long as they are masters ... there can be no communication between masters and slaves until masters *no longer exist as masters.*"[110] And this is, in part, because as W. E. B. Du Bois argued, it is not as though the deception at work, the symbolic and material transformation of a man into a master, has worked on those it was designed to subjugate: "We whose shame, humiliation, and deep insult [the white master's] aggrandizement so often involved were never deceived. *We looked at him clearly,* with world-old eyes, and saw simply a human thing, weak and pitiable and cruel, even as we are and were."[111] In other words, those who suffer the violence of Mather's dream, Sandoval's dream, Augustine's dream, see and seem always to have seen "clearly, with world-old eyes" what Augustine glimpsed partially when he called the master to picture himself "once he has put off his clothes" for the night, in the frailty of his own naked flesh.[112] Indeed, "I see these souls undressed and from the back and side," writes Du Bois, "I see the working of their entrails. I know their thoughts and they know that I know."[113] The splitting the master wants from this flesh, his attempted overcoming of what he shares with the "mass that derives from Adam and Eve"—that is, the flesh in all its frailty—this splitting is what Du Bois recognizes as a "phantasy" of devastating consequences. But "these super-men and world-mastering demi-gods listened ... to no low tongues of ours, even when we pointed silently to their feet of clay."[114] Until the masters can listen to this, look down and see their feet of clay, and alter not their inner disposition but the immense and irreversible violence by which they ground their standing *as* masters, there can be no reconciliation, Cone says. No reconciliation between would-be masters and slaves, and no reconciliation even between the masters and themselves, broken in two by the failures of fantasy.

In speaking of "feet of clay," Du Bois draws our attention to the part of the body that links would-be demigods to the earth. The part of the body that *grounds* you, joins you to plantation grounds—the woods or the road. Agee's shoe, twisting on gravel. Grounding would be the starting point for anyone who would reclaim the virtue of *humilitas* in its complex etymological linkages of *human* with *humus*—compost, earthliness, dirt.[115] "In burial," writes Robert Macfarlane, "the human body becomes a component of the earth, returned as dust to dust—inhumed, restored to humility, rendered humble."[116] This is part of what it would mean to recognize mastery as a standpoint, *standing* as revolt against this return to the ground, a revolt against our ecological intimacies in and *as* earth, revolt rooted in what Augustine would call *timor mortis,* fear of ashes to ashes and dust to dust.[117]

But in the meantime, from this vantage, we can better understand how *unthinkable* the fugitive slave is within the categories set by the master's thought: the fugitive intervenes in this conversation the master has with himself. For if the good master is willing to be humble, willing to "share" while maintaining the terms of the relationship (explicitly: fear and control), and the slave *still runs off anyway,* then what does that say about the master's self-understanding? The object of his care, his generosity, has run off. Can he still be a master in the same way under this situation? No. And so the fugitivity of the fugitive keeps the master, even or especially the good, humble master, lying awake at night when he undresses for bed, fragile flesh that he nevertheless is. And from this vantage, that of the master qua master (as distinct from the master qua flesh and blood), we see the need for what I above called Augustine's *subjunctive Christ* in "the form of the slave" to come to us in the night, to call masters to humility and slaves to obedience, and so to reassure us in our self-deceptions concerning who we are and what we have done.

It remains difficult to grapple with what an Augustinian view onto the present would mean in terms of the project of democratic translation, of translating Augustine's politics into the world race built. In my view, the argument I have developed here on the problem of the master in Augustine and beyond demands from us greater ambivalence—that is, a more critical appreciation of both the possibility and the real limits of what Augustine himself can say to this moment—greater than that, for example, of one recent Augustinian engagement with the era of Black Lives Matter. In an insightful reflection for the *Journal of Religious Ethics* issue titled "COVID-19 and Religious Ethics," Jennifer Herdt interprets the mass uprisings in the wake of the police killing of George Floyd as, in key part, a result of the shared experience of pandemic, quarantine, and heightened vulnerability. Herdt is careful to acknowledge the central importance of the "sustained organizing against police brutality" in the form of the Black Lives Matter movement and to note that the image of Floyd "gasping for breath vividly reminded us of Eric Garner's 2014 death, and of the millions of Black Americans who symbolically struggle to breathe in a systemically racist society."[118] And yet, for Herdt, Floyd symbolizes "more" than this too, and "this more" is linked to Covid-19 and a notion of "vulnerability" which she believes Augustine helps us bring into view:

> Chauvin's knee on his [Floyd's] neck embodied white domination. But not just this; in a context of shared and heightened vulnerability, George Floyd, calling for his mother, *was any of us and all of us,* bewildered, forlorn, alone, with familiar routines upended and the taken-for-granted texture of our lives lying in shambles around us.
>
> Augustine in his sermons often addressed the wealthy in ways that powerfully exposed shared vulnerability.[119]

At issue are two points of concern. First, the Black feminist analytic of fungibility with which I have been engaged throughout—developed in Hartman, Morrison, Spillers, and Lethabo King—invites us to pause over this empathic identification, whereby "George Floyd . . . *was* any of us and all of us," his murdered life exchangeable for "any" of our lives in their pandemic-disrupted "familiar routines." Again, Herdt is careful to underscore the stark racial disparities visible in the different effects of the pandemic upon white and Black people. Yet the critique of fungibility invites us to hesitate over whether something is nevertheless occluded when Black suffering is called upon to facilitate wider ethical meditations by inviting *identification* with a Black person in pain, a tradition which Hartman has theorized as "the precariousness of empathy" in sympathetic white allies like John Rankin (and elsewhere, William Wilberforce).[120] Empathy is "double-edged," Hartman suggests, because "the effort to counteract the commonplace callousness to black suffering *requires that the white body be posited in the place of the black body in order to make this suffering visible and intelligible.*" In other words, "in making the other's suffering one's own," the specificity of the other risks being, paradoxically, "obliterated." Hartman's point is "not to suggest that empathy can be discarded," but rather to "highlight the dangers of a too-easy intimacy" in a social context already marked *not* by alienation or distance or unfamiliarity between Blacks and whites, but precisely by a "monstrous intimacy."[121] Understanding the latter requires grasping the present not only as a generic "this side of the eschaton," as Herdt says (though surely it is this too), but more specifically as haunted by racial slavery's particular afterlife, the deep role of Christian mastery within it, and the risk—inherent in even the most thoughtful attempts to face such histories—of "committing further violence in [one's] own act of narration."[122]

And that brings us to the second point. At the heart of Herdt's brisk pivot to Augustine in the second paragraph quoted above is the ethical value of "exposing shared vulnerability," and in particular the fact that, "again and again, Augustine underscored shared nakedness at birth." Herdt cites four sermons of Augustine's on this point to underscore Augustine's concern with vulnerability as capable of enabling us to "dismantle barriers to sympathetic identification." But I wonder how Herdt would read Sermon 114B above, in which Augustine enjoins masters to consider their shared nakedness. This exhortation does not negate, erase, or even mitigate the master's legitimate need for domination. Rather, it allows humility to *reconcile* the master's inner vulnerability with the outer demands of good social order. Here the frailty of naked flesh, shared between master and slave, forces the master into a split: between his shared frailty and his need as master for "control in the household." Humility in vulnerability allows him to redress this split without any serious alteration to the social order itself. This is not unrelated to one sort of response to the crisis of state violence (especially police violence) against Black people: the response of liberals who find themselves sympathetic to the protestors but resistant to any proposed alternatives *to* (rather than reforms within) the policing system. For such people, the question becomes: How can we respond to unrest and uprising by *reconciling* humane sensibilities with enduring, reformed structures of control—that is, without any serious alteration of the social order itself? Augustine indeed provides a way forward if this is what you want, reconciling these precisely by way of appeal to humility—a humility which need not lose control over the terms of a relation of power. And this clarifies the struggle for those who inhabit the afterlife of the Christian master—can our theological imagination open a space for instead envisioning a world beyond and against this gesture, of mastery *in* humility, humility *in* control? What remains to be seen is whether we can instead embody humility in the form of *abolishing* the structures which inhibit it (without resorting to utopian fantasy), a possibility I return to in the following chapter.

For now, I suggest this begins with a confrontation with the position of the master for Christians today who—especially by way of whiteness, class status, social power—have inherited the afterlife of the master's position and now must confront the lingering effects of mastery upon our forms of life, our theological imaginations, and our attempts to retrieve tradition. To that end, I raise three questions for further inquiry, taking in reverse order the Christological themes above. First, on *obedience.* Amid the global uprising of Black Lives Matter against carceral violence, we might wish to ask, *whose* obedience is demanded by the structures of the world as it presently exists, the world of racial slavery's afterlives? When another Black person is killed by police, how often are we told that if only they had *obeyed* the officer's commands, they would be alive? What is the relation of Christ's obedience to this world of racialized order and racialized criminality, structured by command and obedience? More pointedly, within this world, what does it mean that when Christ "became obedient unto death," his obedience looked like "death on the cross" (Phil. 2:8), which is to say, *it looked like disobedience*—given that the cross was the punishment given precisely to the seditious and the fugitive, to those whose lives in motion could only appear as violent threats to "law and order"?[123] These theological and scriptural considerations must haunt how Christian leaders respond not only to "peaceful" protests, but to the very framing which posits an easy, simple moral distinction of violence from nonviolence, "peaceful" from "disruptive," protest from riot. Second, on *ascent.* If Christ's obedience appears within this world's structures as disobedience, how would this affect the movement of our attention, the formation of our desire and our interior life? Some of us will need to begin to reckon with how our formation, yes, even our theological education, has yet to interrupt our investments in the order of racial hierarchy, in the profit, stability, and coherence it still promises. Others of us will need to reckon with how our very attempts to resist this order often subtly reproduce our attempts to hold onto the position of mastery, while reinscribing the figure of "the oppressed" as an object of thought, rather than a partner in action— as a noun to be looked at, talked about, or helped, rather than a verb to be joined in solidarity.[124] What spiritual disciplines, what practices of social life, what modes of assembly make our lives most open to the divine work of unmaking and remaking, to education into alternative modes of attention, care, and desire? Third, and briefly, on *intimacy*. What would it look like and sound like to press toward the intimacy of human and divine which God made possible in Christ by returning again and again to a scandal: "The real scandal of the gospel," wrote James Cone, "is this: humanity's salvation is revealed in the cross of the condemned criminal Jesus, and humanity's salvation is available *only* through our solidarity with the crucified people in our midst."[125] I return to develop this link between the cross and solidarity more thoroughly in Chapter 5.

In this chapter, I have developed further the portrait of the Christian master by expanding how the grammar of slavery and the position of the master shapes the Augustinian account of the form of the slave Christology and its most resonant Augustinian virtue—humility—as both are drawn inside the structures of the master's house. Understanding the extent to which the three layers of the master's house shape Augustine's thought is crucial as we turn to the next chapter on temporality in Augustine, which explores how Augustine's account of the origins of slavery in the *saeculum* is intelligible only by recognizing again the work of this tripartite cosmology, in which the cosmos is like a Roman household with God above rational creatures and rational creatures above irrational creatures, providing the structure of governance by which divine providence remains sovereign over the world.

FOUR

Abolition's Time

The ghost of Augustine wanders among us. We are suddenly more aware
than before that action—political action, say—is not merely historical in the
familiar contextual senses. It takes place in time, is temporal, temporalizes,
and is therefore always vulnerable to contingency and conflict.... We are
suddenly more aware than before of just how much, and how uncannily,
fictive models of time shape our experience of the past in the present and
our expectations for the future.
—David Scott, *Omens of Adversity: Tragedy, Time, Memory, Justice*

Nor does [God] submit to this temporal order, as though its slave; rather
he rules over it as its Lord and directs it as its Master.
—Augustine, *The City of God*

In one of the few extended comments on Augustine's thought in
contemporary Black Studies, David Scott invokes Augustine's searing
meditations on temporality. It is not merely that political life takes place
in time, but that something about doing politics *temporalizes:* it makes
and unmakes our experience of the passage of time, alters how we
remember the past (or how and why we forget it), and sets conditions for
what we anticipate as possible and impossible in the future. Politics is
responsive to and generative of collective times imagined, times lived—
it cracks open futures, pasts, and presents to ongoing negotiation and
contestation. Scott underscores this politics of temporality as especially
"vulnerable to contingency and conflict," to interminable irresolution,
and in this way, he echoes the distinctly Augustinian sensibility of ambivalence during the world, the ambivalence I identified in Chapter 2 as
marking a key coordinate of political Augustinianism. In this chapter, I turn

to examine in detail how for Augustine, as Scott writes, "fictive models of time shape our experience," that is, not simply how we imagine time, but how imagined temporalities inhabit us, how they foreclose or open lines of theological and ethical inquiry, and thus how they constrain or enable forms of life.

At issue specifically is how the Augustinian "fictive model" of the present time—*saeculum*, and especially what he calls *in hoc saeculo*, "in this age"— shapes his narration of where slavery comes from, what it's for, and how it shapes both human and divine action in the world. But it is not the case that Augustine has a preformed account of *saeculum*, which he then simply applies to his narration of the origins of slavery. Nor that slavery's origins simply provide one event among others in the story of the present age. For Augustine the relation between the two—the temporality of *saeculum* and the existence of slavery—is more intimate.

The *saeculum*, writes Paul Griffiths, is "constituted exhaustively by the set of events that begins with the creation out of nothing of the cosmos as a beautifully ordered whole (*civ. Dei* 11.3–6) and ends with the last judgment."[1] It is at once "beautiful, ordered," Griffiths continues, and "disordered and thereby ugly: that disorder and ugliness came into being with the fall," and from that point on, "the story is one of increasing and spreading decay and violence." Interestingly, on Griffiths's account, the fall is identical with the emergence of "systemic violence," and here for Augustine—though Griffiths does not mention it—slavery enters the plot.

Two statements on slavery from *The City of God* thus provide our initial frame for what follows. In Book 19, Augustine makes clear that there was no slavery of man to man in the beginning: "By nature, then, as God first created man, no one is a slave either to man or to sin."[2] And in Book 4, Augustine makes clear that there will be no more slavery in the age to come: "full happiness will come only in the life where no one will be a slave any longer." No slaves in the beginning, no slaves in the end. Only now. And so, what is it about this now, this post-fall present in the *saeculum*, which provides the conditions of possibility for slavery's emergence? Indeed, which makes slavery not only emerge and not only persist but also attain the status of being divinely "ordained," in Augustine's view, "by precisely the same law which commands that the natural order is to be preserved and forbids it to be disturbed"?[3] And finally, how might attending to the intimacy of slavery and *saeculum* intervene in the endless debate among Augustinians concerning the task of political and ethical life in a "secular" age?

I have noted above that when slavery in Augustine's corpus is discussed by Augustinians at length, it is almost always directed to a discussion of the character of political authority in Book 19 of *The City of God*—especially the question of whether Augustine thinks the particular form of hierarchical subordination such authority introduces into the created order is "natural" or "unnatural." Interpreters have been preoccupied not primarily with the question of slavery in its own right, but with how Augustine's apparent tendency to equate all political authority with slavery shapes any genuinely Augustinian account of the origins of politics itself. I have aimed, in this book, to show the extent to which slavery, in both its symbolic resources and its material realities, permeates Augustine and Augustinianism far beyond this narrow set of questions. By instead attending to the appearance of masters and slaves in Augustine's treatment of wide-ranging topics of ongoing interest to Augustinians—pilgrimage, humility, virtue, agency, and more—I have attempted to let Augustine be stranger than Augustinians have sometimes allowed, and so to let ourselves be stranger too, foremost by showing some of us more clearly to ourselves in the figure of the master. The alignment of much Christian thought with the vantage, interests, and self-deceptions of the master class, I have suggested, neither originated in Augustine nor disappeared after him, but in him we find a window into an enduring problem whose contours we can trace by attending to various reception histories of Augustinian thought and practice. With these pieces in place, I can now turn at last to the place most Augustinians have wanted to begin—Augustine's account of slavery's origins in Book 19. This is especially important for two reasons.

First, the habit among Augustinians, as John Rist emphasizes in his perceptive reading, is to grant that the "strongest point" in Augustine's defense of the institution of slavery is his keen sense for how profoundly *inevitable* slavery or slavelike domination is under the present conditions of fallenness: "Augustine assumes that even if certain forms of slavery, such as he knew in his own society, were to disappear, they would be replaced by others. The name might change; perhaps slaves would no longer be called 'slaves.' The reality would remain unchanged. . . . Slavery in some form is endemic, and there is no point in trying to do the impossible and be rid of it."[4] Rist rightly points out that the same is true of concupiscence—it cannot, on Augustine's own account, be eliminated in this life—yet here, unlike slavery, Augustine insists the struggle against it must be undertaken anyway.[5] Still, the anti-perfectionism of Augustine at the institutional level is indeed partly what renders his thought perennially compelling, perhaps especially in political eras like ours, in which "perfection" seems an especially fanciful notion. (I will argue in the final section for an alternate framing of this issue.) Second, it is precisely at this juncture of his belief in slavery's inevitability that modern interpreters, whether his detractors or his defenders, have been most tempted to explain Augustine's views by chalking them up to psychological temperament (his "conservative cast of mind," his "anxiety" toward social disorder), to overweening frameworks like "pessimism" and "realism" (which purport to explain much but illumine little), or to overdetermined appeals to the totemic power of his historical "context," as when Gervase Corcoran invokes the "general brutality of the age" to account for what he takes to be Augustine's otherwise embarrassing "silence on cruelty toward slaves."[6]

None of these particularly helps us take Augustine's views seriously *as views*—as intellectual positions developed in rigorous engagement with his social world. Nor do they enable the reckoning I pursue in this chapter, a reckoning with how the temporal sensibility of ambivalence still animating contemporary Augustinian politics is implicated in the master's house, with how this risks reproducing the enduring problem of the Christian master, and thus with how this ambivalent temporality must be imagined elsewhere and otherwise in conversation with fugitive Black thought. To pursue this reckoning, we must grasp the link identified—between the origins of slavery and the entrance of sin into the temporality we inhabit—first in relation to the theological account Augustine develops of sin and evil as nonbeing, as the *privatio* of good creation. Next I show how the contours of this grammar of sin emerge in and through the symbolic space of the master's house. This, in turn, prompts the need for particular attention to the concept of God's *providence*, the fitting category for describing divine agency *in hoc saeculo*, and to the concepts of human *hope, patience,* and *waiting,* as the fitting categories for describing human agency *in hoc saeculo.*[7]

Part 1 takes up the way Augustine's conception of providence under sin provides the key site for narrating the role of slavery in God's plan for a sinful age, drawing the connections between providence and the master's house, especially the threefold cosmological structure of the master's house introduced above. Part 2 turns to the enduring problem of the master by attending to how this providence discourse aligns theological reasoning with the position of the master and functions apologetically in the enslavement projects of the New World. And Part 3 then attempts to disrupt, unmake, and remobilize key categories drawn from Augustine's eschatological thought in a constructive direction in conversation with contemporary abolitionist-democratic projects.

Part 1. Sin, Providence, and the Master's House

In Augustine's telling, the story of slavery's coming to be makes sense only as an event within the coming to be of sin.[8] Thorny conceptual issues result, not least since naming sin's coming to "be"—that is, offering an account of the origin of evil—demands an attempt to isolate with words not one thing among others, but precisely "no-thing" within being: the very "presence" of absence, the "existence" of loss. Augustinian grammar draws evil inside these inverted commas—little spaces of the less than real. As I have noted throughout, in coming to terms with Augustine's view of slavery, scholars consistently (and rightly) emphasize sin's intimate linkage with slavery's origins—a "sign of something fundamentally wrong in human relations," as Rowan Williams noted in a *New Statesman* review essay.[9] In short, they emphasize that one cannot make sense of Augustine's slavery discourse without reference to his theological account of a world profoundly damaged, malformed by evil.

But the inverse of this proposition, though rarely considered, may also be true: Just as one cannot grasp Augustine's explanation of slavery without evil, neither can one fully see Augustine's account of evil—and thus, of life under the fallen portion of the *saeculum*—without the logic of slavery. Without reference, that is, to slavery considered not only as historical event but as a set of metaphors permeating Augustine's corpus—what I have termed the symbolic space of the master's house.[10] The master's house thus serves to clarify, stabilize, and resolve crucial aspects of Augustine's grammar of sin, precisely at the point where his other metaphors fail, and so is indispensable for understanding the temporality of life during the fallen time of the *saeculum*. Showing how the master's house accomplishes symbolic work at this site, work which cannot be achieved by other symbolic resources, is worth pursuing, in key part, to underscore one of the recurring contentions of the project: that "excising" slavery language as simply one metaphor among others in Augustine is implausible, and doing so risks obscuring the intimate linkages between Augustine's "theological" concepts (evil, materiality, providence) and his "political" concepts (*saeculum*, cities, subjection, authority). That said, the somewhat technical investigation into Augustine's account of sin as privation in the following two sections may be tedious for some readers, who may wish to skip to the third section, where I make explicit the implications of the account for providence and slavery.

Darkness Visible, Silence Audible: The Logic of Evil as Nonbeing

I presuppose throughout James Wetzel's definition of what he calls the *privatio* thesis, the "supposition that evil is an absence, only a shadow of something real, and so not a thing of its own kind."[11] Offering neither a summary of all Augustine has to say on evil, nor a treatment of the full range of interpretations among contemporary Augustinians, I instead begin by unfolding the implications of one particular refrain I've noticed recurs in the most clear-sighted readings of *privatio:* the Augustinian grammar of evil is not, in any straightforward or unqualified sense, what modern thinkers ideally-typically call a "theodicy." Such approaches in analytic philosophers like Richard Swinburne, John Hick, and Alvin Plantinga—as Ken Surin's fine survey argues—tend to regard theodicy's task "very much as an ahistorical and individualistic quest for logically stable notions, exact axioms, and rigorous chains of deductive inference."[12] My interest here is not in these debates themselves, but in their capacity to force a more precise rendering of Augustine's grammar of sin in relation to the concerns I have introduced above. This grammar, I suggest, resists the name "theodicy" thus conceived in two signal respects. By examining these two aspects, my argument establishes a window into the *privatio* thesis which clarifies the logic of Augustine's widely discussed "deficient" causality passage (*civ.* 12.7), then shows how the "seeing darkness" metaphor employed there reaches its limits, limits which only the symbolic resources of slavery deployed elsewhere (and discussed in the following section) can overcome.

First, modern theodicy projects of the sort Surin describes do not demand that the problem of evil be viewed "as a constituent of an all-encompassing theological . . . reading of history," and certainly not of "a history which is the work of the very God who reveals himself in Jesus Christ."[13] Yet in the anti-Manichaean breakthrough of Augustine's conversion—notwithstanding some obvious help from Plotinus, Porphyry, and Neoplatonism broadly—

Augustine finds that the logic of what evil "is" remains inseparable from how we think about the revealed God of scripture, the creator of Genesis and John 1.[14] What this inseparability entails, in key part, is that "neither [God nor evil] has a *place* in the universe," as Rowan Williams notes, "neither is a subject competing with others."[15] This is so because whatever *is* exists strictly by virtue of God's creative act, God's bringing forth being from nothing and calling it good. And since neither God nor evil can have this act for its source, neither may be said to "exist" in the manner in which exists that class of created things we call (somewhat imprecisely) the cosmos. Neither evil nor God is "in" the being of things in that way. The two explanations work in tandem: jettison Augustine's grammar of God, lose his account of evil as well. I note their inseparability here, in key part, to acknowledge that one cannot engage *privatio*'s social logic without thereby raising "properly theological" matters as well. More on this below.

But second, and of more immediate concern: unlike most modern theodicy talk, Augustine's *privatio* thesis is not an attempt to locate evil within a rationally coherent account of the world. It instead offers a grammar—a lexicon and syntax inextricably tied to a theological metaphysics of *creatio ex nihilo*—which not only explains why "logically stable notions" of evil can't be given, but also makes clear that this impossibility is itself the point. How so?

In Book 12 of *The City of God*, as Augustine aims to clarify how it is that we've come to speak of two cities or societies at all, "one consisting of the good, the other of the evil," each comprised of angelic and human creatures (12.1), he first needs to clarify how evil entered good creation in the first place. Bad angels could not have rebelled from a difference in nature, he reasons, since "the only nature contrary to the nature which supremely is . . . is a nature which has no being at all" (12.2). Bad angels have a good nature, then; they cannot be evil "all the way down," for in that case there would simply be no angel to speak of.[16] Whence their evil, then? Not in nouns, but verbs. On Augustine's account, evil issues not from a difference in nature but a turn in will, a desire to be otherwise than what they are: to be "in their own power" apart from God, "*as if* they were themselves their own good" (12.1). And in that "*as if*"—that subjunctive form of life Augustine calls *superbia* (12.6)—they "fell away from . . . the good which makes blessed" (12.1).

This explanatory account (not nature but will) only kicks the can back further, though, as Augustine recognizes: for if "an evil will is the efficient cause of an evil act," rather than some flaw in the actor's nature, then we find ourselves "look[ing] for the efficient cause of this evil will," indeed, that of "the very first evil will" (12.6). But how can a good nature possibly author an evil will? Whence such an inclination? Or in short: What causes one person to hold fast to her willing of the good, while another of exactly the same disposition turns her will aside to evil? Augustine's answer is striking: nothing.[17] If we "examine the matter carefully, nothing comes to mind." Or most bluntly: "Nothing is the efficient cause of an evil will" (12.6).

Explaining what Augustine means by this gives us the vantage from which to clarify how exactly the *privatio* thesis is working in a manner distinct from modern theodicy: For Augustine, evil occupies *no* position within a logically coherent network of claims. Or more precisely, when we name a will "evil," what we are naming occupies only the "position" of its process of departure from that network. It has for an intelligible description solely its ongoing attempt to abandon intelligibility, to escape the very domain where reasons are given, effects caused.[18] Whatever coherence evil retains is retained only in this: its centrifugal motion—its outward thrust, away from what supremely is—does not yet "succeed." That is, only insofar as its escape from being remains asymptotic, incomplete, still within creation's pull. Goodness is stubborn as hell—maybe more so, one might hope, in the end.

And so from this vantage, as Charles Mathewes contends, the *privatio* argument "is not about solving, and hence dissolving, the problem of evil, but rather about bringing into focus the real problem, the absurdity and inexplicability of evil's reality."[19] The impossibility of explication is precisely the point: Bringing evil "into focus"—a visual metaphor that gets interesting in light of the passage from Augustine discussed below—demands we decline evil a home in the order of things, where coherent causes achieve coherent effects. Banished thus, "evil" is rather the name we give to incoherence itself, the name for acts directed "against the order of nature" (*contra ordinem naturarum*, 12.8), a complex concept which, in this context, may be said to denote simply that created realm in which actions and their meanings may be shared, cognition made common.[20] Evil cannot be explicated within this order, since to do so "would tie it back into the explanatory fabric of the cosmos, the violation of which is what sin quite literally is."[21] And so it's not merely that this or that particular evil act is disordered; rather, by chasing its own "private ends" (12.1), the evil will attempts to reject, abandon, and unmake order as such. In an oft-cited passage, Augustine calls these attempts "defections":

No one, therefore, should look for an efficient cause for an evil will. For it is not an efficient but rather a deficient cause, because the evil will itself is not an effect but rather a defect. For to defect from what has supreme existence to what has lesser existence is itself to begin to have an evil will. And since the causes of such defections . . . are not efficient but rather deficient causes, *to want to discover such causes is like wanting to see darkness or to hear silence.*[22]

To "see" defection, then, to try to bring it "into focus," is precisely to recognize it *as* opacity, *as* the resistance to, or perhaps retreat from, the transparency of order. Evil—to return to Wetzel's definition, now with particular attention to the visual—is "only a *shadow* of something real." Evil's relation to good, like shadow's to light, has its proper definition only in that which it lacks and which, by its very lacking, it serves to remind us of.[23]

Significantly, you'll find "only" or "merely" in nearly all such definitions of the *privatio* thesis ("only a shadow"), and understandably so. Yet the work this "only" does is complicated; it risks misleading. To say "only" is to risk underplaying the way Augustine—especially in *The City of God,* perhaps more so than *Confessions*—treats evil with remarkable sensitivity to the seriousness with which its effects appear to us: Following the passage above, Augustine immediately admits that things like darkness and silence are, indeed, nonetheless "known to us, the one by no other means than the eyes and the other by no other means than the ears . . . somehow known by not-knowing them" (12.7). The nonbeing which is known by not-knowing retains its own sort of reality. Ask the prisoner in solitary confinement if not-knowing seems to her "only" a lack of the real. Instead, it seems clearer to say, as Paul Griffiths does, that "hell is present in the devastation *really,* as darkness visible and silence audible."[24] Darkness is present, and by no other means than my seeing, silence by nothing but my ears. Eyes strain by the former. The latter feels deafening. Not-knowing is never "mere" absence: it's more like being present, really there, in a prison cell unlit and mute, eyes and ears intact.[25]

The Limits of Darkness Visible and "the Slave" as Sign of Living Death

What's the point of putting it this way? Evil demands language make recourse to paradoxical-sounding formulations—darkness visible, silence audible—but the apparent paradox simply indicates, for Augustine, how difficult it is to reconcile descriptions of evil in the order of being ("darkness") with how evil appears to us in the order of knowing ("visible")—that is, evil's ontological description with its phenomenology. Or put another way, it suggests how difficult it is for him to square the "absence" darkness properly is with the stubbornly real "presence" by which it falls upon the subject who encounters it.[26] And *that* the subject encounters evil as real (that she "knows by not-knowing," but in this way nevertheless *does* know) is itself suggestive that the line which splits presence from absence, being from nonbeing, good from evil, order from disorder, is one which—far from being an aloof abstraction—bisects the perceiving subject herself. That line is not external to, but within the very subject who wishes to know evil's cause. The one seeking a cause for evil, dizzyingly, does so from *within* conditions where evil is already present.

This presents serious issues for the Augustinian proposal. In wishing to know evil's cause, the observer stands in a relationship with the observed that is more intimate, I contend, and more complex than the metaphor of "visible darkness" allows. This of course does not mean the metaphor is "wrong." It comes on stage at just the right moment, does just what it was sent to do. But precisely *as* metaphor there are limits to its signifying work; it is implicated in wider questions it cannot address on its own terms. To specify further what serious questions I have in mind is to begin to press the metaphor of "visible darkness" up against its limits in three key ways, for which I'll stipulate as shorthands: issues of evil's *complexity, causality,* and *completeness.* Reckoning with these, I suggest, drives us beyond that metaphor to recognize in slavery the more expansive symbolic resources for evil-as-nonbeing that Augustine needs, and which, in turn, provide the master's house as the frame within which his account of institutional slavery will function.

Limit 1: Complexity

First, there is a *complexity* to what we may call evil's "internal/external dynamic" which eludes the "darkness visible" metaphor. The latter conceives the relation between the act of seeking evil's causality and the existence of the evil being sought as a relation of faculty to object: as sight to darkness, hearing to silence. A faculty-object relation implies an object whose existence is reliably *external* to the faculty which apprehends it. But for Augustine's argument, in terms of what this metaphor seems designed to convey (what semiotic theorists call its "tenor"), the being of the perceiving subject who "sees darkness" is not actually separable from the darkness she sees. That is, the deficiency signified by "darkness" in the metaphor actually lies, so to speak, within the eyes themselves: "My swelling conceit separated me from you," Augustine recalls, "and the gross swelling on my face closed my eyes."[27] The darkness seen by not seeing, known by not knowing, does not reside "out there," then, in an object *external* to, and observable from, a fixed and stable subject-position.[28] There is no darkness as an object strictly independent of me, of my looking. If there were, it would not be the case that, as Augustine says clearly, "these are not defections toward *things that are evil* but are evil defections." The evil lies not in things themselves, external to me which I then perceive as evil. The evil lies in the defecting itself, *internal* to my own will's turning, and thus, in this narrow sense, internal to me.

The intriguing upshot of Augustine's account is this: Evil itself is not a material thing with spatial-temporal properties. But we must hold two thoughts together: we can say evil is "located" as a genuine *exteriority* of creation—it has no proper place in the order of being, it can't be made intelligible within the "explanatory fabric of the cosmos"—while at the same time, we must say it is "located" as genuine *interiority*, for the acts we call evil are traced to the will's turning, a will which of course belongs not to "external things," but the inwardness of my soul.[29] It is as though fragments of the outside, of what is other than creation, have become lodged like shrapnel within the creature and thus within creation itself. As nonbeing, evil finds its proper description, somehow, as that which is more *external* to creation than its distant stars, yet more *internal* to me (who is in creation) than the cells in the organs in my body. If it were other than exteriority (if it belonged within the world), then evil would be a "nature," and we've established this can't be the case. But if it were other than interiority—proceeded from somewhere besides the will—then we would be back to the "nonsensical, or rather insane" Manichaean position of rendering evil a substance.[30] In short, the terms of Augustine's "darkness visible" metaphor in Book 12 implicitly locate evil as external to the perceiving subject, but by the logic of Augustine's broader argument, evil is something rather more complex—the outside of creation *brought* internal. It is creation's outside *interjected*, folded into its interior. Folded precisely at the point most like God—the creature's will—and therefore most porous to prideful defection.

And so Augustine's account of the nonbeing which evil "is" needs a grammar which goes beyond the faculty-object metaphor in order to clarify its status as an exteriority brought into the interior—where it does not belong—thereby forming something like an *internal exteriority,* or an *external interiority.* And it is here, significantly, that we begin to see the logic of conceiving evil as *disorder,* since the exterior now brought inside signals precisely disarrangement: the breakdown of "the arrangement of things equal and unequal that assigns to each its due place"—Augustine's classic definition of order.[31] I am proposing here that this disarrangement, together with a concept of punishment as its realignment into order, is indeed what the slavery metaphors enable Augustine to bring clearly into view.

This can be seen in a careful reading of Augustine's reasoning in the nineteenth book of *The City of God.* There, this logic of evil as an *internal exteriority* is implicitly present in slavery as a consequence of sin, both in what it means, in the imagination of the master, to *be* a slave, and in what it means, again, within the imagination of the master, to *have* a slave. First, to be a slave is contrary to nature since, as Augustine says, "[God] did not want a rational creature, made in his own image, to have dominion except over irrational creatures—not man over man but man over beasts" (19.15). This follows from the fact that "because man has a rational soul, he subordinates everything that he has in common with the beasts to the peace of the rational soul," and this rational act of subordination enables "properly ordered accord of cognition and action" (19.14). To be a slave is to lose this capacity for ordering one's own actions. It is to have someone else's will supplant your own. It is, according to the logic of slavery, according to the fiction of the chattel principle, not only to be made to function like an animal, but to have what is exterior to the rational soul—someone else's will—be made present precisely where it does not belong, in the place of my own free interiority.[32] As such, to be a slave serves as a fitting, extended metaphor for the way nonbeing intrudes as exteriority into the goodness of creation, injecting disorder into the world at the site of the human.

And second, to *have* a slave is to have one who is consummate outsider, even enemy, present in the intimate spaces of domestic life. As Mary Beard notes in *SPQR: A History of Ancient Rome,* the common Roman proverb "All slaves are enemies" indicates the "degree of fear and anxiety [felt by owners] about their dependence and vulnerability" upon the enslaved bodies in their households.[33] A similar sensibility is surely at work when Augustine, several sections earlier, notes the lachrymal quality of Cicero's warning against "insidious treacheries," those which emerge not from "the open enemy . . . but this hidden evil . . . internal and domestic," when members of one's own household disrupt the peace (19.5). Elsewhere, in warning of how "certain imposters worm their way into the Church," Augustine again invokes the slave in the master's house: "Our Master wanted us to regard these sinners as slaves in the house . . . as a slave, as a sly sinner . . . looking for something to steal, or something to denounce or decry."[34] In this sense too, the imagined body of the enslaved is a sign of an exteriority already made interior. The slave's presence marks the site of conflict and instability, the place where tranquility is threatened and maintained, precisely because it is the place where there is an ambiguous contradiction: "the slave" is both a human person with all that entails, *and* fundamentally being governed by what is other than the very thing—the rational soul—which makes her a human person. Her potential disobedience threatens order. Her obedience secures it. Either way, order and disorder are confronting one another there in the complexity of the internal/external dynamic which the figural body of the slave dramatizes. I return to these matters further below.

Limit 2: Causality

Second, on the terms set by the "darkness visible" metaphor, the one observing evil ("seeing darkness") finds herself in a relation to what is observed more intimate than the metaphor allows. What makes the darkness dark is somehow *caused*—inexplicably, deficiently, which, once again, *is* the point—by the very one trying to gaze upon it. For this reason Wetzel calls the "darkness visible" image "both striking and misleading," since "the issue is not how we see darkness, but whether we cause the darkness that we know by not seeing."[35] Augustine needs a syntax and a vocabulary by which to capture the fact that the very one who perceives the lack that is darkness is herself somehow bound up with the very chain of responsibility which leads to it. This responsibility, this causality—Wetzel notes—the metaphor leaves unresolved. Yet in the account Augustine gives of the causality of slavery, it is clear that slaves, that is, those being punished, *are responsible for their own condition*, their own "darkness." This is not so because of the sinfulness of any particular slave—many slaves are righteous, Augustine maintains, many masters wicked. But within the providence of God, we can be assured that "it is on sinners that the condition of slavery is justly imposed," such that "the first cause of slavery, therefore, is sin." It occurs only "by the judgment of God . . . who knows how to assign different punishments according to the merits of the offenders" (19.15). The one suffering evil has indeed caused the evil she is suffering, not individually, but simply by virtue of being present in humanity and thereby nascently present in the chain of events which led to sin's just punishment.[36]

Limit 3: Totality

Third, the "darkness visible" metaphor reaches a limit insofar as it cannot really signify the fact that evil, on Augustine's view, afflicts the human creature in a manner more totalizing, more complete than is suggested by a particular sense faculty. Seeing and hearing are, strictly speaking, "accidental" properties of the human person. (To lack them is to be a blind person or a deaf person, not to forfeit the nature called "human.") They are partial, not total aspects of the human creature. If the "complexity limit" suggests that the metaphor in question cannot adequately represent the way "darkness" is present in the eyes themselves (as the awkwardness of that syntax itself displays), and the "causality limit" suggests that the metaphor says little about the all-important matter of what brought about the darkness in the first place, this third limit concerns the fact that "seeing darkness" concerns only a particular sense faculty, whereas sin concerns the whole person.[37]

We know the latter is the case principally through what Augustine identifies as sin's chief consequence, the punishment promised to Adam and Eve from the beginning: death, which is "undoubtedly the punishment of all who are born in unbroken succession from the first man" (13.6). It seems fitting, then, that death-as-punishment and slavery-as-punishment are closely linked in Augustine's thought, insofar as the slave is, for him, a figure of *living death.* Following a historically influential Latin etymology,[38] Augustine notes that the word *servi* is believed to come from *servando,* signaling that those enslaved have been "saved" or "preserved" when they could have been killed under the laws of war (19.15). Effectively the enslaved person receives a commuted death sentence, an extension of their life under permanent threat of its erasure.[39] The slave thus makes visible through their life the "presence" of the ultimate lack—death itself.[40] The Augustinian logic of evil as nonbeing finds its most powerful symbolic expression neither in the form of darkness seen, nor in silence heard, but in slavery—death being lived. What visible darkness and audible silence approach partially, the slave as the figure of living death renders in full. At the symbolic level of the master's imagination—reflected in law and culture—the enslaved person has no existence outside enslavement.[41]

Abolition's Time

Providence's Twofold Operation and the Master's House

After first aiming to clarify the logic of evil as nonbeing, I have argued that the *privatio* thesis exceeds what can be communicated in the key metaphor developed in one widely discussed passage in Augustine, suggesting that the logical relations of slavery fill this gap elsewhere in Augustine's thought. In sum, I have argued that the figure of the slave—in yet another instance of the analytic of *fungibility* discussed above—here does profound signifying work: more vividly and coherently than other symbolic resources, the figure of the slave depicts an exteriority brought inside (insofar as the household slave is both consummate outsider and intimately familiar), dramatizes the causality of evil (insofar as the sinner must be shown to be responsible for her own punishment), and makes visible the situation of one whose *entire* existence is under the force of the punishment, who thereby signifies a penal condition for human life itself, reducible neither merely to seeing darkness nor to hearing silence, but to a more totalizing slave symbolics—"living death." Why does all of this matter? In what follows I want to make explicit what this entails about the character of the *saeculum* and the theological discourse traditionally deployed for narrating God's ongoing activity within it: providence. Part of the stakes involved, as we will see, is that a closer look at how providence, slavery, and *saeculum* are working in tandem will complicate and refigure the significance of the often-made apologetic claim that Augustine finds slavery unnatural—a "result" of sin.

My starting point is a perceptive contention from Gervase Corcoran's monograph on slavery in Augustine, one whose full implications Corcoran does not pursue.[42] Corcoran writes: "Thus it appears [for Augustine] that the introduction of slavery into the world was no mere arbitrary punishment, but *was called for by the structure of reality itself.*"[43] Here, for all the shortcomings of his treatment of slavery in Augustine, Corcoran cuts to the heart of things: for Augustine, slavery is no arbitrary punishment. The punishment fits the crime, so to speak, a crime which is intelligible only within a certain structure of reality. What is the nature of this sin, and what is that structure of reality which makes slavery intelligible as its fitting punishment?

Reconstructing Augustine's views by weaving together multiple texts (including *On the Trinity, Confessions,* and multiple scriptural commentaries), Corcoran argues that this "structure of reality," the one which makes slavery as a punishment not arbitrary, is a conception of the "hierarchy of being" by which "man holds a midway position between God and the rest of creation."[44] This midway position for man exists in virtue of his bearing the image of God, which, to quote Augustine himself, "of course is reason itself, or mind or intelligence or whatever other word it may more suitably be named by," that is, whatever name is suitable for naming the "factor in which he [man] surpasses non-rational animate beings."[45] Though this midpoint in the hierarchy idea has echoes in Plotinus and others, Corcoran rightly links it further to the distinctly Augustinian moral psychology of loves, whereby one's loves draw one toward the object of desire: "if a man loves God he ascends to him . . . whereas if he loves material things without reference to God, he descends to their level."[46]

In other words, "the structure of reality" in question, the one which makes slavery a fitting punishment for sin, is a cosmological picture of three levels. It is precisely the tripartite hierarchy discussed at length in the previous chapter: at the top is God, figured as the *Dominus* over a *domus*; at the midpoint is man in the image of God, as the only rational soul within the created order, figured as the good and faithful *servus*; at the bottom is all the rest of creation, lacking the capacity of the rational soul, figured in the *servus vicarius*. In *On Genesis: A Refutation of the Manichees*, Augustine again makes this explicit, noting that the serpent's temptation was that they "should be their own masters instead without the Master," and in giving into the temptation, they "make bad use of that halfway centrality," what we have called the midpoint of humble mastery, "by which they were subject to God, and had their own bodies subject to themselves."[47] The master's house, then, is the framework, the structure of reality, within which the crime of sin is imagined as a spatial "fall," a lowering of mankind from his rightful position at level 2 in the hierarchy of being to position 3 with the brute animals: in this fall, Augustine writes in *The City of God*, Adam and Eve are "cast down to life and death at the level of the beasts."[48] More precisely, in their sin, they aimed to exalt themselves to level 1, of being "like God" in accordance with the serpent's promise. But in accordance with scripture (Augustine likes to quote Psalm 73:18, "You cast them down while they were being exalted"), it is precisely this striving upward which "humbles" them by force, brings them low, sends them careening down to level 3 among the beasts of the field.[49] When man "sought to be God, not by lawful imitation but by unlawful pride, he was cast down into the mortal conditions of monstrous beasts."[50] Or yet again: "The tree of life . . . planted in the middle of Paradise signifies the wisdom by which the soul is made to understand that it has been set at *a kind of mid-point in the whole order of things,* so that although it has every material, bodily nature subject to it, it has to realize that the nature of God is still above itself."[51]

And thus, by sinfully turning away from their proper capacity for well-ordered human existence, with the rational soul mastering a body fully obedient to its will, humankind incurs a punishment which corresponds quite perfectly to the nature of the crime: to be a slave is, as I suggested above in discussing the *privatio* thesis, to have another's will standing in the place where one's own, by nature, should be. In other words, by sinfully abandoning the midpoint of the well-ordered rational soul, by disordering his will toward those lower things he shared in common with the beasts, Adam's punishment consists—by a kind of poetic justice—in a condition of enslavement defined precisely by being dispossessed of one's own will. The point: to say that the "first cause of slavery is sin" (*civ.* 19.15), then, is not to call *slaveholding* sinful.[52] It is instead to explain the origins of our *enslavability*. It is to give a theological account of why being enslaved is a fitting, legitimate punishment for the distinct sort of creatures—human, rational—that we are.

Augustine is clear that to call slavery a punishment, fitting for the structure of humankind's place in the cosmos, is to make no crude assessment concerning *which* human beings wind up slaves, as though those who become slaves are sinful in a way that those who wind up masters are not.[53] Augustine repeatedly acknowledges, to the contrary, that there are many wicked masters and many righteous slaves.[54] The point is *all* are sinful, so all are enslavable justly. So whenever and wherever you find a human being enslaved, you can without hesitation recognize the *justice* of the situation, affirm it as the outworking of God's providence, be secure in the knowledge that it "can only happen by the judgment of God . . . who knows how to assign different punishments according to the merits of the offenders" (*civ.* 19.15). Corcoran overstates matters only slightly in concluding that the "question of the origin of slavery . . . held little interest" for Augustine in comparison with "his real interest," namely, "justifying God's action in the affairs of men." In this way, Corcoran notes, the "novelty" of Augustine's account "lies in his integrating this [the origins of slavery] into his teaching on the providence of God."[55]

How exactly does providence get integrated? A tremendous amount of ink has been spilled on whether political life belongs to the order of nature for the Augustine of Book 19.15 in the same way that family and social life do.[56] Most follow R. A. Markus in finding that "what is interesting for our purpose about this passage" is less the defense of slavery itself and more "the equivalence [it posits] between slavery and all political authority" and the implications of this for Christian engagement with politics.[57] Both Corcoran and (more influentially) Markus emphasize that the account of slavery in *The City of God* 19 must be understood in relation to the notion of providence as a *twofold* operation, developed earlier in *The Literal Meaning of Genesis.*[58] There Augustine draws the key conceptual distinction between *providentia naturalis,* by which God's governance works through nature, and *providentia voluntaria,* by which God's governance operates through the acts of wills and the events caused by these wills. "Dependent on the two streams of providence," writes Markus, "there are two kinds of order to be found in the world: the order of nature and the order expressed in human choices and enacted in human action and its results. This duality of order in the world underlay all Augustine's later reflection on society."[59] Markus emphasizes that this introduction of twofold providence marks a clear turn in Augustine's thinking, a breaking away from "the cosmic and political order as conceived in the classical, Hellenistic or neo-Platonic views which had played so great a part in Augustine's early thinking."[60] It marks a turn toward an account of creation and its fallenness in which, instead, institutions of coercion like slavery do not belong to an original state of nature, yet remain fully within the scope of God's governance, insofar as they constitute "God's just punishment for man's transgression," and more to the point, provide "his providential dispensation for coping with its consequences, disorder, strife, and lack of concord."[61] Against this looming disorder, "God's providence rules and administers the whole of creation," writes Augustine, "both natures and wills; natures so that they may simply be, wills on the other hand so that neither the good ones may be unfruitful nor the bad ones go unpunished."[62]

Markus takes pains to emphasize that, in this sense, slavery does not correspond to the natural order. But this has often been misread by interpreters like Corcoran to soften the sting of his subsequent justification of it for modern readers, without recognizing that Augustine justifies slavery's existence precisely on the grounds that our fallen life during the *saeculum* is itself not natural, but rather is nature disordered, such that slavery is all the *more* legitimate for its unnaturalness. Its unnaturalness, again, is precisely what makes the punishment fit the crime. And its paradoxical nature as living death, I suggested above, is precisely what makes it such a powerful symbolic expression of the logic of evil as *privatio*. Here we again recognize the artificiality of separating "literal" from "metaphorical" slavery. It is their interwoven nature which allows Augustine's God to find in slavery the very means for containing the disorder let loose by the sinfulness of human wills, for preserving that minimal order which Augustine calls "earthly peace." Corcoran recognizes this but goes on to insist "this hardly means . . . that [Augustine] was justifying [slavery] more than the other Fathers of the Church, no more than his statement in *Contra Faustum* that even the persecutors of the martyrs had their power from above can be taken to mean that he justifies murder."[63] Corcoran's analogy makes the exact opposite point to what he seems to have intended: when Augustine affirms the providential ordering at work in martyrdom, we can scarcely imagine him going on to offer—as he so often has done in the pages preceding regarding slave masters—specific advice, counsel, and spiritual guidance to emperors for how best to torture and execute martyrs in a humble and loving spirit.

The discourse of providence is best viewed as denying the ground of "nature" to the institution of slavery, precisely so as to place it on *more* stable grounds, to provide an alternative basis for it which is, given the nature of the *saeculum*, in fact *more* secure: it is ordained precisely to contain, through coercion, the disordering of human life which resulted from humankind falling to the level of beasts. It is, once again, God's own "providential dispensation for coping with [sin's] consequences, disorder, strife, and lack of concord."[64] Slavery is needed *more* in this way, not less. And so this form of accounting for slavery's existence, in theory, precludes any claims particular masters might make to the order of nature as legitimating the basis for their mastery, but as we will see in the next section, that form of justification is far from the only way masters account for the legitimacy of their claim to mastery.

Part 2. Providence and the Enduring Problem of the Christian Master

In a recent volume on the theology and ethics of providence, Charles Mathewes writes, "Everyone who thinks about life in time—that is, everyone—has some functional equivalent to the doctrine of providence—some way of giving the shape of history or time meaning and purpose. And anyone who thinks about time and history, in our world, thinks about politics."[65] Everyone, that is, has something like what David Scott called, in my Introduction above, a working "fictive model of time" which both shapes and is shaped by political life. I have argued that Augustinian providential time provides a basis for enslavement that is more, not less justificatory in character for the way it denies slavery a home in the original state of nature. But this is not to suggest this account of providence is crassly instrumental, reductively a slaveholder's "ideology." Nor is it blandly to point out that history is written from the side of the winners. To the contrary, the brilliance of this account of providence and slavery's origins is precisely its *antitriumphalist* character, its seamless convergence with the virtue of humility discussed in the previous chapter. "A providential politics," as Mathewes writes, "is not a triumphalist politics; it is, in certain crucial ways, the opposite of it."[66] This antitriumphalism emerges in the fact that providentialist thinking "both liberates us and obligates us, lifts us up and brings us low, drives us to our knees and causes us to say, 'this is the Lord's doing and it is marvelous in our eyes.'"[67] It really does bring us to our knees, humble us, steal away from us a more purely ideological "naturalizing" of the social order, and instead draw us inside the performance of a more complex and powerful theological work. It clears the ground of cheap, convenient explanations. It denies the stability and transparency of order, throws the task of Christian discernment down into the ambiguities of the world, offering the one who seeks political and theological discernment no simple escape from the conditions of ambivalence. From there one must make sense of oneself and one's political arrangements only with fragments, only in risk.[68]

This is precisely what Augustine himself goes on to do once he has established a providential framework for narration, by offering two explanatory possibilities regarding the more proximate causes of the origins of slavery, one from the domain of his culture broadly conceived, one from scripture (to which I return in a moment). What comes into view is a certain complication of Mathewes's point above: It is certainly true that everyone has some "functional equivalent to the doctrine of providence," but Mathewes underplays the extent to which providential thinking *itself* must always make recourse to the interpretive tools one has ready to hand—to other "functional equivalents" of more or less utility, often without the ability to specify precise criteria for why these explanatory frameworks for discerning God's action, rather than others, are to be recognized as the workings of providential action. This, in turn, troubles even as it underscores Mathewes's point concerning the ineluctable "moral obscurity, moral difficulty" which providential thinking requires: "the rhetoric of 'moral clarity' is typically used to efface the real complexity of a situation, to make us focus on some points and disregard others. In contrast, real moral clarity teaches a deep appreciation for the breadth of the relevant facts about the world, an appreciation that should produce in us a deep and complicated ambivalence. A providence-informed faith offers *moral obscurity*, moral difficulty. It doesn't make things clearer, but rather more vividly ambiguous and complicated."[69] I am moved by this somewhat paradoxical image of a more "vividly ambiguous" scene of political discernment. And yet, it is hard to avoid noticing that for all its ambiguity and obscurity and difficulty, what results from providential thinking must, unavoidably, issue in some highly determinate content which, being highly determinate, will be subject to disputation. What results, in the example Mathewes offers, also happens to be a defense of the nation-state on extremely tendentious grounds that offer no criteria for why *these* "relevant facts about the world," rather than others, provide grounds for his providentially informed judgment that the nation-state is "the most effective bit of political technology humans have invented."[70]

My concern here is neither to endorse nor to refute this contention, but to underscore the *form* of argument which providential discourse provides. What we find is not Mathewes distorting a genuinely Augustinian doctrine of providence, but rather displaying its brilliance quite effectively: the " 'bringing low" enacted in the language of honest, frank assessment of "moral obscurity" is precisely what clears the way for determinate judgment, and that judgment, unavoidably, smuggles in a host of more or less disputable contentions whose reasons providence itself cannot fully provide. This being the case, it is not exactly clear what providence adds to the equation, other than the distinct sense of humility which is imparted by the assurance that whatever is being done, God is intimately involved in the doing. Other claims must do much of the heavy lifting.[71] Other "functional equivalents" *of* providence are not as radically different from the sort of work providence *itself* must do as it initially seemed. Left unresolved, then, is not the question of human agency, for indeed divine providence, as traditionally conceived, does not erase human agency but enables it. Rather, what is left unresolved, in a contemporary Augustinian account like that of Mathewes, is how to assess the normative theological-ethical significance of how Augustine's own discourse of providence enables a legitimation of slavery, underscoring what I have developed throughout as "alignment" with the position of the master, not the enslaved.

The most promising starting point for addressing this in Mathewes's own account is this: "On this picture we are always *in medias res,* with lines of filiation and obligation (and occasionally enmity) drawn before we have a chance to agree to them."[72] To inhabit the afterlife of slavery is to be drawn inside that parenthetical "occasionally" as more than merely occasional—*modern life begins with slavery.* It is to learn to pose the question of providence anew from inside the foundational, if often unacknowledged, conditions of enmity which—invisibly for some and with brutal unavoidability for others—animate one's life: the racial conditions of domination which form modernity's "structures of antagonism."[73] It is this sort of structural antagonism, enmity, indeed violence, which Mathewes's account of providence hints at yet does not confront, even as Augustine's own providential discourse—in the denaturalizing ambivalence it injects into slavery—provides a vivid account of how providence can serve to conceal structural violence.[74]

Conceal how? Augustine's providential framework theologically opens the space for invoking what I mentioned a moment ago, a harmonizing of providence with two more proximate explanations of slavery's origins: two origin stories, one drawn from scriptural texts and another from cultural-linguistic ones, by which implicitly divine providence—in its *providentia voluntaria* channel—links up with human chains of causality in the emergence of slavery as a human institution. In *Questions on the Heptateuch,* Augustine underscores that the slavery of man to man disrupts the natural order by which "reason ought to dominate irrational life." There is the "just slavery and just domination" by which "cattle serve man and man rules over cattle," and there is the "natural order among men, that women should serve men and children their parents, from which derives the justice of the fact that the weaker in reason should serve the stronger."[75] But the slavery of man to man is brought about "in this age" by a "disturbance" in the natural order, a disturbance caused, more proximately, by "iniquity or adversity," with iniquity exemplified in the scriptures by Canaan being cursed, and adversity exemplified by Joseph being sold by his brothers.

Both these examples recur in the more influential *City of God,* Book 19 explanatory account, and in both accounts, Augustine draws these scriptural examples into contact with another set of "relevant facts about the world" drawn from Roman linguistic culture, that is, with another set of the "functional equivalents" which must be appealed to for providential think-ing to do its work: "Thus wars brought about the first slaves, on whom this name was bestowed in the Latin language. For any man who has been conquered by a man could be killed by the right of war, but because he was spared he was called a slave."[76] Likewise, in the Book 19 version, Augustine appeals again to scriptural types, then underscores the explanatory power of war slavery as refracted through the Latin etymology, here developed in additional detail: "the origin of the word for 'slaves' is believed to stem from the fact that those who might have been killed under the laws of war were instead sometimes preserved by the victors and became slaves; thus they were called slaves due to the fact that they were preserved."[77] Augustine's appeal to the idea that the word "slaves" (*servi*), the substantive form of "to serve" (*servire*), originates from "to save" (*servare*) does not imply that he believed that the enslaved people moving through the households, streets, and fields around him were literally former soldiers, defeated but 'saved' rather than killed in war. Editions of *The City of God* sometimes feature an editorial footnote pointing out that the etymology which derives *servi* (slaves) from *servando* (preserved) does not originate with Augustine and is incor-rect, but for me its philological illegitimacy is not the point.

Rather, I am interested in the hidden costs of Augustine's providential narration and a crucial formal quality of providential thinking: Augustine is willing to weave "relevant facts" drawn from his culture into an account of how Christians should think theologically about slavery. Despite its refusal to make recourse to the natural order, it provides a complexly ambivalent but coherent form of stability and legibility to God's rule in time. In this case, Augustine calls upon Roman culture's association of slaves with the conquest of other peoples, condensed into the spurious etymology, to play a role in the assurance that slavery "can only happen by the judgment of God ... who knows how to assign different punishments according to the merits of the offenders."[78] I am interested in what risks being hidden by such rea-soning. To that end, I want to examine two crucial ways in which Augustine's appeal to this Latin etymology to help explain the origins of slavery—not in nature but in the wills through which divine providence yet rules over cre-ated order—reframes Augustinian providential thinking within the endur-ing problem of the Christian master. One is a line of reception histories, the other a consideration of the implications for Augustinianism of a recent development in historical studies of late ancient Roman slavery.

First, Mary Nyquist's *Arbitrary Rule: Slavery, Tyranny, and the Power of Life and Death* gives us a window into the reception of the Augustinian account of slavery's origins in early modernity, with careful analytic attention to the vexed interplay between the discourse of political slavery (among political actors resisting tyranny) and the concomitant emergence of Atlantic chattel slavery.[79] Nyquist notes that "early moderns follow Greek and Roman authorities in assuming that the concentrated, supra legal power held by the individual slaveholder or interstate conqueror depends in some way on war slavery doctrine." Both Florentinus and Gaius define the power the slaveholder holds over the enslaved as "contrary to nature but established by *jus gentium*," then establish the military victor's power over life and death etymologically: "the word *servi* (slaves), substantive form of *servire* (to serve) comes from *servare* (to save)."[80] Early modern thinkers from Hugo Grotius to Thomas Hobbes to John Locke will make use of this etiology, joining a long line of thinkers who find in it a resource for approving discussions of slavery. But "most significant" of these, writes Nyquist, "because he thereby brings it into the Christian fold, [is] Saint Augustine [who] assumes its validity in *The City of God* when with reference to the so-called just war he says, '[T]he latine word *Servus,* had the first derivation from hence: those that were taken in the warres, being in the hands of the conquerours to massacre or to preserve, if they saved them, then were they called *Servi*, of *Servo*.'"[81] If that translation of *The City of God* sounds odd, it is because she is quoting the early modern edition of Juan Luis Vives, *Of the citie of God with the learned comments of Io. Lod. Vives* (translated into English in 1610)—about which more in a moment.

For now, it is most important to note that, notwithstanding the fact that the Latin etymology explicitly serves, in Augustine's account, to locate slavery within God's *providentia voluntaria*, and *not* in the order of nature, Nyquist notes that "its location right after the admission that slavery is against nature gives it an apologetic, justificatory character."[82] Building from Alan Watson's similar reading of its function in his longer study, *Roman Slave Law*, Nyquist contends that "indebtedness" and a "sense of obligation" is what "appears to link *servare* to *servi*, constituting another, major sign of this etymological figure's ideological function," namely, the way it nourishes a connotation of "reciprocity: the victor willingly saves, the vanquished willingly serves."[83] Naturally, in reality, "there is no symmetry whatsoever between the two actors in this minidrama." Reciprocity is instead a self-deception of the emerging master, since, of course, "the vanquished has no choice but to serve."[84] The point is: despite appealing to providence rather than nature, to the ambiguity and ambivalence by which God rules during the *saeculum*, Augustine's use of the etymology of *servus* functions to stabilize, in these reception histories, precisely "the power of life and death that, following Roman jurisprudence, Euro-colonialism assigns the slaveholder." Its association of "saving and enslaving" in military contexts comes to "readily support early modern efforts to *naturalize* slavery."[85] This flexibility of interchange between providential slavery and "naturalizing" slavery should give pause to contemporary Augustinians who attempt to deflect criticism of Augustine's legitimation of slavery by his restricting it to the realm of fallen social life in the *saeculum*.

So too does another, related reception history, by which the Vives version of *The City of God* just cited is taken up, much like the John Henry Hopkins example from Chapter 2, in the context of the U.S. Civil War. In 1861, Rev. Samuel Seabury, professor at the General Theological Seminary in Manhattan, New York, published a defense of American slavery which aimed to distinguish it from previous slave systems, primarily on the grounds that it involved a "contract between masters and slaves" involving reciprocal demands and obligations.[86] Seabury quotes the Vives version of *The City of God*, Book 19 at considerable length, including the *servus* etymology, concluding that in it we find "the theory of servitude luminously developed." He reads Augustine to argue that "the relation of master and servant grows out of the wants of man, and is part of Nature's order." (Indeed, the subtitle of his book is *Justified by the Laws of Nature!*) On the basis Augustine offers, Seabury concludes that Christianity thus "does not abolish the natural relations of mankind, but breathes into them a new SPIRIT—the love of God and man."[87]

It is fair enough to point out that this is clearly a poor reading of the text he has just quoted. Seabury did not have the benefit of reading Robert Markus. Still, the reading he offers, which aims to ground slavery in the order of nature, a grounding Augustine explicitly denies, nevertheless seems less outlandish when juxtaposed to the lines from Augustine which Seabury has just cited: slavery is ordained by "that law which commandeth the conservation and forbiddeth the disturbance of Nature's order."[88] And more, when we read Seabury's own words, "Christianity is led, not to abrogate the relation of master and servant, but to restore it to its ... performance of its reciprocal duties," can we not hear the echoes of Augustine's *Exposi-tions of the Psalms*, "Christ did not come to set slaves free, but to turn bad slaves into good slaves"?[89] From this vantage, it becomes less surprising that Seabury can believe himself truly Augustinian in his defense of slavery, citing Book 19's attribution of slavery to providence under sin, even as he weaves Providence into his own text no less than twenty-eight times, such that a narration of the enslavement of Africans can converge seamlessly with the mysterious workings of God. Bringing on board various relevant facts from the emerging needs of economies sacred and profane, providen-tial thought flows from the position of the master as a powerful vision of fleeting, fragmentary order in a world disordered by sin, a world preserved by God's prudence. It is less surprising from this vantage to recall that the great American religious leader George Whitefield, upon a long and painful discernment process of the economic necessities of his community in St. Paul's Parish, South Carolina, reversed his previous opposition to slavery, purchased a farm, imported enslaved Black labor, and named his plantation Providence.[90]

Second, in addition to these reception histories bringing into view the intimacy of providence and the problem of the master, new historical work in late ancient studies invites us to return to the *servus* etymology from a dif-ferent angle onto slavery's "origins": not the origins of slavery as an institu-tion, but the originating "supply" of enslaved people themselves. Augustine's account of Roman slavery, like most Roman thought, rests upon what more recent historiographical work can recognize as a deeply committed self-deception of Roman imperial culture: that the origin of slaves results from "saving" conquered peoples rather than killing them in war. The emerging consensus of the revisionist view suggests that

> with that math [concerning how many conquered war captives would be necessary to sustain the slave supply at constant levels], there is hardly room left for debate over where the majority of new slaves came from. . . . Sources such as cross-border importation and child exposure were surely significant inputs, but when we consider the likely population figures of human groups bordering the empire, and compare the relative extent of the Atlantic slave trade, the conclusion becomes ever more inexorable. *The Roman slave popula-tion was sustained, above all, by natural reproduction.*[91]

That is, the maintenance and expansion of the population of enslaved people, the supply upon which depend imperial economic and domestic order alike, had for its source not the grand struggle of empires in the grip of the *libido dominandi,* but a quieter source of no less horror: enslaved people entered the world through the wombs of enslaved women.[92] The slave supply relied upon a mother's child being claimed by another as tiny property to be sold, traded, or used as needed, upon the infant as commodity of one's own enslaver, and upon all of this being narrated, including narrated theologically, as routine—the providential rupture of families, the providential protection of order.[93] And so, the material surrogacy of the womb is also the symbolic surrogate of providence, the stand-in for what cannot be named, that what God is sanctioning when God sanctions slavery is child-stealing, the breeding of enslaved women for labor needs, the inability to lay claim to one own's child. The very word " 'kinship' loses meaning" in such contexts, writes Hortense Spillers, *"since it can be invaded at any given and arbitrary moment by the property relations."*[94] I want to trouble Augustinian temporal ambivalence at this site, show its hidden costs, not borne by the master or the pilgrim, but offloaded onto the bodies of the enslaved, and especially the enslaved woman, who must suffer the unspeakable, the theft of one's child, so that this ambivalent forward motion can be sustained, that a modicum of the natural order can be preserved. Who pays the cost of that preservation? The *servus* etymology belongs to a wider "silence amounting to repression about one of the structural features of the slave system. The reproduction of the slave population fell outside the discussion of polite mastery, perhaps for the chilling reason that it was exploitative beyond repair."[95] The *servus* etymology serves to mislead, to misdirect our attention, in its inability to bring into the text of providence the realities of *partus sequitur ventrem*—the Roman law by which the enslaved or free status of the child follows the status of the mother—in its providentializing of the invasion of kin by property, its explanation of stolen life, its invisibilizing of maternal anguish.[96]

Part 3. The Ethics of Temporality: 1968. Or, *nunc* or *tunc*?

Where does this leave the contemporary ethics of temporality? Like David Scott above, I am interested in how the ghost of Augustine yet wanders among us—in how the way he models time inhabits us, cuts into our present, aids or limits our capacity to imagine ourselves. To call him a ghost is itself to conjure what Augustine's sense of temporality implies: that we inhabit, with him, a *shared* age, a time in common. His name for this, *hoc saeculum,* means *this* time rather than *that* time. *This* world, not that one: the time we hold in common together, such that he might haunt us still. So how might Augustinian temporal sensibilities be remade in other directions? How might providence and patience function otherwise for an ethics of *saeculum* life?

In Michael J. S. Bruno's lucid survey text *Political Augustinianism: Modern Interpretations of Augustine's Political Thought,* the year 1968—with "violence and revolt engulfing the streets of many world cities"—plays a surprisingly important role in mapping the Augustinian terrain.[97] There is no direct mention here of race riots in American cities, nor of decolonization rippling across the world, nor still of the assassination of Dr. Martin Luther King, Jr., in Memphis. Nevertheless, 1968 marks a "crossroads" for Augustinianism, Bruno writes. The heart of that crossroads, for Bruno, is the risk of letting the urgencies of social upheaval generate a perennial Augustinian mistake: "a deflation of the two cities into one, [such that] the eschatological *tension* that pervades Augustine's *City of God* is largely ignored."[98] This eschatological tension lies at the heart of the temporal sensibility of ambivalence I discussed in Chapter 2, the distinctly Augustinian attunement to our nature as time-bound creatures, enmeshed in unresolved and unresolvable contingency, frailty, ambiguity. It is that which finds in providential discourse a lexicon of political judgment, at once chastened and enabled, bringing us low, yet offering us a path to merge the workings of God's action in time with other explanatory frameworks, as I have explored above. Here, I want to shift my attention to the other pole of moral thought during the *saeculum,* during the time of slavery, by attending to *human* agency in this temporal frame.

In this section, in particular, I take up that question by pursuing the implications of what Bruno says next, namely, that the primary threat to a genuinely Augustinian temporal sensibility in the 1960s and 1970s was liberation theology, and specifically texts like Gustavo Gutiérrez's *A Theology of Liberation,* which cites Augustine's *City of God.* This text, Bruno continues, "seems to justify the fear of [Henri] de Lubac that the eschatological tension of Augustine would be diminished."[99] Bruno's worry is that the crucial eschatological distance between earthly peace and heavenly peace, between temporal politics and our final ends, will be collapsed. He cites, in this respect, the famous 1984 "Instruction on Certain Aspects of the

'Theology of Liberation' " of the Congregation for the Doctrine of the Faith, which cautioned against the tendency to collapse a properly Augustinian eschatological tension, "to identify the kingdom of God and its growth with the human liberation movement."[100] And so what comes into view is a familiar and influential worry, directed at theological movements centered upon liberation, namely, that in their fierce moral urgency, they aim—futilely and potentially destructively—to lay hold of the fullness of the kingdom *now*.

Against this over-realized eschatology, a world-weary temporal sensibility positions itself as a more *patient* alternative.[101] This latter sensibility is attuned to the way true justice continues to elude our grasp, and so it aims to inject a note of tragedy, of chastening sobriety into liberation theology, especially by noting how often movements for liberation end up reproducing the very violence they oppose in their quest for utopia in the here and now. Paul Griffiths goes so far as to insist that "emphasizing *peregrinatio*" and with it the time-bound sensibility of ambivalence which any genuinely Augustinian thinking must display, "*requires* the judgment that political perfectionism (the view that we can, in this age, get our politics right) and most kinds of political progressivism (the view that we can, in this age, significantly improve our politics) are utopian and may never be endorsed by Christians."[102] And as I have suggested above, when it comes to defending Augustine's regrettable views on slavery, the strongest line of Augustinian defense is simply to point out, as Rist does, that within the fallen *saeculum* we inhabit, relations of domination are inevitable, and so we cannot fault Augustine too harshly for accommodating himself to the institution of slavery. .

What is interesting for my purposes is that when this anti-utopian sort of "Augustinian" chastening of politics is being criticized, even its critics rarely call into question the way it *frames* the relation between temporality and competing visions of ethics. That is, even its critics retain and reproduce a temporal framework in which, put crudely, those who resist and aim to transform unjust social structures are aligned with an eschatology emphasizing *already,* and those with reservations toward such projects are aligned with an eschatology of *not yet*. In this basic temporal framework, the characteristic temptation of the former would be impatience. The latter's: complacency. In this final section, I want to challenge and reconfigure this way of organizing the temporal framework of ethics, drawing out a dissatisfaction with the way it leaves us hamstrung between the limited options of (for lack of a better set of terms) a liberal-reformist ethics grounded in the "already" of progressivist time and a conservatism grounded in the "not yet" of anti-utopian time.[103] Another way of configuring the temporality of ethics is possible, a differently temporalized politics of patience, building from repurposed Augustinian categories of time. This hinges on understanding the performance of mastery, the desire to be a master, as—contrary to its self-narration—a specific form of *temporal performance,* a flawed and illusory way of inhabiting flesh in time.[104] That form we can call brutal impatience. As a way into this argument, I examine one of the type of critics I mentioned above, one who faults Augustine's temporal politics for the way it does not open the possibility of reform in the here and now, even as this critic retains the basic temporal framework I want to challenge.

In the same volume as Griffiths's essay cited above, Margaret R. Miles offers a brilliant examination of female bodies and the prevalence of rape in Augustine's *City of God,* developing something like a sympathetic immanent critique. The "sympathetic" aspect of the critique is the way that Augustine's vision of resurrected bodies in Book 22 is for Miles "profoundly counter-experiential, counter-cultural, and beautiful."[105] And at the heart of her critique is a set of questions which follow from the way Augustine "sharply distinguished resurrected bodies from present bodies," generating a "failure to suggest that Christians work to remedy the ills of the earthly city":

> If he believed that we are to enjoy one another in the heavenly city, not for use, but for each other's beauty alone, why not practice now? If we are to see one another with full transparency—*facie ad faciem*—why not practice now? If present social arrangements are unjust (gender assumptions and arrangements, slavery), why not work to fix them now?[106]

Thus Miles offers a broadly liberal-reformist critique of Augustine's putting off our access to resurrected bodies, instead of seeking them in the earthly city *now*. Given the arguments of previous chapters, one might expect me to join in precisely this line of critique against Augustine on slavery, especially given that the standard modern Augustinian defense on this point is that Augustine had "limited historical horizons of social and economic reform," that is, a limited sense for what sort of changes might be possible in the here and now.[107] But I want to take a different approach. I want to investigate more closely what sort of implicit temporal sensibility is *performed* in the act of mastery, that is, what implied response to the time-boundedness of our flesh is at work in *being* a master, in the act I began to redescribe at the end of Chapter 3: imaginatively and materially splitting oneself off from the "frailty of the flesh" which—in Augustine's own words—masters share with "that mass which derives from Adam and Eve," and thus with the person they have enslaved.[108]

To do this, let us stick with the picture that Miles's essay brings into view. In Augustine's imagining of the glorified "spiritual" bodies of the resurrection, as Miles emphasizes, Augustine posits neither a rejection nor an overcoming of the physical body, but rather its total infusion with spirit: this is "a real body permeated throughout with spirit."[109] When this achievement of the full union of body and spirit arrives, then "evil, inactivity and idleness, toil, constraint, decay, necessity . . . defects, deformities, and ugliness will also disappear, as well as weakness, sluggishness, and corruption."[110] How did Augustine arrive at this conception? "He worked out the 'picture suggested to [his] mind' by beginning with present bodies and subtracting their encumbrances (*civ.* 22.30)." And his scriptural model for this is the verse which Miles claims he "quoted more frequently than any other throughout his oeuvre. . . . 'We see now through a glass darkly; then, however, face to face' (*Videmus nunc per speculum in aenigmate; tunc autem, facie ad faciem*)."[111]

Miles keenly frames the debate I have been referring to above when she notices that "the syncrisis '*nunc* . . . *tunc*' both connects and contrasts present and future experience."[112] Within the temporal framework of ethics I discussed above, that is, of how the interpretive debate over Augustine's notion of eschatological tension often functions, the liberationists are thought to insist on the *nunc* (the now, the already), while traditionalists insist on the *tunc* (the then, the not yet). But Miles's analysis provides us a kind of crease, a wrinkle in the text, which we might step inside to reconfigure the terms of the debate itself. The *nunc-tunc* (now-then) device "creates a textual tension that jars the reader's mind to imagine a body that is both intimately experienced (flesh, bones, internal organs, sexual differentiation) and wholly unknown (invulnerable, weightless, and with an incredible capacity for effortless movement and penetrating vision)."[113]

Stepping inside the space opened by this "textual tension," I suggest that this latter "wholly unknown" possibility of the Augustinian resurrected body, the possibility of having a body that is "invulnerable . . . with an incredible capacity for effortless movement," *is precisely what the structure of the master–slave relation is designed to provide for masters.* But to recognize this demands one have a different account of what mastery is—one other than, against, and beyond the masters' own self-narrations. It demands, that is, reconceiving the master's self-deceived way of framing the master–slave relation as a relation between an independent and a dependent (which a certain misreading of Hegel's dialectic has reinforced), and instead theorizing the relation as most fundamentally predicated on what Delores Williams theorized as *surrogacy*, and what Orlando Patterson (and many in his wake) theorized as *parasitism*.[114] In these alternative theoretical frameworks, I note three things: (1) that both, with the necessary qualifications made, apply to the definitional structure of slavery as such, and so are relevant categories for analyzing the *enduring* problem of the master; (2) that put simply, both refuse the notion of the slave as "dependent" upon the master, and instead foreground how deeply the master needs the slave; and (3) that as such, we see a profoundly violent, yet often neglected *intimacy* between the body of the master and the body of the slave, both in physical reality and within the symbolic world of how the master imagines the relation, and this fact invites closer attention.

Writing in the first century C.E., Pliny the Elder—in a statement rare for its self-awareness among the master class of antiquity—discloses the nature of this intimacy clearly: "We use other people's feet when we go out, we use other people's eyes to recognize things, we use another person's memory to greet people, we use someone else's help to say alive—the only things we keep for ourselves are our pleasures."[115] With remarkable candor, Pliny discloses the structure of the relation as an intimate act composed, at once, of *joining* and *splitting* of flesh: the enslaved person's body is grafted onto the master's as an extension of his will, his power, his life, and so functions to *enhance* his body. The enslaved body is a kind of appendage to the master's, upon which the master relies and so becomes, as Patterson has forcefully argued, *parasitically dependent.* At the same time, by keeping for ourselves "only our pleasures," the master splits his flesh off from the slave's, offloading onto the enslaved bodies all—or asymptotically, as close to all as possible—of the pain, toil, and vulnerability endemic to human existence. The body of the enslaved becomes a *substitute,* a *surrogate,* for these elements of mortal life, especially the gendered dimensions of sexual violence and maternal reproduction, from which the master class now can stand at a remove, in this splitting-joining performance of what Christina Sharpe has

called "monstrous intimacy."[116] Dionne Brand excavates with analytic precision and a poet's sensitivity this disturbing closeness—which Pliny came
close to admitting—of the joining and splitting performed by "the captors
who enter the captive's body":

> Slaves became extensions of slave owners—their arms, legs, the parts of them
> they wished to harness and use with none of the usual care of their own bod-
> ies. These captive bodies represent parts of their own bodies that they wish
> to rationalize or make mechanical or inhuman so as to perform the tasks of
> exploitation of resources or acquisition of territory. These captive bodies
> then become the tools sent out to conquer the natural world. Of course they
> aren't merely tools but the projections of the sensibilities, consciousness,
> needs, desires, and fears of the captor.[117]

To the extent that this joining-splitting performance at the heart of mastery succeeds—and importantly, it never fully does, or can[118]—the master
acquires for himself a bodily existence approaching, asymptotically, the very
body Augustine describes in his fantasies of resurrection: a body which is
resolutely physical, yet "invulnerable, weightless," one which is free from
"toil, constraint, decay," an experience of flesh shorn of "weakness." It is this
very structure of mastery which creates the conditions prompting Augustine, in the sermon discussed in the previous chapter, to call the master's
attention back to "the frailty of his [own] flesh."[119] What is utterly absent from
Augustine's account, which focuses on the inward disposition the master
must have amid this situation, is the immense toll of violence the joining
and splitting scheme has upon the enslaved person, in his or her exponen-
tially heightened exposure to the would-be normal conditions of having a
body in time.[120]

The point, then: when we have recognized this, we can begin to recognize how often Augustine is inadvertently diagnosing the temporal sensibility underlying what mastery is: mastery is the desire to lay claim to
the resurrected body *now* by violently offloading the vulnerability of one's
temporal flesh onto the flesh of a surrogate, onto a host upon whom one
functions as parasite. This opens up the possibility of a radical shift in the
terms of the debate over Augustinian temporal sensibilities: mastery, and
arrangements of social and political life structured by it and built to secure
it, names *the over-realized eschatology* of trying to have the resurrected body

now through the sacrifice of the flesh of another, and thus, an attempt to collapse the very eschatological tension which an Augustinianism conceived otherwise would call us to sustain. Mastery's vice is brutal impatience. It is compounded, as Patterson notes, by the inevitable desire to lie, to *conceal* the terms of the parasitic relation through an "inversion of reality," by which the master "camouflaged his dependence. . . . Paradoxically, he defined the slave as dependent."[121] Rist summarizes Augustine's view fairly: "although all slaves are equal in humanity with their masters . . . their freedom is only to be achieved eschatologically. No one has the right to be 'freed' in this life; indeed in the strict sense no one *can* be free in this life."[122] But if we understand the problem of the master beyond the camouflage, as the attempt to secure a certain *kind* of freedom now—of being freed, however partially and tenuously, from the "toil, constraint, decay" of fleshly life in time—precisely by *intensifying* such realities upon surrogate flesh, then the ethical point of Augustinian eschatology cuts in precisely the opposite direction: no one has the right to finalize their body in this way, to have flesh 'free' and finally at rest, to collapse the then of heaven into the now of earth. Mastery is refusal to be a creature in time, "to live on the way, in imperfect tense."[123]

This enables us to bring on board other texts from Augustine's corpus to develop further this notion of mastery as the inability to carry the weight of one's own porous flesh, the desire to offload that onto another. Writing of a certain type of ascetic, Augustine contends:

> For what they hate is not their body, but its imperfections and its dead weight. What they want is not to have no body at all, but to have one free from corruption and totally responsive; they think that if the body were such a thing it would not be a body, because they consider such a thing to be a soul. When they seem to persecute their own body by a kind of repression . . . their aim . . . is not to have no body at all but to have one that is subservient and ready for necessary tasks.[124]

In describing certain kinds of misguided asceticism, Augustine has (despite himself) diagnosed the desires of the master, the one who imposes violence on the body of the enslaved person in order for his own existence "not to have no body at all but to have one that is subservient and ready for necessary tasks." In other words, mastery is asceticism of the other; the offloading of the body's "dead weight," its temporal vulnerability to chaos and disorder, onto the other as surrogate. And this allows us to reread with new eyes more famous passages, like Augustine's description of the Christian household in *The City of God* 19:

> A household of people who live by faith looks to the eternal goods which are promised for the future. It makes use of earthly and temporal things like a pilgrim. It is not captivated by them, nor is it deflected by them from the path that leads toward God, but it is sustained by them so that *it may more easily bear the burdens of the corruptible body that weighs down the soul and may at least keep those burdens from getting any worse.*[125]

What does it mean that clearly and explicitly, enslaved human beings number among the "earthly and temporal *things*" which make life easier, which provide surrogates for the master's own body in its exposure to this present age of *saeculum*? Consider another example from Sermon 115: "Take away death, the last enemy, and my own flesh shall be my dear friend throughout eternity." It is as though the flesh of the slave becomes a way of dealing, or *refusing* to deal, with this death-bound existence, by offloading one's own fleshliness onto the other, and freeing oneself too quickly. To be a master is to attempt to lay hold of rest for the flesh *now*, before it is time.

Strikingly, then, on this view, the liberationist, or more precisely, the abolitionist—the one who wants to do away with such arrangements of social life, the one who is not invested simply in altering who gets to be included as masters in a master–slave relation, but rather in remaking relation itself—this one, it turns out, *is more patient than the master.* The master wants to move too quickly to the time when his flesh will be invulnerable, or least, at peace once again, as he supposes it was in the beginning. The master wants that now—rest and peace for flesh *now*, where "flesh" is the shorthand for all the vulnerability, the porosity, that quality of being *able to be unmade* by the forces of death, of endings.[126] He cannot have it, but he wants it. In his desperation, he offloads all that death-bound vulnerability onto the bodies of others, even as he draws them, as we have seen, inside a conception of reality in which he believes his mastery echoes, however faintly and imperfectly, the heavenly Master. He thus wants the other's flesh to be a surrogate for his own wounds, while he keeps the benefits all for himself, even as he renarrates that condition within a vision of Christian belonging, of a spiritual nurturing in sovereignty over the household. When we think about the cosmological hierarchy of the master's house, then, with the "bad slaves" inhabiting the third level with the irrational beasts and the land and the rest of the creation, we might suggest that the enslaved body is or anticipates, in a certain way, a kind of "ecological sacrifice zone," a systematic concentration of harm upon some bodies precisely for the benefit to others.[127] Slavery is sacrificial ecology.

Patience, then, might be reconceived as *abolishing* the brutal impatience of the master's project to get invulnerability in the flesh now by conscripting the other's flesh, by substituting it for your own. Patience means bearing the weight of flesh together, holding the flesh in common, or *the flesh as a commons*, the (under)commons of the flesh, and finding there communion, sociality, of a thoroughly unsentimental kind, of a Spillerian kind, the zero-degree of social existence, which cannot be turned into a slogan, but instead requires slow, difficult projects of shared life, of giving care to the borders of the human, the borders between self and other, self and land, self and God. And indeed, this sort of patience is precisely what we find among a key Black feminist strand of contemporary police and prison abolitionists: a sensibility which does not imagine a utopian world where people will not harm or exploit one another; rather, it makes the case for abolishing false carceral "solutions" to the enduring problems of interpersonal harm.[128]

Note how different this is from Augustine's own critique of mastery: the *libido dominandi* is a problem because it cuts back on itself, enslaving the one who wants to be a master; that is one sort of master. But more often, our masters are not like that. Not hungry for glory, for grand displays of imperial power, not in the grip of lust. Instead, masters—whether Christian or post-Christian, that is, secular—are so often weary and petty and self-conscious and scared. And they only want a way to *not have to deal* with the source of their weariness and fear and self-consciousness: that source is their own porous flesh in this time of the *saeculum*, of being subject to the risks of being a creature, with its capacity to be unmade by the earth, by water, by dirt and time, by another. That is what masters are avoiding by setting up *structures* of mastery, that is, social arrangements which aim to localize that porosity strategically to specific bodies, organized along the lines of what we have come to call "race," and thus capitalize off of that targeted vulnerability to death. This is what Ruth Wilson Gilmore's elegantly precise definition of racism sees: "group-differentiated vulnerability to premature death."[129]

In short, that is what this final section of the chapter offers in its suggestive way: a rethinking, in repurposed Augustinian terms, of the enduring problem of the master as a problem to which structures of racism—as a modern strategy of mastery, of joining-splitting—provide an answer. The perennial problem the master faces is the temporal existence of his body—porous flesh, vulnerable, unruly, with the nonexistence of stable borders of the self.[130] The master desires to overcome the temporality of flesh, to lay claim to what Augustine imagines is a "spiritual body" of the future age in two sinful ways: (1) he wants it *now,* and (2) he wants it by *surrogacy,* that is, by the forced relations slavery institutes, such that his own enfleshed existence is bifurcated, with its vulnerability made fungible in the person of the slave, and its pleasures retained in the person of the master, all while drawing both persons inside a vision of Christian belonging.

The spiritual flaw at the heart of the Christian master is not the presence of pride alone, then, but what I have called a brutal refusal of patience, an unwillingness to face the conditions of his own temporal life; and the second flaw is untruth, the unwillingness to name his attempted escape of those conditions *as* an escape from time. Instead, the master inverts the parasite relation to make the body of the host appear to be dependent, with a whole range of cultural and symbolic racialized and gendered signifiers built for this purpose. To begin to rethink mastery as the violent desire to have the resurrected body *now,* and to have it through the violent acts of splitting and joining with the subjugated flesh of another, might be a way of upending or reconfiguring the already/not-yet alignments of eschatological politics, whereby the liberationists are framed in the apocalyptic already camp, and the conservatives in the not-yet camp, which Augustine is often thought to reproduce both by his detractors and defenders.

Instead, our task is to forge the kind of common life in which we can bear the weight of our flesh together *without* seizing control of the other's flesh to use as an extension of, and surrogate for, our own. The aim of mastery, in other words, is to *realize a state of peace, invulnerability, impermeability for the body which cannot be attained until heaven,* and it aims to do this by, to borrow and repurpose more language from Augustine, *intensifying the "pressure" of* saeculum *upon the body of the other.* One thinks of Peter Brown's reading of Augustine as imagining the *saeculum* as "a vast experimental laboratory: to bring this point home, Augustine uses the familiar image of an olive press, squeezing the olives for oil. The religious life . . . is quite inconceivable for Augustine without this constant *pressura*—this constant pressing—inside the *saeculum* . . . for Augustine, [this pressure of the *saeculum*] is all-embracing and inescapable."[131] In Sermon 113A, Augustine invokes this oil press image: "The world now is just like an oil press; it's under pressure. . . . Sometimes pressure is applied in the world; for example, famine, war, want, dearth, poverty, an epidemic, robbery, greed; pressure on the poor brings unrest to the cities—we see it all happening. That these things would happen was foretold, and we see them happening."[132] Yet this pressing in upon the flesh of our temporal condition, with its frailty of flesh, its limits and risks, its ambiguities and ambivalences, is precisely the embrace which masters wish to elude, avoid, and offload onto another. In Sermon 19, Augustine again invokes the olive press of the *saeculum* and connects this image of "pressure" to the fact that, in the form of earthquakes and ruins and random terror, "in addition to being so fragile, this life is under daily threat from enormous dangers."[133] If you do not understand that, Augustine says, if you are not willing to recognize that you cannot achieve this earthly peace now, then you "understand neither what you seek, nor what you are who seek it."[134]

But this is what the fugitive—the maroon who does not reproduce the structures of surrogacy she flees in the community in the woods—knows. She understands what she seeks and what she is who seeks it. She knows the *vita socialis sanctorum* before and after Augustine does. Marronage offers an open-source name for this other than structures of "command and obedience" (*civ.* 19), elsewhere than the master's house. The politics of response to *saeculum*, then, is not a patience that acquiesces to mastery, but rather the space opened for unflinching critique of the master's impatience, and the utter refusal to let or make someone else bear through violence what we can only bear together: the openness of our flesh, where that openness is at once terrifying and the grounds for our communion. That provides the grounds, in a certain sense, for *democratizing* the *saeculum*, not merely as a liberal democratic citizenship, but as what Angela Davis (following Du Bois) called *abolition-democracy:* that is, seeing to it that we all, insofar as we can, abolish the brutal impatience represented in slavery and its afterlives in the carceral state, build institutions for doing social life differently beyond the deformations of mastery, and imagine alternative ways to bear the weight and the pleasure of our flesh together. "Abolition-democracy," writes Neil Roberts as he reads Angela Davis (who in turn is reading Du Bois), "involves imagining the means and methods through which a fractured American democratic project in need of reconstructing after a short-lived Reconstruction can be sutured. . . . Abolish slavery and democracy can materialize."[135] Yet as Davis

and notable contemporary abolitionists underscore, this is not a purely negative impulse toward tearing things down. "Abolition is about presence, not
absence," writes Ruth Wilson Gilmore. "It's about building life-affirming
institutions."[136] Nor is it a utopian impulse that imagines naïvely that the
work can ever completed. Rather, "freedom is a constant struggle," as Davis
famously put it.[137] The project of abolition, to draw from David Scott's reap-
propriation of Greek tragedy to narrate the Haitian Revolution, is "humanity's everlasting struggle with the ineluctable contingencies of evil that . . .
are 'inseparable from social and political organization.' "[138]

I noted above, following Rist, that while "Augustine is regularly prepared
to emphasize both that the struggle against 'concupiscence' is unending,
and that concupiscence (let alone sin) cannot be eliminated in this life," he
seems to consider the endemic nature of human domination to be a reason
to recognize in slavery a divinely ordained purpose—useless, even harmful
to resist. In making the first part of that point, Rist draws our attention to
Sermon 151, where Augustine preached to a congregation in the fall of 419:
"We always have a fight on our hands . . . the very covetousness we are born
with *can never be finished off as long as we live;* it can be lessened day by day,
it can't be finished off completely." This does not lead to resignation, but
is a call to "struggle," to enact "warfare," "to put up a fight," one which can
never be completed in this life, but must be undertaken nevertheless.[139] What
would this Augustinian sensibility look like when *brought out of alignment*
with the master's position? What ethical and political possibilities would
emerge from a "constant struggle" which can never be finished, but must be
begun? There is no substitute for the enduring work of justice, and no easy
answers to be found. In the following chapter, I turn to examine the possibility of rereading the significance of key Christian practices as theological
confrontation with and creative unmaking of the capture imposed by the
position of the Christian master.

FIVE

The Table and the Sea

This gospel that has just been read about Christ the Lord, and how he walked over the surface of the sea, and about the apostle Peter, and how, by growing afraid as he walked, he staggered ... is advising us to take the sea as meaning the present age and this world.
—Augustine, Sermon 76

Just as the Egyptians pursue the Jews as far as the sea, so Christians are pursued by their sins as far as baptism. Observe, brothers, and see; through the sea the Jews are liberated, in the sea the Egyptians are overwhelmed.
—Augustine, Sermon 4

But who are the dead who were in the sea and whom the sea gave up?
—Augustine, *The City of God*

Where are your monuments, your battles, martyrs?
Where is your tribal memory? Sirs,
in that grey vault. The sea. The sea
has locked them up. The sea is History.
—Derek Walcott, "The Sea Is History"

The sea is multivalent. A symbol of the present age and of baptism, imaged by the Red Sea at Passover and the Sea of Galilee where Jesus walks and Peter staggers, Augustine's figural sea is as vast, everchanging, and self-dislocating as the shifting waves themselves.[1] In modern Black and especially Caribbean expressive culture, as in the poem by Derek Walcott above, the sea is often associated with the diasporic lifeworlds emerging from the horrors of the Middle Passage, including the terror of enslaved people thrown overboard.[2] I have argued throughout this book that the task of contemporary Christian thought unfolds in the wake of this ongoing history, that it might in this way be haunted from a new and distinct angle by Augustine's question above: Who are the dead who were in the sea and whom the sea gave up?

Slavery's link to the sea predates the modern. In a letter to Alypius, Augustine bears witness to the unlawful capture of free persons by slave traders, set on ships for "terribly cruel sailings."[3] This cruelty of the slave traders—regarded as unsavory figures in ancient culture even by those who did not oppose slavery itself—is evident in Augustine's finding the sea an image of the present age's disorder: "The sea symbolizes the present age, embittered with salt and tossed by gales." He continues: "Observe the evil sea, bitter sea, with waves violent, observe with what sort of men it is filled. Who desires an inheritance except through the death of another?"[4] The latter point—wealth achieved through another's death—recalls the parasitic surrogacy discussed above. Augustine's sea symbol fits here, not only in signifying disorder and venality, but in that it invokes the Mediterranean, ancient site of global trade, from which multiple, intersecting human civilizations emerged. The sea Augustine gazed upon signals, at once, barbarism and civilization, brutality and flourishing, disorder and culture.[5] "The Mediterranean," Orlando Patterson writes, "central to the development of human civilization and lovingly celebrated in Euro-American historiography, from the viewpoint of human oppression has been a veritable vortex of horror for all mankind, especially for the Slavic and African peoples. The relationship was in no way accidental."[6] Tangled inside the image of the sea are these competing and conflicting uses, terror and freedom, sin and baptism, deliverance and slavery. In this concluding chapter, I want to recapitulate the argument to this point, then turn to reconsider, in the shadows of that argument, the limits and possibilities of this multivalent signification habit of Augustine for constructive theological aims. What are we to do with the lexicon of slavery which has now been built into Christian theological grammar?

To move into this question, I contend that what I will call the table and the sea—echoing the way Augustine himself so often intimately linked the theology of the Eucharist and theology of baptism—is the most promising site in Augustinianism for interrogating these limits and possibilities.[7] Then, in the Epilogue—something like an appendix to this chapter's conclusion—I gesture toward the implications of the argument toward wider contemporary debates in method concerning the relation of traditionalist and liberationist approaches to ethics and political theology.

·

In the first chapter of this book, I introduced the vexed role Augustine's slavery imagery plays in the contemporary Augustinian attempt to appropriate his political thought, a vexation which makes uncertain how to translate the very name of his God into English. I examined how our own slave-haunted past and its ongoing afterlives in the present intervene in our reception of such texts, how they tend to generate an affective register of response among Augustinian interpreters—discomfort, shock, distaste—which in turn leads to a hermeneutic strategy of disavowal: a simultaneous acknowledging of Augustine's slavery discourse, and an attempt to foreclose its relevance in advance. I further located these disavowals in often unmarked, but important epistemic commitments governing how Augustinians read not just Augustine's day but their own; that is, how precisely they construe modernity as a problem to which theological and ethical discourses respond.

Augustinians like Eric Gregory have noted that interpretive disagreements often center not just on competing readings of Augustine's texts, but on competing ways of "assessing the needs of our age."[8] These attune readers to his texts in different ways, in search of the Augustine "we" need for its most pressing challenges. I foregrounded the tenuous nature of that "we" in its neglected internal differentiations. These are brought into view, in key part, precisely by noting the way white Augustinians, unlike thinkers in the Black radical tradition, have not reckoned with modernity either in its founding moments of racial subjugation or in their persistence up to the present. Slavery—and thus also mastery—has afterlives which, when grappled with, would reconfigure the terrain on which we raise questions like agency, virtue, order, and so on. Reckoning with racial modernity in this way attunes us differently to Augustine's texts and their significance for the present. If racial difference is grasped not as simply one variation upon the problem of multiculturalist pluralism, but rather as the shadows master–slave dynamics cast across every corner of the terrain of racial capitalist modernity—echoing Morrison's adage: modern life begins with

slavery—then this invites Augustinian interpretive attention to the slavery
discourse in Augustine's own thought. Just as contemporary questions about
liberal democratic citizenship have sent contemporary Augustinians looking to Augustine's account of citizenship—knowing full well the contexts
are different, yet believing something productive might emerge from the
encounter with difference—so too I have argued that contemporary questions concerning the afterlife of slavery ought to send us more deeply into
Augustine's entanglements with the position of the Christian master.

Thus, the first chapter concludes by proposing a four-step approach
which corresponds to the four major claims of the book. *First,* I identify in
the contemporary political Augustinian conversation a particular Augustinian concept: *peregrinatio* (Chapter 2), *humilitas* (Chapter 3), and *saeculum*
(Chapter 4). In so doing, I make the claim that our understanding of this
concept is furthered when we examine Augustine's treatment of that concept in relation to his slavery discourse. This expands the topic of "slavery
in Augustine" beyond a narrow focus on the status of the institution in Book
19 of *The City of God,* and instead tracks how a slavery discourse permeates
areas of his thought which remain of great interest to constructive theological and ethical reflection. *Second,* I analyze how this slavery discourse
which Augustine employs to develop that concept, when examined closely,
makes it difficult to separate cleanly "figurative" and "literal" slaveries in
his thought, as previous interpreters have been inclined to do. Instead, what
emerges is what I have called *the master's house,* a *domus* ruled by a *dominus,*
functioning as a symbolic structure recurring throughout his thought, inside
which a given concept can be given coherence, specificity, and a point of
contact with the social world Augustine inhabited.

Third, I examine how a given Augustinian concept (whether pilgrimage or humility or *saeculum*), insofar as it is developed inside the master's
house, is not developed inside a politically neutral description of social reality. Once we bracket the master's own self-narrations, as though these were
the only possible description, we can begin to recognize more clearly that
a slave system—definitionally, qua slave system, and not by any accidental
cultural property or moral shortcoming of a particular master—is a relation
predicated on force, domination, and antagonism between master and slave.
Slavery, insofar as it is a definable concept with any legibility at all, must
rest on what formerly enslaved intellectual J. W. C. Pennington termed the
"chattel principle": the transformation of person into property, of the human

into a fungible thing. This principle, in the manifest brutality it unleashes upon the enslaved person, remains "fictive" in the strict sense that it cannot complete (or "make real") the full mastery it posits: this is the case just to the extent that in the life of the enslaved, beneath "things" are human beings, beneath "social death" is insurgent social life, or put simply, "objects" can and do resist.[9] This fictive quality injects an inherent and interminable instability to the master–slave relation, and so, just to the extent that the master has routed his own identity through this relation, his identity becomes for him *a problem*. Discourses of the master—in law, literature, culture, and so on—thus in various ways find themselves attempting to stabilize this instability, and in order to do so, must develop a complex range of narrative tools, of self-deceptions and mystifications and alternative facts—what Orlando Patterson calls "inversions" of the underlying parasite relation. Thus the question haunting the work throughout: What happens when these self-deceptions get built into the grammar of Christian thought and life by God being imagined a good and merciful *Dominus,* Christ taking "the form of the slave" in the incarnation, and acts of human sinfulness being signified as fugitive disobedience?

It must be noted that I speak here in types, for the sake of producing concepts which can only ever be partially adequate to the world they help make visible to thought: there are gradations involved in the extent to which such discourses of mastery approach a hypothetical point of full inversion, full self-deception. They never fully reach it, and never approach it in simplistic or—in the crude sense—"ideological" ways. Certainly not in the case of Augustine. Even so, by close attention to Augustine's own texts and their reception histories in modern Christian thought, we can carefully track the subtle ways in which Augustine's use of the master's house moves him along this spectrum, moves him toward a particular encoding of social reality which is not neutral, but which adopts the masters' vantage in the master–slave conflict. Insofar as this is the case, there is built into the grammar of Christian moral thought this more-or-less self-deceived side of the epistemic break I posited in my Introduction, that side of the master who glimpses, in the shadows, the figure of the fugitive slipping off into the night, and with her, the stable coherence of his own identity *as* master.

So in sum: This *alignment* of Augustine's moral thought with the position of the master, even in his criticism of lustful Roman mastery, together with the self-deceptions and instabilities that that alignment injects into his theological and ethical thought, is what I have proposed to examine under the conceptual heading: *the enduring problem of the Christian master*. The "Christian" in that conceptual heading refers to the way specifically Christian resources—concepts like human life as pilgrimage (Chapter 2), humility as the virtue of Christ's slave form (Chapter 3), and *saeculum* as a time in which slavery is providentially ordained (Chapter 4)—are drawn inside and captured by the ethical project of securing coherence and stability for the master's position, for the inherently unstable social relations which are endemic, by definition, to slave societies. The "enduring" in that conceptual heading refers to the way that, for all the uncapturable ruptures and contingencies of historical transformation which attend the long entanglements of western Christianity and slaveholding, there nonetheless are specific, perennial challenges which attending to reception histories of Augustinian thought can help illumine.

Fourth, and finally, I have argued that the modern afterlife of slavery presents us with a context for ethical life in which *race* marks out the complex and persisting permutations of master–slave relations of domination in the present, such that between Augustine's social world and our own, we might identify parallel moral dynamics animating the conditions in which we do ethical thought. Thus, I have drawn each Augustinian concept into an encounter with Black religious and political thought as the other side of that "break" in the shadows, as the site of Christian ethical life reconstructed elsewhere and otherwise. This is not for the sake of retrieving or "saving" Augustine, but for the sake of homing in on the fact that the problem of mastery, for the reasons developed above, can never fully succeed, never fully capture the social life to which it lays claim. And so Augustine so often bears witness to aspects of ethical life with God and one another that remain threatened but are never fully captured by the position of the master, and it is these aspects which might be drawn out, taken apart into their elemental pieces, and remade through a thinking with and after and alongside fugitive Black texts from James Cone to Delores Williams to Saidiya Hartman to Neil Roberts—moving within and beyond terrain which cannot be captured by "secular" and "religious" distinctions, as important as those often are. And yet, this sort of encounter, this bending and remaking of ethical concepts is by no means simple, and is more complex than my work here has yet accounted for.

In the remainder of this conclusion, then, I want to think through how exactly an approach to reading slavery metaphors in Augustine and elsewhere might generate not only critique but also ways forward for encounter between Augustinian politics and Black religious thought. The end game of an argument like this one, I think, cannot be to eradicate all traces of slavery discourse from Christian thought, as though the problems set forth here could be resolved by erasing certain habits of speech long internal to Christian grammar. As I have suggested above, it is, in a sense, both too late and too early for that: too late in that too much blood is already on the ground—one more disavowal won't work; too early in that we have not yet imagined a social order fully beyond the world race built. The task instead, monumentally difficult, concerns rethinking the relation between the symbolic worlds we have inherited and the position of the master these forms have been called upon to sustain. How might such signs be broken open and deformed, bent and remade? Is there some theological practice which would inhabit the tension and interplay between what Houston Baker called "the mastery of form" and the "deformation of mastery"?[10] As one entry point into these questions, I return here to Augustine's canonical account in *Teaching Christianity* of the multivalence of signification.

•

A two-part question runs through Augustine's *Teaching Christianity*: First, what is the precise relation of *res* and *signum,* or thing and sign, reality and its representation? Second, why does this relation *matter* so much for creatures like us—which is to say, for rational souls enfleshed? Living in flesh means living with limit: our rational natures know nothing purely, but partially and in time, by word, symbol, image. Not in transparency, but by mirrors and shadows.[11] Likewise, we never possess with finality. We desire, acquire, then suffer loss—often sudden and irreparable loss. (Augustine dialogues with his son Adeodatus in the earlier work on signs, *The Teacher* [*De magistro*], from 389; in 390, Augustine buries him in Thagaste at seventeen.) Learning and desiring, beset by grief and lack, we are restless creatures, Augustine thinks.

This restlessness of *peregrinatio*—as a complex theological claim about language, time, and desire, and *not* as a too-familiar portrait of his own psychological profile—provides one way of naming how Augustine parts ways with "the Platonists."[12] Call restlessness the shape of his hope, watch it emerge in fragments across his life's work, a hope remade elsewhere and otherwise than theirs. Rowan Williams notes it is the incarnation, God's own entrance into the world of time, which slowly persuades Augustine to take the risk which animates *Teaching Christianity* as a whole: the risk of trusting that what's to be hoped for in this life is neither an overcoming of our need for signs, nor an escape from temporality, history, or body. Rather, writes Williams, to Augustine "the incarnation manifests the essential quality of the world itself as 'sign' . . . of its maker. It instructs us once and for all that we have our identity within the shifting, mobile realm of representation, non-finality, growing and learning, because . . . the whole creation is uttered and 'meant' by God, and therefore has no meaning in itself."[13]

The upshot is that "we live in a world of restless fluidities in meaning." Signs "refuse to stay still."[14] Symbols bend and rearrange in time. That means the threat of interpretive anarchy is real—as evidenced at times in Augustine's own scriptural exegesis, Williams notes. Yet holding that threat at bay, for Augustine, is the cross of Jesus.[15] For the cross provides the *final* symbolic form. The cross is that "sign" which, Augustine writes in Book 2, "encompasses the whole of Christian activity."[16] The cross marks the sole stable point in this endless play of signs—an anchor, around which churning waves of signification rearrange themselves in time.

Under the pressure exacted by the problem of the master developed up to this point, here I want to press the implications of this Augustinian theory of signs by seizing upon an aspect of "the cross" that neither Williams nor Augustine himself addresses, but one which social histories of Roman antiquity indicate in vividly complex detail: Crucifixion was no mere "res" *waiting* to become "signum" with Jesus. It already held rich symbolic dimensions. Embedded within Roman spectacle culture, it already marked an event charged with signifying power, intensely public, comprising what K. M. Coleman calls a "fatal charade."[17] "When we crucify criminals," wrote Quintilian, the first-century Roman rhetorician, "the most frequented roads are chosen, where the greatest number of people can look and be seized by this fear. For every punishment has less to do with the offence than with the example."[18] At once entertainment and deterrent, crucifixion enacted a brutal imperial parable, a "penal liturgy" performed for watching crowds, as though to say: here is what befalls those who would exalt themselves, here is what rebellion looks like halted, humiliated, and violently realigned with political order—realigned with and by the very order it placed under threat.[19] "The body of the condemned," as classicist Danielle Allen writes in a different context, "must always be made to *mean* something."[20] In the

Roman social imaginary, the cross was a paradigmatic scene of the body condemned, the body devastated, the groaning and silent body, the body which nevertheless *speaks*. Or rather, an empire speaks through it. Crucifixion—prior to its role in a nascent Christian imagination—was no senseless suffering waiting to be made symbolic. Its suffering *was* signification. (Of what, exactly, we return to below.)

What this historical aspect brings into view is a set of constructive-theological questions about what Augustine calls "the Lord's cross" (*crucem Domini*), questions the scriptural accounts invite us to imagine Jesus himself having to face: What do you do when you find your very body *conscripted* to mean and to speak—that is, to serve signifying purposes beyond, even against, your own? And conscripted in this way not by God, but by the demands of the dominant, by those who rule, with their enduring need to produce and make coherent a particular arrangement of social and political life? What do you do with this type of signification which—"restless fluidities in meaning" notwithstanding—came into being precisely to hold your captive flesh in place, pin down its unruly potential to signify, and use this signifying potential to satisfy the immense storytelling needs of empire? And finally, how might this "official" meaning, the signification sanctioned by the dominant, stand in relation to whatever other meanings you might wish to discern in your own flesh?

Such questions have often been important for those whose lives have been made to inhabit symbolic forms across the ages like "slave," "woman," "savage," "queer," "Black." They are not questions a historian asks qua historian. Rather, they are questions which historical work can help to emerge into view, in this case by rendering a clearer picture of how crucifixion functioned in Roman culture. And so also, help to emerge as salient for theological thinkers, especially for those who, with Augustine, think the restless relation of thing to sign lies at the heart of what it means to be human. Nevertheless, the set of core questions above—of the dynamics of signifying flesh under conditions of domination—is yet to appear as a site of sustained inquiry in the modern Augustinian tradition of political theology. By rethinking Augustine's theory of signs in the direction marked by this series of core questions, this final chapter aims to lay the groundwork for future constructive encounters between Augustinian politics and theologies of liberation, or what Charles H. Long calls, with greater precision, "theologies opaque."[21]

As ever, this places me not among historians aiming to reconstruct purely how Augustine thought, but among theological ethicists who try to think about the present in Augustinian ways, while I freely concede both the contested nature of that distinction and the commonly noted dangers of anachronism in the latter sort of work.[22] Working at this vexed crossroads of patristics, Augustinian political theology, and Black thought, I first foreground the historical considerations which elicit the set of questions raised above. Then I turn in the end to a more direct meditation upon the significance, for such questions, of Jesus's words at the last supper. There I develop a constructive theological interpretation of those words as a way into the gifts of the last supper and baptism—the table and the sea—informed both by the Augustinian theory of signs sketched above and by some aspects of Black religious thought.

Understanding the implications of the contention made above, that the cross did not *become* symbolic with Jesus, depends in key part upon grasping the intimate connection in the Roman social imaginary between crucifixion and slavery—or more precisely, between the crucified body and the body of the slave. I underscore the latter way of putting it to emphasize that I am not proposing slavery as a magic interpretive key to the exclusion of other factors like gender and sexuality, or honor and shame, or punishment as part of state terror.[23] Rather, the enslaved body is itself a nexus where such factors necessarily converge (and indeed, wherever the enslaved body does *not* function this way indicates how conceptually distinguishing "slave societies" from "societies with slaves" remains relevant).[24]

It is no accident that the example which both opens and concludes Felicity Harley's recent assessment of the state of the field on crucifixion in Roman antiquity is the mime performance of the crucifixion of Laureolus, fugitive slave turned notorious bandit.[25] Most cases of Roman crucifixion involve enslaved people and, significantly, noncitizens (*peregrini*). (This already gestures tacitly toward the possibility I have raised throughout: solidarity between pilgrims and fugitives, the road and the woods.) Writing nearly twenty years ago, Jean-Jacques Aubert called the link between slaves and crucifixion "a point so well established and documented that it is unnecessary to dwell on it, as recorded cases would add up ad nauseam."[26] More recently, our historical understanding of crucifixion in the Mediterranean world has been greatly expanded, rendered in increasingly granular complexity, yet this basic connection between the Roman practice of crucifixion and the bodies of the enslaved has not been overturned.[27]

This does not imply all victims of crucifixion were enslaved people. The person whose crucifixion is under consideration here, Jesus of Nazareth, by all available evidence, was not.[28] But we are concerned with precisely the symbolic dimensions of crucifixion, as that distinctive penal practice which Valerius Maximus infamously called the *servile supplicium*—the "slave punishment"—and further with the theological significance of those symbolic dimensions. Thus, the crucial upshot is in view when Aubert writes, "crucifixion of nonslaves represented . . . a conscious attempt to *treat* them as slaves and implied for the victim a total loss of legal status."[29] More recent cultural histories of slavery in Rome have not only reaffirmed the general link above—as when classicist Myles Lavan writes, "Crucifixion was the conventional method of executing slaves"—but the further point about non-slaves: "even if it was sometimes inflicted on non-citizens and even citizens of lower social standing (*humiliores*)," Lavan continues, "it was always regarded as a characteristically servile punishment."[30]

In other words, the oft-noted element of extreme shame and humiliation is coextensive with the fact that to crucify was, among other things, *to recast the victim's body as a slave body.* It is this signifying act—a collapse of the all-important distinction between a free body and a slave body—which the crucifixion of nonslaves implied generally, and which the "Christ hymn" of Philippians 2 seems to authorize for Christian thought as a context for interpreting Jesus: the crucified one who is not a slave, but "takes the form of the slave."[31] As I discussed in Chapter 3, for the mature Augustine, the Philippians 2 hymn, especially the "form of the slave" (*forma servi*), would come to be vitally important, providing what Lewis Ayres calls Augustine's "Panzer text."[32] There I suggested that the history of Christian theological uses of the "form of the slave," including Augustine's, must be situated *within,* and not as an exception to, an enduring intellectual habit among masters ancient and modern, namely, of finding slaves "good to think with."[33] Less bloody than crucifixion, using slavery metaphors to reflect on various matters of the human condition nevertheless performs the same logic: the body of the enslaved exists as an object to serve the purposes of the master, including intellectual, theological, literary, or conceptual purposes. As Sandra Joshel points out, this includes not only when the slave serves conceptually as the 'other' to the master, but just as frequently in moments when "the freeborn implicitly or explicitly *identify* with slaves and their condition."[34] I highlighted the way that the analytic of fungibility in Black feminist thought complicates the often-invoked ethical salience of *empathy*. One might object that in the Stoic examples discussed by Joshel, the enslaved person is always castigated by the metaphorical use (the glutton denounced as a "slave" to food, and so on), whereas the Christian "form of the slave" metaphor *celebrates* the enslaved person as a virtuous model of humility and obedience. But whether castigated or celebrated, actually existing enslaved people still remain silent, buried beneath "the slave"—figural bodies silenced which nevertheless speak, or rather, masters speak through them.[35]

Further, the signifying effect discussed in this section—crucifixion as recasting the crucified as a slave body—is all the more significant when we note how deeply unstable, and therefore how anxiously policed, was this all-important border between the free body and the enslaved body in the late Roman period. The conflict between legal text and social reality underscores this point, as Susanna Elm points out: "In fact, the picture of slavery in the later Roman Empire was highly complex: the clear positions of the Roman law, positing and preserving the deep divide through birth between bodies as property and free human beings, was always confronted with a reality in which this divide was crossed and re-crossed. . . . [B]y the time of Augustine . . . a great number of persons lived in a grey zone, in hybrid states as neither true slaves nor really free."[36] That reality, the historical instability of the border between slave and free, is the context in which Jennifer Glancy proposes we understand the two widely discussed Divjak letters in which Augustine addresses the slave system. His opposition to the slave traders sweeping through North Africa, Glancy argues, was rooted not in objection to "the institution of slavery itself," as evidenced by his citing scriptural tradition to enjoin slaves to submit to masters, but rather in a deep "disquiet at the prospect of blurring distinctions between slave and free."[37] This is not to suggest an individual shortcoming but, to the contrary, to underscore how embedded Augustine was in the historical situation posed by the "grey zone" Elm described, how "the confusion of the categories of free and slave crystallizes a fundamental anxiety in the ancient world over the stability of the slave body."[38] I have argued throughout that this context invites us to consider how difficult it is to disentangle, in Augustine's moral and political thought, slavery as *res* from slavery as *signum*. In other words, I have argued that it is not as easy as interpreters have sometimes assumed to separate Augustine's justification of slavery the institution (as a necessity of human life under sin) from the key concepts in his thought which he used slavery metaphors to articulate—the very concepts which political Augustinians reappropriate for contemporary life. Generally, Augustinians lament the former as an unfortunate residue of Augustine being a man of his age, while declining to examine how that context—Augustine's enmeshment in a slave society—has shaped the theological and political concepts they wish to apply to our age.

An issue for constructive appropriations of Augustine, then, is the possibility that certain slave metaphors in Augustine present not merely a neutral depiction of social reality, but rather a particular way of encoding that reality, one which risks aligning Christian thought with the moral vantage of the masters, for whom fugitive slaves are fitting emblems of disorder, sin, and pride, while obedient slaves signify order, virtue, and humility. This alignment with the position of the master poses normative questions for Christian citizenship in political orders premised upon unjust domination, especially for those of us who, by way of whiteness, maleness, class status, and otherwise, have inherited the afterlife of the master's position in the present, and thereby profit from how modern Atlantic slavery's legacies yet shape our common life. Since I began presenting these claims in public a few years ago, I have often been met with variations upon a single, quite appropriate response: *If* it is right to problematize certain metaphorical uses of slaves, as you say, what are we supposed to do now with that language we have inherited? This chapter is, in key part, an extended struggle with that question. My proposal is neither that we excise such language from our theological lexicon, nor that we find in it a reason to stop engaging Augustine's resources for contemporary concerns; to the contrary, I propose we let ourselves be troubled and stay troubled, then build from his own theory of signs to revisit the practices of signification itself, and from there generate something like what follows here.

What I offer is not a description of Augustine's views on the cross, which have been explored by others at great depth elsewhere, so much as a constructive experiment in the sort of fluid, hermeneutical layering across vast historical distances which Augustine himself so often practiced—the multivalence we witnessed in the opening examples of the sea.[39] As Jürgen Hammerstaedt's overview shows, Augustine's meditations upon the cross often stitched together prefigurative images from the Hebrew scriptures, historical events familiar to Roman hearers, nautical metaphors from everyday life, and more.[40]

And so, reading Augustine beyond himself, building speculatively from his notion that all symbolic forms rearrange themselves when the decisive symbol of the cross appears, we might constructively revisit the meaning-making performance Jesus enacts on the night he was betrayed. On that night, we might wish to say, Jesus improvises within the enduring and ongoing signifying possibilities of the Passover meal he has inherited as a child of Israel. He knows what is to come. He is not trying to "find" meaning in the otherwise meaningless violence that awaits him. Instead he seems keenly aware that for those seeking his death, the violence of the cross is not meaningless at all, but already highly charged with narrative power, with value, with desire. The cross, he understands, is *already* a dense site of Roman meaning, a privileged space set up precisely for acts of imperial signification. His broken flesh, he understands, is already scripted—typecast within a melodrama about order and obedience, his death a moralizing spectacle about the threat of seditious bodies, now split apart before the eyes of the crowd.

When Jesus draws his friends close at the table and raises a loaf of bread, the sentence "This is my body" *interrupts* that bland story. "This is my body" *ruptures* that brutal symbol of the transformation of disobedience into obedience, disorder into order—that whole symbolic order of slavery which early Christian thought would, at times, inherit, recalibrate, and in that way, preserve. In saying, "This is my body," Jesus steals from empire the right to route their signifying labors through his captive flesh. It is as though he says: You will not use my body that way. (If there can be natural signs, and given signs, as in Augustine's account, perhaps there can also be *taken* signs.[41]) His flesh instead opens toward something else—an elsewhere his imperial masters neither anticipate nor contain within their existing structures of meaning. The meaning of Jesus's flesh will not be order, but feasting and forgiveness; not spectacle, but covenant. By improvising upon and in this way sanctifying the Passover form of symbolic activity he inherited, Jesus participates in Israel's fugitive theft of the master's meanings, accedes to the divine demand for new signs to bloom within deathly spaces, and invites us into spaces like the table gathered and the sea parted, where violence is not romanticized or redeemed, but unmade on the basis of what it tried to thwart: unsanctioned communion, a being-with prior to and against every symbol of death.[42]

In the cross Jesus seized upon a symbolic instrument designed for his death, stole its meaning away from the masters, and resignified it. With this act at the table, God sanctifies and blesses all those in our world who seize upon symbolic instruments designed for their death—including New World signifiers like Blackness—and instead open them up in new ways, stealing their meaning from the self-deceptions of masters who *knew not what they did* when they made them. "There is absolutely no evidence from the long and dismal annals of slavery," writes Orlando Patterson, "to suggest that any group of slaves ever internalized the conception of degradation held by their masters."[43] This unknowingness indexes an excess to the symbol itself. An inexhaustibility and an "exorbitance"—to invoke Nahum Chandler—this openness of the sign, with its unfinished quality, recalls the Augustinian restlessness above.[44] On the move beneath and beyond their "official" meaning, signs—to repurpose Rowan Williams—"refuse to stay still."[45] Receiving that resignifying potential within the specificity of New World afterlives of slavery, within the persistent gestures of dispossession going under the heading "race," drives us to think with Charles Long about the *opacity* of the sign in the religions of the oppressed: "The oppressed must deal with both the fictive truth of their status as expressed by the oppressors, that is, their second creation, and the discovery of their own autonomy and truth—their first creation."[46] Can a sign's fictive truth be unmade? Bent toward discovery? "Blacks, the colored races, [were] caught up into this net of the imaginary and symbolic consciousness of the West, rendered mute. . . . But"—and everything hangs on this *but*—"even in these symbolic structures there remained the inexhaustibility of the opaqueness of this symbol for those who constituted the 'things' upon which the significations of the West deployed its meanings."[47] That opacity in the symbol—considered in its deep grounding in the openness of language, grounded in the sort of restless creatures we are—is one aspect which critics of so-called identity politics have never understood in Black Studies. Its scope, as Alexander Weheliye writes, folding one more sense into the sea, is "neither as an identitarian land claim concerned with particular borders nor a universal terra nullius, *but instead as a ceaselessly shifting ground that voyages in and out of the human.*"[48] This ceaselessly shifting ground, the open qualities of signification bent and remade—itself at the heart of the human, being a creature in time—is what an Augustinianism broken out of alignment with the master could entail. This is no simple task.

A risk flashes up here, as there always does in attempting to rework an act with as brutal a history as the Eucharist, of bearing a resemblance to what Katie Grimes has incisively called "sacramental optimism," a theological habit by which it is thought "that the church's practices, if enacted and understood properly, possess a demonstrable capacity to resist the atomizing individualism of the modern nation-state . . . [or] counteract racial division and injustice."[49]

But the reading I have begun to sketch above makes no claim that there is an internal coherence to the Eucharist which, when understood properly, relocates the site of resistance and liberation to its rightful place in the church's own practices. Nor does it make claims that such practices enact a "formation" of worshippers which will then translate into better action or better politics in the world race built. I am closer to the inverse. I want to suggest that the remaking of signs which this proposal invokes presses the space and place of theological and ethical reflection elsewhere—out into concrete solidarity with movements for justice *inside which we relearn and remake the meanings of "our own" symbols*—in particular, the movement for Black Lives, transformative justice projects and police-prison abolitionist movements as instances of abolition-democracy, and Black- and Native-led struggles for climate justice.[50]

I suggested in Chapter 3 that if there is to be a repurposing to terms like obedience, ascent, and intimacy, it would arise from the solidarity James Cone identified: "The real scandal of the gospel is this: humanity's salvation is revealed in the cross of the condemned criminal Jesus, and humanity's salvation is available *only* through our solidarity with the crucified people in our midst."[51] From this vantage, we can at once think of solidarity as the precondition for the celebration at the table *and* as the place where participants are formed deeper into the very practices of resignification which open up the cross and the criminal, and with it, link what unfolds in worship with the wider demands of justice in a world haunted by slavery's afterlife—what M. Shawn Copeland calls "eucharistic solidarity."[52] If we revisit the moment when James Cone declared that "God is Black," and later, that the cross is a lynching tree,[53] and if we think about how racial "Blackness" was forged as a symbol of enslavement, only to be stolen, bent, and remade into Blackness as a signifier of belonging, perhaps then we can say that Cone's utterance is not only near to the heart of Christ's own symbolic practice, but something like an Augustinian resignification beyond Augustine himself—a remaking of signs through the break of the shadows, in fugitive flight from the master's house. Augustine glimpsed in signs a restlessness and an errancy he could not fully describe from within the grip of mastery, but the gift of his account of signification is precisely how this incompleteness itself is the ground of hope—signs are held open toward unthinkable futures, remade beyond what you can see.

Tenebrae

Now the knowledge of the creature is a kind of twilight.
—Augustine, *The City of God*

Twilight! That space of unreality between night and day, where spirits
begin to roam . . . that time when transformation happens.
—Carole Boyce Davies, *Caribbean Spaces*

This book began in a scene at sundown, drawn from the image by
which Augustine recasts his life and ours inside the world of scripture—
layering Genesis, Job, and more: *Here is a fugitive slave,* he writes, *fleeing
her master, pursuing a shadow.* Inhabiting dusk, I framed my inquiry as
an attempt to stay with what the enduring picture woven by these three
threads—the master, the slave, the shadows—aims to capture, and especially in what eludes that capture, what slips off silently into the night.
That approach brought into view problems and troubled possibilities
at the site of the Christian master, a point at which Augustinian politics
and modern Black thought encounter one another. To the extent that
the Christian master has woven the figure of the slave into his speech,
his social imaginary, and his sense of himself, it means that when the
fugitive takes flight, the action tears the fabric as a whole—throws into
crisis its lexicon, disrupts that order of speech and self built, in key
part, by its ability to master, to arrange all things equal and unequal, to
hold them in their proper place. Unholding and unheld, his knowledge fal-
ters—even of himself. Having bound his identity to the one he enslaved,
he now faces a fracture, an absence where there will have already been a
doubleness once concealed, the slave's two bodies: there is the figure of "the
slave" within the master's imagination, and there is the person enslaved,

existing at once within and in excess of the brutal conditions set by enslavement.[1] I have suggested, near the end of each chapter, that arising from this excess, this uncaptured vantage, torn out of alignment with the project of mastery, is the possibility of breaking down and reworking key Augustinian themes: *peregrinatio*, humility, temporality, with consequences for how to think theologically about race, death, ecology, democracy, and more.[2]

In this breaking down and reworking, I seek neither to retrieve Augustin-ianism as patrimonial origin, nor to redeem it from its past uses, as though the reworked version somehow recovers the "real" Augustine (or even the real, good, liberatory "core" of Christian doctrine) hidden beneath the actual historical one with all the problems. That is an unhelpful fantasy.[3] Yet there is fantasy work too, I have suggested, in imagining that by casting Augustine aside we could, by the talismanic force of denunciation, place our own lives outside and beyond analogous forces of domination, outside and beyond the afterlives of slavery, those which provide us the very conditions of theo-logical inquiry today. By staying with, by breaking down, by drawing such themes into encounter with particular scenes of modern Black thought, I press toward a different option for theological performance, whereby indi-vidual elements of a tradition are not discarded, but "reduced or ground down *in order to be fashioned anew.*"[4] This is a newness qualified and partial. Fashioning anew holds no promise of success, whatever that would mean, for the problems we seek to banish are the ones we carry with us into every room. The Epilogue aims to render this approach—the fashioning-anew of a tradition's elemental materials—more explicit by relating it to a broader conversation in contemporary theological method which has been implicit throughout.

I want to renarrate this method of fashioning-anew as a way of bringing together two salient currents of the contemporary theological scene, the two modes of inquiry which have displayed the most energy for responding to the challenges of religion in modernity, both of which find the source of that energy in one of western modernity's others: postliberal theologies oriented by "tradition" (particularly what Jeffrey Stout famously called "the new tra-ditionalism," which often recovers resources from *premodern* thought) and contextual theologies oriented by "liberation" (particularly those rethinking categories from the *underside* of modernity).[5] The various inadequacies of this simplistic two-category framing—tradition and liberation, theologies of *before* and theologies of *below*—would not be difficult to name. Both are abstractions. Both would require further specificity depending on the task at hand, but for my task, I find them useful abstractions, abstractions which make it possible to bring something real into view about the viable options for theological work, as well as something about the condition under which this work unfolds, its historical mood and elusive "structure of feeling."[6] That mood in the present, I want to suggest, is marked by an acute awareness of western theological failure.

Such failure itself is nothing new, but there is something historically specific to our sense of theology's having failed—specific to theological work as it presently unfolds from a vexed, marginalized position within the modern western university system it helped bring into existence—pressing us not merely to contend with various shortcomings of individual thinkers, not merely to acknowledge the occasional "complicity" of churches in various historical injustices, but rather, as Linn Tonstad put it recently, "to make the inevitability and seriousness of such theological failures a *programmatic* concern."[7] The founding methodological debates of modern theology are familiar, pertaining to its contested status as *wissenschaftlich* (that is, as scientific, where the German word *Wissenschaft* includes both natural and human sciences). Less attention has been paid, Tonstad contends, to the fact of theology's being marginalized in the university "because theology is in the main pursued by believers committed to what many see as a deeply unjust tradition, the Christianity that in one form or another is frequently held responsible for the making of modernity through the slave trade, colonialism, the wars of religion, and the concomitant rise of the nation-state and transition to full-fledged capitalism."[8]

Moving toward a condition marked by increasing awareness of this failure, the Epilogue here renarrates the sundown of my Introduction in relation to the wider condition in which theological reflection takes place. I do this by redescribing sundown through three wider uses of *twilight* as a symbol for this condition. (My apologies to fans of Rod Serling and Stephenie Meyer: neither's work appears below.) Throughout this narration, I trade upon an ancient triad which links *lighting, naming,* and *life. Lighting:* the conditions of visibility under which objects appear to perception; *naming:* the act of giving language to objects thus perceived; *life:* the mode of living, the social form, in which perception and naming take place, as well as the revised possibilities for living together that naming engenders. "The quality of light," writes Audre Lorde, "by which we scrutinize our lives has direct bearing upon the product which we live. . . . This is poetry as illumination, for it is through poetry that we give name to those ideas which are—until the poem—nameless and formless."[9] It is the *quality* of light, its intensity and color, its tint and shadow, which conditions what can appear, what can be named, how we can live. I call the link ancient because, in addition to the Genesis texts discussed below, Plato's *Republic* gives us a classic lighting-naming-living triad: we are prisoners born in a dimly firelit cave, "giving names" to flickering shadows (7, 515b) until education draws learners out of darkness into a sunlit world, enabling "a good and wise life" (521a).[10] But in the three layers of the narration below, there is no Platonic recourse to a realm of pure sunlight. There is only twilight existence, brought into view in three layers, forming an account of the conditions under which contemporary theological inquiry unfolds and a path forward by bringing together the two strands mentioned above.

Twilight of the Creature

The knowledge of the creature is a kind of twilight, Augustine writes, with the cycle of six days in Genesis ("there was evening and there was morning, the first day") providing him something like genres of illumination.[11] Angels have *morning* knowing—sunlight, pure and direct. Theirs is "bodiless intelligence," notes James Wetzel, immediate intimacy with "divine wisdom itself, the second person of the Trinity." Ours, bound to body and time, is "a crepuscular mode of knowing that Augustine identifies with the first advent of evening *(facta est vespera)*."[12] Crepuscular: neither day, nor night—a partial way of knowing, an in-between illumination, *gloaming.* Twilight offers itself as a symbol of this rich Augustinian sensitivity to the *temporal* constitution of the knowing human subject. Rooted in his partial break from (and lifelong entanglement with) a Platonist metaphysics of unmediated access to eternal forms, he comes to insist on the mixed and time-bound nature of human communities, and with it their historical fragility—their ambivalence, their impurity, their propensity to fail.[13]

This focus upon the temporality of knowing animates the most refined recent engagements with the Augustinian tradition. In it Jonathan Teubner's *Prayer After Augustine* finds an opening for a surprising intervention into well-worn tradition and modernity debates, recasting familiar antagonists like Jeffrey Stout and Alasdair MacIntyre as interlocutors who, Teubner contends, for all their obvious differences share a loosely Hegelian and analytically precise attention to the crucial issue: "the kinematics of tradition, that is, reflection on the motions qua motions of the act of tradition."[14] The kinematics of tradition, for both, means the foremost task of ethics lies not in identifying timeless moral principles by Kantian (or Platonic) reason, but in Hegelian attention to the *Sittlichkeit* of particular moral communities, that is, to how ethical life takes shape *in time*—unfolds within the twilight existence of creaturely life. Tradition for Teubner (and if he is right, for Stout and MacIntyre) poses a question distinct from the "development of doctrine," dealing not with the anxious preservation of some essential content to be safely handed down, but with the *motions* of the handing itself.[15] The twilight of the creature invites us to ask: How do particular traditions come to *move* and be moved in time, and what drives, blocks, or alters that movement?

Teubner takes more seriously than most in the tradition-and-modernity conversation the risk of tradition-talk leading one to "embrace (consciously or unconsciously) a kind of cultural conservatism that leaves little room for marginalized voices" and with it the danger of allowing one to "glide over the unspeakable ills of our societies, including racism, sexism, homophobia, and xenophobia."[16] Yet such voices and ills remain in the background. How did the voices get "marginalized" in the first place? Understandably, this question is not the focus of Teubner's study. Yet it does pose a question internal to his concerns. Is the risk merely that the traditionalist might "glide over" the unspeakable ills, or that she might fail to recognize her tradition's own role in producing them—fail to ask whether and how that tradition has *needed* the very others it placed at the margins in order to exist at the center?[17] If the latter is the case, the further risk would be to self-impose ignorance not of these ills (although that too), but of the very tradition one claims to inhabit. To remain opaque to oneself.

In its awareness of this risk, even as it backgrounds the histories which produced it, Teubner's account of tradition seems to me a kind of barometer of our present mood, displaying a sensitivity to the situation in which theological inquiry takes place for an emerging generation of scholars: something about the present seems to demand *both* a commitment to deploying premodern theological traditions rigorously *and* a refusal to ignore modern vectors of oppression like race, gender, sex, disability, and more. But while a massive erudition attends the former among theologians serious about tradition, the latter often remains merely a topic—an "ethical" problem to be addressed, rather than a fertile site at which fundamental theological questions must be rethought, and from which serious traditions of knowledge have emerged which demand rigorous and extended engagement, not the occasional mention or citation. Much theological work emerges rich in one dimension, bereft in the other. It is tempting to ask: How does one balance both things, not one or the other, doing both in the work? But it is better to ask: How does attending to the latter actually recalibrate and enrich how one does the former? This is where I am headed: to propose that for those concerned with a tradition, "making room" for marginalized voices is not a matter of managing the terms of their inclusion into its hallowed precincts, nor of figuring out which resources from Augustine (or Origen or Thomas or Nicholas of Cusa) might be "applied" to modern forms of oppression, but rather of applying the same rigor to learning the complex and divergent histories *by which* whole ways of knowing get marginalized in the first place, including—and this is crucial—the role of one's very tradition in facilitating (or resisting) that marginalization.[18] I want to suggest that foregrounding such matters of oppression (racism, sexism, homophobia, and histories of marginalization) does not merely provide a particular "context" to which a tradition might then attend, but rather refigures the kinematics of tradition itself, and with it, the task of theological inquiry at the present moment. This will require not dismissing but thickening and transforming the Augustinian twilight inside which "tradition" appears as both an object and mode of inquiry, and this means first pressing deeper into it.

To see how this works, I argue here that attending to such matters (the vectors of oppression mentioned above) exacts pressure upon, then opens possibilities for refashioning, the key analytic distinction Teubner borrows from Edward Shils: between *exogenous* and *endogenous* factors of tradition development. The latter are "changes which originate *within* the tradition and are carried out by persons who have accepted it . . . not forced on them by external circumstances." Such change, he adds, "is an outgrowth of their own relationship to the tradition."[19] Teubner reads both Stout and MacIntyre (at least, post-*After Virtue*) as focused primarily upon exogenous sources of change—for MacIntyre, one tradition defeating its "rival"; for Stout, the pragmatist encounter of traditions in democratic life—while carefully acknowledging the partial, provisional nature of the distinction: "there is likely no pure case of either endogenous or exogenous tradition development."[20] By calling our attention back to the endogenous, to the *internal* dynamism of a particular tradition as the basis for its kinematics, Teubner broadly retains, even as he expands and revises, the "cultural-linguistic" approach of earlier scholars who conceived theology as the internal logic, the "grammar," of Christian speech and practice.[21] For the MacIntyre of *Whose Justice? Which Rationality?*, what displays the line dividing internal from external, *endo* from *exo*—the line coinciding with the boundary of the community itself—is what he will call a community's *"system of naming."* It is because I think he is right to key in on how naming reveals the inner/outer dynamics of tradition, but blinkered by failing to attend to the forms of oppression mentioned above, that I want to examine in some detail this connection between a *tradition's internal/external dynamic* and what is revealed in its *system of naming*, before turning to offer an alternative twilight construal incorporating his insights.

•

There is no English-as-such or Latin-as-such, MacIntyre argues, only Latin-as-written-in-the-Rome-of-Cicero (MacIntyre's example) or English-as-spoken-by-college-students-on-TikTok (not MacIntyre's example). So if "the boundaries of a language," he continues, are always "the boundaries of some linguistic community which is also a social community," then two crucial features of languages-in-use help us see how, from them, what we come to call *traditions* emerge: "their practices of naming persons and places, and the particular ways in which by saying something a speaker or writer communicates more and other than he or she has actually said."[22] (I leave aside for now this tantalizing second feature—saying more than one has said—and return to it below in the third section.) The boundaries of a community, the lines which make it possible to distinguish *endo* from *exo* in the first place, come into view in its naming of people and places. How so?

MacIntyre's example is the Irish in use on Tory Island, with its three sets of names: one in Irish for formal occasions, one in Irish for local everyday life, and one in English for dealing with "outside bodies as employers in Britain or Irish government agencies." In the second set, there is a string of names (one's first name added to one's father's, mother's, grandmother's, and so on), which is "as long as it needs to be to convey the information necessary to distinguish that person from everyone else in the community." Indeed, importantly (though MacIntyre makes little of it), this name can also include a detail like one's grandfather being an immigrant; the string thus includes not only one's familial relations, but traces of one's social position within the community via histories of movement. It is thus inadequate to suggest a name is merely "referential," that it stands abstractly in a "unique, single relationship to its bearer," MacIntyre contends, for such names require a particular *mode of life* for the name to make sense at all: "the mode of life in which the name is related to its bearer in all these different ways provides a necessary background for understanding what makes *this name* the name of *that* particular person." And what in particular of the background links *this* to *that*—joins name to person? *Community* and *kin.* "Naming in this scheme is naming someone *as* a member of the local community [and] *as* a member of his or her kinship group. In the use of the name beliefs about kinship are necessarily presupposed."[23] To name-*as* is to presuppose a being-together. Naming-as distinguishes one person from all the others and in this way joins her irrevocably to them. A mode of life with particular beliefs is what makes naming-as, distinction and joining, possible. "Beliefs about kinship," in a suitably MacIntyrean "thick" sense, foremost involve not propositions, but adherence to a particular form of sociality—within twilight, timebound life—which makes one's own selfhood, literally *one's very name,* a possible site of communion, and so of one's own human flourishing. I want to do something new with this affecting and powerful account of naming, but to do so, it must first be located within a wider frame.

On Tory Island, four surnames cover 80 percent of the population.[24] It is not surprising to learn the community is tiny and close-knit and relatively homogenous, and it is this fact that has led many readers, not entirely unfairly, to detect in MacIntyre a romantic attachment to the local, a nostalgic longing for an (imagined) premodern coherence indistinguishable from sameness, as well as to point out that this mood is *itself* distinctly modernist. Here Jeffrey Stout's trenchant critique, mentioned earlier, has been found compelling, as has his alternative: not of one tradition outnarrating its rivals, but the democratic encounter among differences as itself a kind of tradition—the precise sort we need in order to respond, above all else, to what Stout considers secular modernity's central challenge: "the facts of pluralism." In narrating how this challenge came to be, Stout wants to eschew the misguided "intellectualism" in many influential antimodern genealogies of secular modernity—for "history rarely works in the theory-driven way that philosophers and theologians imagine." He is "trying to tell a story of a more down-to-earth sort."[25] But the elisions of his story are, strikingly, what joins his account most decisively to MacIntyre's

"According to my account," Stout writes, "secularization was not primarily brought about by the triumph of a secularist ideology.... What drove the secularization of political discourse forward was the increasing need to cope with religious plurality discursively on a daily basis under circumstances where *improved transportation and communication were changing the political and economic landscape*."[26] Quite a lot hangs on whether we narrate the forces driving modernity as "improved transportation and communication," or as a global system of racial capitalism emerging from Iberian conquest, Atlantic slavery, settler colonialism, and imperial warfare waged to extract resources from every corner of the globe.[27] The issue is not that Stout's narration is bloodless. The issue is which scenes of violence, whose blood, shape the narration. Stout frames his opposition to MacIntyre through a historical narrative of early modern Europe in which two options for dealing with plurality were tried: one involved coercion to compel theological agreement, the other the sort of discursive ethical deliberation Stout commends. "The bloodshed, unrest, and spiritual misery caused by the former made the latter increasingly attractive."[28] He points out the moment in *Whose Justice?* where MacIntyre, too, highlights the wars of religion in early modern Europe as the "savage and persistent conflicts of the age," suggesting this amounts to MacIntyre's "admission" of the decisive factor of "the facts of pluralism" in rejecting Aristotle, while lamenting that "the rest of the book shows no traces of this thought." But what neither book shows traces of— the absence that joins them together—is what might come into view if the "story" expanded its frame beyond "the educated classes of early modern Europe" as the scene in which modernity unfolds. Absent from both Stout and MacIntyre is the violence between an emerging North Atlantic order and its colonial others, as well as any attempt to examine how this—a more global "down-to-earth story"—would refigure the notions of tradition that emerge from it.[29]

The very fact that Stout—unlike MacIntyre, Teubner, and many of the Augustinians I've engaged in this book—actually talks about race matters at length underscores a vital point for the contemporary situation of theological inquiry: it is not enough to think about "race" as one more marker in a sequence of various kinds of "difference," as one subset of what Stout calls "the facts of pluralism," while remaining locked within the analytic frame of the American nation-state. (Indeed, the seriousness with which Stout takes certain Black thinkers, while neglecting these questions, indicates no lack of intensity in his commitment to justice, but a hesitancy to engage Black life and thought beyond its specific relation to the nation form of the American project.[30]) What is needed is an analytic frame for making sense of *how* race emerges as a problem at all, and for this, "pluralism"—religious, ethnic, racial, or otherwise—will not do. Following Willie James Jennings, we might stipulate here a crucial distinction between *challenges* and *troubles*. "People groups have always existed," he writes,

> but it was not until the modern colonial moment that those people were forced to think themselves in the troubled togetherness of race, religion, and nation in a world being stolen, privatized, segmented, segregated, commoditized, and bordered. We inherited troubles. *The troubles were not the differences in peoples, in their different ways of being in the world, in believing in the gods or not believing, in acting, or in thinking, or even in negotiating with or struggling within those differences. These were and yet are the challenges that come with being creatures.*[31]

In their neglect of what Jennings elsewhere calls "traditioned imperialist modernity," western philosophers and theologians have misunderstood the situation in which their inquiry takes place, conflating the perennial *challenge* of human difference with the particular *troubles* of the very colonialist order western Christianity helped produce.[32] What I have called the twilight of the creature—Augustine's sign for the temporal and embodied constitution of the human knower, and with it, the grounds for acknowledging the irreducibly partial and ambivalent nature of human moral communities—has launched, for modern Augustinianism, a robust and theologically sophisticated engagement with modern pluralist societies, as I discussed in Chapter 2. And yet, it has been able to think the contemporary situation only through the general prism of what Jennings calls "the challenges that come with being creatures." Augustinian twilight helpfully signifies this general creaturely challenge, even as modern Augustinianism has mostly ignored (or, as I argued in Chapter 1, *disavowed*) what Jennings calls the troubles—the specific dimensions this twilight condition takes on in the modern colonial moment: of whiteness as an epistemic and moral frame, of the enduring legacies of slavery, of the violent transformation of lands, watersheds, minerals, animals, and peoples into property relations. In Chapter 4, I made a case for turning an Augustinian temporal sensibility against Augustine's project of mastery. We need a twilight otherwise, another way of imagining the situation of our vespers reality, to press into the troubles and find better theological approaches for engaging them. It is precisely this to which I will turn in a moment, but to do so, I need to return to MacIntyre's account of naming.

I have wanted to see what comes into view if we assume MacIntyre is descriptively right in what naming does and how it works, but face in the foreground what often remains in the background—the sort of "ills" and "marginalization" Teubner gestures toward, what Jennings calls the troubles. MacIntyre's account of naming loads a tremendous amount of ethical and existential weight upon the historical *form* that a mode of life enacts. Modes of life can be damaged; they involve to varying degrees violence, marginalization, and arbitrary domination of some by others. What does this mean for the status of the name?

I suggest MacIntyre is more serious about this question than many of his conservative defenders (and leftist critics) sometimes realize, even as he has lacked the historical and conceptual tools to draw his narration of modernity's moral malaise into a less superficial account of its global colonial realities.[33] But glimmers appear. In the passage I discussed above, he selects an especially illuminating example to show that "there may be rival systems of naming, where there are rival communities and traditions, so that to use a name is at once to make a claim about political and social legitimacy and to deny a rival claim." His example: "Doire Columcille" in Irish and "Londonderry" in English are competing attempts *to name the same place.* The former identifies it for an Irish and Catholic community by placing it inside "a continuous identity ever since it became St. Columba's oak grave in 564," while the latter identifies it for an English-speaking Protestant community in order "to name a settlement . . . whose commercial origin [is] in London, England." And so: "To use either name is to deny the legitimacy of the other." Condensed within the contested place name is a *modern struggle for legitimacy in an emerging global system of settlement,* a vexed contestation involving violence and conflict, a site of pain and loss. "The naming of persons and places is not only naming-as; it is also naming-for. Names are used *as* identification *for* those who share the same beliefs, the same justifications of legitimate authority, and so on."[34] Not just naming-*as,* but naming-*for*—making claim to legitimate authority. The question that obsessed MacIntyre is a palimpsest beneath the title on the cover: Whose names matter? Which claims count?

I had been grappling with this affecting notion of naming for years, but only recently went to look at the 1963 article he cites about Tory Island in *Man*—the journal of the Royal Anthropological Institute. And as I read, I found it almost poignant to imagine MacIntyre arriving at, though not citing, the self-assured closing lines on its final page: "The world at large is not interested in the particular antecedents of a man and the islanders recognize this in their use of surnames with the outside world. The old 'family' or clan names placed a man in his wider kinship group in the days when this was important—it no longer matters today."[35] What MacIntyre, at his best, most vociferously resisted—on grounds moral, political, and philosophical—was not the claim of the English name over and against the Irish one, but rather that hidden epistemic and moral frame, embodied in the apparently neutral narration of what "matters today," which presumed its adequacy to adjudicate such conflicts *by claiming not to be an epistemic and moral frame at all.* Impoverished by a Eurocentric education, MacIntyre called this frame simply "liberal modernity." But what he was pressing toward naming is a kind of diffuse and shared catastrophe, an emerging global system whose commodifying effects rippled out, quite differently to be sure, to the Tory Islanders as they were gazed upon by the colonialist standpoint of a racial modernity, which redescribes itself as though it were no standpoint at all—just rationality itself, moral and scientific. "The problem," MacIntyre wrote recently, "has been that the characteristic habits of thought of modernity are such that they make it extremely difficult to think about modernity *except in its own terms,* terms that exclude application for those concepts most needed for radical critique."[36] Tools for such critique proliferate from modernity's underside.[37] I am suggesting that Augustinian twilight, awareness of the timebound constitution of the human knower, helpfully drives much modern thought in search not just of tradition but of its kinematics, of how it moves in time, but that in its most eloquent defenders like MacIntyre, the kinematics of tradition raises issues in naming whose historical contours it cannot narrate, whose movements it cannot discern. It remains locked in modernity's own terms. In search of other terms, beyond and against what

Cedric Robinson would call "the terms of order," MacIntyre pressed first toward modern Europe's *counter*modernity, Marxism; then, disillusioned, to modernity's *before:* Aristotelianism, Thomism.[38] But what if he had taken up modernity from *below*, by engagement with the displacement and trans- formation of terms enacted in the thought-world of, for example, the Black radicalism which the much-later MacIntyre, by way of his respect for C. L. R. James, came to recognize *as* a complex set of traditions?[39]

There, he would find for instance that since the early 1960s, Sylvia Wynter has been struggling precisely toward "those concepts most needed for radical critique" by pressing outside colonial modernity's own terms, by refusing, as she puts it, to conflate the map modernity offers of itself with the territory it occupies. Insurgent movements are doomed, she claims, so long as they remain "defined in terms of our present liberal . . . order of knowledge."[40] Wynter's work not only makes visible what I above called the moral and epis- temic frame by which the (aptly titled) journal *Man* claims to narrate what "matters today," but crucially for our theological situation, she also identifies the great "paradox" which lies at the root of any attempt to do what Mac- Intyre and many of his inheritors want: to think modernity outside its own terms, to " 'exoticize' Western thought by making visible its 'framework' from 'another landscape.' "[41] That paradox is the fact that the most "penetrating insights" *into* western modernity have been "gained by the very nature of a wide range of globally subordinated peoples moving *out of* their Western assigned places." That is, the sharpest understanding of modernity emerged among those it subordinated, those who were at once "assimilated into and excluded from the social order," exacting further pressure upon the coherence and stability of internal and external, *endo* and *exo* notions.[42] They did this by "calling into question what was, in effect, the structures of a global world system, as well as the multiple social movements of other groups internal to the West, such as feminists, gay activists, Native Americans, Chicanos, Asian-Americans, and students, all mounting similar challenges—insights, therefore, *into the nature of that absently present framework which mandated all their/our respective subjections,*" that framework concealed and displayed by the self-assured closing lines in *Man*.[43] Wynter goes on to detail and diagnose the failures of such movements, their defeat by various strategies—including, notably, the multicultural framework of pluralist difference.[44]

Among such movements, though Wynter does not dwell on them, were theologies from below, theologies opaque, especially Black theologies of liberation which were—as Jennings argues in an underappreciated essay called "The Traditions of Race Men"—met in the theological academy with various and powerful "strategies of containment." Depending on the needs of the moment, the "contextualism" of such theologies could either be framed as a bland, commonsense invocation of the situatedness of *all* inquiry, or function "as a disciplinary boundary wholly subsuming the intellectual work of people of color and marked off from what is alleged to be more foundational, developed, and rigorous theological, philosophical, or religious scholarship."[45] The deployment of "tradition," Jennings argues, must be grasped within this frame as one of the theological academy's premier strategies of containment. Thinkers responsive to the mood of this present historical moment, that is, who are both serious about traditioned inquiry and unwilling to ignore modern forms of oppression, must enact a refusal. They must refuse the notion that the intellectual work Jennings describes is provincial, relevant only to particular contexts, particular "bodies," and they ought to do this not out of some misguided charity impulse toward minoritized scholars, but precisely in order to understand their own world, and only on this basis, to generate new forms of encounter with their own traditions. One further strategy of containment must be refused, and this marks the turn from Augustinian twilight as a mood of theological inquiry to another layer of twilight, an alternate construal of this historical situation which does not reject Augustinian twilight but incorporates it within a more encompassing sense of the present. This strategy of containment "positions the discursive practices of people of color as bound to critique (as a subtle signature of nihilism) and devoid of an authentically constructive heart aligned with historic Christian orthodoxy, or with serious heterodoxical alternatives, or even serious engagement with the real intellectual problems or questions of the Western world."[46] I am not so much rejecting the twilight of the creature among modern traditionalist thinkers, that is, their turn to the particular, the partial, the social, over and against the universality of the modern, as much as I am proposing that in order to fulfill their own aims, to think modernity outside modernity's own terms, such thinkers must turn to resources from modernity's underside. What would it look like to redescribe a scene for theological inquiry accordingly—another twilight inside which naming and living appear otherwise—one that refuses containment and presses toward constructive modes of encounter?

Twilight of the Modern

The knowledge of the creature is a kind of twilight: it involves irresolution—what William James called "unclassified residuum," the sites of elision and ambiguity which resist being seamlessly integrated within a completed system of knowledge.[47] Augustine does not have to read far in Genesis to find one: Adam's naming of the animals. He wants to know why "all the beasts of the field and all the flying things of heaven had been brought to Adam for him to put names to them," what the point of all that was, then suggests rather tentatively, "it seems to me that it was done on account of some prophetic significance—but still it was actually done, so that once the historical fact has been established, *the field is left free for its figurative interpretation.*"[48] He considers several possible reasons for this Adamic need to name, rejecting each in turn, then leaves us with the notion that the indeterminacy itself is mystical: "Where, however, something is apparently possible," but where it might "strike some people as what you could call superfluous, or even plain silly," in such cases we should simply let it "be entrusted to our hearts . . . as something mystical (because plain silly it cannot be)—though as a matter of fact, I have either already presented this kind of interpretation or inquiry elsewhere, or else must put it off to some other time."[49] That last bit is interesting, his hedging of bets. In a footnote the translator points out, first, that in his youthful work, *On Genesis: A Refutation of the Manichees,* Augustine had briefly suggested the animals were brought to Adam for naming in order "to show Adam his superiority over the animals, in virtue of his possessing reason," and second, "as for any further 'mystical' or 'prophetic' interpretation, I doubt if he ever bothered later on to attempt it. So the field remains wide open to the imaginative skills of modern typological exegetes."[50] On the first point, we might note how odd it is that, if the capacity to name was meant to display the obvious, self-evident fact of man's superiority and mastery over the other animals, including "every animal of the field" (*Gn. adv. Man.* 2.20), it is precisely one of these animals who turns around and, as though just moments later, immediately outsmarts the human who named him. It is noteworthy that the man did all the naming, and all the listening to God's commands, *before* the woman is created. And so when she is deceived, when they are deceived, it is difficult to avoid noticing the obvious: they are so bad at using language, so helpless before the creation he tried to name alone. A fall: naming as impotent, naming gone awry. By the time of the evening breeze, as twilight stretches over the garden, God calls out and they confess they have been "tricked" by one of the very animals the man had named, had asserted his mastery over. Thus on the second point, as Hill notes, since it is doubtful whether Augustine ever bothered another attempt, since "the field remains wide open to the imaginative skills of modern typological exegetes," I want to move into this open field, proposing here that what *challenges* are to *troubles*, in Jennings's terminology, Augustine's twilight is to the twilight of Caribbean poet and critic Derek Walcott.

In Walcott's *What the Twilight Says,* we encounter a second kind of twilight—a historical condition different from but not unrelated to Augustine's own, an image for the intellectual mood of colonial modernity, whose contours we glimpsed in Jennings and Wynter. Theological inquiry has only begun to think this second twilight. It has done even less to think the specific nature of the relation between twilight 1 and twilight 2, that is, between the perennial challenge of the creature's partial and ambiguous knowing in this temporal life and the particular trouble of trying to do Christian thought in the aftermath of a decaying western Christian civilizational project.[51] Writing in the early 1970s, Walcott theorizes the intellectual and political condition of the colonized Caribbean as a strange, interstitial time: *after* the heyday of an empire upon which the sun never sets, *before* its final disappearance from the earth. Neither day nor night. (Residuum: *It has been dusk for four hundred years,* Hartman writes.) "When dusk heightens, like amber on a stage set, those ramshackle hoardings of wood and rusting iron which circle our cities," Walcott writes, when "one walks past the gilded hallucinations of poverty" with its "orange-tinted back yards," here the strange softness of twilight, "with the patience of alchemy, almost transmutes despair into virtue."[52]

Alchemy—*almost.* Something about walking through the favelas at this time of day makes visible the problem: around him "the dusk was a raucous chaos of curses, gossip, and laughter ... but the voice of the inner language was reflective and mannered, as far above its subjects as that sun which would never set until its twilight became a metaphor for the withdrawal of empire and the beginning of our doubt."[53] A gap unsettles his nerves: between the inner language the poet has mastered, the refined and mannered classics of the English language he loves, and the outer language he overhears, its fecundity bursting forth in the chorus and chaos of the streets. Doubt intrudes: to be colonized is to approach the poetic task with a "malarial enervation: that nothing could ever be built among these rotting shacks."[54] That shacks provide "no standing ground, no place for enquiry," as MacIntyre might say (in the lines Jennings selects as epigraph to "Tra ditions of Race Men"), that orange-tinted back yards yield only "a state of intellectual and moral destitution."[55] Many come into the university or the theological academy told the spaces they come from are places from which *nothing could ever be built.* What to do in the face of this? Where to turn for new language, new resources for the "forging of a language that went beyond mimicry"?[56]

Walcott's twilight reveals—then refuses to resolve—an unyielding tension in how one might answer that question: the tension between anteriority and newness.[57] Between the poet's desire to assimilate the "literatures of empires, Greek, Roman, British," drawing richness from the language of the Old World, and his simultaneous desire toward invention, toward the spontaneity of *curses, gossip, and laughter* exploding from the favelas of the New. Caliban's dilemma emerges: how to turn language learned from Prospero in a radically new direction.[58] Some of Caliban's children assimilate Prospero's traditions wholesale. Others outright "reject [them] as the language of the master." Walcott finds both options illusory in equal measure, full assimilation or groundless self-invention.[59] Twilight permits neither purity of origin nor totality of break. And in this irresolution, this need instead for an "electric fusion of the old and the new," I am suggesting we find an account of what our situation demands, one which can hold together both Audre Lorde's most cited insight, "the master's tools will never dismantle the master's house"—sometimes reduced, slogan-like, to *down with the old!*—and her most neglected one: "Sometimes we drug ourselves with dreams of new ideas. . . . But there are no new ideas waiting in the wings to save us as women, as human. *There are only old and forgotten ones,* new combinations, extrapolations and recognitions from within ourselves—along with the renewed courage to try them out."[60] In this refusal to bow either to the anteriority of the master's tools or to the newness of "new ideas," in the courage to experiment, risking new combinations of old ideas, here emerges an Augustinian twilight sensibility redrawn—creaturely finitude fashioned anew for the troubles of the task in slavery's afterlife, amid the shadows of the modern colonial world.

I am struck by how carefully, how subtly, Lorde refuses to be constrained by the opposition of universal ("human") to particular ("women")—that oppositional relation of universalism to particularism upon which strategies of containment, as Jennings notes, so often turn.[61] Instead she quietly places them in *apposition:* "as women, as human."[62] There is no tension in that comma, in the relation between her writing as a woman, as Black, as lesbian, and her writing as human *unless* one assumes in advance the human is white, straight, or male. She does not. "My audience is every single person who can use the work I do," Lorde says in a 1986 interview. "Anybody who can use what I do is who I'm writing for."[63] Likewise Walcott theorizes the specificity of Saint Lucia and Haiti and Martinique, dissects the situation of "the New World Negro," illumines Frantz Fanon and Aimé Césaire, yet refuses to restrict twilight to the "particular" condition of the colonized alone.[64] Twilight suffuses France and England, marks colonizers and migrants, inhabits Whitman, Neruda, Borges. For "the *common* experience of the New World," he writes, "is colonialism." And if this is the case, "who in the New World does not have a horror of the past, whether his ancestor was torturer or victim? Who, in the depth of conscience, is not silently screaming for pardon or for revenge?" Such screams index differentiated experiences of a *shared* history, from which emerges "a literature of revenge written by the descendants of slaves or a literature of remorse written by the descendants of masters."[65] The theological literature—when it is not silencing or ignoring such histories and theology's role in them—often mirrors these options. Walcott thinks another option is possible for poets, and I think it offers a way forward for constructive theological method too. It brings us back to the vexed status of the name.

The option which allows us to refuse the "literature of recrimination and despair," to press toward a task shared with the great poets of colonial modernity, is what Walcott calls *Adamic naming:* it means "awe at this elemental privilege of naming the New World . . . an elation *common to all of them, whether they are aligned by heritage to Crusoe and Prospero or to Friday and Caliban.*" This vision of renaming the world *in* common is inseparable from remaking it *as* a commons. It is "not metaphorical, it is a social necessity," at once poetics and politics. For "a political philosophy rooted in elation would have to accept belief in a second Adam, the re-creation of the entire order, from religion to the simplest domestic rituals." Would this risk utopian fantasy—an ill-fated attempt to return to Eden? The work of Adamic naming "does not pretend to such innocence, its vision is not naïve. Rather"—and here it is as though Walcott has incorporated the Augustinian sensibility of twilight fully into his description of the mood of the modern colonial world—"Rather, like its fruits, *its savour is a mixture of the acid and the sweet,* the apples of its second Eden have the tartness of experience. In such poetry there is a bitter memory and it is the bitterness that dries last on the tongue. It is the acidulous that supplies its energy. The golden apples of this sun are shot with acid."[66] All of them, all of us, whether aligned by heritage to the colonizers and masters or the colonized and the enslaved, must "know that the old vision of Paradise wrecks here." It is twilight, and there is no going back. The only task is the renaming, the re-creating of a world together in the wake of wreckage. Between day and night, with sweetness cut by acidity, the task of Adamic naming demands we hold together both elation and "the anguish that every noun will be freshly, resonantly named."[67]

Elation *and* anguish. Anguish because this link between twilight and naming, between the quality of light and the practice of language, as suggested in the ancient triad, is not separate from *life.* Anguish because Adamic naming is not removed from and does not redeem the *lived,* shattered histories by which Christian masters enact brutal impatience, as I argued in Chapter 4, laying claim to a utopian life and an invulnerable body now by violently offloading the burdens of the *saeculum* onto the flesh of the subjected other. Anguish because whole peoples, Walcott writes, were subjected to "a Manichean God: *Dominus illuminatio mea,*" subjected to *the Lord is my light,* to Psalm 27, to University of Oxford's motto, and so to the fact that the empire upon which the sun never sets "was brought to this New World under the guise of divine light, the light of the sword blade."[68] An Augustinian twilight sensibility of ambiguity and obscurity, of loss, of goodness real but tainted, is what I have wished to fashion anew rather than jettison, in part because I think it has the surprising effect of helping us take less seriously the temporal framing by which the defenders of various unjust hierarchies are world-weary realists (or "pessimists"), while those who resist them are utopians (a framing the latter have themselves often endorsed). On the contrary, it is the Christian masters who move into the New World "under the guise of divine light," utopian and brutally impatient in their morning knowing.[69] The desire for pure divine light is the Christian master's overrealized eschatology, made visible in "the light of the sword blade," enacted in its refusal of the temporal life of the creature, which the Christian master resists, cannot bear, and so forces onto the body of the enslaved, in hopes of seizing a taste of the life to come—sweetness with no trace of acid, a life of invulnerability, utopia, *now*. An ecology of sacrifice.

Anguish *and* elation. Elation because in resistance to this impatience, this grasping for fleshly existence free from the normal pains and ambiguities and ordinary goods of life, Walcott finds cause for celebration in "what was also brought in the seeded entrails of the slave . . . a darkness which *intensified* the old faith," the intensifying transformation of Christian belief in the faith of the converted enslaved person. It was already the case, when Walcott was writing in 1974 (and is surely even more the case today), that "a new generation looks back on such conversion with contempt," but for him "it is the beginning of the poetry of the New World. And the language used is, like the religion, that of the conqueror of the God. But the slave had wrested God from his captor." When the fugitive runs off into the dusk, I've argued, she carries off with her—wrests away—the master's own God. In this, Walcott says, the slave "changed weapons, spiritual weapons, and as he adapted his master's religion, he also adapted his language. . . . Now began the new naming of things."[70] Walcott's twilight of course challenges Augustinian twilight. It alters and refashions its deepest insights within colonial modernity, shows what it might reveal, might *do* when torn out of alignment with mastery. But in this it also issues a very explicit challenge to those who would hold this new naming—which in order to remake old traditions requires deep engagement with them—in contempt. It challenges those who believe they have no use for old traditions at all, for to Walcott, they share with some of tradition's blandest defenders a belief in what kind of thing a "tradition" is which, in fact, "is *not* tradition, which is alert, alive, simultaneous, but history." By neglecting the fact that traditions *move,* by ignoring their kinematics, alive not inert, such "prophets of bitterness" feel not "elation but cynicism, a despair at the vices of the Old."[71] Despair and cynicism are surely reasonable, utterly human places to find oneself, in my view, but I am unnerved, challenged, driven in directions I cannot fully name, by how decisively Walcott links them to bad politics and boring language. "The older and more assured I grew," Walcott writes, "the more I needed to become omnivorous about the art and literature of Europe to understand my own world. I write 'my own world' because I had no doubt that it was mine, that it was given to me, by God, not by history, with my gift." *Elation.* The re-creation of this world of a gift, the gift of this world.[72]

Epilogue

•

Amid all this talk of obscurity and shadows, I wish to be clear: The ambiguity which the twilight bespeaks, the ambivalent conditions Walcott conjures for theological work, *is* not an ambiguity regarding the colonialist western Christian (and western secular) project. I am not ambivalent about mastery or whiteness. I concur with Baldwin: "All of the Western nations have been caught in a lie, the lie of their pretended humanism; this means that their history has no moral justification, and that the West has no moral authority."[73] That project itself, its ongoing history of domination, is unjustifiable and irretrievable. What remains ambivalent is one's relation to the *forms,* the *names,* the philosophical concepts and artistic resources which emerged out of these irreducible histories. I am ambivalent toward Christian categories drawn from Augustine and elsewhere (as well as categories drawn from Enlightenment humanism) precisely *because* I am unambivalent about abolishing mastery. It is my considered view that attempts to establish oneself "against" a problematic historical figure (in this case Augustine, but others apply too) are typically likelier to *reproduce* one's own standing of mastery—to preserve, rather than dissolve, the illusion of one's own distance from domination.[74]

What remains is the fact that while the relation of the subjected to the dominant is often *not* ambiguous (or at least, not *as* ambiguous as members of dominant groups wish to believe), the relation of those who inherit these histories—both those aligned by heritage to Prospero and Caliban—to the *names* which emerge from them "*is* marked completely by ambivalence."[75] What remains is the question of what to do with the terms of art by which the project of mastery has been, at once, *advanced and resisted.* This ambivalence, having been used both to advance the cause of mastery *and* struggle against it, suffuses (to take a few examples at random) the category of the human, the Christian as an identity, the ethic of love, ideals like liberation and freedom, Thomism, Marxism, democracy, notions of agency and personhood—all these are deeply implicated in historical failure, deeply tainted by and internal to the very forces many of us oppose, or wish to oppose. And yet it is among the most enduring and proven strategies of the insurgent not to abandon them, not to concede their use to the oppressor. To do so would be to cut oneself off from those forebears who, as both "conscripts of modernity" and conscripts of tradition, resisted enemies precisely by seizing upon their terms and transforming them anew—by Caliban's remaking of Prospero's tongue. "Conscripts of modernity" is David Scott's term, coined in part, to help anticolonial thinkers refuse what he calls (following Foucault) the " 'blackmail of the Enlightenment': the coercive demand to respond to a 'simplistic and authoritarian alternative: you either accept the Enlightenment and remain within [it] . . . or else you criticize the Enlightenment and then try to escape from [it]."[76] Theological inquiry has been boxed in, sapped of vitality, and contained by a comparable blackmail of the Tradition (capital T), but we need not be. Discerning which specific elements to reject and leave behind, which to take up and fashion anew, is always a matter of discernment, of risk, and this is what it means to think, name, and live in time, under the creaturely and colonial ambiguities of twilight. This brings us back, now from a new angle, to how traditions move, how names change, and so to the kinematics of naming itself, to language straining at its own edges.

Twilight of Language

"Twilight!," writes Caribbean feminist Carole Boyce Davies in the epigraph above, echoing and going beyond Walcott: "That space of unreality between night and day, where spirits begin to roam and objects that seem perfectly normal in the daylight assume strange patterns and shapes, that gap between different realities, that zone of instability between darkness and light, that time when transformation happens."[77] In this third movement, twilight is the quality of illumination inside which *normal objects become strange.* Twilight is the time *when transformation happens.* Spirits roam, familiar becomes uncanny, shadows take a ghostly cast. I want to reach further into what Adamic naming, what refashioning old names anew, looks like more concretely inside this haunting "gap between different realities." Haunting is not a register of language most Christian thinkers employ, yet here it will press us into the very zones of experience at the edges of life and death, of mourning and loss, of time and timelessness, with which Christian thought, at its most serious, has always been engaged. I have been writing toward three twilights, three configurations of *lighting-naming-living* which, when layered together, mark the present situation of thought. Augustinian twilight, that is, the twilight of the creature, offers a symbol for the temporal constitution of the human knower. It generates a sensibility which centers the ambivalent, the partial, and the particular over and against the false timelessness and universality of much modern thought, and in so doing, puts forth the necessity not just of traditions, but of attention to their kinematics—to how they move in time. Walcott's twilight, the twilight of the modern, incorporates and goes beyond this, outlining the unique contours of racial modernity, the afterlives of slavery and colonialism, in which the forms of the old world and the new world intermingle, and with them emerges a distinct task for the children of Caliban and Prospero alike: Adamic naming, the fusion of language old and new in the remaking of social life. In this third section, I want to think about what haunts the language itself, the grammar and syntax traditions carry within them, and how these ghosts transform the possibilities of living which particular traditions yield—how they alter our sense of how tradition moves and is moved. The third twilight is this: that what we must name, the life toward which our names move, waits at the borders of what language can do. It waits at the edge of words, not because it is speech about God (with all its well-worn issues), but because it is speech about one another in the context of shattered and negated social life, because it is speech not from scratch. It moves in the wake of violent misnaming. It is speech by and about lives which enter into language precisely in the moment of their disappearance.[78] And so our naming response, our Adamic naming—the sort of naming which presupposes, as MacIntyre shows, a mode of life and claims about whose lives matter—this naming also must stand perilously close to the edges of language. I will suggest this twilight of language brings us to the border of what is there and not there in the archive of history, the border of noun and verb in the grammar of tradition, and the border of writing and other expressivities—bleeding over into drawing, into liturgy, into life.

•

Once in a workshop, a colleague introduced the paper I was to present with a reminder to the group: *Of course,* he said, *the ancient world was not nearly so troubled as we are by slavery and by coercion more broadly.* I understood his point: that in antiquity slavery was an almost unimaginably normal part of daily life; that Augustine was hardly alone in his attitude to slavery. Within the archives of the intellectual culture of Augustine's period, we find few if any texts with a moral anguish equivalent to nineteenth-century abolitionism or to our own today. It was this intellectual culture, these archives, I think, that my colleague meant when he said "the ancient world." In this subtle and important conflation of the ancient world with the cultural archive it left behind, a certain limit of language comes into view, a condition which shapes how we encounter a world and its traditions of thought. What can we know, and what eludes us? (As ever: who is that *we*?) What is the theological significance for fashioning anew, for Adamic renaming, of this conflation—the hidden gap between an archive's language and its living world?

Consider one of the key objects of material evidence we have from the archive of Augustine's day: the Roman slave collar—a metal ring riveted about the enslaved person's neck. Many of them were inscribed with Christian iconography—a chi-rho, a palm frond, an alpha and omega—and the words *tene me quia fugi:* "hold me because I have run away."[79] Western scholars have collected these since the late sixteenth century, with interpretive debates over their origin, use, and significance reflecting the shifting intellectual and moral currents of the scholars themselves as much as their object of study.[80] Seventeenth-century archaeologists "drew the logical inference and assumed that many of the slaves to which the *collaria* were attached were the chattel of Christian owners," D. L. Thurmond notes, while their nineteenth-century counterparts proved "reluctant to credit the possibility of slave ownership among a group to whom the institution of slavery was supposedly anathema."[81] (They must have been dog collars, some insisted.) As we've seen throughout this book, one's own historical and social position with respect to slavery tends to shape how one interprets slavery's appearance elsewhere. And yet in either case, whether regarded as an artifact of Christian masters or rejected in an abolitionist apologetics of special pleading, what remains hidden from the inquiry, unavailable to us, is the negative space: the empty center of the iron ring. The collar offers vital insight into the intellectual culture of the ancient world—material, visual, and textual evidence. Its empty center reflects "that which eludes us in the literature, namely, the daily lives of millions of ancient persons who lived and died with no other record."[82]

I am asking why and how it matters for theological method that our traditions contain many more empty centers than we have yet acknowledged—absences which are not ignored, not excluded, but *filled in.* Filled with speech. "*Hold me because I have run away.*" Who is the *I* in that sentence, forced to speak against herself? How did this *I* conceive of her resistance or submission? And is it plausible to imagine her way of thinking might be "not nearly so troubled as we are by slavery and coercion more broadly"? I do not find that plausible. It is the case that her way of thinking is mostly unavailable in the archive, negated, overwritten by the master's inscription in iron. In the third layer of twilight, we ask: What is the theological significance of all the absent *I*'s, the elsewhere *I*'s, in their fugitive movement through that negative space, those empty centers, which can appear to us as salient only if we refuse to conflate the archive's language with its living world? My proposal: By preserving both the collar and its empty center, the tradition *holds* more than it can *contain*. When objects like these are endogenous to a tradition, a tradition cannot grasp what it holds within itself. It can neither anticipate nor control its hidden vitalities, for what is endogenous to it is its own exteriority, lives human and more-than-human in motion elsewhere, and in this surplus, this exorbitance beyond the limits of its direct control, is the starting point for each fashioning-anew, each act of breaking down and drawing upon elements of a theological tradition to Adamically rename the world. In this study I have identified "the slave" as one name where the tradition holds within it lives it cannot wholly contain. Here I am exploring the possibility that the break I identified at dusk, the space where the master's perception of the moral and theological life of the enslaved runs aground on the fugitive's own motion, indexes *a wider set of absences in the tradition.* In the third layer of twilight, we confront the fact that in order for the transformation of familiar names to occur—the breaking down and fashioning anew of Adamic naming—we must encounter these empty centers of the tradition, the open circles, cast in iron, where a particular life is not ignored by the tradition but deeply needed by it, and for this reason is not unnamed, but *overnamed* and *misnamed.*

Any attempt to find a constructive task for theology in Adamic naming must proceed first through these negations: What happens when we are misnamed? Misnamed badly, and brutally, and in ways deemed *necessary* to the coherence of the community as presently constituted? The misnamed, as a class of people, poses a different question to "tradition" than a rival tradition, than the encounter with some other community. In this case, the question is emerging at the site of those who are, as I said above, "assimilated *into* and excluded *from* the social order." This site of assimilation and exclusion, where the very coherence of *endo* and *exo* is strained, this site—as we saw in Wynter's paradox above—is also a place of immense generativity: for the greatest insights *into* the emerging modern mode of life and its names of subjection, along lines of race, gender, sexuality, and so on, came precisely from "a wide range of globally subordinated peoples moving *out of* their Western assigned places." These subordinated peoples, in the fullness of their breadth and difference, also share the condition of being subjected to a name which relates "to its bearer," writes MacIntyre, such that "he or she answers to it, when addressed by it, may be summoned by its use."[83] What does it mean when one is summoned by a name that is false, degrading, opposed to one's own flourishing, and in precisely ways that the dominant community finds integral to its own benefit?[84]

This is what it means to be subjected to what Hortense Spillers calls "*over-determined* nominative properties." She begins her famous essay "Mama's Baby, Papa's Maybe: An American Grammar Book" with an intentionally "confounding" series of names: "Let's face it. I am a marked woman, but not everybody knows my name. 'Peaches' and 'Brown Sugar,' 'Sapphire' and 'Earth Mother,' 'Aunty,' 'Granny,' God's 'Holy Fool,' a 'Miss Ebony First,' or 'Black Woman at the Podium.'" Such names, she continues, are "so loaded with mythical prepossession that there is no easy way for the agents buried beneath them to come clean." That is, "the names by which I am called in the public place" are already so loaded, so "overdetermined," that the task of Adamic renaming runs *deep*: "I must strip *down* through layers of attenuated meanings . . . and there await whatever marvels of my own inventiveness."[85] Spillers links the contemporary naming dynamics present to her as a Black woman at the podium to the enduring cultural-symbolic effects of the chattel principle, the reduction of person to thing, as glimpsed in the text of the law. There, she notes, "the 'slave' is movable by nature, but 'immovable by the operation of law.'" That is, the enslaved human being named "the slave" *moves, acts, feels, thinks.* But as property, "the slave" is "the essence of stillness."[86] The name, the language, in this way, comes to bear witness to the very thing it cannot contain: not just the familiar gap posited by semiotic theorists between signifier and signified, but the less abstract gap involved in this overdetermined nominative act between "the slave" and what the quotation marks of that locution cannot hold within them. "The slave" is a *noun,* but moving beneath that name is a *verb*—a human being who moves, thinks, feels, cannot be located or pinned down in advance.[87] Borrowing this notion of noun and verb from Nathaniel Mackey, I am suggesting that this injects instability and unanticipated motion—*verbness*—into any theological sentence whose grammar rests upon the syntactical use of this locution as noun for thought, but I am also raising here the question of what other overdetermined nouns lie dormant in the tradition. In the ancient light-name-life triad, it is suggestive that "the term usually translated into English as 'name' (*onoma*) covers not only proper names such as *Hermogenes* and *Socrates* but also what would nowadays be classified as common nouns (*man, horse,* etc.)," in a context with just two parts of speech: *onoma* and *rhemata,* usually translated "verbs" or "predicates."[88] A tradition of Black fugitive thinking attunes us to this dynamic of naming: that in the very place where a noun appears by daylight, there emerges at twilight a verb—a life in motion.

There is an important implication of this gap between noun and verb which we can bring into view through Avery Gordon's *Ghostly Matters: Haunting and the Sociological Imagination.* On one hand, the real existence of this human life, this verb, beneath "the slave" is *needed* for a concept to gain widespread intelligibility among its hearers in the first place (for if there never had been a society with "actual" slaves, nor could there be a society with slave metaphors). On the other hand, by virtue of the specific character of *this* relationship—one of domination by which a person must be regarded as precisely what she is not: a thing—there is a very real sense in which the actual human life buried beneath is and must be *elsewhere,* uncaptured by what I earlier called the "subjunctive" fantasy in the master's mind. The enslaved person is at once *there* and *not-there* in the names we have inherited—at once known to us and radically unknown, made visible in the very act of vanishing. It is this quality which Avery Gordon offers us in the notion of *haunting.* "The ghost," writes Gordon, gives us a way of speaking "not simply [of] a dead or a missing person, but a social figure, and investigating it can lead to that dense site where history and subjectivity make social life." What sort of social figure? The sort which, like Spillers's notion of being at once marked and misnamed, overdetermined and yet elsewhere, *"makes its mark by being there and not there at the same time."*[89] What ghosts haunt the tradition, what ghosts come out and roam at twilight?

Every noun will be freshly, resonantly named—in both elation and anguish. While underscoring the specificity of slavery and its afterlives, we might open out too onto other questions about the "social figures" of thought which derive their intelligibility only from within social orders premised upon domination—where the dominant have a vested interest in distorting the nature of the domination.[90] This might press us to attend to the particular contexts in which "the tradition" is haunted by social figures who are at once present and absent, there and not there. I am wondering what might emerge into view if we stay with the implications of this for theological method, first with the figure of "the slave" in its contradictory demands upon the grammar of faith, and with the wider question of reading—with attention to their distinctive contexts—other overnamed and misnamed "nouns" which we find in the scriptural and theological traditions we have inherited, other places where real human lives are at once needed and elsewhere, at once *there* and *not there*, known and unknown. The figure of "the woman" in scripture is at once there to be identified with, there insofar as Ruth and Esther and Mary have all shaped the actual lives of flesh-and-blood women across the ages, and also not there, in that there has always been an elsewhere and otherwise to the gendered experience of women than how they appear within texts constructed by men in the patriarchal symbolic system that shaped their actual lives. Overnamed and misnamed figures and images are internal to the tradition, waiting to be opened up, reanimated, made new. So Cone seizes upon and resignifies "the cross" in its relation to the criminalized lynching victim, Delores Williams upon Hagar as figure of survival and resistance "congruent with" Black women's lives, queer and trans Christians upon the eunuch (as Linn Tonstad has observed), and more, in a deeper mode of interrupting, unmaking, haunting, and Adamically renaming the order of signs one inherits, where one lives and is elsewhere.[91] In these places, traditions are predicated upon massive knowledge and a powerful unknowing, and at the border of this knowing and unknowing, ghosts await. There is so much the tradition cannot afford to know. By containing the iron ring, the tradition also contains the absence at its center—a powerful absence whose hand rises and grips the sunlit tradition which imagines it is merely "handing" on material from one generation to the next. "That the slaveholding class is forced, in time," writes Spillers, "*to think and do something else* is the narrative of violence that enslavement itself has been preparing for a couple of centuries."[92] It is up to us to imagine whether theological discourse could be part of imagining and living this something else.

Only a tradition which understands it is haunted can be *reanimated*—brought back into troubled and vital contact with its hidden animacies, the lives elsewhere and present, existing here and not here within the language we inherit. Not redeemed, uncleansed of its past, a tradition is brought into a new and more richly differentiated present life, where the ongoing voice of the absent, the irrecoverable, makes concrete ethical demands upon life in the present. We might think of this procedure of refashioning the tradition as a specific turn within the long "negative" tradition of speech in Christian thought, a turn toward the apophaticism of the human. This long tradition has emphasized, as Denys Turner notes, that "we have no access to the *invisibilia* of God except through the *visibilia* of creation."[93] And yet here we have paused over the difficulties posed by relations of domination to encountering, without distortion, without falsehood, even the so-called *visibilia* of creation—the misnamed social figures who animate the tradition and allow its problematic symbolic work to continue. And so, if Turner's apophatic tradition yielded not just intellectual critique, but rather "consciously *organized* a strategy of disarrangement as a way of life, as being that in which alone God is to be found," perhaps we might read in certain contextual theologies a refashioned "disarrangement as a way of life," an "apophaticism of the other"—the *right to opacity,* to not be known in advance as a noun, but rather to exist as a verb. This would be the basis for the renaming, which is to say *disarrangement* of various "nouns" in Christian theology by those who both identify, in some way, with the analogous status of that "noun," *and* disidentify with what it has signified in its dominant use as noun, and so comprise a *verb,* a movement away from or beyond or against its arrangement. A movement—a verbing—in the interstice of twilight, the gap of transformation from noun to a new name, a new life.

If Adamic renaming, the reanimation of form—in its struggle at the borders of what language can do—presses us beyond the normal grammar of noun and verb, it also presses toward other expressive forms. I suggest we might think of it as aspiring to the status not of painting, but of drawing. "Paintings," John Berger writes, "with their colours, their tonalities, their extensive light and shade, compete with nature. They try to seduce the visible, to *solicit* the scene painted." This is what a naïve and scholastic theology tries: to seduce, to solicit, to lure the reader into trying out other ways of life. "Drawings cannot do this. They are diagrammatic; that is their virtue. *Drawings are only notes on paper.*" Theology's naming—can you imagine—is just *notes on paper.* Diagrams, notes, sketches. But at this modest point, something strange happens. "The paper becomes what we see through the lines, and yet remains itself." How? "A drawing made around 1553 by Pieter Bruegel is identified in the catalogues as a *Mountain Landscape with a River,*

Village and Castle. . . . It was drawn with brown inks and wash. The grada-tions of the pale wash are very slight." Why does this matter? Because "the paper lends itself between the lines to becoming tree, stone, grass, water, cloud. Yet it can never for an instant be confused with the substance of any of these things, for evidently and emphatically, it remains a sheet of paper with fine lines drawn upon it." By way of the lines, the sheet of paper beneath them transforms into life—tree, stone, grass—and yet it remains exactly what it is, a sheet of paper with some lines on it. It cannot be confused with the life it briefly became. So it is with all attempts to write about, or write toward, something like renaming anew amid haunting. These are *brown inks and wash*, slight gradations. But between the lines another life approaches. Who are you, such that this takes place, despite the fact that "it remains a sheet of paper with fine lines drawn upon it"? "This is both so obvious and, if one reflects upon it, so strange that it is hard to grasp. There are certain paintings which animals could read. No animal could ever read a drawing." You can look at this sheet of paper, know it as paper, take note of its lines, and be met by a world. It is *you* for whom the world arrives, you who bring to life whatever stones, grass, waters these faint lines aspire faintly to trace.[94] (I recall Augustine's worry, that certain questions prove that the asker under-stands neither what they seek nor *what they are* who seek it.)

This bring us to what some church traditions have called Tenebrae (dark-ness) as a liturgical moment in which, I suggest, shadows invite us into an apophaticism of the human. That is: not that human things are inadequate or imprecise in their ability to signify God, but that even the created things which image God—above all, the human person—remain, to a significant degree, unknown to us, misknown to us. As the moment of Holy Saturday in which celebrants blow out each candle while Jesus lies dead in the tomb and not yet resurrected, Tenebrae invites us into the moment in which those who knew Jesus, or who seemed to know Jesus, now have a question mark placed over their knowledge. The names we attached, he evades. We *thought* he would restore the kingdom to Israel. We thought. Now he is elsewhere, he is gone, utterly gone, and the lights are going out, one by one. We tarry with a figure who is not here and yet here, dead and elsewhere, in front of us and absent—not because we can save ourselves by doing so. We tarry, we wait because only by doing this might we walk toward the other world where he will lead us.

Tenebrae is the moment in the liturgical calendar when the dynam-ics of God being, at once, *there and not-there* are brought to their sharpest point. Christ is fully there, we could open the tomb, look at his body lying there, eyes closed, observe the arch of his neck, the fold of his hands. No metempsychosis enters to comfort us. He is there, altogether there. And he is entirely absent, as not there as one can be, not only because he is dead, but because he is (it came to be known) elsewhere in motion—on his way to the depths and back. Here and not here, presence and absence, Christ lies in excess of our attempts to name, fix, or bring to stillness his motion. The mixture of hope and fear this elicits, a feeling of ambiguous longing, is a mood deeply Augustinian. Tenebrae would be not dusk brought inside and resolved, but rather, an indication that life with God will now take place in the context of this dusk, where alone the meaning of the key words of faith will be found. It would mean not saying that there are social problems which traditionalist retrieval theology has neglected, nor only that there are "subjugated knowledges" that such theology needs to learn from (though that is surely the case). It is that, by linking the twilight image to Tenebrae, the liturgy itself is already exogenous—already *outside* itself, already out in the world where signs live and move and have their being, and if we wish to understand *our own liturgy*, we will discover it out there, out here in struggling toward another arrangement of the world in the dusk, in the breaks of social life, even or especially social life damaged badly by domination. One cannot do Christian theology rigorously without deep engagement with so-called minoritized discourses, because the categories, symbols, and names "internal" to theology in the present attain their intelligibility only by being already *out there* in the world, in forms of life which generate minoritized and minoritizing structures in the first place, and so lend only unstable and shifting legibility to "our" terms. These can be confronted and remade only by deeper forms of solidarity as creatures always already on the way, fugitives and pilgrims together, embedded in time and in twilight and in the particular relations by which, entangled, we live.

ACKNOWLEDGMENTS

It is a pleasure to acknowledge my immense and unpayable debts. I am grateful to the Dean's Graduate Fellowship program at Duke University, whose generous support provided the time and space in which this project developed. I also want to thank the Duke Graduate Program in Religion for the financial support provided for international and domestic research travel, which was indispensable to the project. A special word of thanks is due to Stephen Chapman, whose rare brilliance as both a scholar and administrator made an enduring difference to my work and life at Duke, as well as to Carol Rush for her tireless patience, attention to detail, and words of encouragement. I am especially happy to acknowledge the American Council of Learned Societies and the Mellon Foundation for the generous support provided by the ACLS/Mellon Dissertation Completion Fellowship, which enabled my final year of graduate study to be centered fully upon the task of writing.

With particular delight I acknowledge my debt to the faculty members whose brilliance and kindness made this project possible. Since my time as an M.Div. student in the Divinity School at Duke, Jay Kameron Carter has been a model of boundless intellectual energy, creativity in thought, and generosity in dialogue. I began my Ph.D. amid the pain of a divorce, then completed it in the grief of my father's unexpected death. At both these moments and many in between, Dr. Carter enacted the practices of care he theorizes so powerfully. I am deeply grateful. Without my coadvisor Luke Bretherton, this project would not exist. It was in a directed study with him on political Augustinianism that I first found in the bishop of Hippo a profound, if unnerving, account of Christian political life and thought. The tension, rigor, and complexity with which Luke thinks with and beyond (and not merely about) Augustine is a model I have attempted, in my own limited way here, to emulate. The influence of Willie James Jennings is on every page. From a Duke Divinity seminar on slavery and obedience, to his incisive questions at my exam defense, to his ongoing participation in my dissertation defense despite having moved institutions, Dr. Jennings's brilliant voice—even from afar—felt like a constant companion. Rey Chow looked at me quizzically when I wandered into her Foucault seminar in the Literature Department at Duke, then became an indispensable interlocutor, teacher, and friend. If the project reflects, even faintly, something of Rey's intellectual style—the elegance and clarity of how she thinks and writes—I will be most grateful. I first met Charles Mathewes on a pirate ship. (I will not explain further.) Chuck was last to join the committee, yet responsible somehow for two-thirds of its footnotes. I regularly woke up to his emails sending me to literature I'd never have encountered otherwise, and this, together with his own immense body of published work, provoked a great many of the questions taken up in this book. Beyond this stellar dissertation committee, I remain in the debt of many other wonderful faculty members at Duke and beyond for conversations and support: Joseph Winters, Eboni Marshall Turman, David Gushee, Amy Laura Hall, Willis Jenkins, Maurice Wallace, James Wetzel, James Alison, Terrence Johnson, John Bowlin, Greg Lee, and many more. Lastly, a very special word of thanks is due to my grand-Doktorvater, the brilliant Eugene F. Rogers. In teaching and writing, in generosity with his time and wisdom, and in understated sartorial flair, Gene remains without peer.

Thank you to the wonderful team at Yale University Press, including Eva Skewes and Abbie Storch, and most especially to Jennifer Banks for her rare combination of brilliance, kindness, and patience. Thank you to Harry Haskell, whose stellar manuscript editing clarified and improved my writing at every turn. Thank you to Ann-Marie Imbornoni for expertly guiding the book through the production process.

Innumerable friends and colleagues in far-flung places have read my work, shared theirs with me, and remained in conversation with me for years: Sean Larsen, Amey Victoria Adkins, Tomi Oredein, Marvin Wickware, Wolff, Samantha Fong, Kara Slade, Amaryah Armstrong, Heath Carter, Rhody Walker-Lenow, Thomas Williams, Alejandra Azuero-Quijano, Emily Dumler-Winckler, Michael Lamb, Marika Rose, Jonathan Teubner, and (with Jay Carter) my fellow members of the band: Candice Marie Benbow and Sarah Jane Cervenak. (Pie > Cake.) My crew of friends at the University of Virginia read much of this book, welcomed me into their winery outings, allowed me into their AAR housing arrangements, and introduced me to the concept of the luxurious writing retreat: Joe Walker-Lenow, Christina McRorie, Paul Gleason, and Greta Matzner-Gore.

Acknowledgments

Finally: my partner Ashleigh Elser. She read every word of this book when it began as a much less readable dissertation. Her wisdom and insights steered the project at every turn. Her support and companionship helped me find my voice. She is a true teacher through and through, and I continue to learn from her every day. With affection and admiration in equal measure, I dedicate this to her.

NOTES

INTRODUCTION. Dusk

Epigraph 1: *civ.* 19.6. Augustine's phrase is *tenebris vitae socialis.* The translation used is *The City of God,* trans. William Babcock, *WSA* I/7 (Hyde Park, NY: New City Press, 2013). All extracts from the *WSA* are reprinted with the permission of the publisher.

Epigraph 2: Saidiya Hartman, "The Time of Slavery," *South Atlantic Quarterly* 101, no. 4 (Fall 2002): 760.

1. "*ecce est ille servus fugiens dominum suum et consecutus umbram. o putredo. . . .*" See *conf.* 2.6.14. Unless otherwise noted, the references here are to *Confessions,* trans. Henry Chadwick, Oxford World Classics (New York: Oxford University Press, 1992).

2. For background, see Chris L. De Wet, *Preaching Bondage: John Chrysostom and the Discourse of Slavery in Early Christianity* (Oakland: University of California Press, 2015), Chris L. De Wet, *The Unbound God: Slavery and the Formation of Early Christian Thought* (London: Routledge, 2018), Jennifer Glancy, *Slavery in Early Christianity* (Oxford: Oxford University Press, 2002), and Peter Garnsey, *Ideas of Slavery from Aristotle to Augustine* (Cambridge: Cambridge University Press, 1996).

3. In all that follows, my use of the concept of "slave society" is informed by recent rigorous theoretical and empirical work which has interrogated the status of Moses Finley's famous binary distinction between "Slave Societies" and "Societies with Slaves." See *What Is a Slave Society?: The Practice of Slavery in Global Perspective,* ed. Noel Lenski and Catherine M. Cameron (New York: Cambridge University Press, 2018), especially the proposal in chapter 1 ("Framing the Question") not to do away with, but to modify "Finley's tidy binary" into "a scale, or rather, a series of scales" in which we speak of ideal-types and gradations in relation to slavery. See also chapter 3 of the same volume, Kyle Harper and Walter Scheidel, "Roman Slavery and the Idea of 'Slave Society,'" for a helpful historiographical account which underscores the significance of Finley's "slave society" idea when it emerged as an alternative to Marxist and Weberian frameworks in the mid-twentieth century and defends its ongoing usefulness as a way of grasping the complexity of ancient Roman slavery, including during the period of Augustine. I return to Harper's broader historical work in Chapter 1 below.

4. Here I follow the wisdom of Peter Brown, who, in charting "new directions" for the study of Augustine in the new edition (2000) of his classic biography (1968), warns that to "demonize" Augustine "is to take an easy way out—as if by abandoning Augustine we have freed ourselves, by magic, from a malaise whose tangled roots lie deep in our own history. We have made our own bed over long centuries. Augustine did not make it for us. Denunciations of Augustine usually misrepresent him and, in any case, they get us no further in the serious, slow task of remaking that bed." See Brown, *Augustine of Hippo: A Biography* (Berkeley: University of California Press, 2000), 502.

5. Richard John Neuhaus, *The Naked Public Square: Religion and Democracy in America* (Grand Rapids, MI: Eerdmans, 1984); Robert Audi and Nicholas Wolterstorff, *Religion in the Public Square: The Place of Religious Convictions in Political Debate* (Lanham, MD: Rowman and Littlefield, 1997); Rowan Williams, *Faith in the Public Square* (London: Bloomsbury, 2012).

6. On the auction block, the public square, and the churches, see Walter Johnson, *Soul by Soul: Life Inside the Antebellum Slave Market* (Cambridge, MA: Harvard University Press, 1999), 136, and more recently, Anne C. Bailey, *The Weeping Time: Memory and the Largest Slave Auction in American History* (New York: Cambridge University Press, 2017). For a powerful and expansive theoretical examination of the auction block in the context of Black geographies, see Katherine McKittrick, *Demonic Grounds: Black Women and the Cartographies of Struggle* (Minneapolis: University of Minnesota Press, 2006), esp. chapter 3, "The Authenticity of This Story Has Not Been Documented: Auction Blocks."

7. My use of the word "worldmaking" here is indebted to Adom Getachew, *Worldmaking After Empire: The Rise and Fall of Self-Determination* (Princeton, NJ: Princeton University Press, 2020). "Under duress" is indebted to Fred Moten, *Stolen Life* (Durham, NC: Duke University Press, 2018).

8. It is important to note that Black Studies is a distinct formation with its own particular historical lineage(s) as a space of inquiry in the university and its own contested pre-university roots, in distinction from often conflated disciplinary formations like "critical race theory" or "critical race and ethnic studies." For a starting point, see Armstead L. Robinson, Craig C. Foster, and Donald H. Ogilvie, eds., *Black Studies in the University: A Symposium* (New Haven, CT: Yale University Press, 1969), and an insightful discussion of it in Sylvia Wynter, "Proud Flesh Inter/Views: Sylvia Wynter," *Proud Flesh: New Afrikan Journal of Culture, Politics & Consciousness* 4 (2006), as well as Sylvia Wynter, "On How We Mistook the Map for the Territory, and Reimprisoned Ourselves in Our Unbearable Wrongness of Being, of Desêtre: Black Studies Toward the Human Project," in *A Companion to African-American Studies,* ed. Lewis R. Gordon and Jane Anna Gordon (Malden, MA: Blackwell, 2006), 107–18. More recently, Joshua Myers has written a brilliant account of the genesis of Black Studies in its relation to the institutional forms of the U.S. academy, while also charting a deeper and richer genealogy of Black Study as a mode of pursuing a conceptual and epistemic freedom at once within and beyond these institutional forms. See *Of Black Study* (London: Pluto Press, 2023).

9. This turn is associated with prominent figures in contemporary Christian thought who have trained an emerging generation of Augustinian scholars; to name just a few: Rowan Williams at Oxford and Cambridge, Robert Dodaro at the Patristic Institute in Rome, Eric Gregory at Princeton, and Charles Mathewes at the University of Virginia.

10. The second translation mentioned here ("the shady parody") comes from *The Confessions,* trans. Maria Boulding, O.S.B., *WSA* I/1, ed. John E. Rotelle, O.S.A. (Hyde Park, NY: New City Press, 1997). In Chapter 1, I take up the question of translating slave and master terms in the *Confessions* and beyond at length.

11. Job 7:1 reads: "Has not man a hard service upon earth, and are not his days like the days of a hireling?" Commentators tend to note this as a poetic deployment of common ancient Near Eastern mythic tropes.

12. Norman C. Habel, *The Book of Job: A Commentary* (Philadelphia: Westminster, 1985), 158.

13. He is working with the Latin translation made by Jerome from the Greek Septuagint, though the differences in translation are surely not solely responsible for the divergent reading offered. See the discussion in the introductory notes to Augustine, *Writings on the Old Testament*, trans. Joseph T. Lienhard, S.J., *WSA* I/14, 632.

14. *Adnotationes in Iob (Notes on Job)* 7, in *Writings on the Old Testament*, *WSA* I/14.

15. Paul Griffiths, *Lying: An Augustinian Theology of Duplicity* (Grand Rapids, MI: Brazos Press, 2004), 71.

16. For the purpose of my argument here, I defend no view about which is the "correct" reading. The point is to examine the difference between the two as giving rise to thought.

17. As I will explore at length in Chapter 1, the figure of the *Dominus* provides Augustine's favored name and image for God.

18. The phrase "lengthening evening shadows" is from Marvin H. Pope, *The Anchor Bible: Job* (New York: Doubleday, 1965), 59.

19. This phrase comes from James Baldwin, "How One Black Man Came to Be an American: A Review of 'Roots,' " *New York Times*, Sept. 26, 1976: "Perhaps, all hard things considered, it was wealthier in the slaves' cabins. We had to face whatever was in there, and, while we might call each other [n-----], we knew that a man was not a thing."

20. Dwight N. Hopkins, *Down, Up, and Over: Slave Religion and Black Theology* (Minneapolis: Fortress Press, 2000), 107–8. It is easy enough to acknowledge that the slavery depicted in Job is not identical to that confronted by later African American interpreters, which in turn is not identical to the slavery of Augustine's era. What is more difficult and interesting to reckon with is the fact that both Augustine and later African American interpreters themselves were surely quite aware of this fact, and nonetheless negotiated their own eras' slave systems in relation to their ancient counterpart in Job, knowing both its differences and underlying similarities. Contemporary readers often deploy a broad critique of "anachronism" by presuming without evidence that readers like Augustine were naïvely equating slaveries across time, while declining to do the work themselves of showing what specific differences are in play and how they would materially alter the interpretations which emerge. I return to questions of anachronism, comparative studies, and the politics of history throughout.

21. Hopkins, *Down, Up, and Over*, 108. My use of "otherwise" is indebted to Ashon T. Crawley, *Black Pentecostal Breath: The Aesthetics of Possibility* (New York: Fordham University Press, 2017), 2.

22. Clifton Ellis and Rebecca Ginsburg, *Cabin, Quarter, Plantation: Architecture and Landscapes of North American Slavery* (New Haven, CT: Yale University Press, 2010), 3–4.

23. The scholar is renowned French lexicographer Jean Pruvost, as cited by journalist Adeline Sire in "The Time of Day When I Used to Think a Dog Could Turn into a Wolf," *The World* 3 (August 2018), https://theworld.org/stories/2018-08-03/time-day-when-i-used-think-dog-could-turn-wolf (accessed July 27, 2023).

24. Elma Stuckey, *The Collected Poems of Elma Stuckey* (Chicago: Precedent Publishing, 1987), 40. Used with permission.

25. Both ancient and modern Christian masters shared this habit, rooted in a reading of the New Testament household codes which historian Keith Bradley summarizes thus: "It was no longer a question of the [human] master eliciting from the slave by material rewards

and incentives a pattern of behavior the master laid down, but of the slave having to behave as the [divine] Master told him to—and coincidentally what master and Master desired was exactly the same." See Keith Bradley, *Slavery and Society at Rome* (New York: Cambridge University Press, 1994), 151, as cited in Sheila Briggs, "Engaging Keith Bradley," *Biblical Interpretation* 21 (2013): 519.

26. Further layers of meaning unfold when we recall that many enslaved people, as Stephen Marshall notes, "refused to address their owners as master and . . . chose, instead, to address them with 'massa' or 'marse' as a way to withhold respect and veil contempt." Stephen Marshall, "Taking Liberty Behind God's Back: Mastery as the Central Problem of Slavery," *Polity* 44, no. 2 (April 2012): 180. One thinks of David Walker's words in 1829: "Have we any other Master but Jesus Christ alone? Is he not their Master as well as ours?— What right then, have we to obey and call any other Master, but Himself?" See *Walker's Appeal, in Four Articles* (Boston, 1829), 20.

27. See Sandra R. Joshel, "Slavery and Roman Literary Culture," in *Cambridge World History of Slavery*, vol. 1, ed. Keith Bradley and Paul Cartledge (Cambridge: Cambridge University Press, 2011), 230–34. Below, I pursue in much greater detail the analytic steps involved in such a claim, concerning the ways "identifying" with the position of the slave obscures the agency of enslaved persons. Saidiya Hartman calls this the "double edged" nature of empathy; see her *Scenes of Subjection: Terror, Slavery, and Self-Making in Nineteenth-Century America* (New York: Oxford University Press, 1997), 19–20.

28. Vincent Brown, "Social Death and Political Life in the Study of Slavery," *American Historical Review* 114, no. 5 (December 2009): 1241 (emphasis mine).

29. For a starting point to these reception histories, see the magisterial *Oxford Guide to the Historical Reception of Augustine*, ed. Karla Pollmann and Willemien Otten (New York: Oxford University Press, 2013), esp. 1750–53, Fábio Duarte Joly's entry on slavery. I will draw frequently upon reception histories of Augustine's thought to illumine the problems I am interested in, while carefully drawing distinctions between Augustine's own views and these vast, complex, often conflicting interpretations of "the Augustinian tradition" (if we can speak of such a thing in the singular). For a sophisticated recent intervention into the notion of Augustinianism as a tradition, see Jonathan D. Teubner, *Prayer After Augustine: A Study in the Development of the Latin Tradition* (Oxford: Oxford University Press, 2018), esp. 14–16, for his helpful distinction between what he terms "Augustinianism 1" (explicit citations, allusions, and references to textual particulars of Augustine's corpus) and "Augustinianism 2" ("certain general orientations and constellations of thought from Augustine").

30. Prominent recent Augustinian books have centered upon this theme: Sarah Stewart-Kroeker, *Pilgrimage as Moral and Aesthetic Formation in Augustine's Thought* (New York: Oxford University Press, 2017); James K. A. Smith, *On the Road with Saint Augustine: A Real-World Spirituality for Restless Hearts* (Grand Rapids, MI: Brazos, 2019); Miles Hollingworth, *The Pilgrim City: St. Augustine of Hippo and His Innovation in Political Thought* (London: T. & T. Clark, 2010).

31. For the most iconic instance of this scene, see *conf.* 7.27.

32. Lewis Ayres, *Augustine and the Trinity* (Cambridge: Cambridge University Press, 2010), 146, 144.

33. John Rist, *Augustine: Ancient Thought Baptized* (Cambridge: Cambridge University Press, 1994), 236.

34. The need to face one's own embodied position, and the matter of understanding what community one is accountable to, is a key contribution of womanist thought which I encountered powerfully years ago in a guest course lecture of Eboni Marshall Turman (then at Duke), and was reminded of recently in the words of Emilie Townes: "I welcome allies in this enterprise. However, my work cannot be their work and vice versa. Where we meet and touch and spark and burn—this is good. However, we each have our own communities, as well, that we must be responsive and responsible to as we challenge old paradigms of hegemony within them." Emilie Townes, "The Womanist Dancing Mind," in *Deeper Shades of Purple: Womanism in Religion and Society,* ed. Stacey M. Floyd-Thomas (New York: New York University Press, 2006), 247.

35. Saidiya Hartman, "Near a Church at Dusk," in *Cahiers d'art: Arthur Jafa* (2020), 102-3. The italicized portions in the remainder of the section reflect Hartman's style for direct citations to *Let Us Now Praise Famous Men* (Boston: Houghton Mifflin, 1945; New York: Mariner Books, 2001), and I retain them here.

36. Hartman, "The Time of Slavery," 760.

37. Hartman, *Scenes of Subjection,* 12 (emphasis mine). For an incisive, empirically and historically rigorous treatment of this enduring plantation system in the wake of slavery's juridical abolition, see Clyde Woods, *Development Arrested: The Blues and Plantation Power in the Mississippi Delta* (New York: Verso, 2017). See also Christina Sharpe, *In the Wake: Blackness and Being* (Durham, NC: Duke University Press, 2016), 12.

38. Hartman, *Scenes of Subjection,* 12-13.

39. On hiddenness, I think of what Kevin Young calls "a hiding tradition" in *The Grey Album: On the Blackness of Blackness* (Minneapolis: Graywolf, 2012), 23. On "racial enclosure," see Saidiya Hartman, *Wayward Lives, Beautiful Experiments: Intimate Histories of Social Upheaval* (New York: Norton, 2019).

40. Cedric Robinson, *Black Marxism: The Making of the Black Radical Tradition* (Chapel Hill: University of North Carolina Press, 2000).

41. Saidiya Hartman, *Lose Your Mother: A Journey Along the Atlantic Slave Route* (New York: Farrar, Straus and Giroux, 2007), 6.

42. See Hazel V. Carby's critique of the gendered commodification of Black Studies in "The New Auction Block: Blackness and the Marketplace," in *A Companion to African-American Studies,* ed. Lewis R. Gordon and Jane Anna Gordon (Malden, MA: Blackwell, 2006), especially these lines from p. 124: "Black women's expressivity, argues [Ann] duCille 'is not merely discourse; it has become lucre in the intellectual marketplace, cultural commerce. What for many began as a search for our mother's gardens, to appropriate Alice Walker's metaphor, has become for some a Random House harvest worth millions in book sales and university professorships.'" I remain grateful for the generosity and brilliance of Prof. Oluwatomisin Oredein, who, years ago when we were graduate students at Duke, pressed me to begin a process of thinking much more carefully and critically about these matters than I had previously done, a process which continues.

43. I have benefited from conversations with Amaryah Armstrong on this point. See also these lines from Sylvia Wynter, drawing from Lewis Gordon: "we live in an anti-Black world—a systemically anti-Black world; and, therefore, whites are not [simply] 'racists.' They

too live in the same world in which we live. The truth that structures their minds, their 'consciousness,' structures ours.'" Wynter, "Proud Flesh Inter/Views," 7.

44. Chuck Morse, "Capitalism, Marxism, and the Black Radical Tradition: An Interview with Cedric Robinson," *Perspectives on Anarchist Theory* 3, no. 1 (Spring 1999): 6.

45. Hartman, "Near a Church at Dusk," 103.

46. A ubiquitous theme in Black Studies, this notion of the plantation is brilliantly theorized in Katherine McKittrick, "Plantation Futures," *Small Axe* 17, no. 3 (November 2013): 1–15.

47. Toni Morrison, *Playing in the Dark: Whiteness and the Literary Imagination* (New York: Vintage, 1993), 11–12.

48. The opening sentences of an essay of the late Prof. Katie Geneva Cannon, one of the founding luminaries of womanist theological ethics, cuts straight to the relevant point: "My work as a scholar in Christian ethics took a decidedly new turn when I became aware of the White academic community's flourishing publishing monopoly of the writing of Black history, Black thought, and Black worldview. Black scholars did not abdicate their roles in these fields to White academicians. Blacks have written monographs, theses, conference papers, proposals, and outlines for books on various aspects of Black reality since the 1700s, but White publishers did not give them serious consideration until the 1970s." See Cannon, "Racism and Economics: The Perspective of Oliver C. Cox," in *Womanist Theological Ethics: A Reader*, ed. Katie Geneva Cannon, Emilie M. Townes, and Angela D. Sims (Louisville: Westminster John Knox, 2011), 3.

49. This too follows a long strand of Black thought, of which perhaps the most famous example is Toni Morrison's *Playing in the Dark*; also see Marshall, "Taking Liberty Behind God's Back."

ONE. The Master's House

Epigraph 1: As quoted in Robin Lane Fox, *Augustine: Conversions to Confessions* (New York: Basic Books, 2015), 22.

Epigraph 2: *civ.* 19.14. Translation by Henry Bettenson, emended by correcting his "servants" to "slaves," since the meaning of *serviunt* must be read in light of the end of the previous sentence's treatment of order and obedience given from masters to slaves (*servi dominis*, which he also mistranslates as servants in accordance with longstanding habits of softening slavery language in ancient texts), and the next section's famous, extended treatment of the origins and nature of slavery (19.15). On the history of scholars softening slavery language, see Richard A. Horsley, "The Slave Systems of Classical Antiquity and Their Reluctant Recognition by Modern Scholars," *Semeia* 83–84 (1998): 19–66. My altered translation here accords with Margaret Miles, who emends R. W. Dyson's translation to arrive at "those who give orders are, in fact, the slaves (*servi*) of those they order." See Miles, "From Rape to Resurrection," in *Augustine's* City of God: *A Critical Guide*, ed. James Wetzel (New York: Cambridge University Press, 2012), 85. The more recent translation by William Babcock goes even further than Bettenson in muting the slavery image of the passage: "those who give commands are *at the service of* those whom they appear to command," bringing to mind Victorian-era butlers or present-day restaurant wait staff, not the Roman household slavery which, as the present chapter will show, was central to Augustine's thought.

Epigraph 3: James Cone, *A Black Theology of Liberation* (Maryknoll, NY: Orbis Books, 2010), 12.

1. Peter Brown, "Dialogue with God," *New York Review of Books,* Oct. 26, 2017, http://www.nybooks.com/articles/2017/10/26/sarah-ruden-augustine-dialogue-god (accessed Dec. 1, 2017).

2. Kyle Harper, *Slavery in the Late Roman World: 275–425 AD* (Cambridge: Cambridge University Press, 2011).

3. James K. A. Smith, "Translation and the Afterlife of Words: A Few Thoughts on Ruden's New Translation of the Confessions," *Fors Clavigera,* Blogspot, Oct. 10, 2017, http://forsclavigera.blogspot.com/2017/10/translation-and-afterlife-of-words-few.html (accessed Oct. 30, 2017).

4. Colson Whitehead, *The Underground Railroad* (New York: Doubleday, 2016).

5. "If slavery persists as an issue in the political life of black America, it is not because of an antiquarian obsession with bygone days or the burden of a too-long memory, but because black lives are still imperiled and devalued by a racial calculus and a political arithmetic that were entrenched centuries ago. This is the afterlife of slavery—skewed life chances, limited access to health and education, premature death, incarceration, and impoverishment. I, too, am the afterlife of slavery." Hartman, *Lose Your Mother,* 6.

6. Smith, "Translation."

7. Sarah Ruden, Introduction to Augustine, *Confessions,* trans. Sarah Ruden (New York: Modern Library, 2017), xxxiii.

8. Here we might push Smith's reflections further by noting Jean Luc-Marion's observation that the "strangeness" of Augustine's *Confessions* "increases to the measure of the efforts to appropriate it," and this strangeness unfolds—significantly in the context of this debate over "master" language—regardless of "whether one translates ever again anew by imposing on it each time the more or less conscious prejudices of impassioned choice, contemporary fashion, or ideological rectification; *or* one buries the brilliant kernel in a coffin of precise but peripheral information, so as to prudently protect oneself from it by keeping it at a distance" (emphasis mine). See Luc-Marion, *In the Self's Place: The Approach of Saint Augustine,* trans. Jeffrey L. Kosky (Stanford, CA: Stanford University Press, 2012), xiv.

9. The connections posited here under the heading of "racialized crises" should make clear that "race"—in all that follows—must be grasped capaciously, not in isolation from but in its intimate entanglements with gender and class and labor, with migration and borders, with policing and state violence, and especially with climate change and ecological devastation. Analyzing these connections requires complex and rigorous multidisciplinary work. For a point of entry into the state of the current conversation on race conceived in this capacious way (with much of the relevant literature pointed to), one might start with "Becoming Black: A Conversation with Olúfémi Táíwò and Achille Mbembe," *Roar Magazine,* May 25, 2021, https://roarmag.org/essays/becoming-black-olufemi-taiwo-achille-mbembe/ (accessed July 1, 2021). For another way of theorizing these connections under the heading of "catastrophe" theorized as "a structural condition, and a way of life imposed as a form of political and social domination, beginning with the New World colonial encounter(s)," see Bedour Alagraa, "The Interminable Catastrophe," *offshoot journal,* March 1, 2021. For my own attempt to reckon with the challenges posed to religious ethics (and the oft-invoked concept

of "solidarity") by the imbrications of race and climate change, see Matthew Elia, "Climate Apartheid, Race, and the Future of Solidarity: Three Frameworks," *Journal of Religious Ethics* 51, no. 4 (December 2023).

10. As R. A. Markus notes, this turn from historical to normative matters seems to prove nearly inescapable with Augustine: "it is very hard to treat [Augustine's] text in its frozen fixity, without engaging in the kind of problems that concerned him. Almost inevitably, the reader is drawn into a dialogue of some kind with Augustine—a dialogue that will also be a conversation with one's own past self." See Markus, *Christianity and the Secular* (Notre Dame, IN: University of Notre Dame Press, 2006), 41. This also resonates with Jean Bethke Elshtain's notion of thinking not merely "about" but "with" Augustine in order to apply his thought to contemporary matters of political and ethical concern. See Jean Bethke Elshtain, "Why Augustine? Why Now?," *Theology Today* 55, no. 1 (April 1998): 6. For a helpful recent survey of modern political Augustinian thought, see Michael S. Bruno, *Political Augustinianism: Modern Interpretations of Augustine's Political Thought* (Minneapolis: Fortress Press, 2014).

11. Eric Gregory and Joseph Clair, "Augustinianisms and Thomisms," in *The Cambridge Companion to Political Theology,* ed. Craig Hovey and Elizabeth Philips (Cambridge: Cambridge University Press, 2015), 191. Similarly, in Rowan Williams's slightly revised 2016 version of his landmark essay "Politics and the Soul" (originally published in 1987), he suggests much of "what Augustine says about the proper spiritual formation of the ruler can be adapted to the formation of the *citizen* in the modern context." See Williams, *On Augustine* (New York: Bloomsbury, 2016), 128. Moreover, Augustinian ethics shows little sign of slowing down. See for instance D. Stephen Long, *Augustinian and Ecclesial Christian Ethics: On Loving Enemies* (Minneapolis: Fortress Academic, 2018).

12. When I speak of "excising" slavery, I am drawing upon Alasdair MacIntyre's framing of certain "unfortunate" beliefs Aristotle held about slaves and women. MacIntyre finds it "important to ask whether such assertions can be excised from Aristotle's thought without denying his central claims about the best kind of *polis,*" then immediately proposes that "it seems clear that they can." See *Whose Justice? Which Rationality?* (Notre Dame, IN: University of Notre Dame Press, 1988), 104–5.

13. Keith Bradley, a major historian of ancient slavery, advances a strong case for the value of responsible comparative work. See the discussion in Bradley, "Resisting Slavery at Rome," in *Cambridge World History of Slavery,* vol. 1, 369–70, 376, as well as Bradley, "Engaging with Slavery," *Biblical Interpretation* 21 (2013): 541–46. For more general discussion, see Enrico Dal Lago and Constantina Katsari, *Slave Systems: Ancient and Modern* (Cambridge: Cambridge University Press, 2008).

14. The best recent discussion of the complex issues involved in this claim is Daniel Boyarin, "The Concept of Cultural Translation in American Religious Studies," *Critical Inquiry* 44 (2017): 17–39. Particularly resonant with my argument here is this: "The point is surely not the mutual unintelligibility of languages or forms of life but the very hard work necessary to render them intelligible to each other and the necessity to do so, as much as possible, without imposing the terms of one on the other. . . . I do believe that we can learn to understand others with a great deal of difficulty and that the effort is worth it—neither to leave the texts in ancient Greek nor to translate them into English but to make English speak Greek" (34–35).

15. In this respect, I think of Charles Mathewes's striking provocation: "It is an interesting fact that we still lack a term for the interpretive flaw that is the opposite of anachronism. 'Historically reductionist' will not quite do; a better contrasting term would be something like 'aphilosophical' or 'atheological,' or some phrase that would include all that they gesture at and more—a phrase, for example, like 'intellectually inert.' " See Mathewes, *Evil and the Augustinian Tradition* (New York: Cambridge University Press, 2004), 61n2.

16. On this question of what's translatable (and what's not), I think of Naomi Seidman's *Faithful Renderings: Jewish-Christian Difference and the Politics of Translation* (Chicago: University of Chicago Press, 2006), which conceives "translation as a border zone, a transit station, in which what does not succeed in crossing the border is at least as interesting as what makes it across" (2). A short, slightly polemical way of putting my argument: Political Augustinians are invested in the border separation of concepts; they stand at the transit station, selectively importing Augustinian goods while severing them from the bundle they came with, namely, the form of life—a thoroughgoing slave society—which made them intelligible in the first place.

17. Here, again, my approach echoes Boyarin's specific conception of a Foucauldian "history of the present" as "seeking to illumine our own predicaments through investigation of the past," a seeking which demands we "find ourselves transformed in the effort to listen to the other, in which we become strangers to ourselves." Part of this involves seeing slave metaphors as bundled within a form of life, where different "forms of life" are conceived, in conversation with the recent work of Rahel Jaeggi, as responding to potentially similar "functional" challenges—in this case, the functional challenge shared by Augustine's period and our own being the need to respond to, and stabilize the contradictions of, a social life organized around the ruptures and interminable instability of master–slave relations. See Jaeggi, *On the Critique of Forms of Life*, trans. Ciaran Cronin (Cambridge, MA: Belknap Press of Harvard University Press, 2018).

18. See Alexander Weheliye, "After Man," *American Literary History* 20 (2008): 322. See Weheliye's wider argument on the salience of Black Studies and the human in his brilliant *Habeas Viscus: Racializing Assemblages, Biopolitics, and Black Feminist Theories of the Human* (Durham, NC: Duke University Press, 2014). My thinking on this point is also indebted to comments made by Eboni Marshall Turman in response to a version of this research presented years ago at the Duke Theology and Ethics Colloquium, as well as to numerous conversations with Willie James Jennings.

19. I am thinking, for instance, of the way "the fact of pluralism" functions in Jeffrey Stout, *Democracy and Tradition* (Princeton, NJ: Princeton University Press, 2004), 127, reflecting the limits of speaking of "racial" and "religious" as modifiers of something called diversity or pluralism: "Religious diversity, like racial diversity, has been a source of discord throughout American history" (63). I think too of the wider, overwhelming dominance of modernity genealogies which focus on the intellectual and political conflicts among competing conceptions of life internal to Europe, with very little interest at all in the contemporaneous global colonial encounters, disruptions, and transformations occurring under the heading of race in the New World. I'm thinking of Brad Gregory's *Unintended Reformation* and Charles Taylor's *A Secular Age*—and many more could be named. I acknowledge, very seriously, that these explore vital and legitimate centering concerns for ethical thought,

while undertaking the difficult work of situating them in relation to the broader framework of Black fugitive thought, which has focused less on pluralism than on racial domination.

20. Hartman, *Scenes of Subjection*, 12–13.

21. "Living Memory: Meeting Toni Morrison," in Paul Gilroy, *Small Acts* (London: Serpent's Tail, 1993), 178. A small sampling of where the adage appears: Lawrie Balfour, *Democracy's Reconstruction: Thinking Politically with W. E. B. Du Bois* (Oxford: Oxford University Press, 2011), 115; David Roediger, "Afterword: What Douglass Knew," in *The Meaning of Slavery in the North*, ed. David Roediger and Martin H. Blatt (New York: Garland Publishing, 1998), 177; James Clifford, *Routes: Travel and Translation in the Late Twentieth Century* (Cambridge, MA: Harvard University Press, 1997), 265; and Couze Venn, *Occidentalism: Modernity and Subjectivity* (London: Sage Publishing, 2000), 187.

22. Paul Gilroy, *The Black Atlantic: Modernity and Double Consciousness* (Cambridge, MA: Harvard University Press, 1993), 221.

23. The literature I'm referencing here is, of course, enormous. On the new school of economics concerning capitalism and slavery, see Sven Beckert, "Slavery and Capitalism," *Chronicle for Higher Education*, Dec. 12, 2014, http://www.chronicle.com/article/SlaveryCapitalism/150787 (accessed Nov. 1, 2017). For another accessible introduction to the growing literature, see Greg Gandin, "Capitalism and Slavery," *The Nation*, May 1, 2015, https://www.thenation.com/article/capitalism-and-slavery/ (accessed Nov. 1, 2017). See also Sven Beckert and Seth Rockman, *Slavery's Capitalism: A New History of American Economic Development* (Philadelphia: University of Pennsylvania Press, 2016). On slavery and the American university, see Alfred L. Brophy, *University, Court, and Slave: Pro-Slavery Thought in Southern Colleges and Courts and the Coming of Civil War* (New York: Oxford University Press, 2016), and Craig Steven Wilder, *Ebony and Ivy: Race, Slavery and the Troubled History of America's Universities* (New York: Bloomsbury, 2013). On slavery and medical science, see Harriet A. Washington, *Medical Apartheid: The Dark History of Medical Experimentation on Black Americans from Colonial Times to the Present* (New York: Knopf, 2008), and Deirdre Cooper Owens, *Medical Bondage: Race, Gender, and the Origins of American Gynecology* (Athens: University of Georgia Press, 2017).

24. Oliver O'Donovan, *The Desire of the Nations: Rediscovering the Roots of Political Theology* (New York: Cambridge University Press, 1996), 184–85. Cf. O'Donovan's further remarks on slavery in *The Ways of Judgment: The Bampton Lectures, 2003* (Grand Rapids, MI: Eerdmans, 2005), 247–48, and in "Liberté B: Théologie morale," in *Dictionnaire critique de théologie*, ed. Jean-Yves Lacoste (Paris: Presses Universitaires de France, 1998), 654–66.

25. For a helpful survey of O'Donovan's considerable contributions and their reception within political Augustinianism, see Bruno, *Political Augustinianism*, 191–93.

26. Gilroy, "Living Memory," 179.

27. My thanks to Charles Mathewes for pushing me on this point.

28. O'Donovan, *The Desire of the Nations*, 184–85. Whatever differences may exist between the Greek and Roman sets of slave terms, historian Myles Lavan is right to conclude that both "*douleia* and *seruitus* always retain the force of their connection within the domain of chattel slavery." His discussion of the cluster of Latin words, expressions, and images of Roman slavery (*seruus, seruire, seruitus*, etc.) as well as their "mutually entailing antonyms in the domains of freedom on the one hand (*liber, libertas*) and mastery on the other

(*dominus, domination, dominari*)," together with his analysis of related imagery like chains and the yoke, has strongly informed my thinking throughout. See *Slaves to Rome: Paradigms of Empire in Roman Culture* (New York: Cambridge University Press, 2013), 75ff. For an example of a text from Augustine which thoroughly relies upon the imagery of slavery not with *servitus* language, but by an extended, somewhat convoluted metaphor about shackles and iron fetters, see *en. Ps.* 149.15. *Expositions of the Psalms,* trans. Maria Boulding, *WSA* III/14–17 (Hyde Park, NY: New City Press, 2000-2004).

29. Again, this view cannot support the evidence now presented by the new school of slavery and capitalism referenced in note 23 above, though it's worth noting that the would-be "newness" of that school conceals the much earlier work of Black historians like Eric Williams, C. L. R. James, and Walter Rodney, a fact Edward E. Baptist acknowledges and reflects upon thoughtfully in the Afterword to his *The Half Has Never Been Told: Slavery and the Making of American Capitalism* (New York: Basic Books, 2014), 424-25.

30. O'Donovan, *The Desire of the Nations,* 184-85.

31. These conditions of life are so widely known about the daily life of most ancient slaves that it is difficult to cite one particular source, but I have learned most from the careful scholarship of Jennifer Glancy, Keith Bradley, Kyle Harper, Peter Garnsey, and J. Albert Harrill.

32. This sensibility, animating the project as a whole, is deeply indebted to a certain intellectual style which, as Joshua Myers argues, is concerned with interrogating "whether the silences at the center of this corrective work [of filling in the 'silences' of Black intellectual history] were *constitutive* of the disciplines that were subject to their exposure? What does it mean to expose a silence if it was not simply overlooked, but intentionally ignored in order to advance a particular regime of truth? Put another way, given the interests that disciplines serve and the political function that the university performs both historically and currently, do the silences that we believe call for our correction actually exist for a purpose?" (emphasis mine). See Myers, "The Order of Disciplinarity, the Terms of Silence," *Critical Ethnic Studies* 4 (2018): 108.

33. O'Donovan, *The Desire of the Nations,* 183ff.

34. Neil Roberts, *Freedom as Marronage* (Chicago: University of Chicago Press, 2015), 28.

35. After all, according to O'Donovan, modern slavery was merely "a recidivist movement within later Christendom," since it never "re-enter[ed] its mainstream economic organization." O'Donovan, *The Desire of the Nations,* 264.

36. For a careful analytical philosophical treatment of this epistemic dynamic of social cognition, see Charles W. Mills, "White Ignorance," in *Black Rights / White Wrongs: The Critique of Racial Liberalism* (New York: Oxford University Press, 2017).

37. Audre Lorde, "A Litany for Survival," in *The Collected Poems of Audre Lorde* (New York: Norton, 1997), 255.

38. Eric Gregory, *Politics and the Order of Love: An Augustinian Ethic of Democratic Citizenship* (Chicago: University of Chicago Press, 2008), 54.

39. Lane Fox, *Augustine,* xi.

40. Rowan Williams, "Patriarchal Villains? It's Time to Re-think St Paul and St Augustine," *New Statesman,* Nov. 10, 2015, https://www.newstatesman.com/politics/2015/11/patriarchal-villains-it-s-time-re-think-st-paul-and-st-augustine (accessed Oct. 3, 2017).

41. I am again indebted to chapter 1 of Roberts's *Freedom as Marronage* for this line of argumentation.

42. Consider for instance the moral reflections of James W. C. Pennington, better known as the "fugitive blacksmith," an excerpt of which is published under the fitting title "Great Moral Dilemma" in *African American Religious History: A Documentary Witness*, 2nd ed. (Durham, NC: Duke University Press, 1999), 81–88. Here Pennington offers a critical analysis of the moral situation he faced upon being accused of being a fugitive: must he lie, remain silent, or tell the truth? The point is not that Augustine or Augustinians have not reflected upon such questions, but rather, they have not reflected upon what it means that the *enslaved* person himself or herself engages in moral reasoning, enacts moral agency, and thus poses a set of questions back upon the masters themselves.

43. Charles Mathewes, *The Republic of Grace: Augustinian Thoughts for Dark Times* (Grand Rapids, MI: Eerdmans, 2010), 8.

44. Mathewes, *Republic of Grace*, 4.

45. As Danielle S. Allen writes, with characteristic subtlety concerning the racial dimension of the "two-pronged citizenship" she theorizes: "All citizens must confront the paradox that they have been promised sovereignty and rarely feel it. Herein lies the single most difficult feature of life in a democracy. Democratic citizens are by definition empowered only to be disempowered. As a result, democratic citizenship requires rituals to manage the psychological tension that arises from being a nearly powerless sovereign. For a long time, in this country, the solution to this paradoxical fact that most democratic citizens are, at the end of the day, relatively powerless sovereigns was the two-pronged citizenship of domination and acquiescence. These old bad habits dealt with the inevitable fact of loss in political life by assigning to one group all the work of being sovereign, and to another group most of the work of accepting the significant losses that kept the polity stable." See Allen, *Talking to Strangers: Anxieties of Citizenship since Brown v. Board of Education* (Chicago: University of Chicago Press, 2004), 41.

46. Another recent account of the Black struggle for citizenship presses beyond the often singular focus upon the *Dred Scott* decision to reckon with the movement among African Americans, beginning in the 1820s, to claim birthright citizenship amid calls for colonization (resettling African Americans in Africa). See Martha S. Jones, *Birthright Citizens: A History of Race and Rights in Antebellum America* (New York: Cambridge University Press, 2018).

47. I thank Amaryah Armstrong for this line of argument.

48. Kyle Harper's translation. See Harper, *Slavery in the Late Roman World*, 347–48.

49. For an overview of the household in Augustine's political thought, particularly in its relation to the *civitas*, see Kevin L. Hughes, "Local Politics: The Political Place of the Household in Augustine's City of God," in *Augustine and Politics*, ed. John Doody, Kevin L. Hughes, and Kim Paffenroth (Lanham, MD: Lexington, 2005), 145–64. The treatment of the *dominus* and of the issue of slavery is underdeveloped.

50. My use of "the master's house" to suggest a shared symbolic space which encompasses both Augustine's literal and metaphorical uses of slavery broadly echoes what historian Kate Cooper notes about the double-valence of the *domus* concept itself within Roman culture. *Domus* at once names a "physical space" *and* a way of "represent[ing] the household

as a lived social reality . . . [as] the crucial unit in the pyramid of social order." See Cooper, *The Fall of the Roman Household* (New York: Cambridge University Press, 2007), 110.

51. I appropriate the concept of "symbolic space" from Pierre Bourdieu with several key reservations. Loïc Wacquant offers a helpfully technical definition of Bourdieu's conception of symbolic space as "the grid of mental classifications that guide persons in their cognitive and conative construction of the world," while underscoring the need to identify correspondences and distortions between symbolic space, social space, and physical space. I find this framework useful for thinking through "the master's house" in Augustine, even as I note the following reservations: (1) I am skeptical of the tendency among scholars of slavery to borrow "high" sociological concepts while refusing to engage the sophisticated theoretical frameworks which have emerged specifically to analyze slavery, often from the experiences of the formerly enslaved themselves; (2) there is a temptation to "speak Bourdieuse," which, as Loïc Wacquant has observed, often functions without rigorous engagement with the conceptuality itself; and (3) by borrowing from the sociology of knowledge, there is the temptation of suggesting that Augustine's thought is being treated less as a partner in an ongoing intellectual conversation, and more as an object of critique, or worse, deconstructed (in the crude sense) as a purveyor of ideology. This is not the case. Instead, concepts like social space and symbolic power are useful to me only insofar as they bring us closer to Augustine as a thinker and ongoing interlocutor for ethical theory, not insofar as they would reduce his concepts to a mere effect of his world (Pierre Bourdieu, "Social Space and Symbolic Power," *Sociological Theory* 7 [1989]: 14–25; Loïc Wacquant, "Four Transversal Principles for Putting Bourdieu to Work," *Anthropological Theory* 18, no. 1 [2018]: 3–17). My thinking here is also informed by Willie James Jennings's appropriation of Henri Lefebvre's "threefold idea of space as perceived, conceived, and lived." See Jennings, *The Christian Imagination: Theology and the Origins of Race* (New Haven, CT: Yale University Press, 2010), 350n63.

52. This framework often rests upon idyllic pastoral tropes—cheerful mammy figures, kindly old masters, white and Black children playing together in the yard outside—which served to bolster proslavery ideology. "These images are problematic," write Clifton Ellis and Rebecca Ginsburg, "not because such events never happened, but because when these caricatures serve as stand-ins for all enslaved workers . . . we lose sight of the brutality and violence that was at the system's core. These lingering images are an injustice to the contributions made by enslaved workers and to the debt owed them." See Ellis and Ginsburg, Introduction, in *Cabin, Quarter, Plantation: Architecture and Landscapes of North American Slavery,* ed. Clifton Ellis and Rebecca Ginsburg (New Haven, CT: Yale University Press, 2010), 1–2.

53. On the postbellum plantation household as an illuminating window into the ongoing transformations of race and gender, citizenship and nation which emerged in the wake of slavery's juridical abolition, see especially Thavolia Glymph's pathbreaking *Out of the House of Bondage: The Transformation of the Plantation Household* (New York: Cambridge University Press, 2008). For a classic treatment of menial service in the postbellum house of the master, see W. E. B. Du Bois, "The Servant in the House," in *Darkwater: Voices from Within the Veil* (New York: Washington Square Press, 2004). And for a more recent foray into postbellum Black women domestic workers as a scene of untold political and social imaginings, see Hartman, *Wayward Lives.*

54. Peter Brown, "Dialogue with God."

55. *conf.* 2.6.14.

56. For instance, in the passage just quoted, Chadwick gives "Lord" the first time and "Master" the second, yet the word is *dominum* both times, clearly comprising a single, extended image.

57. On this trope of the enslaved body's vulnerability to violence functioning metaphorically, see Glancy, *Slavery in Early Christianity*, 102ff.

58. In *The City of God*, to illustrate the just correlation of temporal sin and eternal punishment, Augustine points out "it is entirely just that a slave should pay the penalty of years in shackles when he has provoked his master with no more than a passing word" (*civ.* 21.11).

59. In the first sentence here, I am quoting from *Homilies on the Gospel of John*, trans. Edmund Hill, *WSA* III/12 (Hyde Park, NY: New City Press, 2009), 224. But in the second sentence, Hill's translation oddly obscures the brutal imagery at work by rendering the Latin (*Cognoscat se Agar, ponat cervicem*) as "Let Hagar come to know herself, and set aside her disdain." Therefore, I have used the more literal translation found in *Nicene and Post-Nicene Fathers*, vol. 7, trans. John Gibb, ed. Philip Schaff (Buffalo, NY: Christian Literature Publishing, 1888).

60. *ep.* 185.15, as cited in Harper, *Slavery in the Late Roman World*, 183.

61. For background, see Garnsey, *Ideas of Slavery*, chapter 9. For a recent treatment of Augustine as offering an "immanent critique" of Stoicism, see Gerald P. Boersma, "Augustine's immanent critique of Stoicism," *Scottish Journal of Theology* 70, no. 2 (May 2017): 184–97.

62. *civ.* 19.15 and throughout. Cf. *In Johannis Evangelium tractatus* 41.4: "The slave of a man who is oppressed by the harsh domination of his master seeks respite in flight. But where is the slave of sin to flee? . . . Sometimes men flee to the church, and lawless as they are, wishing to be without a master, but not without their sins, generally give us a lot of trouble. On the other hand, it sometimes happens that men who are subject to an illegal and shameful yoke, flee to the church because they are freeborn men held in slavery, and they appeal to the bishops. The bishop is considered unmerciful if he does not make efforts to prevent the suppression of free birth. Let us all flee to Christ, let us appeal to God to free us from sin. . . ." See *Homilies on the Gospel of John* 41–124, trans. Edmund Hill, *WSA* III/13, ed. Allan D. Fitzgerald, O.S.A. (Hyde Park, NY: New City Press, 2009).

63. Susannah Elm, "Sold to Sin through Origo: Augustine of Hippo and the Late Roman Slave Trade," *Studia Patristica* 98 (2016): 15.

64. See, for example, *De libero arbitrio* 1.4.9.25 on sin, order, and providence; *De utilitate credendi* 12.27 on epistemology, the foolish, and the wise; *De doctrina Christiana* 3.4.8 on metaphorical and literal senses of texts; and *De bono conjugali* 17.19 on order and marriage.

65. *Contra Iulianum opus imperfectum libri sex* 4.12.61. Here Augustine is quoting Cicero with (not uncomplicated) approval, particularly noting his highly suggestive distinction: the soul rules the body as a king commands his subjects, but the soul rules *lust* as masters their slaves: "Masters harass their slaves as the best part of the soul, which is wisdom, harasses the vicious and weak parts of the same soul, such as lusts, anger, and the other disturbing forces."

66. *civ.* 18.2.

67. Conceptualizing the imperial project of Rome in terms of master–slave relations is by no means unique to Augustine, nor is it self-evident that such a conceptualization is *necessarily* a subversive "critique" of empire, as is often supposed. To the contrary, as Myles Lavan's excellent recent work has shown, the elite men who governed the Roman Empire themselves were happy to use the rhetorical and symbolic tools of slavery to describe their own imperial project. See Lavan, *Slaves to Rome: Paradigms of Empire in Roman Culture* (New York: Cambridge University Press, 2013).

68. Oliver O'Donovan, "The Political Thought of *City of God* 19," in *Bonds of Imperfection: Christian Politics, Past and Present,* ed. Oliver O'Donovan and Joan Lockwood O'Donovan (Grand Rapids, MI: Eerdmans, 2004), 72. On those pushing for a different "textual center of gravity," one which does not restrict Augustine's political thought to a realm separable from his doctrinal thinking, see Charles Mathewes, *A Theology of Public Life* (Cambridge: Cambridge University Press, 2008), 20. Concurring with that expansion, I have been pressing the matter of slavery in Augustine beyond Book 19-centric discussions of natural subordination versus political subordination which were so important in the work of R. A. Markus and his interpreters. See Markus, *Saeculum: History and Society in the Theology of St. Augustine* (Cambridge: Cambridge University Press, 1970), especially Appendix B, "*De civitate Dei,* XIX, 14–15 and the Origins of Political Authority."

69. *civ.* 19.15.

70. Williams, "Patriarchal Villains." It is not immediately clear how to read this statement in relation to Williams's recently updated version of his classic "Politics and the Soul" essay: "Augustine does not envisage a situation in which anyone is able to *decide* about the structures of governmental authority ... he is conspicuously a man of the *bas-empire,* assuming, unclassically, the givenness of the existing order. Indeed, the most disturbing and uncongenial feature of this analysis for most modern students is probably the absence of any idea that the actual *structures* of government and society are answerable to some critical principle." See Williams, *On Augustine,* 123–24.

71. Florentinus, *Digest* 1.5.4. Cf. Ulpian, *Digest* 50.17.32. Both as cited in Garnsey, *Ideas of Slavery,* 64; for the general overview, see chaps. 5 and 6. Garnsey's basic conclusion about the upshot of attributing slavery to sin is simplistic, but essentially correct: "Sin had issued in slavery, but slavery was not itself sin; it could not be if it was an aspect of God's (just) judgment of men" (241). I return to these issues at length in Chapter 4. For a fuller comparative intellectual history of Augustine's thinking on slavery relative to his philosophical and theological predecessors and contemporaries, see Toni Alimi, *Slaves of God: Augustine and Other Romans on Religion and Politics* (Princeton, NJ: Princeton University Press, forthcoming).

72. *civ.* 19.15.

73. *en. Ps.* 102.14, as quoted in Harper, *Slavery in the Late Roman World,* 230. Similarly, in *civ.* 19.16, Augustine notes that if a slave "disrupts domestic peace by his disobedience," then whipping him is "for the benefit" of the slave himself, to bring him "back into line with the peace from which he had broken away."

74. Throughout the book, I reference several illumining examples drawn from the reception histories of Augustine's political thought, especially entries from the magisterial *Oxford Guide to the Historical Reception of Augustine,* ed. Karla Pollmann and Willemien Otten (New

York: Oxford University Press, 2013), including the School of Salamanca, Robert Bellarmine, eighteenth-century slaveholding Jesuits in the Americas, and U.S. Civil War–era clerics like John Henry Hopkins (whose appropriation of Augustine for defending slavery I discuss in Chapter 2).

75. Thomas Aquinas, Supplement to the *Tertia Pars* of the *Summa Theologiae*, q. 52, a. 1, ad 2. The citation here is to the Benziger Bros. edition, 1947, translated by Fathers of the English Dominican Province, available at the website of the Thomistic Institute at the Dominican House of Studies in Washington, D.C.: aquinas101.thomisticinstitute.org.

76. See Christopher Tomlins, *Freedom Bound: Law, Labor, and Civic Identity in Colonizing English America, 1580–1865* (Cambridge: Cambridge University Press, 2010), 420–23. See also the mention of Augustine in conversation with these later retrievals in Robert A. Williams, Jr., *The American Indian in Western Legal Thought: The Discourse of Conquest* (Oxford: Oxford University Press, 1992), 101. I thank Gregory Lee for bringing my attention to Williams's book. For another striking historical view into the complex relation, but ultimate compatibility, between the Augustinian view and a fully elaborated "natural slave theory," see Anthony Pagden's treatment of Sepúlveda: "Sepulveda's main rhetorical device in the dialogue, Aristotle's theory of natural slavery (to which I shall return), is omitted and in its place we find the Augustinian argument, with which few of the Salamanca theologians could have taken issue, that slavery is a punishment for sin. This Sepulveda maintained could be applied to the Indians because of their crimes against nature." Anthony Pagden, *The Fall of Natural Man: The American Indian and the Origins of Comparative Ethnology* (Cambridge: Cambridge University Press, 1982), 112.

77. Many Black thinkers have advanced this claim. For one starting point, see B. Anthony Bogues, "Reflections on African-American Political Thought: The Many Rivers of Freedom," in *A Companion to African-American Studies,* ed. Lewis R. Gordon and Jane Anna Gordon (Malden, MA: Blackwell, 2006), 427: "The matter is not as simple as Du Bois's argument that liberalism was a sham for the black population; instead, it is to understand that liberalism, as it unfolded in America, was and is also a part of white supremacy. In other words, American liberalism is *racial liberalism.*" He further cites the now classic work of Charles Mills, *The Racial Contract* (Ithaca, NY: Cornell University Press, 1997). For a recent, accessible introduction to the compatibility of modern political liberalism with slavery, see Andrew Zimmerman, "When Liberalism Defended Slavery," in *Race Capitalism Justice,* ed. Walter Johnson (Cambridge, MA: MIT Press, 2018), 83–89. See also Laurent Dubois, "An Enslaved Enlightenment: Rethinking the Intellectual History of the French Atlantic," *Social History* 31, no. 1 (2006): 1–14.

78. Ruden, Introduction to Augustine, *Confessions,* xxxiii.

79. Brown, "Dialogue with God."

80. Toni Morrison, *Playing in the Dark: Whiteness and the Literary Imagination* (New York: Vintage Books, 1993), 37.

81. Morrison, *Playing in the Dark,* 17.

82. Morrison, *Playing in the Dark,* 38.

83. Hortense Spillers, "Notes on an Alternative Model—Neither/Nor," in *Black, White, and in Color* (Chicago: University of Chicago Press, 2003), 302 (emphasis mine). Also influencing my thought along related lines is the following from Spillers: "The captive body, then,

brings into focus a gathering of social realities as well as a metaphor for *value* so thoroughly interwoven in their literal and figurative emphases that the distinctions between them [literal and figurative senses] are virtually useless" (208).

84. Hartman, *Scenes of Subjection*, 38.

85. Hartman, *Scenes of Subjection*, 34.

86. For an introduction to the concept of fungibility, a window into its crucial role in wide-ranging debates within Black Studies (not only between Afropessimists and their critics, but in its recent redeployments in Jennifer Morgan and C. Riley Snorton), and a striking ecological reading of fungibility which refuses "reducing . . . Black figures and porous flesh as abject objects" and instead "reveals the ways that all bodies are already embedded in and run conterminously with nonhuman life," see Tiffany Lethabo King, *The Black Shoals: Offshore Formations of Black and Native Studies* (Durham, NC: Duke University Press, 2019), chapter 3, "At the Pores of the Plantation," 111–40 (the portion cited here is from p. 114). Stephen Marshall suggests that the hard-to-pin-down conflict between so-called Afropessimists and Black optimists is rooted in a struggle for how to interpret Black fungibility as an analytic framework. See Marshall, "The Political Life of Fungibility," *Theory and Event* 15, no. 3 (2012).

87. Joshel, "Slavery and Roman Literary Culture," 215.

88. *en. Ps.* 124.7.

89. Cf. Charles Mills's philosophical account of social cognition under conditions of racial domination, whereby "the conceptual array with which the cognizer approaches the world needs itself to be scrutinized for its adequacy to the world, for how well it maps the reality it claims to be describing . . . in most cases *the concepts will not be neutral* but oriented toward a certain understanding, embedded in sub-theories and larger theories about how things work." See Mills, "White Ignorance," 60 (emphasis mine).

90. Jennings, *The Christian Imagination*, 183–84.

91. James Wetzel, *Augustine and the Limits of Virtue* (Cambridge: Cambridge University Press, 1992), 65.

92. Indeed, as Jennifer Glancy writes, the virtues which have been called "slave morality" since Nietzsche—obedience, humility, fidelity, respect, and so on—are more rightly called *slaveholder* morality: "the attitudes that slaveholders desired to inculcate in the enslaved bodies of their households" (Glancy, *Slavery in Early Christianity*, 142; cf. 131ff.). She further notes that Roman jurists proscribe causing a negative moral influence on another master's slave, "not only for making a good slave bad, but also for making a bad slave worse," a fact which casts new light on the statement I quoted from Augustine above, that "[Christ] has not made slaves free, but turned bad slaves into good slaves."

93. For more, see the section on the contrast between good slaves and bad slaves as a trope of Roman law and literature in the work of Sandra Joshel, who writes: "As modern readers are all too aware, law is not literature, yet in Rome law reflects literature—and literature law—in a society where *elite buyers, lawyers and authors were all masters, participants in the same discourse and rooted in the same interests and values.* In literature as in law, loyalty, obedience, good service and deference to a master mark good slaves; the opposite qualities identify bad ones." See Joshel, "Slavery and Roman Literary Culture," 217.

94. See Bradley, "Resisting Slavery at Rome," 362–84.

95. For a lucid, extended overview of the scholarly debates concerning the comparative approach, see Enrico Dal Lago and Constantina Katsari, "The Study of Ancient and Modern Slave Systems: Setting an Agenda for Comparison," in *Slave Systems: Ancient and Modern*, ed. Enrico Dal Lago and Constantina Katsari (New York: Cambridge University Press, 2008), 3–31.

96. For example, Roberts, *Freedom as Marronage*; Lawrie Balfour, *Democracy's Reconstruction: Thinking Politically with W. E. B. Du Bois* (New York: Oxford University Press, 2011); and Getachew, *Worldmaking After Empire*.

97. James underscores that American universities must discover in Black Studies neither an intellectual sideshow, nor a mere "concession to black students but a great opening and penetration into *their own* intellectual life and understanding. That here is an opportunity to extend the field of intellectual inquiry which they have neglected up to now, a chance to penetrate more into *the fundamentals of Western civilization*, which cannot be understood unless black studies is involved." See C. L. R. James, "The Black Scholar Interviews: C. L. R. James," *Black Scholar* 2, no. 1 (September 1970): 42–43 (emphasis mine).

98. See the discussion in O'Donovan, *The Desire of Nations*, of "The Southern School" and the retrieval of tradition as the two most powerful alternatives to secular liberalism on the relation of religion to politics. Yet O'Donovan strangely lumps many things into the so-called Southern School, so that he often seems to believe he has dealt with liberation theology across multiple fields of inquiry—feminism, Black thought, queer theology—despite having shown no evidence in the argument of having read, let alone seriously engaged, the major texts in the discourses he purports to explain.

TWO. The Road and the Woods

Epigraph 1: *civ.* 19.17.
Epigraph 2: Hartman, *Scenes of Subjection*, 151.

1. *en. Ps.* 55.9.

2. "Augustine . . . provide[s] properly political guidance, mostly by giving the lexicon and syntax of a Christian account of the public thing. . . . This grammar has *peregrinatio* as its central term of art." Paul J. Griffiths, "Secularity and the *Saeculum*," in Wetzel, ed., *Augustine's* City of God, 52.

3. In deliberating upon how to characterize his move from London to the United States, Luke Bretherton illustrates the dangers of conflating, for instance, peregrination with exodus: "I thought of using the word *exodus*, but that would imply that London was a place of oppression from which I was liberated. To say that would not only be a misnomer, it would also deeply offend my mother, who is, as you can imagine, somewhat sensitive on these matters." Luke Bretherton, "From London to Durham: A Theological Peregrination," *Other Journal* 22 (May 9, 2013).

4. I thank Luke Bretherton for the phrase "density of meaning" and the related idea. For a summary of the translation issues, see Sarah Stewart-Kroeker, "Excursus: On Pilgrimage," in *Pilgrimage as Moral and Aesthetic Formation in Augustine's Thought*, 10–17.

5. My use of the phrase "the shape of human life" is indebted to Kathryn Tanner, who finds in it "the fundamental question of ethics." See Tanner, *Jesus, Humanity and the Trinity: A Brief Systematic Theology* (Minneapolis: Fortress Press, 2001), 67.

6. For a recent summation of the history of Augustinian scholarship on the relation of the image to Plotinus and the Platonists, see Stewart-Kroeker, *Pilgrimage as Moral and Aesthetic Formation in Augustine's Thought,* chapter 1.

7. Leszek Kolakowski, "In Praise of Exile," *Times Literary Supplement,* Oct. 11, 1985: 1133–34, reprinted in Kolakowski, *Modernity on Endless Trial* (Chicago: University of Chicago Press, 1990), 57.

8. This was the theme of a 2017 panel of the Augustine and Augustinianism group at the American Academy of Religion annual meeting, entitled "Augustine on Exile and Migration," at which I presented an early draft of this chapter.

9. *conf.* 7.27, 131–32, as quoted in Stewart-Kroeker, *Pilgrimage as Moral and Aesthetic Formation in Augustine's Thought,* 19 (ellipsis original). Stewart-Kroeker quotes the same passage without ellipsis on p. 37.

10. Matthew Levering, *The Theology of St. Augustine: An Introductory Guide to His Most Important Work* (Grand Rapids, MI: Baker, 2013), 101; Annemaré Kotzé, *Augustine's Confessions: Communicative Purpose and Audience* (Leiden: Brill, 2004), 160; Michael Barnes, "Way and Wilderness: An Augustinian Dialogue with Buddhism," in *Augustine and World Religions,* ed. Brian Brown, John Doody, and Kim Paffenroth (Lanham, MD: Lexington, 2008), 115–40, at 130. See also Eugene TeSelle, *Augustine* (Nashville: Abingdon, 2006), 7, which, in a chapter called, notably, "Augustine's Journey," makes reference to the passage in question, but alludes only to "rebel angels," leaving no trace of the imagery of fugitives, those who had deserted either their master or their military duties.

11. Although it would raise an interesting and distinct set of issues, for the sake of space I leave aside here the military aspect of the image and focus on slaves. For one starting point on thinking the soldier in Augustine, see R. W. Dyson, *St. Augustine of Hippo: The Christian Transformation of Political Philosophy* (New York: Continuum, 2005), 116–41. For my purposes, what matters is that both groups comprising this image—deserters and fugitives—*can* be grouped together for Augustine, implying not merely a sociological fact about Augustine's time, but that within his moral imagination, both are similarly *elsewhere* than they belong: both have rejected their obligation to and defected from their assigned place within existing social and political order, the only chance of securing earthly peace. This is suggested, for instance, in *ep.* 189, where Augustine writes to a military tribune who was considering becoming a monk, urging him to remain a soldier: "Augustine was not about to have the gifts of a good soldier closeted or cloistered while barbarians were at the gate," writes Peter Iver Kaufman, "Augustine's Dystopia," in Wetzel, ed., *Augustine's City of God,* 68–69.

12. Late in the process of revising this chapter, I discovered that James K. A. Smith's recent popular book on Augustine uses just this term to describe the road: "The road is iconic because it is the symbol of liberation." He mentions in passing a few pages later the contrast figure of the runaway in Augustine without identifying the figure as a runaway *slave,* and without going deeper into the questions posed by slavery in the metaphor, or by the way its afterlives in the present shape our political imaginaries. See *On the Road with Saint Augustine: A Real-World Spirituality for Restless Hearts* (Grand Rapids, MI: Brazos Press, 2019), 59. The chapter is entitled "Freedom: How to Escape."

13. The classic and still-influential example is R. A. Markus, *Saeculum: History and Society in the Theology of St. Augustine* (New York: Cambridge University Press, 1970), esp.

chapter 7. See also Peter Iver Kaufmann, *Redeeming Politics* (Princeton, NJ: Princeton University Press, 1990), 132–35.

14. In 1939, T. S. Eliot famously pondered whether we have arrived at a place "at which practising Christians must be recognized as a minority . . . in a society which has ceased to be Christian." *The Idea of a Christian Society* (New York: Harcourt, Brace and Company, 1940). As cited in Robert A. Markus, *Christianity and the Secular* (Notre Dame, IN: Notre Dame University Press, 2006), 1.

15. See Jennings, *The Christian Imagination*, 8. For prominent examples of such assessments, see Richard John Neuhaus, *American Babylon: Notes of a Christian Exile* (New York: Basic Books, 2009), and R. R. Reno, *In the Ruins of the Church: Sustaining Faith in an Age of Diminished Christianity* (Grand Rapids: Brazos Press, 2002). A more recent (and far more painfully superficial) example is Rod Dreher's widely discussed *The Benedict Option: A Strategy for Christians in a Post-Christian Nation* (New York: Sentinel, 2017), which urges Christians, who comprise just over 70 percent of the U.S. population, to "embrace exile and the possibility of martyrdom" (120). "We faithful orthodox Christians didn't ask for internal exile from a country we thought was our own, but that's where we find ourselves. We are a minority now, so let's be a creative one" (99). Where I build upon Jennings is to explore how the pilgrimage/exile image as a model for Christian politics, from its *earliest* elaborations in Augustine, has long provided Christian moral life an idiom in which to reconcile eternal longings and real temporal power within a theologically and scripturally intricate frame.

16. For instance, Johannes van Oort's often-cited *Jerusalem and Babylon: A Study into Augustine's* City of God *and the Sources of His Doctrine of the Two Cities* (Leiden: Brill, 1991) exhaustively documents every occurrence of keywords *peregrinus, peregrinatio,* and *peregrinari,* even indicating each of the occurrences deemed *unrelated* to his subject matter "for the sake of completeness" (132n608). By contrast, van Oort mentions slaves just once, writing: "the citizen of the city of God . . . orders his earthly relationships in accordance with this peace: in his household, in his relations with slaves, in the proper exercise of power in his household and toward his slaves," offering no further explanation (147).

17. "The symbol gives rise to thought" comes from Paul Ricouer, *The Symbolism of Evil,* trans. Emerson Buchanan (Boston: Beacon Press, 1969), 237.

18. I use the term "agency" with a set of reservations hinted at in the Hartman epigraph above and explored with great clarity and precision in Walter Johnson, "On Agency," *Journal of Social History* 37 (2003): 113–24, surrounding the ways in which aiming to restore "agency" to human lives constituted as objects under racial slavery is fraught.

19. *civ.* 19.15.

20. I adapt the notion of moral-symbolic universe here from Peter L. Berger and Thomas Luckmann, *The Social Construction of Reality: A Treatise in the Sociology of Knowledge* (London: Penguin Press, 1967), 110–22.

21. Jennings, *The Christian Imagination*, 183.

22. Charles Mathewes, for instance, writes, "If the fundamental problem of modern politics is pluralism, this is a fundamentally religious problem, and it must be confronted as such." See Mathewes, *A Theology of Public Life* (Cambridge: Cambridge University Press, 2007), 111. The chapter that follows is, in some sense, an extended argument that the set of issues contained within the conceptual framing of "pluralism" hardly exhausts, much

less constitutes the "fundamental" aspect of, the "problem of modern politics," and that recognizing this attunes us to a different set of concepts—slavery and mastery—in Augustine.

23. Here, as above, it may be necessary to reassure some readers that to proceed in this fashion does not entail uncritically or anachronistically positing an *equivalence* or a relation of identity between ancient and modern slave systems, as though only in such a situation of pure equivalence would the "point of contact" I identified be possible. By definition, no two historical scenes are equivalent. What is necessary to begin the conversation I want is not to establish that ancient Mediterranean and modern Atlantic slave systems are "the same," only to establish that both *are* slave systems—where "slave systems" is not a general invocation of slavery, but a technical and precise category used by historians of slavery, which makes judicious comparison possible. (See Lago and Katsari, "The Study of Ancient and Modern Slave Systems.") To bring a successful objection to my particular use of comparative perspective, one would need to (a) identify a particular difference between ancient and modern slave contexts and (b) specify how this difference alters or challenges a specific site of my argument. This is in principle entirely possible to do, and an entirely fair mode of critique. Yet in my experience thus far, the sort of critic who worries about anachronism has not completed this work, nor seems particularly interested in starting it. They have not identified, say, how differences in legal procedures of manumission, or the difficulties of established enslaved birth rates in antiquity, or the ambiguities of honor culture in the U.S. South would specifically challenge either my reading of Augustine, or my reading of Atlantic social worlds. Instead, the objection nearly always concerns the sheer *fact* of nonequivalence between ancient slavery and modern slavery itself, as though this fact alone can stop the conversation before it begins. Yet this bare fact of nonequivalence is not thought to preclude *starting* a conversation about the contemporary significance of Augustine's views on culturally bound, historically nonequivalent matters like civic authority, marriage, citizenship, ecclesial offices, and so on. And so it is worth exploring why slavery alone *must* remain locked in the attic of the past, and it is this very desire to do so which, perhaps more than most things, displays the very cross-temporal connections it denies.

24. Robin D. G. Kelley, *Freedom Dreams: The Black Radical Imagination* (Boston: Beacon Press, 2002).

25. Sarah Jane Cervenak and J. Kameron Carter, "Untitled and Outdoors: Thinking with Saidiya Hartman," *Women & Performance: A Journal of Feminist Theory* 27 (2017): 45–55. A question I will return to, but flag now briefly: How might we avoid the temptation to assimilate pilgrimage to fugitivity and instead first confront the intimacy of the pilgrims and masters? That is, how do we refuse to jump straight toward a fugitive model of the City of God and instead confront "the problem of the master"?

26. Cedric Robinson, *Black Marxism: The Making of the Black Radical Tradition* (Chapel Hill: University of North Carolina Press, 2000), 73, as quoted as an epigraph in Fred Moten, *In the Break: The Aesthetics of the Black Radical Tradition* (Minneapolis: University of Minnesota Press, 2003).

27. For careful disentangling of the various uses and misuses of this highly contested link—between *saeculum* and "the secular"—see Griffiths, "Secularity and the *Saeculum*."

28. James Wetzel, Introduction to *Augustine's City of God*, 4. The critics Wetzel cites are Rowan Williams, John Milbank, Oliver O'Donovan, and Robert Dodaro, and to these we might add Charles Mathewes, Luke Bretherton, and Eric Gregory.

29. Robert Markus, *Christianity and the Secular* (Notre Dame, IN: Notre Dame University Press, 2006), 73.

30. See the exchanges across multiple article and book chapters between Peter Iver Kaufman and Eric Gregory, including Kaufman, "Christian Realism and Augustinian (?) Liberalism," *Journal of Religious Ethics* 38, no. 4 (2010): 706–13; "Augustine's Punishments," *Harvard Theological Review* 109 (2016): 550–66; Eric Gregory, "Strange Fruit: Augustine, Liberalism, and the Good Samaritan," in *Christianity, Democracy, and the Shadow of Constantine*, ed. George E. Demacopolous and Aristotle Papanikolaou (New York: Fordham University Press, 2017), 98–110, at 106–8.

31. Gregory and Clair, "Augustinianisms and Thomisms," 191.

32. Gregory, "Strange Fruit," 107.

33. It is worth noting that this is hardly unique to political Augustinianism. For a treatment of this absence in political theory more widely, see Lawrie Balfour, *Democracy's Reconstruction: Thinking Politically with W. E. B. Du Bois* (New York: Oxford University Press, 2011), esp. chapter 1.

34. Gregory, "Strange Fruit," 107.

35. A classic and influential instance of this sensibility comes from Jean Bethke Elshtain's aptly titled *Augustine and the Limits of Politics*: "If Augustine is a thorn in the side of those who would cure the universe once and for all, he similarly torments cynics who disdain any project of human community, or justice, or possibility. We time-bound creatures, doomed or compelled to narrate our lives within temporality, within what Augustine calls the *saeculum*, can gather together the self and forge a compelling if not conflict-free identity. Wisdom comes from experiencing fully the ambivalence and ambiguity that is the human condition." See Elshtain, *Augustine and the Limits of Politics* (Notre Dame, IN: University of Notre Dame Press, 2018), 91.

36. On the important phrase "during the world," see Mathewes, *Theology of Public Life*, 15–23. Similarly, Gregory and Clair write: "It is Augustinian liberals and antiliberals' shared sense of the *temporality* of politics—as fundamentally rooted in the murky origins of sin—that eliminates any *natural* antecedent for political society" (Gregory and Clair, "Augustinianisms and Thomisms," 186).

37. I am indebted here to Joseph Clair, who suggests that this "pair of principles (to prefer and to refer)" provides "in a nutshell, the heart of Augustine's ethical advice," then goes on to probe thoughtfully the unresolved ambiguities and tensions with this framework. See Clair, *Discerning the Good in the Letters and Sermons of Augustine* (New York: Oxford University Press, 2016), 36–37.

38. "[W]hat all of this means for the relationship of citizens of the Heavenly City to the earthly city lies somewhere in between the two extremes of completely abandoning the earthly city and looking to the earthly city to achieve utopian-like harmony and peace." Kristin Deede Johnson, *Theology, Political Theory, and Pluralism: Beyond Tolerance and Difference* (New York: Cambridge University Press, 2007), 169.

39. Luke Bretherton, *Christianity and Contemporary Politics: The Conditions and Possibilities of Faithful Witness* (Malden, MA: Wiley-Blackwell, 2010), 82.

40. By ambivalence, then, I mean to signal the connotations of the whole "lexicon" mentioned above, even as I think "ambivalence" succeeds in holding together the positive and

negative dimensions I discuss below, and enables staying with the language contemporary Augustinians most often rely upon. In addition to the examples already cited, I think, for instance, of the fact that Charles Mathewes uses the words "ambivalent" or "ambivalence" no fewer than eight times in the span of a few paragraphs in the Introduction to *Republic of Grace*, 10–11.

41. Mathewes, *Republic of Grace*, 11.

42. Brown, *Augustine of Hippo*, 323–24.

43. Stewart-Kroeker, *Pilgrimage as Moral and Aesthetic Formation in Augustine's Thought*, 10.

44. Similarly, Rowan Williams identifies the *peregrinatio* as "the basic form of discipleship," then immediately specifies its positive and negative dimensions, or perhaps better, its backward-facing and forward-facing direction: as a sign of our temporal condition, *peregrinatio* marks each moment as one "God obliges me to leave" *and* as "necessary prompt or stimulus to the journey of desire, not as something simply to be negated." See Williams, "Wisdom in Person: Augustine's Christology," in *On Augustine*, 144.

45. Most famously in *civ.* 19.14–17.

46. This assessment of pluralism as the central "need of the present," of course, is not unique to Augustinians or even to Christian political thinkers. In what remains a sorely neglected treatment of liberalism among political theologians, for instance, Paul Kahn writes, in the opening lines of his book, "Every age has its own point of access to ethical and political deliberation. For us, that point is the problem of cultural pluralism." See *Putting Liberalism in Its Place* (Princeton, NJ: Princeton University Press, 2005), 1.

47. This is not to suggest that the emphasis on Augustine's account of earthly peace is the *only* resource Augustinians deploy for engaging modern pluralism. For an engagement with pluralism predicated on other—and in my view, more compelling—Augustinian resources, see Charles Mathewes, "Pluralism, Otherness, and the Augustinian Tradition," *Modern Theology* 14, no. 1 (January 1998): 83–112, which draws more deeply from Augustine's anthropological meditations on the sinful self and his properly theological meditations on God as absolute other.

48. Despite Augustine's critique of Rome's pretensions, Gregory writes, "Augustine could still see that its imperfect peace revealed a natural law in the order of nature. Robbers themselves maintain 'some shadow of peace.' And, by God's providence, 'even the heavenly city . . . while in its state of pilgrimage, avails itself of the peace of earth.' Temporal peace is known both by comparison and contrast with this eternal peace." See Gregory, "Strange Fruit," 101–2.

49. Deede Johnson, 170–71.

50. "On their pilgrimage [citizens of the Heavenly City] are part of the earthly city and share some of its earthly goods. . . . The recognition that earthly peace and the institutions and laws that contribute to that peace are a good desired by heavenly citizens supplies sufficient motivation for the pilgrims of the Heavenly City to support and engage the temporal world." Deede Johnson, 172.

51. Markus, *Christianity and the Secular*, 49–50.

52. Markus, *Saeculum*. James Wetzel suggests, nonetheless, that "his reading remains fundamentally the same." See Introduction to Wetzel, ed., *Augustine's City of God*, 3n5. Cf. Wetzel, "Review of Markus," in *Church History* 76 (2006): 395–97.

53. Markus, *Christianity and the Secular*, 58.

54. Note that this marks a departure from the Augustine of Markus's *Saeculum*, for whom, as Gregory and Clair summarize, "the political is an antiperfectionist institutional arrangement set up merely to secure physical survival" (Gregory and Clair, "Augustinianisms and Thomisms," 181).

55. Markus, *Christianity and the Secular*, 64, 65.

56. Gregory and Clair, "Augustinianisms and Thomisms," 191–92 (emphasis mine).

57. Gregory and Clair, "Augustinianisms and Thomisms," 192.

58. Nor do the authors present it as novel—the point that *is* a novel and significant provocation is their suggestion that it is this move which enables bringing together Thomists and Augustinians beyond the standard interpretations which divide them at the point of their perceived opposition on the "naturalness" or "sinfulness" of political authority.

59. Gregory and Clair rightly identify this turn as the "trend in contemporary political Augustinianism since the work of Dodaro, Gregory, and Mathewes" (Gregory and Clair, "Augustinianisms and Thomisms," 193). Another commonly identified watershed moment is the extraordinarily influential 1987 article by Rowan Williams, "Politics and the Soul: A Reading of the City of God," *Milltown Studies* 19–20 (1987): 55–72.

60. Gregory and Clair, "Augustinianisms and Thomisms," 188–89. For "textual center of gravity" and a related summary of the shifts in both historical and constructive studies of Augustine beyond Book 19, see Mathewes, *Theology of Public Life*, 19ff., and for the related literature, see especially footnotes 26 and 27.

61. Peter Brown, *Religion and Society in the Age of St. Augustine* (New York: Harper and Row, 1972), 42–43. Significantly, Eric Gregory appeals specifically to this passage's notion of the "middle distance" in specifying the overarching framework and central driving concerns of his influential *Politics and the Order of Love: An Augustinian Ethic of Democratic Citizenship* (Chicago: University of Chicago Press, 2008), 56.

62. Brown, *Religion and Society*, 43. Another name for such a bond might be *solidarity*, raising the troubling question of whether those who inhabit the pilgrim path through the world can be in solidarity with the fugitives in the woods so long as they remain bound in loyalty to the master's house. I return to this below.

63. Peter Iver Kaufman has remained, perhaps, the fiercest (if also the most good-humored and liveliest) critic of the citizenship turn, underscoring on historical grounds and close textual readings, again and again, the pessimistic and even "dystopian" strands which most civic Augustinians have tried to overcome. See Kaufman, "Christian Realism and Augustinian(?) Liberalism"; *Incorrectly Political: Augustine and Thomas More* (Notre Dame, IN: University of Notre Dame Press, 2007), 99–132; "Augustine's Dystopia"; and most recently "Stepping Out of Constantine's Shadow," in *Christianity, Democracy, and the Shadow of Constantine*, 202–17.

64. Markus, *Christianity and the Secular*, 62.

65. Again, here the locus classicus is Markus, *Saeculum*, Appendix B, "*De civitate Dei*, XIX, 14–15 and the Origins of Political Authority." In particular, Markus states clearly that his interest lies not with slavery itself, and explicitly not with what it means for good slaves to be ruled by bad masters, but rather with how Augustine's words about slavery illumine his views of political authority as such: "What is interesting for our purpose about this

passage is not Augustine's defence of such a state of affairs [that described in *en. Ps.* 124.7], which rests on his view that it is God's dispensation *ad tempus*, and will be done away with at the end; it is the equivalence between slavery and all political authority, secular power, and dignity on which some stress is laid" (200).

66. See the discussion in Chapter 1 of this habit in Eric Gregory, Rowan Williams, and Robin Lane Fox.

67. Illaria L. E. Ramelli, *Social Justice and the Legitimacy of Slavery: The Role of Philosophical Asceticism from Ancient Judaism to Late Antiquity* (Oxford: Oxford University Press, 2016), 1.

68. Chris L. de Wet, *The Unbound God: Slavery and the Formation of Early Christian Thought* (New York: Routledge, 2018), 7–8. See Ramelli, *Social Justice and the Legitimacy of Slavery*, esp. 1–25. Ramelli's account is valuable, though her treatment of Augustine suffers from occasional misunderstandings, or at least imprecision, regarding key features of Augustine's thought. For instance, she attributes to Augustine the view that "slaves deserve to be slaves due to their own sins (which, at least in the case of a person born a slave, is hard to explain, especially if one, like Augustine, rejects the pre-existence of souls)" (155), but this is to misconceive the penal nature of slavery as pertaining to an individual's "own sins," rather than to the fallen condition of humanity as such. I concur with Boniface Ramsey's editorial notes to *The City of God*, Book 19: "Augustine does not intend to say that a particular slave's sinfulness is responsible for the fact that he is enslaved but rather that the very existence of slavery is the result of human sinfulness in general." See *WSA* I/7, 372n48.

69. The literature of the debates on this shift among social historians is immense. For an excellent intervention into the project to "recover" enslaved agency, see Walter Johnson, "On Agency," *Journal of Social History* 37 (2003): 113–24. One key aspect of the problem is the conflation of liberal notions of "agency" and universal conceptions of "humanity," such that, "by continuing to frame their works as 'discoveries' of Black humanity, indeed, historians unwittingly reproduce the incised terms and analytical limits of a field of contest (black humanity: for or against) framed by the white-supremacist assumptions which made it possible to ask such a question in the first place" (114).

70. For a succinct and lucid response to the well-worn accusation of "anachronism" which is so often directed toward critical studies of slavery in ancient contexts, see De Wet, *The Unbound God*, 6–7.

71. Indeed, one undertheorized index of the *global* significance of the household concept for Augustine is his suggestion that, if the Roman Empire's "neighbors had been peaceful and just," then there would have been no cause to wage just wars against them, and hence, "human affairs would have been happier" as the relation among "the peoples in the world" would be modeled after that of "houses among the citizens in a city." *civ.* 5.15.

72. Markus, *Christianity and the Secular*, 58. Likewise, in Jean Bethke Elshtain's appeal to something rather like the middle distance we've been speaking of, she attributes to Augustine the view that "no single man can create a commonwealth. There is no ur-Founder, no great bringer of order. It begins in ties of fellowship, in households, clans, and tribes." Elshtain, *Augustine and the Limits of Politics*, 97.

73. Markus, *Christianity and the Secular*, 58.

74. Williams, "Politics and the Soul: Reading the *City of God*," in *On Augustine* (London: Bloomsbury, 2016), 119. Citations heretofore are to this slightly revised 2016 version.

75. Williams, "Politics," 119. I note that Williams is speaking of the connection of *imperare* to *consulere* here, and to the extent that *imperare* pertains to the relation of master to slave, it is fittingly called, as I do here unreservedly, *mastery*. Williams avoids the terms "master" and "mastery" throughout this section. Also, I return to the question of the *libido dominandi* in the next chapter's treatment of virtue, *humilitas*, and the vexed question of the inner dispositions of pagan and Christian masters.

76. Williams, "Politics," 119.

77. *civ.* 19.16.

78. Williams, "Politics," 124–25.

79. This is not to suggest that the enslaved, in Augustine's thought, cannot be pilgrims too. They most explicitly *can*, and indeed, it is their temporal orientation toward seeking the fragments of earthly peace as they long for God as their eternal peace which joins them into a band of pilgrims with their enslavers. I return to this at length in what immediately follows here.

80. *civ.* 19.13. It is perhaps suggestive that this definition, which achieved classic status in the tradition and was mobilized by Thomas Aquinas (*Summa Theologiae* II–II, q. 29, a. 1), appears so infrequently in contemporary Augustinian retrievals. Instead, for instance, Deede Johnson perpetually refers to "earthly peace *and justice*" even though Augustine rarely uses the two terms together.

81. Harper, *Slavery in the Late Roman World*, 253–54. In service to an extended metaphor on the proper storage of one's "treasure," Augustine uses the omnipresent worry among masters of thieving slaves to illustrate a theological point: "So you trust in God, but do not believe him? 'I trust in Christ, that what I left at home will be safe, and no one will break in or steal it.'... You will be much safer if you believe Christ, and put your money where he advised you to put it. Do you trust your slave, yet feel suspicious of your Master?" *en. Ps.* 38.12.

82. Cf. *In Johannis Evangelium tractatus* 41.4: "The slave of a man who is oppressed by the harsh domination of his master seeks respite in flight.... Sometimes men flee to the church, and lawless as they are, wishing to be without a master, but not without their sins, generally give us a lot of trouble."

83. *civ.* 19.16.

84. *civ.* 21.11.

85. *en. Ps.* 102.14, as quoted in Harper, *Slavery in the Late Roman World*, 230.

86. Harper, *Slavery in the Late Roman World*, 288.

87. *civ.* 19.16.

88. Garnsey, *Ideas of Slavery*, 214.

89. Glancy, *Slavery in Early Christianity*, 9; see also Harper, *Slavery in the Late Roman World*, 257ff.

90. Harper, *Slavery in the Late Roman World*, 260.

91. W. W. Buckland, *The Roman Law of Slavery: The Condition of the Slave in Private Law from Augustus to Justinian* (Cambridge: Cambridge University Press, 1908), 267.

92. Buckland, *The Roman Law of Slavery*, 45, 55.

93. When I speak of "waywardness," I am thinking of Saidiya Hartman, *Wayward Lives*. My use of "otherwise" here and throughout is directly indebted to Ashon T. Crawley, *Black Pentecostal Breath: The Aesthetics of Possibility* (New York: Fordham University Press, 2017), 2.

94. See Bradley, "Resisting Slavery at Rome," 370–72.

95. Roberts, *Freedom as Marronage*, 28.

96. James Cone, *The Spirituals and the Blues* (Maryknoll, NY: Orbis Books, 1972), 25.

97. Compare yet another example of this "good slave / bad slave" framework in Augustine: "Put the question to yourself. what kind of slave do you regard as worthy of your love? Perhaps you have a good-looking slave, very tall and well-built, but he is a thief, a bad character, deceitful. And you have another slave, perhaps, who is short, disfigured in the face, repulsive in color, but he is faithful, thrifty, and sober. Think about it: which of the two do you rate more highly? If you consult your bodily eyes, the handsome, dishonest fellow will come out on top; if you go by what the eyes of your heart tell you, the ugly but faithful slave wins." *en. Ps.* 33(2).15.

98. Cone, *The Spirituals and the Blues*, 26.

99. Charles Mathewes, "Faith, Hope, and Agony: Christian Political Participation Beyond Liberalism," *Annual of the Society of Christian Ethics* 21 (2001): 140.

100. Griffiths, "Secularity and the *Saeculum*," 53ff.

101. Cone, *The Spirituals and the Blues*, 28.

102. For this point on resistance, I am indebted to the work of Kevin Quashie, *The Sovereignty of Quiet: Beyond Resistance in Black Culture* (Rutgers, NJ: Rutgers University Press, 2012). Saidiya Hartman, "The Belly of the World: A Note on Black Women's Labors," *Souls* 18 (2016): 171.

103. Hartman, *Scenes of Subjection*, 103.

104. Stewart-Kroeker, *Pilgrimage as Moral and Aesthetic Formation in Augustine's Thought*, 68–69. Cf. *civ.* 10.32 on "the royal road which alone leads to a kingdom that does not totter on a temporal summit but stands fast on an eternal foundation."

105. "This fugitive movement is stolen life, and its relation to law is reducible neither to simple interdiction nor bare transgression." Fred Moten, "The Case of Blackness," *Criticism* 50 (2008): 179.

106. Harper, *Slavery in the Late Roman World*, 35.

107. On the notion that this necessary legal fiction is among those cross-cultural aspects of slave societies present in both ancient Roman antiquity and New World modernity (whereas other aspects are markedly different), cf. Keith Bradley: "My understanding is that slavery is an extreme form of a universal human tendency for some members of society to exercise domination over others. It is an institution in which all humanity and personhood are denied the powerless by the powerful. It has manifested itself in many different times and places; and in view of its historical prevalence it is *a priori* likely to have had common features wherever it has appeared, though predictably its specific manifestations will have varied according to time and place in keeping with the historically and culturally contingent factors that have distinguished one society from another. The historian's function accordingly is to identify the specific features of a given society and to define the particularist elements or emphases within it of a universal social formation that has generic and constant characteristics." See Bradley, "Roman Slavery: Retrospect and Prospect," *Canadian Journal of History* 43, no. 3 (December 2008): 482.

108. For one small example, Jennifer Glancy notes: "The appearance of slave bodies in census returns is a curiosity that underscores the ambivalent legal status of slaves: classified

as things, classified as persons." A certain household records in its census declaration that it holds " 'Elpis . . . aged 26, having a scar on the left shin, and half of a slave Sarapammon born in the house of Isis also called Memphis, 20 years old, whose other half belongs to Kroniaine and Taorsis in the Syrian quarter.' Counted as a person, Sarapammon merits inclusion in the census. Counted as a thing, Sarapammon appears as jointly owned property." Glancy, *Slavery in Early Christianity*, 11. For a careful textual window into a relevant modern analogue, see Michel-Rolph Trouillot's analysis of a specific "ambivalence" found in the journals and correspondence of the slaveholding planter class: "On the one hand, resistance and defiance did not exist, since to acknowledge them was to acknowledge the humanity of the enslaved. On the other hand, since resistance occurred, it was dealt with quite severely on the ground, within or around the plantations. Thus, next to a discourse that claimed the contentment of slaves, a plethora of laws, advice and measures, both legal and illegal, *tried to curb the very resistance denied in theory*." See Trouillot, "From Planters' Journals to Academia: The Haitian Revolution as Unthinkable History," *Journal of Caribbean History* 25, no. 1 (June 1991): 85–86.

109. Philip goes on to speak of this ability to decree as a "conversion," an "act of transubstantiation the equal of the metamorphosis of the eucharistic bread and wine into the body and blood of Christ." M. NourbeSe Philip, *Zong!* (Middletown, CT: Wesleyan University Press, 2008), 196.

110. John Henry Hopkins III, "John Henry Hopkins, First Bishop of Vermont," *Historical Magazine of the Episcopal Church* 6, no. 2 (June 1937): 187.

111. John Henry Hopkins, *A Scriptural, Ecclesiastical and Historical View of Slavery, from the Days of the Patriarch Abraham to the Nineteenth Century: Addressed to The Rt. Rev. Alonzo Potter, D.D., Bishop of the Protestant Episcopal Church, in the Diocese of Pennsylvania* (New York: Pooley & Co., 1864), 102 (italics original). On the ambiguity of the pronoun in the line from Psalm 124, John Rist also believes that it refers to "Christ" (not Paul) (Rist, *Augustine: Ancient Thought Baptized*, 236).

112. *en Ps.* 124.

113. David Bentley Hart, *Atheist Delusions: The Christian Revolution and Its Fashionable Enemies* (New Haven, CT: Yale University Press, 2009), 177. Other citations from Michael Lamb, *Commonwealth of Hope* (Princeton, NJ: Princeton University Press, 2022), 1. See Garry Wills, *Saint Augustine: A Life* (New York: Penguin, 1999), 129.

114. Figgis, *Political Aspects*, 43.

115. Figgis, *Will to Freedom*, 293.

116. *Sermo Denis* 16.1, as cited in Gregory, *Politics and the Order of Love*, 356.

117. Figgis, *Will to Freedom*, 294–95.

118. In the context of an essay on domination, Eric Gregory writes: "I think it is not hyperbole to think that if Augustine had not begun this reevaluation of classical philosophy and its world, we would live in a very different moral and political universe. He furnished a deeply humanitarian ethic premised on concern for the suffering of creatures who bear the image of God." Gregory, "Sympathy and Domination," 37.

119. Gregory, *Politics and the Order of Love*, 54.

120. Gregory, "Sympathy and Domination," 37.

121. Harper, *Slavery in the Late Roman World*, 209ff.

122. *De moribus ecclesiae catholicae* 1.30.63, as quoted in Garnsey, *Ideas of Slavery*, 7.

123. Harper, *Slavery in the Late Roman World*, 210.

124. *New Sermon (Mainz 54)*, Ch. 4, lines 91–125, as quoted in Garnsey, *Ideas of Slavery*, 225.

125. *en. Ps.* 124.7. Although texts like *The City of God* and *Confessions* are more well known to modern readers, it is worth remembering that Augustine's *Expositions of the Psalms*, as one scholar points out, "dominat[ed] the interpretation of the Psalms in the West for more than a thousand years." Allan D. Fitzgerald, O.S.A., ed., *Augustine through the Ages: An Encyclopedia* (Grand Rapids, MI: Eerdmans, 1999), 290.

126. One recent essay which takes this approach is Joseph E. Capizzi, "From Slave to Friend: John 15, Philemon, and Slavery in Augustine," in *Sacred Scripture and Secular Struggles*, ed. David V. Meconi (Leiden: Brill, 2015), 235–49.

127. It is all the more striking that here Augustine explicitly stages an instance of Christ "speaking" given that, as Rowan Williams notes (drawing from the work of many others), "in the *Enarrations* . . . the Psalms represent the unifying of the divine and the human voice in Christ." In other words, for Augustine's *Enarrations*, the Psalmist is *already* speaking in the voice of Christ, so that to explicitly invoke what Christ would say may be usefully read as an intensifying of the Christological significance of the statements issued here to masters and slaves. Further, it is all the more striking that for Augustine's hermeneutics of the Psalms, "Jesus speaks in the voice of the suffering Christian" according to Williams, since in this passage (*en. Ps.* 124), I am arguing that Jesus's voice is essentially the voice of the master *camouflaged* in the voice of the slave. See Williams, "Augustine as Interpreter of the Psalms," in *On Augustine*, 27.

128. Spillers, "Mama's Baby, Papa's Maybe," 235. I anticipate objections here from readers who believe the semantic and syntactical dynamics Spillers identifies cannot retain any intellectual force when applied elsewhere—in this case, to Augustine. In response, I offer two points: First, there certainly *are* features of her analysis specific to the modern context, but *this* aspect pertains to the central definitional feature of slavery itself—the contradictions which must be resolved as a result of slavery's central premise, the transformation of person into property—apart from which slavery is not slavery at all; thus, such an objection would need to go beyond simply reminding us that Augustine's slavery was in some sense "different" from what Spillers is analyzing, and instead identify some specific feature which, when considered properly, would materially alter the account offered here. Second, it is worth simply pausing over the fact that categories of analysis drawn from other domains of modern thought—philosophical, psychoanalytic, anthropological, etc.—are regularly employed to illumine ancient thinkers, but there seems to be something about Black thought, and especially Black feminist thought, that is often assumed to be *bound* to context in a special way, insufficiently rigorous and expansive to do intellectual work more broadly.

129. Lest this be misunderstood along the lines of those inclined to insert an entirely preposterous "just" in front of "construct"—those who say things like "race is just a social construct"—we should remember that slavery's wobbly construct is, as Fred Moten reminds us, indeed a "necessarily fictional, but materially brutal, standpoint." To call it a construct is not to call it less than real. See Fred Moten, "Blackness and Nothingness (Mysticism in the Flesh)," *South Atlantic Quarterly* 112 (2013): 738–40.

130. Plato, *Phaedo* 62b–c, as quoted in Garnsey, *Ideas of Slavery*, 16.

131. Plato, *Laws*, Book 6, lines 776b–c.

132. My use of opacity here is directly indebted to the work of Charles Long. See *Significations: Signs, Symbols and Images in the Interpretation of Religion* (Minneapolis: Fortress Press, 1986), esp. the essay "Freedom, Otherness, and Religion: Theologies Opaque."

133. Aimé Césaire, *Discourse on Colonialism*, trans. Joan Pinkham (New York: Monthly Review Press, 1972), 42; Bill Brown, *Other Things* (Chicago: University of Chicago Press, 2015), 249.

134. As discussed in note 3 to the Introduction, "slave society" is an influential concept associated with Moses Finley, distinguishing the great many societies who had slaves from the few "slave societies," which possess not only large numbers of slaves but a system of economic life ordered around slavery, together with a culture in which slavery is a significant aspect. See Harper, *Slavery in the Late Roman World*, 37ff.

135. James W. C. Pennington, *The Fugitive Blacksmith* (London: Gilpin, 1850). See also Walter Johnson, *Soul by Soul: Life Inside the Antebellum Slave Market* (Cambridge, MA: Harvard University Press, 1999).

136. "Blacks, the colored races, caught up into this net of the imaginary and symbolic consciousness of the West, rendered mute through the words of military, economic, and intellectual power, assimilated as if by osmosis structures of this consciousness of oppression. This is the source of the doubleness of consciousness made famous by W. E. B. Du Bois. *But even in these symbolic structures there remained the inexhaustibility of the opaqueness of this symbol for those who constituted the 'things' upon which the significations of the West deployed its meanings.*" Long, *Significations*, 204 (emphasis mine). In some sense, what I have put on display is the way that, from its earliest formative moments, the emerging Latin Christian theological tradition put in place a set of interpretive habits by internalizing slave metaphors from the side of the master, namely, a set of habits which invoked the meanings of "bodies" under one's control, oblivious—criminally so—to the ways the persons "caught" in the net of those meanings remained opaque, fugitive, *elsewhere.*

137. This superficially resembles the problem of "recognition" in Hegel's master/slave dialectic, but I suggest that what it poses is a slightly different dilemma. Although exploring this claim fully would lie far beyond my scope here, my sense is that the difference relates to the fact that, in Hegel's framework, "the slave" reciprocates the master's struggle for recognition, such that the conflict is driven by the slave's longing for *standing*, for occupying the position of the recognized. Orlando Patterson famously noted that historically masters mostly got recognition from one another, not from their slaves. But what happens when the enslaved too does not want recognition from the master, nor desires what the master has—moves elsewhere and in excess of this desire for standing? This open question is indexed in the movement of the fugitive and in the outlaw spaces of the woods beyond the roadside. I benefited tremendously from discussing these matters with Hegelian philosopher Jay Bernstein at a seminar in 2016 entitled "Of Masters and Slaves" at the New School as part of the Institute for Critical Social Inquiry (ICSI).

138. Cedric J. Robinson, *Black Marxism: The Making of the Black Radical Tradition* (Chapel Hill: University of North Carolina Press, 2000), 125.

139. Robinson, *Black Marxism*, 125.

140. Cf. Walter Johnson, "On Agency."

141. Robinson, *Black Marxism*, 125 (italics and ellipsis original).

142. On this point, my thinking is indebted to Hortense Spillers, who tracks this specific dynamic—the opacity which racial thinking imposes on both the dominant and the subjugated—in a profound and searching excavation of the "tragic mulatto/a figure" in American culture: "The fictions and realities of domination are not only opaque (not everywhere and at once visible) to the subject (and *narrated*) community, but also remain evasive, in their authentic character as raw and violent assertion, to the dominant (and *narrating*) community" (emphases original). See Spillers, "Notes on an Alternative Model—Neither/ Nor," in *Black, White, and in Color*, 310.

143. Anne Anlin Cheng, *The Melancholy of Race* (Oxford: Oxford University Press, 2001), 12 (emphasis mine).

144. Cedric Robinson, *Forgeries of Memory and Meaning: Blacks and the Regimes of Race in American Theater and Film Before World War II* (Chapel Hill: University of North Carolina Press, 2007), xiii.

145. I am here thinking with Fred Moten's brilliant theorizations of the notion that "objects can and do resist." See Moten, *In the Break*, 1.

146. Frederick Douglass, for example, wrote: "Slavery has been fruitful in giving itself names . . . and you and I and all of us had better wait and see what new form this old monster will assume, in what new skin this old snake will come forth next." As cited in Dorothy E. Roberts, "Foreword: Abolition Constitutionalism," *Harvard Law Review* 133, no. 1 (November 2019): 3. The literature on Afropessimism is enormous, but for an important critical perspective on the influential work of Frank Wilderson, see Nick Mitchell, "The View from Nowhere: On Frank Wilderson's Afropessimism," *Spectre* (Fall 2020): 110–22. Mitchell underscores the university as the problematic site of Wilderson's interventions, which often neglect the complex global and class-based material histories which disrupt his "ontological" formulations.

147. Hartman, "Venus in Two Acts," 11.

148. Ashon T. Crawley, *Black Pentecostal Breath: The Aesthetics of Possibility* (New York: Fordham University Press, 2017), 2.

149. Moten, "Blackness and Nothingness," 744.

150. As cited in Roberts, "Foreword: Abolition Constitutionalism," 3.

151. This imagery comes from Octavia Butler's 1979 novel *Kindred*, which enacts in literature the enduring problem of the master, its violent reach into the present, in the form of a time-traveling Black woman named Dana. I unfold some of these connections in an essay entitled "The Trouble with Antiracist Whiteness: Reading the Afterlife of Mastery in Octavia Butler's *Kindred*" (currently in preparation).

152. Long, *Significations*, 204.

153. There is ample evidence of wide-ranging tactics of everyday resistance, as Keith Bradley's "Resisting Slavery at Rome" shows, displaying a striking resemblance to the "array of tactics" Saidiya Hartman describes: "work slowdowns, feigned illness, unlicensed travel, the destruction of property, theft, self-mutilation, dissimulation, physical confrontation with owners and overseers." See *Scenes of Subjection*, 51.

154. Here again, it is vital to continue to track with Long's words about the *opacity* of oppressed persons in their experience, ever mindful of the tendency to make them again "transparent."

155. Barbara Ransby, *Making All Black Lives Matter: Reimagining Freedom in the Twenty-First Century* (Berkeley: University of California Press, 2018), 149.

156. *s.* 4.9, from *Sermons*, trans. Edmund Hill, *WSA* III/1–11 (Hyde Park, NY: New City Press, 1990–97).

157. Stewart-Kroeker, *Pilgrimage as Moral and Aesthetic Formation in Augustine's Thought*, 88.

158. Stewart-Kroeker, *Pilgrimage as Moral and Aesthetic Formation in Augustine's Thought*, 68–69.

THREE. The Form of the Slave

Epigraph 1: *ep.* 118.22.

Epigraph 2: *civ.* 19.15.

1. *conf.* 7.9.14.

2. Cornelius Mayer, "Humilitas," in *Augustinus-Lexikon*, ed. Cornelius Mayer et al., 5 vols. (Basel: Schwabe, 1986), 3.443–56. As cited in Katrin Ettenhuber, *Donne's Augustine: Renaissance Cultures of Interpretation* (Oxford: Oxford University Press, 2011), 109n14.

3. "It is not that there are no other commandments that should be mentioned [besides humility], but unless humility precedes and accompanies and follows upon all our good actions and is set before us to gaze upon, set alongside for us to cling to, and set over us to crush us down, pride tears the whole benefit from our own hand." *ep.* 118.22. See *Letters*, trans. Roland Teske, S.J., *WSA* II/1–4 (Hyde Park, NY: New City Press, 2001–5).

4. The centrality of obedience to Augustine's ethics, especially conceptions of justice, has generally been underappreciated and undertheorized. "In human beings and in every rational creature," writes Augustine, "obedience is the source and the perfection of all justice. So true is this that obedience is singled out as the major difference between" Adam and Christ. See *en. Ps.* 71.6. Elsewhere Augustine writes, "This [obedience], I can indeed say with absolute truth, is the one and only virtue for every creature that is a rational agent under the authority of God." See *The Literal Meaning of Genesis (De Genesi ad litteram)* 8.6.12, in *On Genesis*, trans. Edmund Hill, *WSA* I/13 (Hyde Park, NY: New City Press, 2002).

5. Lewis Ayres, *Augustine and the Trinity* (Cambridge: Cambridge University Press, 2010), 146.

6. Ayres, *Augustine and the Trinity*, 144.

7. Kyle Harper concludes his massive study of slavery during Augustine's era with a restatement of this central point: "The inhabitants of the Roman world insisted on the centrality of slavery in sexual rules, in habits of violence, in the economy of honor, in the material realm of production, in the legal order. In the mind of the preacher whose words have so often served as our guide, the world was inconceivable without slavery. The household and the city, the rich and the poor, the urban and the rural: *slavery was implicated in every aspect of social life.*" Harper, *Slavery in the Late Roman World*, 509 (emphasis mine).

8. Glancy, *Slavery in Early Christianity*, 132.

9. R. W. Dyson, *St. Augustine of Hippo: The Christian Transformation of Political Philosophy* (London: Continuum, 2005), 90.

10. Dyson, *St. Augustine of Hippo*, 110.

11. Charles Mathewes notes a relevant, common misperception: "[Augustine's] magisterial *De civitate Dei* is commonly read as a 'Charter of Christendom' for an era safely converted

to the church and in which wise bishops counsel pious emperors; but recent historical research, and the recently rediscovered Divjak letters, depict a setting far more superficially, partially, and provisionally Christian than this, suggesting that Augustine's massive work was more an attempt to attain some small influence with an imperial administration largely indifferent to the squealing of bishops." See *Evil and the Augustinian Tradition*, 62n5.

12. *civ.* 19.15.

13. *civ.* 1, preface.

14. Orlando Patterson, *Slavery and Social Death: A Comparative Study, with a New Preface* (Cambridge, MA: Harvard University Press, 2018).

15. Stewart-Kroeker, *Pilgrimage as Moral and Aesthetic Formation in Augustine's Thought*, 33–35.

16. Recently republished in Charles Norris Cochrane, *Augustine and the Problem of Power: The Essays and Lectures of Charles Norris Cochrane*, ed. David Beer (Eugene, OR: Cascade, 2017), 92.

17. Cooper, *Secular Powers*, 1.

18. Cooper, *Secular Powers*, 23.

19. Cooper, *Secular Powers*, 27.

20. O'Donovan, *Desire*, 219.

21. O'Donovan, *Desire*, 278.

22. Michel Foucault, *Discipline and Punish: The Birth of the Prison*, trans. Alan Sheridan (New York: Vintage, 1995). On the latter, see as one starting point Angela Y. Davis's classic essay "From the Prison of Slavery, to the Slavery of Prison: Frederick Douglass and the Convict Lease System," in *The Angela Davis Reader*, ed. Joy James (Malden, MA: Blackwell, 1998), 74–95. A more recent treatment of the relevant issues is Khalil Gibran Muhammad, *The Condemnation of Blackness: Race, Crime, and the Making of Modern Urban America* (Cambridge, MA: Harvard University Press, 2010).

23. See Mark Christian, "African Diaspora Connections and Gilroy's Denial," in *Racial Structure and Radical Politics in the African Diaspora*, ed. James L. Conyers, Jr. (New Brunswick, NJ: Transaction Publishers, 2009), 3:48.

24. O'Donovan, *Desire*, 278.

25. Mathewes, *Evil and the Augustinian Tradition*, 142.

26. Mathewes, *Republic of Grace*, 167.

27. Mathewes, "Pluralism, Otherness, and the Augustinian Tradition," 102.

28. Gerald W. Schlabach, "Augustine's Hermeneutic of Humility: An Alternative to Moral Imperialism and Moral Relativism," *Journal of Religious Ethics* 22, no. 2 (1994): 299–330.

29. Deborah Wallace Ruddy, "Christian Humility and Democratic Citizenry: St. Augustine and Jacques Maritain," in *Reassessing the Liberal State: Reading Maritain's Man and the State*, ed. Timothy Fuller and John P. Hittinger (Washington, DC: American Maritain Association, 2001), 209–10, 223, 227. Cf. Mark Button, " 'A Monkish Kind of Virtue'? For and Against Humility," *Political Theory* 33, no. 6 (2005): 840–68, who writes: "Democratic humility may be one of the most important qualities for late-modern societies marked by ethical and political pluralism" (841).

30. Paul Weitham, "Toward an Augustinian Liberalism," *Faith and Philosophy* 8 (1991): 461–80, at 469; Judith N. Shklar, *Ordinary Vices* (Cambridge, MA: Belknap Press of Harvard University Press, 1984).

31. Weitham, "Toward an Augustinian Liberalism," 464.

32. A good place to begin reconsidering the limits of Rawls's framework and the implicit appeal to "ideal theory" that Weitham makes here is Charles W. Mills, " 'Ideal Theory' as Ideology," in *Black Rights / White Wrongs: The Critique of Racial Liberalism* (Oxford: Oxford University Press, 2017), 72–90.

33. Eric Gregory, *Politics and the Order of Love: An Augustinian Ethic of Democratic Citizenship* (Chicago: University of Chicago Press, 2008), 54.

34. For an example of the ideology critique approach which tends to attribute clean causal links between theories and practices, see Stephen F. Brett, *Slavery and the Catholic Tradition: Rights in the Balance,* American University Studies, Series 5, Philosophy 157 (New York: Peter Lang, 1996): "generations of slaves lost their rights because of theories upheld by well-meaning but critically inadequate scholarship" (ix). Often associated with the work of Louis Althusser, the approach of "ideology critique" is more complex than crass claims of causality, however. See Michael Morris, *Knowledge and Ideology: The Epistemology of Social and Political Critique* (Cambridge: Cambridge University Press, 2016), 1–5.

35. Robert Dodaro, "Augustine's Secular City," in *Augustine and His Critics: Essays in Honour of Gerald Bonner,* ed. Robert Dodaro and George Lawless (London: Routledge, 2000), 244, 247.

36. Dodaro, "Augustine's Secular City," 247.

37. Robert Dodaro, *Christ and the Just Society in the Thought of Saint Augustine* (Cambridge: Cambridge University Press, 2004), 183.

38. For one example of Augustine as villain in relation to slavery, see Arthur A. Rupprecht, "Attitudes on Slavery Among the Church Fathers," in *New Dimensions in New Testament Study,* ed. Richard N. Longnecker and Merill C. Tenney (Grand Rapids, MI: Zondervan, 1974).

39. Jaroslav Pelikan, *The Christian Tradition: A History of the Development of Doctrine,* vol. 1: *The Emergence of the Catholic Tradition (100–600)* (Chicago: University of Chicago Press, 1971), 256.

40. For an introduction, see Wanda Cizewski, "Forma Dei—Forma Servi: A Study of Thomas Aquinas' Use of Philippians 2:6–7," *Divus Thomas* 92 (1989): 3–32. For a wider look, one would consult various entries in the massive *Oxford Guide to the Historical Reception of Augustine,* ed. Karla Pollmann and Willemien Otten (New York: Oxford University Press, 2013).

41. For one recent overview of the scholarly literature, see Joseph A. Marchal, "The Hymn Within (and Among the) Philippians," in *Philippians: Historical Problems, Hierarchical Visions, Hysterical Anxieties* (London: Bloomsbury, 2017), 13–28.

42. *civ.* 19.16–17.

43. Linn Tonstad, *Queer Theology: Beyond Apologetics* (Eugene, OR: Cascade Books, 2018), 33 (emphasis mine).

44. *De Trinitate (The Trinity),* trans. Edmund Hill, O.P., WSA I/5 (Hyde Park, NY: New City Press, 2012), 1.3.14.

45. Ayres, *Augustine and the Trinity*, 169.

46. Ayres, *Augustine and the Trinity*, 146.

47. Ayres, *Augustine and the Trinity*, 121, 41, See, for a classic example, his engagement with the Platonists, referenced above, in *conf.* 7.

48. *Trin.* 2.1.3.

49. Chris L. de Wet, *The Unbound God: Slavery and the Formation of Early Christian Thought* (New York: Routledge, 2018), 15. It is worth noting, however, that contemporary metaphor theory has moved far beyond the "substitution" theory of metaphor alluded to above. Treatments abound, but the most lucid starting point remains Janet Martin Soskice, *Metaphor and Religious Language* (New York: Oxford University Press, 1985), 24–25.

50. *Summa Theologiae* I, q. 13, a. 7, ad 5.

51. Using "the master's house" as a symbolic space which encompasses both Augustine's literal and metaphorical uses of slavery echoes historian Kate Cooper, *The Fall of the Roman Household* (New York: Cambridge University Press, 2007), on the double-valence of the *domus* concept within Roman culture. It names a "physical space" and a way of "represent[ing] the household as a lived social reality . . . [as] the crucial unit in the pyramid of social order" (110). My thinking here is also indebted to conversations with Sean Larsen.

52. *s.* 159B, from *Sermons*, trans. Edmund Hill, *WSA* III/1–11 (Hyde Park, NY: New City Press, 1990–97).

53. *s.* 159B.4. This image of slave beating as an act of mercy is fairly standard for Augustine, as we saw above in discussing *en. Ps.* 102.14. Similarly, in *civ.* 19.16, Augustine notes that if a slave "disrupts domestic peace by his disobedience," then whipping him is "for the benefit" of the slave himself, to bring him "back into line with the peace from which he had broken away."

54. *s.* 159B.5.

55. For an illuminating discussion of these three categories in the writings of Paul and their contested theological significance, see the debate among Jennifer Glancy, Albert Harrill, and Dale Martin, in Jennifer A. Glancy, "Review Essay: Slavery, Historiography, and Theology," *Biblical Interpretation* 15 (2007): 200–211.

56. *s.* 159B.7.

57. In this section I generally retain Augustine's use of gender-exclusive pronouns advisedly, in order not to erase the gendered nature of some aspects of his thought.

58. *s.* 159B.5.

59. *s.* 159B.7.

60. *In Iohannis evangelium tractatus* 17.16, from *Homilies on the Gospel of John 1–40*, trans. Edmund Hill, *WSA* III/12 (Hyde Park, NY: New City Press, 2009).

61. *civ.* 13.3. Crucially, the figure of the beast—the nonhuman and ostensibly irrational animal—works in intimacy with the figure of the slave. In Sermon 359 (discussed below), for example, the figure of obedience provided to Augustine's hearers is the *donkey* upon which Christ rides into town in the gospel narratives. In my second book project, provisionally titled *We Are Each Other's Harvest: Solidarity at the End of the World*, I return to the question posed to Christian theological ethics by the "irrational" animal in light of two fields of inquiry: (a) the astonishing advances in evolutionary anthropology's comparative animal cognition studies, which render untenable the idea of a clean distinction between

"rational" and "irrational" which maps onto human and nonhuman animals; (b) the turn to the question of animality in Black Studies as a way into the haunted category of "the human" in western humanistic thought. On (a), I have benefited immensely from my collaborative work with research scientists Brian Hare and Vanessa Woods at Duke University's Evolutionary Anthropology Department and Center for Cognitive Neuroscience, especially at the Canine Cognition Laboratory. And on (b), for a point of entry, see the brilliant work of Joshua Bennett, *Being Property Once Myself: Blackness and the End of Man* (Cambridge, MA: Harvard University Press, 2020).

62. *conf.* 7.7.11.

63. Patterson, *Slavery and Social Death*, 184. The classic study by Heinrich Erman remains valuable, especially the discussion of Augustine's use of *servus vicarius* in framing the questions of ecclesiastical authority in terms of the obedience of slaves to other slaves. See *Servus vicarius: L'esclave de l'esclave romain* (Lausanne: F. Rouge, 1896), 408–9.

64. Patterson, *Slavery and Social Death*, 184.

65. Patterson, *Slavery and Social Death*, 184.

66. Luke Bretherton, *Resurrecting Democracy: Faith, Citizenship, and the Politics of a Common Life* (Cambridge: Cambridge University Press, 2015), 106. Though sometimes lumped in with the "political Augustinians," Bretherton often thinks with and against Augustine while refusing the "political Augustinian" label and differing sharply with the Augustinian liberals. For his engagement with the problems posed to citizenship by the legacies of modern racial slavery, see Bretherton, *Resurrecting Democracy*, 252–57, and "Exorcising Democracy: The Theopolitical Challenge of Black Power," *Journal of the Society of Christian Ethics* 38 (2018): 3–24.

67. Cf. *conf.* 7.7.11, *vera rel.* 35.65. The latter is translated by Edmund Hill as *True Religion*, in *WSA* I/8 (Hyde Park, NY: New City Press, 2005).

68. *s.* 159B.

69. "Agricultural handbooks [of the period] assign a central role to the *vilicus*, the elite slave manager/bailiff who exercised authority over the slaves beneath him while subordinating himself to the authority of the slaveholder. . . . [T]he householder of the household codes, at least of the household codes that address slaveholders, serves in a parallel position to the *vilicus*, guaranteeing the orderly conduct of subordinates while submitting to a higher authority." Brent D. Shaw, "Body/Power/Identity: The Passions of the Martyrs," *Journal of Early Christian Studies* 4, no. 3 (1996): 208.

70. *civ.* 14.14.

71. Most notably in Peter Lombard's *Sentences*, which would shape generations of medieval thinkers.

72. *Jo. ev. tr.* 17.16. Augustine's intertextual reading, weaving the slave Christology of Philippians 2 together with the account of the devil's fall in Isaiah 14 and humankind's fall in Genesis 3, would set the terms of medieval interpretation for centuries. See Cizewski, "Forma Dei—Forma Servi," 7–8.

73. Harper, *Slavery in the Late Roman World*, 254.

74. *s.* 113.4.

75. Theft by enslaved people was an omnipresent threat in the Roman household. See Harper, *Slavery in the Late Roman World*, 254.

76. Ayres, *Augustine and the Trinity*, 133.

77. Jennings, *The Christian Imagination*, 183–84.

78. *s.* 359B.7.

79. *s.* 359B.

80. *s.* 359B.10.

81. *Jo. ev. tr.* 17.16. On the complexity of Augustine's relationship to the Jewish people, see Paula Fredriksen, *Augustine and the Jews: A Christian Defense of Jews and Judaism* (New Haven, CT: Yale University Press, 2010).

82. *en. Ps.* 124.7.

83. *en. Ps.* 124.7.

84. Gregory anticipates this charge and defends against it. See *Politics and the Order of Love*, 46.

85. *s.* 359B.

86. *civ.* 1, preface.

87. *vera rel.* 35.65.

88. A similar conclusion is reached in Cassandra M. M. Casias, "Sinful Slave-Owners in Augustine's Sermons," *Journal of Late Antiquity* 11, no. 1 (Spring 2018): esp. 116.

89. Harper writes: "Manumission was an important incentive, but like the spectrum of punishments and rewards, its use as a motivational technique was camouflaged in ambiguous and moralized terms." Given that it "was dangled as the reward for a long period of obedient service," its somewhat ambiguous valence in the cultural imaginary seems to have resulted, in part, from the apparent possibility of "broken promises and betrayals," as well as from the strategic, self-serving habit among masters of manumitting slaves in their old age, after decades of body-breaking service, precisely at the moment at which they no longer could provide labor and instead would require care. See Harper, *Slavery in the Late Roman World*, 242.

90. Gregory, *Politics and the Order of Love*, 57n50. He cites Barry Alan Shain, *The Myth of American Individualism: The Protestant Origins of American Political Thought* (Princeton, NJ: Princeton University Press, 1994), and Graham Walker, "Virtue and the Constitution."

91. Rick Kennedy, *The First American Evangelical: A Short Life of Cotton Mather* (Grand Rapids, MI: Eerdmans, 2015), 60. For a recent, extended meditation both on the limits and possibilities of Perry's notion, see W. Clark Gilpin, "The Augustinian Strain of Piety: Theology and Autobiography in American History," in *Augustine Our Contemporary: Examining the Self in Past and Present*, ed. Willemien Otten and Susan E. Schreiner (Notre Dame, IN: University of Notre Dame Press, 2018), 233–47.

92. In one of the earliest such biographies (1744), for instance, David Jennings produces the power of Mather as a narrative model of virtue by juxtaposing his achievements with his humility. That is, the telling of Mather's numerous achievements (literally giving the numbers of books written, sermons preached, vigils kept) in the narrative is followed immediately by citing Mather's own self-censures for ongoing sinfulness and sloth despite these achievements: "Notwithstanding his amazing Diligence ... and the many valuable Services with which he filled up every year, and every Day, his Humility has filled his Diary with continual Censures upon himself, and his Defects." Jennings, *An Abridgement of the Life*

of the Late Reverend and Very Learned Dr. Cotton Mather (London: Oswald and Brackstone, 1744), 26.

93. *Diary of Cotton Mather,* vol. 8, *1709–1724* (Boston: Massachusetts Historical Society, 1812), 272.

94. The congregants somehow understood this, Mather insists with a hint of defensiveness, "without any Application of mine to them for such a Thing."

95. *Diary of Cotton Mather,* 272.

96. Patterson, *Slavery and Social Death,* 334.

97. Nor still is my concern reducible to, though it does involve, some early traces of certain dynamics on full display in the antebellum "slaveholding paternalism" of the South, as in the work of Eugene D. Genovese and Elizabeth Fox-Genovese.

98. Patterson, *Slavery and Social Death,* 334.

99. Cotton Mather, *The Negro Christianized: An Essay to Excite and Assist That Good Work, The Instruction of Negro Servants in Christianity* (Boston: B. Green, 1706).

100. *Diary of Cotton Mather,* 342.

101. *Diary of Cotton Mather,* 363n1.

102. See Steven J. Niven, "Onesimus," in *African American Lives,* ed. Henry Louis Gates, Jr., and Evelyn Brooks Higginbotham (New York: Oxford University Press, 2004), 640–41; and Kathryn S. Yoo, "Strangers in the House of God: Cotton Mather, Onesimus, and an Experiment in Christian Slaveholding," *Proceedings of the American Antiquarian Society* 117 (2007): 143–75.

103. Mather, *The Negro Christianized,* 10. It is worth noticing too that the sort of verses which contemporary progressive Christians are likely to invoke in opposition to the history of mastery often were found compatible with it. Mather cites and discusses in support of his position Colossians 3:11: "there is neither Greek nor Jew, circumcision nor uncircumcision, Barbarian, Scythian, bond nor free: but Christ is all, and in all." See the discussion in Tomlins, *Freedom Bound,* 462–64.

104. Though it lies beyond my scope here, one might wish to explore the possible reverberations of this Augustinian tripartite structure of mastery *beyond* "the religious." That is, to view its possible legacies in the imaginative frameworks of modernity's emerging secular humanism, whereby various agents will come to stand in what looks rather like position 1 of the cosmology, without changing the structure of the master's house itself. These agents include, for instance, a certain hegemonic conception of scientific reason, a naturalized-biological evolutionary "providence," a Hegelian force of Absolute Spirit realizing itself in and as history, and finally, the impenetrable forces of the invisible hand—the global market. In each case, the agency of "the human," an overrepresentation of western man, is narrated inside these latently Augustinian frames at position 2: the one able and willing to submit to what occupies position 1, and therefore capable of ruling what remains below in position 3: the indigenous and African peoples of the world, the animals and waters and lands. The wide-ranging theoretical and historical interventions of Sylvia Wynter provide key resources for these dense and admittedly ambitious arguments. One starting point her work suggests, given the tripartite cosmological hierarchy I've tracked here, is the turn from medieval to modern at the juncture of an emerging Renaissance humanism, represented for her in the following statement from Pico della Mirandola's often-cited *Oration on the Dignity of Man:*

Now the highest Father, God the master-builder, . . . took up man . . . and placing him at *the midpoint of the world* . . . spoke to him as follows: "We have given to thee, Adam, no fixed seat, no form of thy very own, no gift peculiarly thine, that thou mayest feel as thine own, have as thine own, possess as thine own the seat, the form, the gifts which thou thyself shalt desire. A limited nature in other creatures is confined within the laws written down by Us. In conformity with thy free judgment, in whose hands I have placed thee, thou art confined by no bounds; and thou wilt fix limits of nature for thyself. . . . Neither heavenly nor earthly, neither mortal nor immortal have We made thee. Thou, like a judge appointed for being honorable art the molder and maker of thyself; thou mayest sculpt thyself into whatever shape thou dost prefer. Thou canst grow downward into the lower natures which are brutes. Thou canst again grow upward from thy soul's reason into the higher natures which are divine."

This imaginative cosmology at the birth of the global colonial world positions western man at "the midpoint of the world," the hinge of the universe, linking and thereby also dividing divinity from beasts, higher reason from sensate nature, and therefore fit to rule over an emerging colonial scene. See Wynter, "Unsettling the Coloniality of Being/Power/Truth/Freedom Towards the Human, After Man, Its Overrepresentation—An Argument," *CR: The New Centennial Review* 3, no. 3 (Fall 2003): 259–60, 276–83 (emphasis mine). Notably, Charles Taylor's more widely influential account of the turn from medieval to modern, *Sources of the Self*, also invokes Mirandola's statement as a key moment in the story, yet lacks the analytic resources, or perhaps the interest needed, to grasp the emerging racial and colonial order of man vis-à-vis his subhuman others. See *Sources of the Self: The Making of the Modern Identity* (Cambridge, MA: Harvard University Press, 1989), 199–200.

105. An effort to rehabilitate a conception of humility sensitive to its racialized and gendered dimensions and in conversation with Black Studies would need to confront the crucial task of distinguishing between humility and *humiliation*. For one rich, subtle recent discussion, see Danielle Allen's engagement with Ralph Ellison's *Invisible Man* in "Ralph Ellison: Democratic Theorist," in *African American Political Thought: A Collected History*, ed. Melvin L. Rogers and Jack Turner (Chicago: University of Chicago Press, 2021), 466–69. In an explicitly theological context, see Stacey Floyd-Thomas, "Black Joy and Oppressive Humility: Folk Wisdom, Womanist Theory, and Black Life," podcast for the *Yale Center for Faith and Culture* (Dec. 12, 2020), https://faith.yale.edu/media/black-joy-and-oppressive-humility (accessed March 15, 2021).

106. *s.* 114B (emphasis mine).

107. *s.* 114B.

108. *s.* 114B.

109. Alonso de Sandoval, *Treatise on Slavery: Selections from* De Instauranda Aethiopum Salute, trans. Nicole von Germeten (Indianapolis, IN: Hackett Publishing, 2008), 76 (emphasis mine).

110. James Cone, from a video recording of a lecture given at the University of Richmond on October 7, 1971, available at https://www.tiktok.com/@blkamerican/video/7168940311639575850?is_from_webapp=1&sender_device=pc&web_id=7280166764267570734. A contemporaneous article

in the school newspaper, titled "Black Liberation Means an End of White Power" (*The Collegian*, October 8, 1971), reported on Cone's lecture.

111. W. E. B. Du Bois, "The Souls of White Folk," in *Darkwater: Voices from Within the Veil* (New York: Washington Square Press, 2004), 25.

112. *s.* 114B.

113. Du Bois, "The Souls of White Folk," 21.

114. Du Bois, "The Souls of White Folk," 25.

115. See for example Bruno Latour's *Down to Earth: Politics in the New Climatic Regime*, trans. Catherine Porter (Medford, MA: Polity, 2018), 86.

116. Robert Macfarlane, *Underland: A Deep Time Journey* (New York: Norton, 2019), 31.

117. No one has explored the crucial salience for Augustine's politics of *timor mortis*—fear of death—as brilliantly as Robert Dodaro. See *Christ and the Just Society*, 30–43. I return to this theme in the following chapters.

118. Jennifer Herdt et al., "COVID-19 and Religious Ethics," *Journal of Religious Ethics* 48, no. 3 (2020): 356–57.

119. Herdt et al., "COVID-19," 357.

120. Hartman, *Scenes of Subjection*, 21–23. On Wilberforce, see Hartman, *Lose Your Mother*, chapter 7, "The Dead Book," which makes visible the disturbing intimacies among white responses to Black suffering which are normally thought to be in opposition to one another, in this case, that of the slave ship captain, a surgeon, and the abolitionist Wilberforce.

121. Hartman, *Scenes of Subjection*, 19. Christina Sharpe, *Monstrous Intimacies: Making Post-Slavery Subjects* (Durham, NC: Duke University Press, 2010).

122. Hartman, "Venus in Two Acts," 2.

123. I thank Willie James Jennings for continually pressing me to think through these questions of obedience and disobedience in the "form of a slave." I explore this theme of the cross, the fugitive, and Augustine's thought in Chapter 5 below.

124. I use the terms noun and verb in reference to Nathaniel Mackey, "Other: From Noun to Verb," *Representations* 39 (Summer 1992): 51–70, and I return to this in my Epilogue.

125. James Cone, *The Cross and the Lynching Tree* (Maryknoll, NY: Orbis, 2011), 162 (emphasis original).

FOUR. Abolition's Time

Epigraph 1: David Scott, *Omens of Adversity: Tragedy, Time, Memory, Justice* (Durham, NC: Duke University Press, 2014), 28.

Epigraph 2: *civ.* 4.33.

1. Griffiths, "Secularity and the *Saeculum*," 34.

2. *civ.* 19.15. Of course, what Augustine means by "nature" here is infamously difficult to determine. As R. A. Markus writes, "The looseness of his conception of 'nature' is too notorious to require comment." See Markus, *Saeculum*, 209. Cf. Gervase Corcoran, O.S.A., *Saint Augustine on Slavery* (Rome: Institutum Patristicum 'Augustinianum,' 1985), 79–80, as well as C. Boyer, "La notion de nature chez saint Augustin," *Doctor Communis* 8 (1955): 65–75.

3. *civ.* 19.15. Further, Augustine states elsewhere that within the present ordering of things, owning slaves is a human right. See *Io. ev. tr.* 6.25.

4. Rist, *Augustine: Ancient Thought Baptized*, 236.

5. Rist, *Augustine: Ancient Thought Baptized*, 238.

6. Corcoran, *Saint Augustine on Slavery*, 89.

7. There are, of course, a number of ways of translating *saeculum, in hoc saeculo, saecularis,* and related terms. For a discussion, see Paul J. Griffiths, "Secularity and the *Saeculum*," 33–34.

8. *civ.* 19.15.

9. Rowan Williams, "Patriarchal Villains? It's Time to Re-think St Paul and St Augustine," *New Statesman*, Nov. 10, 2015, http://www.newstatesman.com/politics/religion/2015/11/patriarchal-villains-it-s-time-re-think-st-paul-and-st-augustine (accessed Nov. 12, 2017).

10. One way of saying this is that vis-à-vis the Augustinian account of sin, slavery plays the role of an extended instance of "symbolic signification" in Ricoeur's sense. Following Ricoeur's terminology, I suggest the ubiquity and style of slave language in Augustine occupy a status not of "allegory" but of "symbol": "Allegory is a rhetorical procedure that can be eliminated once it has done its job. Having ascended the ladder, we can then descend it. Allegory is a didactic procedure. It facilitates learning, but can be ignored in any directly conceptual approach. In contrast, there is no symbolic knowledge except when it is impossible to directly grasp the concept and when the direction toward the concept is indirectly indicated by the secondary signification of a primary signification." Ricoeur, *Interpretation Theory: Discourse and the Surplus of Meaning* (Fort Worth: Texas Christian University Press, 1976), 55–56.

11. James Wetzel, "Augustine on the Origin of Evil: Myth and Metaphysics," in Wetzel, ed., *Augustine's City of God*, 168.

12. Kenneth Surin, *Theology and the Problem of Evil* (Oxford: Blackwell, 1986), 13. Surin's work has the further advantage of insisting upon the "unique historical specificity of these ancient texts" (i.e., theological responses to evil like Augustine's and Irenaeus's), a point which bolsters this chapter's attempt to read the *privatio* thesis within the symbolic world of a society in which, as Kyle Harper concludes, "slavery pervaded every aspect of social thought and practice." See *Slavery in the Late Roman World*, 508–9.

13. Surin, *Theology and the Problem of Evil*, 13.

14. *conf.* 7, especially.

15. Rowan Williams, "Insubstantial Evil," in Dodaro and Lawless, eds., *Augustine and His Critics*, 120. Cf. *civ.* 12.5.

16. Cf. *conf.* 7.12.18: "all things that are corrupted suffer privation of some good. If they were to be deprived of all good, they would not exist at all."

17. For a more detailed summation and analysis of the steps of reasoning by which Augustine arrives at this answer, see William S. Babcock, "The Human and the Angelic Fall: Will and Moral Agency in Augustine's *City of God*," in *Augustine: From Rhetor to Theologian*, ed. Joanne McWilliam (Waterloo, ON: Wilfrid Laurier University Press, 1992), esp. 135–39.

18. I follow Rowan Williams in conceiving evil as properly spoken about in temporal ("process") rather than spatial ("position") language. "Insubstantial Evil," 120.

19. Mathewes, *Evil and the Augustinian Tradition*, 77.

20. "They are not defections toward evil natures but rather are evil precisely because, against the order of nature [*quia contra ordinem naturarum*], they defect from that which has supreme existence and defect to that which has lesser existence." *civ.* 12.8. For a discussion of natural order and Augustine's important use of "second nature," see Rist, *Augustine: Ancient Thought Baptized*, 138, 175.

21. Charles Mathewes, "Augustinian Anthropology: *Interior Intimo Meo*," *Journal of Religious Ethics* 27, no. 2 (Summer 1999): 206.

22. *civ.* 12.7 (emphasis mine).

23. Cf. Mathewes, "Augustinian Anthropology," 205.

24. Paul Griffiths, *Decreation: The Last Things of All Creatures* (Waco, TX: Baylor University Press, 2014) (emphasis mine).

25. The phrase "darkness visible" appears in Milton, *Paradise Lost*, Book I, line 63. I take the image of the prison cell in part from this passage: "a dungeon horrible / on all sides round."

26. I signal here what I take to be perhaps the chief, perennial difficulty in attempts to apply the Augustinian grammar to contemporary instances of evil, viz., the apparently unsatisfying (at least to some), almost obscene character of naming as "mere absence" what appears to our sense of things to be so monstrously "real."

27. *conf.* 7.8.12.

28. Cf. "Deprived of their participation in the eternal light, they are no longer light in the Lord but rather *darkness in themselves.*" *civ.* 11.9 (emphasis mine). Note that angelic rather than human creatures are under discussion here, but this does not seem to substantively alter the point.

29. *conf.* 7.

30. *civ.* 11.22.

31. *civ.* 19.13.

32. This is not to say, of course, that Augustine thinks slaves are animals, or even animal-like in nature. (He explicitly denies this; see, for instance *lib. arb.* 3.9.26.96.) That's just the point: the slave's body is a sign of disorder *precisely because* none other than a human being is being made to operate in the world in the way an animal does, that is, by being ruled not by his own rational soul (in free obedience to God), but by another human will. Still, the relation between the figure of the nonhuman animal and the figure of the slave in Augustine and in Christian theological thought more broadly remains sorely neglected.

33. Mary Beard, *SPQR: A History of Ancient Rome* (New York: Liveright, 2015), 330. The saying also appears notably in Seneca's *Epistulae* 47.2–5, as quoted in Garnsey, *Ideas of Slavery*, 55.

34. *en. Ps.* 55.9.

35. Wetzel, "Augustine on the Origin of Evil," 178.

36. "What man became—not when he was created but when he sinned and was punished—is what man begot, so far as the origin of sin and death is concerned." *civ.* 13.3. Ramelli's otherwise sharp treatment misses the mark on this specific point of Augustine's views on slavery. See the discussion at Chapter 2, note 68 above.

37. Again, there is certainly no reason why one metaphor "should" capture all aspects or angles of the concept it involves, but given how widely discussed and crucially important this particular passage is in Augustinian thought, its argument can be made clearest when its edges (limits) are brought most sharply into focus.

38. For this fascinating history, one which in my view casts new light on the standard readings of this passage in Augustine, see the section entitled "Etymology as Ideology: *Servire* from *servare*, or Enslaving as Saving," in Mary Nyquist, *Arbitrary Rule: Slavery, Tyranny, and the Power of Life and Death* (Chicago: University of Chicago Press, 2013), 218ff.

39. This aspect of slavery of course forms the basis of Orlando Patterson's now-classic *Slavery and Social Death*, with which I have been in conversation throughout.

40. I aim here, as throughout, to restrict my discussion to how this "living death" framework discloses the *enslavers'* imaginary, as reflected in culture and law, in part to indicate the unresolved (and perhaps unresolvable) debates concerning whether Patterson's influential "social death" framework obscures more than it clarifies when it comes to that form of *life* which moves beneath the epithet of "the slave." An illuminating criticism of Patterson along these lines is found in Vincent Brown, "Social Death and Political Life in the Study of Slavery," *American Historical Review* 114, no. 5 (December 2009): 1231–49. In Brown's view, "it is often forgotten that the concept of social death is a distillation from Patterson's breathtaking survey—a theoretical abstraction that is meant not to describe the lived experiences of the enslaved so much as to reduce them to a least common denominator that could reveal the essence of slavery in an ideal-type slave, shorn of meaningful heritage" (1233).

41. What Chris de Wet says of the slave metaphors in Pauline literature is no less true of Augustine: "The point is that the metaphor does not work if it is reduced to a form of paid servanthood.... The potency and radicalism of the metaphor lie in its extremity. The slave is one who has no agency outside of the volition of the master; the will of the slave is renounced and totally subservient to that of the slaveholder. Any authority the slave has is not his own; it is a transplanted and surrogate authority." Chris L. de Wet, *Preaching Bondage: John Chrysostom and the Discourse of Slavery in Early Christianity* (Berkeley: University of California Press, 2015), 47.

42. Though Corcoran's *Saint Augustine on Slavery* remains valuable as one of the few monograph-length treatments of slavery in Augustine's thought, its usefulness is significantly hampered in two respects. First, the historical account its first chapter (there are only two) offers of the social realities of slavery in Augustine's day is now severely dated. Since its publication in 1985, a wealth of analysis in late ancient studies has decisively enhanced our view of the social, political, and economic dimensions of Augustine's world, rendering the survey Corcoran's first chapter offers of little value to the contemporary reader. Second, Corcoran's theological and ethical assessment of Augustine's views on slavery is hobbled by the decidedly confessional, even apologetic character of Corcoran's approach. His desire to defend Augustine against modern critics often leads to special pleading on Augustine's behalf, as for instance when Corcoran, upon noticing Augustine's "lack of eloquent denunciation of cruelty to slaves," offers the conjecture that this must mean there simply was not much such cruelty! It must be "due to the comparative rarity of the problem rather than evidence of his indifference to their lot . . . his silence on cruelty towards slaves can reasonably be interpreted to mean that this was rare"(89). On this tendency toward "indulg[ing] in special pleading on behalf of Augustine," see Peter Brown's "New Directions" appendix to the 2000 edition of *Augustine of Hippo*, 494.

43. Corcoran, *Saint Augustine on Slavery*, 78 (emphasis mine).

44. Corcoran, *Saint Augustine on Slavery*, 79.

45. *Gn. litt.* 3.20.30. I retain Augustine's gender-exclusive pronouns here and throughout advisedly, in view of the fact that gender subjection *is* natural for him in the order of nature, whereas it is specifically the subjection of man to man that is the element introduced by sin.

46. Corcoran, *Saint Augustine on Slavery,* 79.

47. *Gn. adv. Man.* 2.15.22, published in *On Genesis,* trans. Edmund Hill, *WSA* I/13 (Hyde Park, NY: New City Press, 2004).

48. *civ.* 13.3. I am currently at work on a project which involves thinking theologically about the figure of the domesticated animal, its intimate linkages with the notion of slavery as domesticating (as "animalizing") human beings, and the ecological implications of this history for Christian political and ethical thought.

49. Cf. *civ.* 14.13.

50. *Gn. litt.* 2.32. Cf. Augustine's words on the justice of the subjection of animals, in his commentary upon Genesis which notes that the patriarchs were "breeders of herds": "And rightly so, for without any doubt this is just servitude and just domination, since cattle serve man and man rules over cattle." He then invokes Genesis 1:26 on being made in the image of God and notes: "Here it is implied that reason ought to dominate irrational life." See *Quaestiones in Heptateuchum* (hereafter *qu. Hept.*), in *Writings on the Old Testament,* trans. Joseph T. Lienhard and Sean Doyle, *WSA* I/14 (Hyde Park, NY: New City Press, 2016), 1.53.

51. *Gn. litt.* 2.9.12.

52. Cf. the discussion of Augustine's own relationship to slaveholding by way of his monastic community and the outrage of his parishioners at this fact, "not out of concern for the slaves' freedom. . . . His congregation seems to have objected to the monks' ownership of slaves for the same reason that they were outraged at their ownership of land: Augustine and his brethren were supposed to have relinquished earthly riches." See Casias, "Sinful Slave-Owners in Augustine's Sermons," 119.

53. As Markus summarizes, "it is clear that the service and subjection which a man owes another in virtue of being subject to him as to his legitimate ruler is an instance of subjection in virtue of status only; it has nothing to do with any possible moral or intellectual superiority of the ruler over his subject." Markus, *Saeculum,* 203. And elsewhere: "The bare superiority of being established in a controlling position is the only kind of superiority Augustine could concede to the master over his slaves or to the ruler over his subjects; in no other sense were his 'inferiors' inferior" (93).

54. See for instance *en. Ps.* 124.7.

55. Corcoran, *Saint Augustine on Slavery,* 81.

56. The debate continues in Veronica Ogle's recent critique of the notion, found in Miikka Ruokanen and others, that Augustine draws "a conceptual distinction between the political and the social," one which Ogle contends "rides on a modern conception of politics," whereas Augustine "comes at his study of politics from a premodern perspective." See Ogle, *Politics and the Earthly City in Augustine's City of God* (Cambridge: Cambridge University Press, 2021), 147.

57. Markus, *Saeculum,* 200.

58. "This extensive Commentary on the book of Genesis contains the first germs of many of the ideas which we meet later in the De civitate Dei." Markus, *Saeculum,* 203.

59. Markus, *Saeculum,* 87.

60. Markus, *Saeculum,* 86.

61. Markus, *Saeculum,* 205.

62. *Gn. litt.* 8.23.44.

63. Corcoran, *Saint Augustine on Slavery*, 81.

64. Markus, *Saeculum*, 205.

65. Charles Mathewes, "Providence and Political Discernment," in *The Providence of God: Deus habet consilium*, ed. Francesca Aran Murphy and Philip G. Ziegler (New York: Bloomsbury, 2009), 257.

66. Mathewes, "Providence and Political Discernment," 271.

67. Mathewes, "Providence and Political Discernment," 271.

68. "... this discernment is always provisional and ambiguous, especially so in politics, and underscores the importance of a humble confessionalism." Mathewes, "Providence and Political Discernment," 260.

69. Mathewes, "Providence and Political Discernment," 261.

70. Mathewes, "Providence and Political Discernment," 262.

71. Cf. John Rist: "Augustine is able to back this appeal [to accept rather than resist slavery] to a *combination* of 'providence' with the Stoic 'Lazy Argument' with a further set of 'Stoicizing' attitudes with which his Christian as well as his pagan contemporaries were familiar." Rist, *Augustine: Ancient Thought Baptized*, 237 (emphasis mine).

72. Mathewes, "Providence and Political Discernment," 265.

73. Frank Wilderson, *Red, White & Black: Cinema and the Structure of U.S. Antagonisms* (Durham, NC: Duke University Press, 2010).

74. This point has come to be associated with the wide-ranging conversation among thinkers gathered under the heading "Afropessimism," especially Frank Wilderson, but it's worth noting, as Jesse McCarthy has in a thoughtful essay, that the "structural antagonism thesis" has deep and significant forebears in Black thought, including the work on anti-Blackness of Lewis Gordon's *Bad Faith and Antiblack Racism* and the expansive psychoanalytic and philosophical thought of Frantz Fanon. See Jesse McCarthy, "On Afropessimism," in *Who Will Pay Reparations on My Soul?* (New York: Liveright, 2021), 202–3.

75. *qu. Hept.* 1.153.

76. *qu. Hept.* 1.153.

77. *civ.* 19.15.

78. *civ.* 19.15.

79. Mary Nyquist, *Arbitrary Rule: Slavery, Tyranny, and the Power of Life and Death* (Chicago: University of Chicago Press, 2013). I thank Luke Bretherton for bringing this work to my attention.

80. Nyquist, *Arbitrary Rule*, 219.

81. Nyquist, *Arbitrary Rule*, 219.

82. Nyquist, *Arbitrary Rule*, 219.

83. Alan Watson, *Roman Slave Law* (Baltimore: Johns Hopkins University Press, 1987), 7–8. Underdeveloped in my account is a theorization of indebtedness, the history of debt-slavery, and the relation of both to the present conditions of ethical life. For a starting point, see the special focus on debt in the *Journal of Religious Ethics*, especially the introductory essay by Luke Bretherton and Devin Singh, "The Axes of Debt: A Preface to Three Essays," *Journal of Religious Ethics* 46, no. 2 (2018): 207–16; and "Economy, Debt, Citizenship" in Bretherton, *Resurrecting Democracy*.

84. Nyquist, *Arbitrary Rule*, 220.

85. Nyquist, *Arbitrary Rule*, 222 (emphasis mine).

86. Samuel Seabury, *American Slavery distinguished from the Slavery of English Theorists, and Justified by the Law of Nature* (New York: Mason Brothers, 1861). See also the discussion in Carole Pateman, *The Sexual Contract* (Cambridge: Polity Press, 2018), 68 ff.

87. Seabury, *American Slavery*, 91–92.

88. Vives edition of *De civitate Dei*, as quoted in Seabury, *American Slavery*, 90.

89. Seabury, *American Slavery*, 91. en. Ps. 124.7.

90. For a discussion of the centrality of providential thinking to the defense of slavery in the eighteenth century, see Philippa Koch, "Slavery, Mission, and the Perils of Providence in Eighteenth-Century Christianity: The Writings of Whitefield and the Halle Pietists," *Church History* 84, no. 2 (June 2015): 369–93. Her conclusion is worth quoting: "The Christian acceptance of slavery in colonial Georgia *depended on the providential thought and language* that was developed in Christian missionary efforts and writings. In the end, a strong commitment to God's providence and the accompanying practice of retrospective narration allowed Christians to accept an abhorrent system of labor, whether because they saw it as a God-devised means of evangelism or as a system created by a divinely-appointed temporal government that Christians must obey" (393, emphasis mine).

91. Harper, *Slavery in the Late Roman World*, 67 (emphasis mine).

92. Through a series of diffuse but salient historical afterlives (on these see Jennifer Morgan in note 96 below), I have in the background Saidiya Hartman's notion of the captive woman as "the belly of the world," and Hortense Spillers's description of the Black American woman as "the principal point of passage between the human and the non-human world. Her issue became . . . the route by which the dominant modes decided the distinction between humanity and 'other.'" See Hartman, "The Belly of the World: A Note on Black Women's Labors," *Souls* 18 (2016), and Hortense Spillers, "Interstices: A Small Drama of Words," in *Black, White, and in Color*, 155.

93. Walter Scheidel is similarly cautious about the empirical limits imposed by the nature of the evidence available, yet shares the same conclusion: "General conditions in the Roman period permitted natural reproduction on a large scale: for mathematical reasons alone, it is hard to imagine that it was not at least as important as all other sources of slaves combined." See Scheidel, "The Roman Slave Supply," in *Cambridge World History of Slavery*, ed. Keith Bradley and Paul Cartledge (Cambridge: Cambridge University Press, 2011), 1:287.

94. Spillers, "Mama's Baby," 218 (emphasis original).

95. Harper, *Slavery in the Late Roman World*, 69.

96. On the afterlives of the *partus sequitur ventrem* doctrine in modern colonial law and in the early production of the meanings of race, see Jennifer L. Morgan, "*Partus sequitur ventrem*: Law, Race, and Reproduction in Colonial Slavery," *Small Axe* 55 (March 2018): 1–17.

97. Michael J. S. Bruno, *Political Augustinianism: Modern Interpretations of Augustine's Political Thought* (Minneapolis: Fortress Press, 2014), 59.

98. Bruno, *Political Augustinianism*, 57 (emphasis original).

99. Bruno, *Political Augustinianism*, 60.

100. As cited in Bruno, *Political Augustinianism*, 60.

101. See, for example, Mathewes, *Evil*, 202, where he narrates "the frustrated rage" of Augustine's critics as "rooted in a basic disposition of impatience with the way things are."

102. Griffiths, "Secularity and the *Saeculum*," 52 (emphasis mine).

103. There are intriguing historical reasons for this. The American Civil War over slavery might be understood as not only a "theological crisis"—as Mark Noll famously argued—but as a more specific theological conflict over competing *eschatologies*: broadly, between postmillenarian optimism and premillenarian pessimism, as is suggested in the uneven but interesting work of John H. Matsui, *Millenarian Dreams and Racial Nightmares: The American Civil War as an Apocalyptic Conflict* (Baton Rouge: Louisiana State University Press, 2021).

104. I am grateful to Rey Chow for discussions pressing me to think more carefully about mastery as a kind of *performance*.

105. Miles, "From Rape to Resurrection," 89.

106. Miles, "From Rape to Resurrection," 90.

107. Gregory, *Politics and the Order of Love*, 54.

108. Here I am referring back to the last part of Chapter 3, quoting s. 114.

109. Miles, "From Rape to Resurrection," 89.

110. Miles, "From Rape to Resurrection," 90.

111. Miles, "From Rape to Resurrection," 90. The passage quoted is 1 Cor. 13:12.

112. Miles, "From Rape to Resurrection," 90.

113. Miles, "From Rape to Resurrection," 90.

114. Delores S. Williams, *Sisters in the Wilderness: The Challenge of Womanist God-Talk* (Maryknoll, NY: Orbis, 1993). Patterson, *Slavery and Social Death*, 334–42. In the wake of Patterson, more recent sociologists and theorists have expanded the analytic of parasitism further. Among these, perhaps the most striking in its focus upon the longitudinal validity of the framework and its significant *gendered* dimensions is Fiona Greenland, "Long-Range Continuities in Comparative and Historical Sociology: The Case of Parasitism and Women's Enslavement," *Theory and Society* 48, no. 6 (December 2019). I am also thinking of the notion of "extractive parasitism," which draws out the specifically *ecological* dimensions of parasitism, as Greenland develops it in conversation with Achille Mbembe, *Critique of Black Reason* (Durham, NC: Duke University Press, 2017), 40.

115. Pliny the Elder, *Natural History* 29.8.

116. Delores Williams, "Social-Role Surrogacy: Naming Black Women's Oppression," in *Sisters in the Wilderness*, 54. Christina Sharpe, *Monstrous Intimacies: Making Post-Slavery Subjects* (Durham, NC: Duke University Press, 2010).

117. Dionne Brand, *A Map to the Door of No Return: Notes to Belonging* (Toronto: Vintage Canada, 2001), 30–31.

118. We are always dealing with a "continuum ranging from a point just prior to true mutualism to one just this side of total parasitism," as Patterson notes (*Slavery and Social Death*, 336).

119. s. 114.

120. For one extremely powerful account of this toll and of the theological imaginaries which arise from and respond to it, see M. Shawn Copeland, *Enfleshing Freedom: Body, Race, and Being* (Minneapolis: Fortress Press, 2010), esp. 23–53 and 110–24.

121. Patterson, *Slavery and Social Death*, 337.

122. Rist, *Augustine: Ancient Thought Baptized*, 237.

123. It is perhaps not accidental that this poignant phrase from Charles Mathewes comes in the context of an appreciative but firm critique of Oliver O'Donovan's "oddly ahistorical" account of ethical life, especially when it comes to our "inescapably, racialized, gendered, and sexualized" selves: "Yet despite the strong affirmation of temporality . . . it remains curiously abstracted from the concrete history of our world, and it does not talk about the complicated heritage of the concepts and categories that we, O'Donovan included, use to describe our lives these days." See Mathewes, "A Response to Oliver O'Donovan's *Ethics as Theology* Trilogy," *Modern Theology* 36, no. 1 (January 2020): 169–71. It is regrettable that in O'Donovan's response in the same issue, he can hear in Mathewes's critique only an "anguished consciousness" animated by something he calls "guilt at past disregard for cultural identities" (196), rather than the incisive and historically grounded invitation to more rigorous ethical thought that it is. Sarah Coakley, in her contribution to the same issue, likewise avoids a more serious engagement, reducing Mathewes's point to the status of "certain predictable criticisms," while declaring that she "deliberately eschew[s] the 'cheap' course of chiding him for these apparent oversights from an assumed position of liberal egalitarian rectitude" (187).

124. *doct. Chr.* 23.22.49. See *Teaching Christianity,* trans. Edmund Hill, O.P., WSA I/11 (Hyde Park, NY: New City Press, 1996).

125. *civ.* 19.17 (emphasis mine).

126. I am clearly drawing from the account of flesh in Hortense Spillers and Tiffany Lethabo King, and alongside this, there is also a rich precedent in early Christian theological tradition for speaking of flesh as a synecdoche for the human creature as such. Cyril of Alexandria, interpreting John 1:14—"the Word became flesh"—defends scripture's habit of "understanding the whole by the part" (the human by "the flesh") because it was "necessary that that which was most endangered in us [the flesh] should be the more urgently restored and by interacting again with that which has life by nature [the flesh of the Word] should be recalled to immortality." See Cyril of Alexandria, *Commentary on John,* ed. and trans. Norman Russell (New York: Routledge, 2000), 104–5.

127. Charles Mill, "Black Trash," in *Faces of Environmental Racism,* ed. Laura Westra and Bill E. Lawson (Lanham, MD: Rowman and Littlefield, 2001). This is, of course, a complex claim. I develop it further in "Climate Apartheid, Race, and the Future of Solidarity."

128. In a comment which at once echoes Augustine's point about the endemic nature of domination *and* yet draws a radically different conclusion, abolitionist organizer and intellectual Mariame Kaba writes: "A world without harm isn't possible and isn't what an abolitionist vision purports to achieve. Rather, abolitionist politics and practice contend that disposing of people by locking them away in jails and prisons does nothing significant to prevent, reduce, or transform harm in the aggregate." See Kaba, *We Do This 'Til We Free Us: Abolition Organizing and Transforming Justice* (Chicago: Haymarket, 2021), 3–4.

129. Ruth Wilson Gilmore, *Golden Gulag: Prisons, Surplus, Crisis, and Opposition in Globalizing California* (Berkeley: University of California Press, 2007), 28.

130. Behind my contention that this is "perennial," even as there are significant historical differences across various slaveholding societies, I am thinking of Keith Bradley's comment on how he approaches slavery in both its universal and particular dimensions: "My understanding is that slavery is an extreme form of a universal human tendency for

some members of society to exercise domination over others. It is an institution in which all humanity and personhood are denied the powerless by the powerful. . . . The historian's function accordingly is to identify the specific features of a given society and to define the particularist elements or emphases within it of a universal social formation that has generic and constant characteristics." See Bradley, "Roman Slavery: Retrospect and Prospect," *Canadian Journal of History* 43, no. 3 (December 2008): 482. Working in a theological register, I am suggesting that the dynamic I have been highlighting in this section—the master's desire to have invulnerability now through surrogate parasitism—belongs to this "universal human tendency" with "generic and constant characteristics."

131. Peter Brown, *Religion and Society* (New York: Harper and Row, 1972), 38.

132. *s.* 113A.11.

133. *s.* 19.6.

134. *De consensu Evangelistarum,* ii, 20, as cited in Brown, *Religion and Society,* 39, who notes, "The statement is all the more poignant as Augustine in his early days had once hoped for just such fulfilment."

135. Neil Roberts, "Angela Y. Davis," in Rogers and Turner, eds., *African American Political Thought,* 676–77.

136. As cited in adrienne maree brown, *We Will Not Cancel Us and Other Dreams of Transformative Justice* (Chico, CA: AK Press, 2021).

137. Angela Davis, *Freedom Is a Constant Struggle: Ferguson, Palestine, and the Foundations of a Movement* (Chicago: Haymarket, 2015).

138. David Scott, *Conscripts of Modernity: The Tragedy of Colonial Enlightenment* (Durham, NC: Duke University Press, 2004), 214.

139. *s.* 151.5.5–7 (emphasis mine).

FIVE. The Table and the Sea

Epigraph 1: *s.* 76.1.

Epigraph 2: *s.* 4.9.

Epigraph 3: *civ.* 20.15. Augustine is interpreting Revelation 20:13: *"And the sea gave up the dead that were in it."*

Epigraph 4: Excerpt from "The Sea Is History" from *The Star-Apple Kingdom* by Derek Walcott. Copyright © 1979 by Derek Walcott, Reprinted by permission of Farrar, Straus and Giroux. All Rights Reserved.

1. *s.* 76.1.

2. For one starting point, see chapter 12, "The Sea Is History: On Temporal Accumulation," in Ian Baucom, *Specters of the Atlantic: Finance Capital, Slavery, and the Philosophy of History* (Durham, NC: Duke University Press, 2005). See the poetic treatment of the infamous "Zong" case in M. NourbeSe Philip, *Zong!* (Middletown, CT: Wesleyan University Press, 2008).

3. *ep.* 10.4*, in *Letters,* vol. 4, trans. Roland J. Teske, S.J., *WSA* II/4 (Hyde Park, NY: New City Press, 2005).

4. On the point about slave traders, I have heard a comparison drawn to used car salesmen in the present: the fact that they are often stereotyped as dishonest or manipulative implies no particular critique of the auto industry, still less a commitment to building a

world beyond cars. See *en. Ps.* 65.9. The first sentence is from the *WSA* translation, the latter from the older, more stylized translation of J. E. Tweed, in *Nicene and Post-Nicene Fathers,* vol. 8, ed. Philip Schaff (New York: Christian Literature Company, 1888), 271.

5. Fernand Braudel, *La Méditerranée et le monde méditerranéen à l'époque de Philippe II* (Paris: Armand Colin, 1949). Peregrine Horden and Nicholas Purcell, *The Corrupting Sea: A Study of Mediterranean History* (Malden, MA: Wiley-Blackwell, 2000). Harper, *Slavery in the Late Roman World,* 508.

6. Patterson, *Slavery and Social Death,* 171.

7. "Augustine's theology of baptism could at the same time be a theology of the Eucharist. In his Easter morning sermons of the newly baptized, Augustine compared the stages of Christian initiation to making bread. . . . Thus Augustine would point to the bread on the altar and insist that 'the mystery that you are lies there on the table; it is your own mystery that you receive.' The rites of initiation had, in essence, made them the body of Christ; and he exhorted the newly baptized, in receiving communion, to 'Be what you see and receive what you are.' " See M. A. Tilley, "Baptism," in Fitzgerald, ed., *Augustine through the Ages,* 84–92, at 88.

8. Gregory, "Strange Fruit," 107.

9. Moten, *In the Break,* 1.

10. Houston Baker, *Modernism and the Harlem Renaissance* (Chicago: University of Chicago Press, 1987), 50–56.

11. As many commentators have noted, 1 Corinthians 13:12—"For now we see in a glass darkly, but then we shall see face to face"—figures centrally in Augustine's account of knowledge, especially knowledge of God. See for example Dodaro, *Christ and the Just Society in the Thought of Augustine,* 169.

12. For an excellent account of Augustine's evolving relation to Platonist thought across his oeuvre, see Stewart-Kroeker, *Pilgrimage as Moral and Aesthetic Formation in Augustine's Thought,* chapter 1, "The Plotinian Heritage of Augustine's Peregrinatio Image."

13. Williams, *On Augustine,* 45. My preceding paragraph is also indebted to his essay as a whole, "Language, Reality and Desire: The Nature of Christian Formation."

14. Williams, *On Augustine,* 46.

15. Williams, *On Augustine,* 49, 51.

16. *doct. chr.* 2.41.62.

17. K. M. Coleman, "Fatal Charades: Roman Executions Staged as Mythological Enactments," *Journal of Roman Studies* 80 (1990): 44–73.

18. Quintilian, *Declamationes* 274, in *The Lesser Declamations,* ed. and trans. D. R. Shackleton Bailey, vol. 1 (Cambridge, MA, and London: Harvard University Press, 2006), 259: "Quotiens noxios cruci figimus, celeberrimae eliguntur viae, ubi plurimi intueri, plurimi commoveri hoc metu possint. Omnis enim poena non tam ad delictum pertinet quam ad exemplum."

19. On the notion of crucifixion as "penal liturgy," a term from Michel Foucault which is usefully appropriated, see Joel Marcus, 'Crucifixion as Parodic Exaltation,' *Journal of Biblical Literature* 125 (2006): 73–87. Cf. John Granger Cook's fine article "Crucifixion as Spectacle in Roman Campania," *Novum Testamentum* 54 (2012), 68–100, which underscores that grasping the fact that crucifixion was a public spectacle provides scholars with "additional tools for understanding the scandalous nature of Paul's gospel of the crucified Christ" (68).

20. Allen, "Envisaging," 149 (emphasis mine).

21. As I explored in the previous chapter, such encounters are often staged in a flat-footed way as the clash of the eschatological tension Augustinianism preserves between earthly and heavenly cities and the supposed collapse of that tension in liberationism's urgent engagement with the demands of the present. Charles Long elaborates the term "theologies opaque" in chapter 12, "Freedom, Otherness, and Religion: Theologies Opaque," of *Significations: Signs, Symbols, and Images in the Interpretation of Religion* (Aurora, CO: Davies Group, 1999). I return to it below. Justo L. González has published an interesting book entitled *The Mestizo Augustine: A Theologian Between Two Cultures* (Downers Grove, IL: IVP Academic, 2016). But the framework of *mestizaje* (intermixture) upon which he relies does not allow the central conflict with which I am concerned here—namely, the violent asymmetry of power which enables the symbolic use of the dominated body to serve the self-deceptions of the dominator—to come into view as a problem for thought. For an exploration of why *mestizaje* tends to function this way, see Néstor Medina, *Mestizaje: (Re)Mapping Race, Culture, and Faith in Latina/o Catholicism* (Maryknoll, NY: Orbis, 2009), esp. 47–50.

22. As Charles Mathewes puts it, "By using the phrase 'the Augustinian tradition,' I mean to draw guidance from Augustine's thought, without being trapped in the historical cul-de-sac of debates about what Augustine 'really meant.' " Mathewes, *Theology of Public Life*, 19. Cf. Gregory, *Politics and the Order of Love*, 7–8. For one insightful discussion of the complex negotiations between what "the historical Augustine" said and meant, and how the Augustine of political Augustinianism animates and inspires wide-ranging engagements with modern projects (liberalism, populism, civic republicanism, and so on), see Kaufman, "Christian Realism and Augustinian (?) Liberalism."

23. On crucifixion in relation to gender and specifically masculinity, see Brittany E. Wilson, *Unmanly Men: Refigurations of Masculinity in Luke-Acts* (Oxford: Oxford University Press, 2015), 201–13. On the interrelation of sexualized dishonor and state violence, see David Tombs, "Crucifixion, State Terror, and Sexual Abuse," *Union Seminary Quarterly Review* 53 (1999): 89–110.

24. Comparative scholarship of slavery continues to employ Moses Finley's classic distinction, but has largely shifted toward speaking of the two as ideal types, locating particular societies on a spectrum between them, with various gradations and shades, rather than as a tidy binary in the way Finley and some inheritors tended to. See Noel Lenski and Catherine M. Cameron, eds., *What Is a Slave Society?: The Practice of Slavery in Global Perspective* (Cambridge: Cambridge University Press, 2018).

25. Felicity Harley, "Crucifixion in Roman Antiquity: The State of the Field," *Journal of Early Christian Studies* 27, no. 2 (Summer 2019): 303–23.

26. Jean-Jacques Aubert, "A Double Standard in Criminal Law?: The Death Penalty and Social Structure in Late Republican and Early Imperial Rome," in *Speculum Iuris: Roman Law as a Reflection of Social and Economic Life in Antiquity*, ed. Jean-Jacques Aubert and Boudewijn Sirks (Ann Arbor: University of Michigan Press, 2002), 113.

27. A classic, influential treatment of the subject is chapter 8, "The Slaves' Punishment," of Martin Hengel, "Mors turpissima crucis: Die Kreuzigung in der antiken Welt und die 'Torheit' des 'Wortes vom Kreuz,' " in *Rechtfertigung, Festschrift für Ernst Käsemann*, ed. J. Friedrich, W. Pohlmann, and P. Stuhlmacher (Tübingen and Göttingen, 1976), 125–84,

translated by John Bowden as *Crucifixion in the Ancient World and the Folly of the Message of the Cross* (London and Philadelphia, 1977). Harley's "Crucifixion in Roman Antiquity" notes that Hengel's volume has been decisively superseded by four works on crucifixion in Roman antiquity: David Chapman, *Ancient Jewish and Christian Perceptions of Crucifixion*, Wissenschaftliche Untersuchungen zum Neuen Testament II/244 (Tübingen, 2008), which reaffirms but does not dwell upon the connection to the enslaved body on p. 44; David Chapman and Eckhard Schnabel, *The Trial and Crucifixion of Jesus*, Wissenschaftliche Untersuchungen zum Neuen Testament 344 (Tübingen: Mohr Siebeck, 2015); John Granger Cook, *Crucifixion in the Mediterranean World*, Wissenschaftliche Untersuchungen zum Neuen Testament 327 (Tübingen: Mohr Siebeck, 2014); and Gunnar Samuelsson, *Crucifixion in Antiquity: An Inquiry into the Background and Significance of the New Testament Terminology of Crucifixion*, Wissenschaftliche Untersuchungen zum Neuen Testament II/310 (Tübingen: Mohr Siebeck, 2011).

28. Winsome Munro has argued that Jesus of Nazareth was in fact a slave, though most have not found the case persuasive. See Munro, *Jesus, Born of a Slave: The Social and Economic Origins of Jesus' Message* (Lewiston, NY: Edwin Mellen, 1998). For a counterargument, see Glancy, *Slavery in Early Christianity*, 100–101. I side with the unpersuaded critics.

29. Aubert, "A Double Standard in Criminal Law?," 114 (emphasis mine).

30. Lavan, *Slaves to Rome*, 124–25.

31. For a helpful overview of the sprawling critical landscape addressing Philippians 2:5–11, see Gregory P. Fewster, "The Philippians 'Christ Hymn': Trends in Critical Scholarship," *Currents in Biblical Research* 13, no. 2 (2015): 191–206. While many New Testament scholars have examined the close relation of crucifixion and slavery in the passage, David P. Moessner applies the very point I've been making in this section—that to crucify is to recast the victim's body as an enslaved body—to the specific context of Philippians 2: "The agent[s] of Christ Jesus' crucifixion . . . treated him as 'the form of a slave' (2:7b—μορφή δούλου) when they crucified him." See "Turning Status 'Upside Down' in Philippi: Christ Jesus' 'Emptying Himself' as Forfeiting Any Acknowledgment of His 'Equality with God' (Phil 2:6–11)," *Horizons in Biblical Theology* 31 (2009): 140.

32. Ayres, *Augustine and the Trinity*, 144–46.

33. J. Albert Harrill, *Slaves in the New Testament: Literary, Social, and Moral Dimensions* (Minneapolis, MN: Fortress Press, 2006), 26.

34. Joshel, "Slavery and Roman Literary Culture," 230 (emphasis mine).

35. Jennifer Glancy's work has been especially powerful in underscoring how the absence of enslaved voices in the historical archives bears witness to this erasure and silence, producing real epistemic limits for the historical researcher of slavery who must hear only the masters' side of the story. See Glancy, *Slavery in Early Christianity*, 130.

36. See Susannah Elm, "Sold to Sin through Origo: Augustine of Hippo and the Late Roman Slave Trade," *Studia Patristica* 93 (2016): 11–12.

37. Glancy, *Slavery in Early Christianity*, 71–72.

38. Glancy, *Slavery in Early Christianity*, 72.

39. For an excellent introduction to the literature, see Jürgen Hammerstaedt, "Crux," in *Augustinus-Lexikon*, vol. 2, ed. Cornelius Mayer (Basel: Schwabe, 1986), 143–52, esp. the bibliography on 151.

40. Augustine spoke of the cross as a boat amid "this river of the horrible wickedness of the human race," and as wood which we must reach out and "grasp" so that we are not "pulled down by so vast a whirlpool of this world." See *ep.* 138.17. Augustine uses the image again similarly in *Homilies on the Gospel of John* 2.62.

41. For the notion of "taken" signs, I thank Ashleigh Elser.

42. I owe the phrase "unsanctioned communion" to a conversation with Willie James Jennings.

43. Patterson, *Slavery and Social Death*, 97.

44. Nahum Chandler, "Of Exorbitance: The Problem of the Negro as a Problem for Thought," *Criticism* 50, no. 3 (Summer 2008): 345–410.

45. Williams, *On Augustine*, 46.

46. Long, *Significations*, 184.

47. Long, *Significations*, 184. On the ongoing salience of Long's thought, see the wide-ranging theorizations of J. Kameron Carter, "Anarchē: Or, the Matter of Charles Long and Black Feminism," *American Religion* 2, no. 2 (Spring 2021): 103–35.

48. Weheliye, "After Man," 322 (emphasis mine).

49. Katie Grimes, *Christ Divided: Antiblackness as Corporate Vice* (Minneapolis: Fortress Press, 2017), 205. I share Grimes's broad commitment to pressing beyond sacramental optimism, but diverge from her alternative proposal of "sacramental realism." I might be closer to what she calls "sacramental pessimism."

50. For a starting point, see the policy proposals of the Movement for Black Lives (https://m4bl.org/resources/), the work of Interrupting Criminalization: Research in Action (https://www.interruptingcriminalization.com/), and Climate Justice Alliance (https://climatejusticealliance.org/get-involved/).

51. James Cone, *The Cross and the Lynching Tree* (Maryknoll, NY: Orbis, 2011), 162 (emphasis original).

52. Copeland, *Enfleshing Freedom*, 124–28. What is entailed by solidarity, both conceptually and practically, is immense and complex. I leave it here open, as my next book project, provisionally titled *We Are Each Other's Harvest: Solidarity at the End of the World*, turns to explore the subject at length. A portion of this book appears as "Climate Apartheid, Race, and the Future of Solidarity."

53. James H. Cone, *A Black Theology of Liberation* (Maryknoll, NY: Orbis, 1970), and *The Cross and the Lynching Tree* (Maryknoll, NY: Orbis, 2013).

EPILOGUE. Tenebrae

Epigraph 1: *civ.* 11.8. This translation is from Henry Bettenson, *Concerning the City of God Against the Pagans* (Harmondsworth, UK: Penguin, 1972). Babcock has "a creature's knowledge is like the dusk of evening," while Dyson has "the knowledge of the creature is like a kind of evening light."

Epigraph 2: Carole Boyce Davies, *Caribbean Spaces: Escapes from Twilight Zones* (Chicago: University of Illinois Press, 2013), 19.

1. I borrow this elocution—the slave's two bodies—from Stephen M. Best's brilliant book *The Fugitive's Properties: Law and the Poetics of Possession* (Chicago: University of Chicago Press, 2004), but it is important to note a distinction in my usage here. Best is referring

specifically to the two bodies "*recognized by law*—the first mortal and the second ('considered as immoveable by the operation of law' . . .) implicitly immortal. As it was often suggested, the slave was an object of property as well as a subject of sentiment" (4, emphasis mine). Within the order of slavery, as I have emphasized throughout, the slave occupies this vexed position as living property, as human commodity, both object and subject. Given that this racial order is modified, not eradicated, after slavery's juridical abolition, the subjecthood imputed to the enslaved after (and *as*) emancipation was a circumscribed humanity of recognized personhood, liberal agency, and individual responsibility, one which "extended and intensified servitude and dispossession, rather than conferring some small measure of rights and protection," as Saidiya Hartman so influentially argued in *Scenes of Subjection* (Preface, xxxii). Therefore, the second body I am referring to here is not the slave's second body recognized by law—not the legal recognition of subjecthood/subjection—but rather the fleshly life of the enslaved person. Immensely difficult to name, describe, or encounter given her appearance within the very archives coextensive with her subjection, this is the life Hartman aims to bring into view by attending carefully to "the tactics that comprise the everyday practices of the dominated." See Hartman, *Scenes of Subjection*, 83, and the entirety of the sections entitled "The Centrality of Practice" and "The Character of Practice" (83–93). I am interested in the way the latter—the everyday practices of the enslaved—engender a break between the first body (the figure of the slave in the texts of the master class, whether legal, literary, or theological) and the second body (the life we meet in the traces of everyday practice).

2. My use of "excess" in this sentence is indebted to Christina Sharpe's description of "Black being that continually exceeds all of the violence directed at Black life; Black being that exceeds that force." Sharpe, *In the Wake*, 134.

3. Here I join Marika Rose in aiming "to refuse the temptation to distinguish between a pure and ideal form of Christianity to which we aspire and the oppressive and lethal Christianity of which we are a part." See Rose, *A Theology of Failure: Žižek Against Christian Innocence* (New York: Fordham University Press, 2019), 178.

4. In this repurposing of Victor Turner's account of the performance process, taken up in Saidiya Hartman's *Scenes of Subjection*, it is worth noting that the breakdown marks a state not of redemption, but of expenditure—of "bodies exhausted and restored, broken and unsovereign, anguished and redressed" (133).

5. On the former (broadly, postliberal engagement with "tradition"), for a general entry to the debates, see John Webster and George P. Schner, *Theology After Liberalism: A Reader* (Oxford: Blackwell, 2000); see also Jeffrey Stout, *Democracy and Tradition* (Princeton, NJ: Princeton University Press, 2004), esp. 92–161; and for an interesting account of how Stout's work helped enable many of the Augustinian interlocutors I've engaged throughout, Jonathan Tran, "Assessing the Augustinian Democrats," *Journal of Religious Ethics* 46, no. 3 (2018): 521–47. On the latter (broadly, contextual engagement with "liberation"), there are by its very nature many starting points, but in addition to texts I will engage with in more detail below in the body of the text, see the Controversies in Contextual Theology series, coedited by Marcella Althaus-Reid and Lisa Isherwood. Their series introduction is worth quoting in its entirety, for it articulates with precision the real risk I run (or perhaps the trap I fall into) of imagining too much homogeneity, of underplaying the internal differentiations

not just between, say, Black liberation theology and Latin American liberation theology, but among competing visions *internal* to each. "Contextual theologies such as Liberation, Black or Feminist theologies have been the object of critical studies in the past. Such critiques, especially when mounted by western academics, have tended to adopt an essentialist approach to these distinct theologies, assuming homogeneity in their development. In reality, on closer inspection, they display profound differences of both content and method. Controversies in Contextual Theology is the first series to highlight and examine these divisions. Each volume brings together two protagonists from within one form of contextual theology. The issues which divide them are openly addressed. Arguments are developed and positions clarified, but there is no guarantee that reconciliation can be achieved." See Marcella Althaus-Reid and Lisa Isherwood, *Controversies in Feminist Theology* (London: SCM Press, 2007), vii. That said, given various developments in the intervening years since the series emerged, my own sense of our intellectual situation does not suggest a rampant lack of awareness among scholars of how radically heterogeneous the state of the field is; on the contrary, there are real risks too in the possibility that hyperawareness of this fragmentation, perhaps counterintuitively, actually hinders the flourishing of difference, insofar as the field comes to be composed of various silos which rarely encounter one another.

6. On "structures of feeling," a contested concept, see Raymond Williams, *Marxism and Literature* (Oxford: Oxford University Press, 1977), 128–35, though more recently scholars have highlighted its much earlier emergence in his thinking. See James Chandler, "I. A. Richards and Raymond Williams: Reading Poetry, Reading Society," *Critical Inquiry* 46 (Winter 2020): esp. 344–50.

7. Linn Tonstad, "(Un)wise Theologians: Systematic Theology in the University," *International Journal of Systematic Theology* 22, no. 4 (October 2020): 504.

8. Tonstad, "(Un)wise Theologians," 504.

9. Audre Lorde, "Poetry Is Not a Luxury," in *Sister Outsider: Essays and Speeches* (New York: Penguin, 2020), 24.

10. Plato, *The Republic*, ed. G. R. F. Ferrari, trans. Tom Griffith (Cambridge: Cambridge University Press, 2000). It is unavoidable here to mention the wide-ranging debates on how to read Augustine in relation to Platonic thought with all the staggering complexity it entails. Though my intention is not to stake out a position in such debates, my thinking has been shaped by John Cavadini's critique of Philip Cary, Brian Stock, and others in the (fittingly titled) essay "The Darkest Enigma: Reconsidering the Self in Augustine's Thought," *Augustinian Studies* 38, no. 1 (2007), especially his argument that Augustine, in the metaphor of the *interior homo*, gives an account of human life which "defies reduction to a pure metaphysical entity to which the accidents of history and body are essentially irrelevant" (124).

11. The phrase "genres of illumination" is from Felicia Denaud, "Into the Clear, Unreal, Idyllic Light of the Beginning | A Will of the Night," *Caliban's Readings*, the blog of the Caribbean Philosophical Association (December 2022), https://caribbeanphilosophy.org/blog/idyllic-light (accessed Feb. 6, 2023).

12. Wetzel, "Augustine on the Origin of Evil," 177.

13. "More so than many of his contemporaries, Augustine was aware not only of his own ability to go astray but also, in the aftermath of Rome's invasion, of the likelihood that all human projects will fail. . . . To think about tradition with Augustine is always to keep in

mind the fragility of any human project, including the symbolic construction of the Augustinian tradition itself." Jonathan Teubner, *Prayer After Augustine: A Study in the Development of the Latin Tradition* (Oxford: Oxford University Press, 2017), 6. Of course, the precise relation of Augustine to Platonism, as well as how it evolves over the course of his very long writing life, remains fiercely contested, as it should be. What follows here does not depend on taking a particular position within these debates. The work of Robert Crouse remains an important point of entry; see "Paucis Mutatis Verbis: St. Augustine's Platonism" in Dodaro and Lawless, eds., *Augustine and His Critics*, 37–50.

14. Teubner, *Prayer After Augustine*, 6.

15. "The kinematics of the Augustinian tradition must therefore be carefully distinguished from modern accounts of so-called 'doctrinal development' in which an anxiety about essence and accretion is at the centre of the reflection. When distinguished from 'traditionalism,' tradition is the very process by which change occurs." Teubner, *Prayer After Augustine*, 214.

16. Teubner, *Prayer After Augustine*, 4.

17. Here, as throughout this project, I emphasize that the point is not simply to fill in a previous absence, to listen for voice where there has previously been silence, but to interrogate *what work that absence was doing*, what productive role the "silence" is playing for the dominant approach. I think of Sylvia Wynter's approach to the absence of Caliban's woman in the *Tempest*: "In effect, rather than only voicing the 'native' woman's hitherto silenced voice, we shall ask: What is the systemic function of her own silencing, as both woman and, more totally, as 'native' woman?" See Sylvia Wynter, "Afterword: Beyond Miranda's Meanings: Un/silencing the 'Demonic Ground' of Caliban's Woman," in *Out of the Kumbla: Caribbean Women and Literature*, ed. Carole Boyce Davies and Elaine Savory Fido (Trenton, NJ: Africa World Press, 1994), 365.

18. I imagine Teubner would view this as compatible with the notion of tradition as duty with which he concludes his fine study: "If it requires repair, we repair; if it requires emendation, we emend; if it requires pruning, we prune. The genealogical exercise, when used only to pick out bogeymen, is a childish game. We need to learn to accept the blame for our traditions and meet their challenges." Teubner, *Prayer After Augustine*, 224. My thinking on inclusion here is indebted to Linn Marie Tonstad, "The Limits of Inclusion: Queer Theology and Its Others," *Theology and Sexuality* 21, no. 1 (2015), which I engage at some length in Matthew Elia, "Sarah's Laugh, Sodom's Sin, Hagar's Kin: Queering Time and Belonging in Genesis 16–21," *Biblical Interpretation* 28 (2020): 414–17.

19. Edward Shill, *Tradition* (Chicago: University of Chicago Press, 1981), 213 (emphasis mine).

20. Teubner, *Prayer After Augustine*, 7–8.

21. See Hans Frei, *Types of Christian Theology*, 2; Tanner, *Theories of Culture*, 105; and most recently, "Appendix: Objections to the Cultural-Linguistic Approach," in Eugene F. Rogers, *Elements of Christian Thought: A Basic Course in Christianese* (Augsburg Fortress, 2021), 195–201. Of course, notably, Teubner's key innovations—tradition1 and tradition2, speaking of "Christian existence," focusing on a practice like prayer, as well as on different levels of traditions and subtraditions—radically expands the cultural-linguistic approach by extending our sense of what a tradition is beyond "texts," language, and grammar in a

narrow sense. My point here is that placing the emphasis upon the *internal* rather than *external*, by my reading, places Teubner within this broad approach when compared with other influential alternatives in modern theological method, notably, the broadly "correlationist" approaches associated with Paul Tillich, David Tracy, and the University of Chicago. For one point of entry to the latter, see David Tracy, *Filaments: Theological Profiles* (Chicago: University of Chicago Press, 2020), chapters 8 and 12.

22. MacIntyre, *Whose Justice?*, 373 and 376.

23. MacIntyre, *Whose Justice?*, 376–77 (italics original).

24. Robin Fox, "Structure of Personal Names on Tory Island," *Man* 63 (October 1963): 153.

25. Stout, *Democracy and Tradition*, 101–2.

26. Stout, *Democracy and Tradition*, 102 (emphasis mine).

27. In this, I echo the final point of Cornel West's deeply appreciative critique of *Democracy and Tradition* in a session of the 2003 AAR Annual Meeting: "Last but not least, I think the book needs to highlight the degree to which America has always had expansionist impulses and has always had imperial ends and aims—so that our discussion of the present moment is not one in which this is somehow so new and novel." I also follow West in siding, in a very deep and serious way, with Stout over and against MacIntyre, Hauerwas, and Milbank in the specific respect that the latter, in their "castigating modernity, castigating democracy," and so on, "don't recognize the degree to which democracies are so fragile." See Jason Springs, Cornel West, Richard Rorty, Stanley Hauerwas, and Jeffrey Stout, "Pragmatism and Democracy: Assessing Jeffrey Stout's *Democracy and Tradition*," *Journal of the American Academy of Religion* 78, no. 2 (June 2010): 416–18. Recent years make this concern appear especially clear-sighted, even prescient. Writing nearly twenty years after its publication, my regard for *Democracy and Tradition* has only grown, even as our situation—in a moment of the emerging climate catastrophe's magnifying global injustices rooted in colonialism—also intensifies the need to examine Stout's neglect of the colonial and imperial histories of race beyond the nation-form, precisely in order to take seriously his immense insight into the genuinely fragile nature of democratic political life and the role of virtue and tradition in sustaining it. For an introduction to this way of interpreting the moral significance of climate change, see Olúfẹ́mi O. Táíwò, *Reconsidering Reparations* (Oxford: Oxford University Press, 2021), esp. chapters 2 and 5.

28. Stout, *Democracy and Tradition*, 127.

29. The lines Stout quotes from MacIntyre in this paragraph are found in *Whose Justice?*, 209, as cited in *Democracy and Tradition*, 127. This account of how traditions work remains almost shockingly distant from what I have proposed, following Black Studies, as the signature encounters of the modern world. One could say of MacIntyre's account of tradition, and to a lesser but real extent Stout, what Sylvester Johnson recently noted of J. Z. Smith: "Oddly, one gets little sense of any violent reality when reading Smith. Rather, Smith's scholarship on religious taxonomy renders a benign portrait of European thinking and contemplating rather nonviolently. If we assume that Smith was not exceptional in rendering such a benign and thus ahistorical account of European intellection, then the explanation becomes rather obvious. Smith was merely leveraging a common practice of most white academics. Throughout his career, he ignored the scholarship of those who have

taken seriously the colonial plight of non-white peoples as crucial data for interpreting the record of human history and for gauging the human condition. What is most dismal about this, in fact, is arguably the quotidian nature of such Eurocentric bias." Sylvester A. Johnson, "Religions in All Ages and Places: Discerning Colonialism with Jonathan Z. Smith," *Journal of the American Academy of Religion* 87, no. 1 (March 2019): 34.

30. Relevant here is Hazel Carby's brilliant critique of the recently influential work of Isabelle Wilkerson: "After the Abolition Act of 1833, the British repurposed slave ships to transport more than a million indentured labourers from India to work on plantations in their colonies around the globe, resulting in the complex entanglements of caste and race in British Guiana, Jamaica and Trinidad. Wilkerson sees caste as both cause and symptom of a Manichean division between black and white in the early days of North American colonisa-tion, but this division tells us little about the effects of gender and class, and can't account for indigeneity. If we broaden our understanding to include the history of racial geographies across the Americas, rather than uncritically accepting national boundaries established long after the European invasions, encounters with indigenous inhabitants become central to any attempt at making sense of the classification and division of humanity. . . . *Instead of think-ing in exclusionary national units,* our work and our institutions should acknowledge these interconnected histories and forge links between black, indigenous and Latinx communi-ties." See "Between Black and White," *London Review of Books,* Jan. 7, 2021, https://www.lrb .co.uk/the-paper/v43/n02/hazel-v.-carby/between-black-and-white (accessed Jan. 12, 2021).

31. Willie James Jennings, *After Whiteness: An Education in Belonging* (Grand Rapids, MI: Eerdmans, 2020), 136 (emphasis mine).

32. Jennings, *The Christian Imagination,* 71.

33. My reading of MacIntyre (here especially) has benefited immensely from conversa-tions with Luke Bretherton and especially his placing of MacIntyre within the context of debates among the British New Left in "Political Theology, Radical Democracy, and Virtue Ethics; or Alasdair MacIntyre and the Paradoxes of a Revolutionary Consciousness," *Political Theology* 22, no. 7 (2021): esp. 635–39.

34. MacIntyre, *Whose Justice?,* 378.

35. Fox, "Structure of Personal Names on Tory Island," 155.

36. MacIntyre, *Ethics in the Conflicts of Modernity: An Essay on Desire, Practical Reasoning, and Narrative* (Cambridge: Cambridge University Press, 2016), 123.

37. For example, in the " 'today" of *what matters today,* we hear echoes of what Johannes Fabian called "the denial of coevalness," that unacknowledged temporal framework of colo-nial knowledge by which an emerging world system locks nonwestern peoples forever in the past. See Fabian, *Time and the Other: How Anthropology Makes Its Object* (New York: Columbia University Press, 1983).

38. Cedric Robinson, *The Terms of Order: Political Science and the Myth of Leadership* (Chapel Hill: University of North Carolina Press, 2016).

39. It should be acknowledged that moments in his otherwise robust portrait of James risk approaching a kind of just-so story that illustrates, a little too conveniently, MacIntyre's own intellectual positions, as when he narrates James thus: "By the 1960s this individualist conception of himself had been displaced. He now understood those same choices as an expression of his formation by and his allegiance to a complex tradition or set of traditions."

I am not sure MacIntyre stands in a position to declare authoritatively that by doing so, James "recognized himself for what he was." See *Ethics in the Conflicts of Modernity*, 293.

40. Wynter, "On How We Mistook the Map for the Territory," 116.

41. Wynter, "On How We Mistook the Map for the Territory," 112. The internal quotation marks are Wynter citing Amiri Baraka.

42. The very useful phrase "both assimilated into and excluded from the social order" comes from Joseph R. Winters, *Hope Draped in Black: Race, Melancholy, and the Agony of Progress* (Durham, NC: Duke University Press, 2016), 19–20.

43. Wynter, "On How We Mistook the Map for the Territory," 112 (emphasis mine).

44. Wynter, "On How We Mistook the Map for the Territory," 109. For a way into the present state of the field in the tradition of Black Studies Wynter here engages, see Joshua Myers, *Of Black Study* (London: Pluto Press, 2023).

45. Willie James Jennings, "The Traditions of Race Men," *South Atlantic Quarterly* 112, no. 4 (Fall 2013): 622.

46. Jennings, "The Traditions of Race Men," 622.

47. William James, *Essays in Psychology* (Cambridge: MA: Harvard University Press, 1984), 247.

48. *Gn. litt.* 9.20–21 (emphasis mine). Citations are to *The Literal Meaning of Genesis*, trans. Edmund Hill, O.P., in *On Genesis*, WSA I/13 (Hyde Park, NY: New City Press, 2002).

49. *Gn. litt.* 9.22.

50. *Gn. litt.* 9.22, 388n21.

51. The recent resurgence of interest in defending colonialism explicitly (Nigel Biggar et al.), though a sad and unfortunate embarrassment for the defenders themselves, has the welcome effect of elegantly proving what is so often denied: that the sort of theological projects aligned with them, the sort which previously would claim to be on the side neither of the formerly colonized nor of the formerly colonizing, can now be recognized for what they are and, as such, their intellectual contributions—if not the reality of their enduring power and resources in the academic world—need not be taken very seriously. What is more difficult, when moving against and beyond this sort of traditionalist project, is what to do on the other side.

52. Derek Walcott, *What the Twilight Says: Essays* (New York: Farrar, Straus and Giroux, 1998), 3–4.

53. Walcott, *What the Twilight Says*, 4.

54. Walcott, *What the Twilight Says*, 4.

55. As cited in Jennings, "The Traditions of Race Men," 613.

56. Walcott, *What the Twilight Says*, 15.

57. The phrase "anteriority and newness" is Bedour Alagraa's, and I am indebted throughout this section and beyond to her brilliant work, especially "Homo Narrans and the Science of the Word: Toward a Caribbean Radical Imagination," *Critical Ethnic Studies* 4, no. 2 (Fall 2018): 169–70. See also Alagraa, *The Interminable Catastrophe* (forthcoming from Duke University Press).

58. In Shakespeare's *Tempest*, his most direct engagement with the emerging colonization of the New World, the native inhabitant Caliban says to his new master Prospero: "You taught me language, and my profit on't / Is I know how to curse. The red plague rid

you / For learning me your language!" (1.2.362–64). A tremendous amount of postcolonial writing has been dedicated to revisiting, unmaking, and reconfiguring this primal scene of modernity. See for instance Aimé Césaire's 1969 play *Une Tempête*; and Wynter, "Afterword: Beyond Miranda's Meanings."

59. For Walcott, both require an attenuated view of Caliban solely as "enraged pupil": "they cannot separate the rage of Caliban from the beauty of his speech when the speeches of Caliban are equal in their elemental power to those of his tutor." Walcott, *What the Twilight Says*, 38–39.

60. The latter is from Lorde, "Poetry Is Not a Luxury," 26 (emphasis mine). The more famous line appears in both Lorde, "Age, Race, Class, and Sex: Women Redefining Difference" and "The Master's Tools Will Never Dismantle the Master's House." See Lorde, *Sister Outsider*, 113.

61. "Pivoting on the couplet of the particular and the universal, this strategy dehistoricized the moment of critique of white male hegemony. It turned and turns contextuality into a commonsense vision of situatedness. The idea that we all speak from a particular context now functions ideologically, concealing rather than disclosing ideological operations." Jennings, "The Traditions of Race Men," 622. Examples of Jennings's point abound. I think of the following from David Ford, as he steps back to reflect broadly on twentieth-century theology: "The global character of twentieth-century theology lay not just in types that had a global reach and participation, but also in the range of theologies that were often highly specific in their orientation or local in context. In the third edition of *The Modern Theologians* some of these are labeled 'Particularizing Theologies,' including black theology of liberation, Latin American liberation theology; African, South Asian, and East Asian theologies; and postcolonial biblical interpretation. . . . There is also a feedback effect on other theologies that might not have seen themselves as 'particularist.' . . . *In a sense, we are all particularist now,* encouraged to be more aware of what has shaped us, such as origins, contexts, interests, perspectives, and limitations." See David F. Ford, *The Future of Christian Theology* (Malden, MA: Blackwell, 2011).

62. This notion of the appositional is indebted to J. Kameron Carter, "Paratheological Blackness," *South Atlantic Quarterly* 112, no. 4 (Fall 2013): 591.

63. As cited in Jack Turner, "Audre Lorde's Anti-Imperial Consciousness," *Political Theory* 49, no. 2 (April 2021): 246.

64. In his 1956 letter of resignation from the French Communist Party, Aimé Césaire writes: "Provincialism? Not at all. I am not burying myself in a narrow particularism. But neither do I want to lose myself in an emaciated universalism. There are two ways to lose oneself: walled segregation in the particular or dilution in the 'universal.' My conception of the universal is that of a universal enriched by all that is particular, a universal enriched by every particular: the deepening and coexistence of all particulars." See "Letter to Maurice Thorez," *Social Text* 28, no. 2 (2010): 152.

65. Walcott, *What the Twilight Says*, 36–39.

66. Walcott, *What the Twilight Says*, 40–41.

67. Walcott, *What the Twilight Says*, 42, 15.

68. Walcott, *What the Twilight Says*, 39.

69. For one example, one might consider Cambridge-educated philosopher Francis Bacon, who "connected utopian thought with practical projects, writing *New Atlantis*, 'Of

Empire,' and 'Of Plantations' while investing in the Virginia Company," which would enact the early project of English colonization and expropriation of the New World. See Peter Linebaugh and Marcus Rediker, *The Many-Headed Hydra: Sailors, Slaves, Commoners, and the Hidden History of the Revolutionary Atlantic* (Boston: Beacon Press, 2000), 37.

70. Walcott, *What the Twilight Says*, 39, 46–48.

71. Walcott, *What the Twilight Says*, 42.

72. Walcott, *What the Twilight Says*, 63. Informing my thinking here are two other texts. In *Who Will Pay Reparations on My Soul?: Essays* (New York: Liveright, 2021), Jesse McCarthy addresses the book's essays "very expressly, to the younger generations struggling right now to find their footing in a deeply troubled world. If there is one thing I would wish for them to take from these essays it is the basic premise that nothing is outside our purview, that there are no limits to the ideas, realms of knowledge, creative traditions, or political histories that we can lay claim to and incorporate. And that the knowledge of the accumulated genius of our literary, intellectual, political, and religious traditions is crucial to determining a course not only through the present crisis but through those still to come" (xviii–xix). In a recent essay, Hilton Als retells a classroom story of George W. S. Trow, in which, when a great artistic work from European tradition is taught as though it belonged to white students, in a way in which it did not belong the Black students, the "idea was seized on by white members of the class. They acknowledged that they were at one with Rembrandt. They acknowledged their dominance. They offered to discuss, at any length, their inherited power to oppress. It was thought at the time that reactions of this type had to do with 'white guilt' or 'white masochism.' No. No. It was white euphoria. Many, many white children of that day felt the power of their inheritance for the first time in the act of rejecting it, and they insisted on rejecting it . . . so that they might continue to feel the power of that connection." Hilton Als, "My Mother's Dreams for Her Son, and All Black Children," *New Yorker*, June 21, 2020, https://www.newyorker.com/magazine/2020/06/29/my-mothers-dreams-for-her-son-and-all-black-children (accessed June 27, 2020). It seems worth considering whether the rejection of whole domains of knowledge as latently white, or whole theological traditions as proto-European, is related not to white guilt but to this sort of white euphoria—a claiming of power in the act of rejecting it. Sometimes you check your privilege like you check a suitcase; set it down and declare it, precisely so you can pick it up later and retain it indefinitely.

73. James Baldwin, "To Be Baptized," in *No Name in the Street*, in *James Baldwin: Collected Essays*, ed. Toni Morrison (New York: Library of America, 1998), 404.

74. Here I am grateful to the comments of the second anonymous reader commissioned by Yale University Press, who pressed me to think more clearly on this point.

75. Hortense Spillers, "Moving on Down the Line: Variations on the African-American Sermon," in *Black, White, and in Color*, 252. Spillers, notably, is speaking specifically of "the African-American's relationship to Christianity and the state," and in this context, given the argument I have made to this point, I am suggesting this specific sort of ambivalence is what those who wish to defect from their inherited positions of white mastery should take seriously, should allow to shape how they relate to the intellectual traditions they inherit.

76. Scott, *Conscripts of Modernity*, 179.

77. Davies, *Caribbean Spaces*, 19.

78. I take the phrase "edge of words" from Rowan Williams, *The Edge of Words: God and the Habits of Language* (London: Bloomsbury, 2014). The latter part of the sentence riffs on a line from Saidiya Hartman: "to reckon with the precarious lives which are visible only in the moment of their disappearance." See Hartman, "Venus in Two Acts," 12.

79. Jennifer Trimble, "The Zoninus Collar and the Archaeology of Roman Slavery," *American Journal of Archaeology* 120, no. 3 (July 2016): 460–61.

80. Trimble, "The Zoninus Collar and the Archaeology of Roman Slavery," 450.

81. D. L. Thurmond, "Some Roman Slave Collars in *CIL*," *Athenaeum* 82 (January 1994): 459.

82. Thurmond, "Some Roman Slave Collars in *CIL*," 459.

83. MacIntyre, *Whose Justice?*, 377.

84. There is remarkable difficulty, Jennifer Morgan points out, in trying to recover what the archive holds and describes and endlessly details, and yet which it cannot truly reveal: "So many reams of paper, so much flotsam, and yet we still are faced with secrets and silences that testify to how crucial those archival erasures are to the construction of an exclusionary 'human.' Perhaps the surprise is rather in the degree to which we are constantly *thwarted in our efforts to name*—to unearth the person or persons referred to as only *negro* or indeed misnamed something much, much worse." Jennifer L. Morgan, "Archives and Histories of Racial Capitalism: An Afterword," *Social Text* 33, no. 4 (December 2015): 157 (emphasis mine).

85. Spillers, "Moving on Down the Line," 203 (emphasis mine).

86. Spillers, "Moving on Down the Line," 224–25. Spillers notes suggestively that "stillness" is an "early version of ethnicity."

87. Nathaniel Mackey, "Other: From Noun to Verb," *Representations* 39 (Summer 1992): 51–70.

88. Roy Harris and Talbot J. Taylor, *Landmarks in Linguistic Thought: The Western Tradition from Socrates to Saussure* (London: Routledge, 1989), 3.

89. Avery F. Gordon, *Ghostly Matters: Haunting and the Sociological Imagination* (Minneapolis: University of Minnesota Press, 2008), 5–8.

90. The background philosophical context on which this claim depends is known broadly as "standpoint theory," originating in both feminist and Black thought.

91. Williams, *Sisters in the Wilderness*, 3ff. Tonstad is ambivalent about such identifications. See Tonstad, *Queer Theology*, 24.

92. Spillers, "Moving on Down the Line," 225.

93. Denys Turner, *The Darkness of God: Negativity in Christian Mysticism* (Cambridge: Cambridge University Press, 1998), 253.

94. John Berger, "To Take Paper, to Draw," in *Landscapes: John Berger on Art* (London: Verso, 2016), 25–26.

INDEX

abolitionism (abolitionist): abolition-
democracy, 157, 174; and the archive,
197-98; Augustine not a, 25, 69; Black,
11, 78; and Black radical thought, 57;
and Christian ethics, 108; contemporary,
11, 158; and patience, 154; prison, 155, 174;
Roman, 28; time, 120-24

Abraham, 29

absence, 13, 20-22, 49-50, 69, 81, 88, 109-10,
124-25, 128-29, 158, 175, 183, 198-205

Adam, 5, 98, 100, 102, 111-14, 133-36, 150.
See also naming, Adamic

Africa (Africans), 17, 64, 110, 114, 145, 160,
170; North Africa, 170

Agee, James, 12-13, 115

agency (agent): Augustinian conceptions of,
122-23; and capitalism, 65-66; divine,
123; of the enslaved, 25, 44, 57, 59,
62-63, 75, 77; and failure, 195; human,
123, 140, 147; and mastery, 49, 64, 161,
195; moral, 19, 41-46, 51, 57, 108; political, 45; and slavery, 11

Allen, Danielle, 166

Alypius, 160

ambivalence: and Augustine, 1, 120; in
Augustinian studies, 62, 107; of human
moral communities, 178, 184; and mastery, 5, 19, 115, 123, 139-40, 157, 195;
and the modern, 197; and pilgrimage, 55,
57, 64, 80; preservation of, 49-52; and
slavery, 13; and time, 139-48

Ambrose, 95, 100

anachronism, 19, 22-23, 32-33, 49, 57, 65,
70-71, 91, 96, 168

angels, 29, 100, 126, 178

anguish, 1, 146, 193-94, 197, 201

Aquinas, Thomas (Thomist), 32, 53, 97, 180,
187, 195

archive, 34-35, 67, 78-79, 92, 107, 197-99

Arendt, Hannah, 58, 68, 81

Aristotle, 183; Aristotelianism, 187

ascent, 94-100, 103-4, 118, 135, 174

Asian Americans, 187

Aubert, Jean-Jacques, 168-69

audible, 125-28, 133

Augustine of Hippo: Divjak letters, 170;
Dolbeau sermons, 87; as ghost, 120,
146-47; historical, 48-49, 57; Mather's
dream as Augustinian dream, 110; and
middle distance, 53-57, 61-62, 79, 84,
111; and the needs of our age, 48, 51, 161;
not absolved for views on slavery, 2-3; oil
press image, 157; organizing structure of
thought, 33, 37; pessimism, 47, 49, 55,
68-71, 123; psychology, 123, 125, 165;
wretchedness, 44

authority: ecclesial, 56; and the Enlightenment, 195-96; of God 105; and humility,
88, 98, 100, 104-5, 114; legitimacy
of, 186; over other humans, 67-68, 73;
political, 30, 122, 125; and punishment,
29; and slavery, 137, 143; of texts, 24,
32, 56

Ayres, Lewis, 10, 84, 95, 169

Baker, Houston, 165

Baldwin, James, 195

baptism, 11, 79, 82, 86, 159-60, 168

Barnes, Michael, 42

Beard, Mary, 131

Black feminist theology, 34-35, 72, 116,
155, 169

Black Lives Matter, 11, 18-19, 34, 81, 115-18,
174

Black radicalism, 14, 43-44, 57, 77, 91,
161, 187

Index

bodies: and crucifixion, 168–72; and earth, 114–15; as ecological sacrifice zone, 155; enslaved body as body politic, 30; enslaved body made to speak the master's truth, 34–35, 73–75, 156, 175, 193; figurative, 74; and fugitivity, 9; and humility, 85; imagined body of the enslaved, 132; and knowledge of the creature, 178; and meaning, 166–67; and obedience, 102; as property, 23, 35, 65–66, 87; and punishment, 135; racialized, 24, 116, 155; and resurrection, 149–50; spiritual, 150, 156; submission to soul, 58–59, 136, 156; as surrogate, 151–55; "this is my body," 172; and tradition, 188; and women's bodies, 146, 149

Boniface, 30

Borges, Jorge Luis, 192

Boulding, Maria, 4

Brand, Dione, 152

Brown, Bill, 75

Brown, Peter, 16–18, 28, 34, 50–51, 54–55, 64, 84, 156

Brown, Vincent, 8, 35

Bruegel, Pieter, 203

Bruno, Michael J.S., 147

Buckland, W. W., 60

Caliban, 191–92, 195–97

capitalism, 21, 65, 76, 161, 177, 183

Caribbean, 82, 109, 159, 190, 196

Carter, J. Kameron, 46

Cervenak, Sarah Jane, 46

Césaire, Aimé, 75, 192

Chadwick, Henry, 4, 42

Chandler, Nahum, 173

Chicanos, 187

Christology: of Augustine, 27, 33, 36, 71, 85, 87, 93–96, 103, 118; Black, 11–12; slave Christology, 36, 85, 93–97, 100–104, 119

Chrysostom, John, 101

Cicero, 92, 131, 181

citizenship (citizens): in the afterlife of slavery, 19; in Augustinian thought, 3, 18, 61; and Black intellectual traditions, 77; Christian, 9, 26, 41–44, 52, 86, 88, 171; democratic, 2, 18, 36, 55, 157, 162; and the household, 28; and humility, 92; noncitizens (*peregrini*), 168–69; and obedience, 58; and pilgrimage, 46, 63, 79, 81; and pluralism, 84, 90–91; sovereign, 26, 90; virtue ethics, 54–57, 64

Clair, Joseph, 18, 47, 53, 55

climate, 18, 174

Cochrane, Charles Norris, 88

Coleman, K. M., 166

colonialism, 3, 21–24, 43, 45, 77, 81, 144, 147, 183–87, 190–97

colonization, 32, 64, 147, 190–93

Cone, James, 10–11, 16, 61–62, 80, 114, 119, 164, 174, 202

Connolly, William, 92

conservatism, 85, 123, 156, 185

Cooper, Julia E., 88

Copeland, M. Shawn, 174

Corcoran, Gervase, 123, 134–38

cosmology, 96, 98, 105–6, 119, 123, 135, 154

Council of Chalcedon, 94

Council of Nicea, 95

COVID-19, 115–16

Crawley, Ashon, 79

creation (creatures): and dominance, 39; dusk as doctrine of, 7; *ex nihilo*, 121, 126; God as creator, 29, 31, 94; God as master of creation, 97–100, 103, 105, 142; "good" or "evil" creation, 123, 126, 130–31, 135, 155; humans created free, 32; and intimacy, 94; and knowledge, 189–91; natural or unnatural, 122; and punishment, 136–37; rational/irrational, 119, 131; re-creation, 192–94, 205; and restlessness, 165–66, 173; and seeing, 133; and time, 147, 153, 173; twilight of the creature, 178–81, 184, 188–89, 196; *visibilia* of, 203

crucifixion (the Cross), 118–19, 166–74, 202

curses, 141, 190–91

Index

darkness visible (metaphor), 125, 128-33
Davies, Carole Boyce, 175, 196
Davis, Angela Y., 11, 79, 157-58
Davis, David Brion, 75
De Wet, Christopher L., 96-97
death: of Christ, 172; as "elemental realm," 8, 35; living death, 133-37; and mastery, 46, 176; and obedience, 102, 118; power of life and death, 143-44; preferred to slavery, 30; as silence, 4; slave as sign of living death, 128-29; social death, 163; and surrogacy, 154-55, 160
democracy: abolitionist-democratic, 124, 157, 174; and the Black radical tradition, 77; carceral state a threat to, 11; crisis, 2-3, 18; and ethics, 8; liberal, 18, 53-54, 106, 162; and mastery, 195; and pluralism, 90-91; and theology, 10, 176; and tradition, 180, 182; translation of Augustine to, 19, 26, 28, 36, 48, 55, 57, 61, 86, 115
dimension (defined), 49-51
disability, 179
disavowal, 12, 19-27, 33, 37, 43, 56, 64, 76, 88-89, 161, 165, 184
disobedience. *See* obedience, disobedience
Dodaro, Robert, 92-93
domination: and Black theology, 176; colonialist, 43; and crucifixion, 171; damage inflicted by, 205; and fallenness, 122; *libido dominandi*, 30, 58, 66, 86, 88, 104-6, 146, 155; and God, 39, 103; and the household, 100; and humility, 107, 162; imperial, 82; and mastery, 34-35, 73, 167, 195, 201-3; and peace, 59; and pilgrimage, 62; and punishment, 63; and race, 111, 116-17, 141, 164; Roman ethics of domination, 84-88, 111, 141-42, 163; and slavery's sinful nature, 11, 158; and time, 148
domus. See household (Roman)
Donatists, 29-30, 50
Douglass, Frederick, 9, 43
Du Bois, W. E. B., 10, 13, 21, 76, 114, 157
Dyson, R.W., 85

ecclesiology, 56, 66, 101
ecology, 7, 82, 115, 147, 155, 176
elation, 192-94, 201
Ellis, Clifton, 6
Elm, Susanna, 30, 170
empathy, 25, 116, 170
empire (imperial), 30, 53, 63-64, 81-82, 85, 90, 145-46, 155, 166-67, 170, 172, 183-84, 190-93
epistemology, 24, 87, 90, 161, 163, 185-87
eschatology, 33, 47, 96, 117, 124, 147-53, 156, 193
eternality (eternal), 47, 49, 51, 53, 64, 71, 103, 154, 178
ethics: in the afterlife of slavery, 76; in Augustinian studies, 21, 25, 33, 51, 69, 140, 183; Black, 87-88, 116-17; and crucifixion, 168-70; of democratic citizenship, 2, 19-20, 28, 115, 161; and ecclesiology, 101; ecological, 7; ethics of slavery do not exist, 2, 8; and fugitivity, 61-63, 78-79; and humility, 88, 92-93, 108, 111; of longing, 8; and mastery, 26, 33, 38, 43, 57, 64-65, 71, 113; and naming, 195; and pilgrimage, 45-46, 51; and providence, 138; and race, 14, 20, 164; Roman, 86; and secularism, 122; and time, 1, 121, 146-50, 153, 158; virtue ethics, 48, 53-56
ethnicity (ethnic), 20, 45, 184
Eucharist, the, 11, 101, 160, 173-74
eunuch, 202
Europe (European), 24, 32, 64, 89, 183, 187, 194
Evans, Walker, 12
Eve, 100, 111-14, 133, 135, 150
evil: avoidance of, 50; and bodies, 150; causality, 125, 129-34, 141; completeness, 129, 133; complexity, 129-33; as internal exteriority, 129-32; and Plato, 74; and politics, 158; *privatio*, 5, 123-28, 134, 136, 138; and slavery, 29, 34-37, 44-45, 101, 104
exegesis, 10, 84, 95, 166, 189-90
exodus, 42, 80, 82

Index

fallenness, 5, 11, 32, 68, 94, 96, 122, 124, 137, 144, 148

Fanon, Frantz, 192

fantasy, 45, 72, 76, 78–79, 114, 118, 152, 176, 192, 201

feminism, 187, 196. *See also* Black feminist theology

Figgis, J. N., 69–70

Florentinus, 31, 143

Floyd, George, 115–16

forgetting, 10, 21–24, 120

Foucault, Michel, 78, 89, 196

Fox, Robin Lane, 25

fugitivity (fugitive): as Augustinian metaphor, 28–29, 42–45; and "bad" slaves, 36, 44–45, 72–75; in Black thought, 6, 9–10, 14–15, 77, 123, 164, 174, 201; and crucifixion, 168; and disorder, 56–66; and dusk, 25; *fugitivis desertoribus*, 42–43; and mastery, 163, 171, 175, 194; in Mather's dream, 110, 114; and naming, 199; negative associations with, 44, 82; and pilgrimage, 12, 46–49, 55, 60–67, 205; positive associations with, 44, 82; possibilities in the afterlife of slavery, 78–82; and punishment, 118; as rottenness, 1, 4–5, 29; and sundown, 7; and time, 157; unthinkable nature of, 115

Gaius, 143

Garner, Eric, 116

Garnsey, Peter, 31, 60

gender, 13, 27–28, 149, 151, 156, 168, 177, 179, 200, 202

genocide, 45

Gentili, Alberico, 32

ghetto, 14, 64

Gilmore, Ruth Wilson, 155, 158

Gilroy, Paul, 20–21

Ginsburg, Rebecca, 6

Glancy, Jennifer, 85, 170

global warming, 18

Gordon, Avery, 201

Greece (Greek) *or* Hellenism, 96, 137, 143, 158, 191

Gregory, Eric, 18, 25, 47–55, 69, 91–92, 106, 161

Griffiths, Paul, 5, 62, 121, 128, 148–49

Grimes, Katie, 11, 173

Grotius, Hugo, 142

Gutiérrez, Gustavo, 147

Hagar, 29, 202

Haitian, 81, 158, 192

Hammerstaedt, Jürgen, 171

Harley, Felicity, 168

Harper, Kyle, 17, 60, 69–70, 101

Hart, David Bentley, 68

Hartman, Saidiya, 1, 9, 12–14, 17, 20, 34–35, 41, 46, 62, 72, 79, 116, 164, 190

Hebrew, 4, 171

Hegel, G. W. F., 27, 97, 151, 179

Herdt, Jennifer, 115–17

Hick, John, 125

Hilary of Poitiers, 95, 100

Hobbes, Thomas, 143

Homoians, 95

homophobia, 179–80

hope, 26, 33–34, 82, 86, 90, 107, 110–11, 123, 165–66, 174, 205

Hopkins, Dwight N., 6–8, 13

Hopkins, John Henry, 66–67, 70, 78, 144

household (Roman): *servus*, 10, 27, 31, 60, 87, 97, 99, 102, 135, 143–46; three-layered hierarchy, 87, 96–101, 105, 119; two figures of the Roman household, 10. *See also* master's house, the

humanism, 40, 68–70, 88, 195

humiliation, 110, 114, 166, 169

humility: of Christ, 82, 102–6; in contemporary Augustinian political thought, 87–88; as defense of Augustine himself, 91–93; as elemental realm, 35; of enslaved peoples, 37, 85–86, 109; and the form of the slave, 84–87; as goodness, 36; *humilis*, 83, 87; and lowliness, 99; and masters/mastery, 10, 86, 112–15,

138; and the master's house, 96–100, 135, 162; and Mather's dream, 107–10; Nietzschean critique of, 85; and obedience, 101–2, 170–71; and pilgrimage, 71, 164; and pluralism, 90–91; politics of, 85, 94; and secular pride, 88–89, 97, 99; and slave Christology, 93–94; as surest base of mastery, 104; as virtue, 10, 122, 139–40; and vulnerability, 111–19

icon (iconic), 42–44, 55, 59–60, 63, 80–82, 107, 198
immigration, 18, 41–42, 64, 182, 192
incarceration, 3, 18, 89, 103
Indigenous (Native Americans) 45, 174, 187
innocence, 98, 192
intimacy: and crucifixion, 168; ecological, 115; between enslaver and enslaved (the master's house), 27, 79, 107, 131–34; of Eucharist and baptism, 160; monstrous, 117, 152; in personage of Jesus Christ, 94–96, 102–4, 119, 174, 178; and pilgrimage, 41, 50–51; of sin and slavery, 124–25, 129, 140; social, 110; and surrogacy, 151; and time, 121
Irish, 181–82, 185–86
Israel, 42, 80, 82, 94, 172, 204

James, C. L. R., 14, 21, 39, 187
Jennings, Willie James, 36, 43, 45, 101, 184–85, 188–92
Jerusalem, 42
Jesus Christ: body of Christ, 110; in Cotton Mather's dream, 108–11; as criminal, 119, 174, 202; of the enslaver, 76, 78; equal with Father, 96, 100–105; and fugitivity, 79–80; God revealed through, 125; humilitas, 10, 33, 55, 82–87, 92–93, 115, 162; and household order, 100–106; Incarnation, 10, 84, 92–96, 100, 163–66; and metaphors of slavery, 28, 67, 71–72, 145, 174; obedience to the Father, 82, 94–96, 102, 105, 118; as slave, 36, 93–95, 163–64, 174; as Son

of the Master, 10, 94–95; as Son of the Paterfamilias, 105; subjunctive Christ, 72–80, 115; "this is my body," 172; in the tomb, 204–5; two natures, 94–96. See also Christology; crucifixion (the Cross)
Jews (Jewish), 56, 102, 159
Johnson, Kristin Deede, 52
Joshel, Sandra, 35, 169–70
justice, 3, 13, 20, 31–32, 90, 136, 141, 148, 158, 174, 184; injustice, 13, 19, 173, 177

Kant, Immanuel, 179
Kelley, Robin D. G., 46, 79
Kennedy, Rick, 107
Kincaid, Jamaica, 13
King, Lethabo, 116
King, Martin Luther Jr., 147
kinship, 146, 182, 186
Kotzé, Annemaré, 42

landscape, 6–7, 45, 187, 203
Latin, 1, 5, 7, 16, 93, 133, 142–43, 181
Lavan, Myles, 169
law (legal): of God, 114; illegal seizure, 98, 100; inheritance, 27–28; manumission, 110; power of, 13; and pride, 135; property, 21, 23, 72; and race, 57; Roman, 31, 60–62, 65–68, 101, 143–46, 170; and slavery, 31, 66, 70, 72, 75, 133, 169–70, 200; voting, 18; of war, 142
Leo (Pope), 100
Levering, Matthew, 42
LGBTQ+ individuals, 167, 187, 192, 202
liberal modernity, 88, 186
liberalism, 3, 51–52, 86–91
liberals, 53, 91, 117
liberationist, 19–20, 39, 150, 154, 156, 161
lighting, 177–78, 196
liturgy, 12, 166, 197, 204–5
Locke, John, 143
Long, Charles H., 80, 167, 173, 187

Index

Lorde, Audre, 24, 178, 191–92
Lubac, Henri de, 147

Macfarlane, Robert, 115
MacIntyre, Alasdair, 53, 179–87, 191, 197, 200
Mackey, Nathaniel, 200
Markus, Robert (R. A.), 47, 52–55, 58–59, 137, 144
marriage, 29–30; husbands, 26, 29, 58; wives, 26, 29, 58
Martinique, 192
martyrs, 138, 159
master's house, the: Augustine's slave metaphors, 26–33, 36, 77–80, 163; and Augustinian studies, 16–26, 48, 55–56; confrontations with, 78; and cosmology, 106, 154–55; defined, 38, 162; and gratitude, 103; and the household of God, 107–9; and humility, 93, 110–13; and obedience, 103–4, 110–11, 157; and order, 37, 56–66, 108, 111, 117, 154–55; and orders of slavery, 102; peace's centrality to, 45, 71–73, 131–32; and pilgrim/fugitive dichotomy, 46; and politics, 70; and providence, 123–29, 134–35. See also household (Roman)
mastery: and agency, 49, 64, 161, 195; and ambivalence, 5, 19, 115, 123, 139–40, 157, 195; and Christian violence, 113–14, 152–53, 157, 185, 193; enslaved body made to speak the master's truth, 34–35, 73–75, 156, 175, 193; libido dominandi, 30, 58, 66, 86, 88, 104–6, 146, 155; as parasitism, 151–53, 156, 160, 163; and pilgrimage, 65, 67, 71, 78–82, 146, 154, 162; Roman ethics of, 84–88, 111, 141–42, 163; and secularism, 155; standpoint of the master, 3, 9, 67, 115; and surrogacy, 34, 151–57, 160; and whiteness, 17, 108, 114–17
Mather, Cotton, 10, 106–10, 114
Mathewes, Charles, 26, 50, 62, 90, 127, 138–41
Mediterranean, 64, 160, 168

Miles, Margaret R., 149–50
Monica, 29
moral-symbolic contrast, 9, 36–37, 44
Morrison, Toni, 15, 20–23, 26, 34–35, 91, 116, 161

names (naming): Adamic naming, 189–96, 199–200; and Black thought, 201; as categorization of the slave, 68, 122; of evil, 125, 127; Irish example, 181–82, 185–86; of Jesus, 204–5; and language, 177–78, 181–82, 185–86; made new, 196–97; of mastery, 195; misnaming, 197–203; overnamed, 199, 202
Native Americans. See Indigenous (Native Americans)
neighbors, 26, 47, 53, 69, 88
Neruda, Pablo, 192
Nicholas of Cusa, 180
nouns, 50, 118, 126, 193, 197, 200–3
Nyquist, Mary, 143

Obama, Barack, 45
obedience, 10, 36–37, 45, 58–61, 82, 84, 94, 98–106, 109–10, 115, 118, 132, 136, 157, 170–74; disobedience, 9, 36, 44–45, 59–60, 82, 98, 102–5, 110, 118, 132, 163, 172
O'Donovan, Oliver, 20–26, 30, 55, 89
Onesimus, 107–11
ontology, 75, 95, 129
Origen of Alexandria, 180

Panzer text. See Philippians, as Panzer text
Passover, 159, 172
patience, 11, 29, 85, 123, 147–49, 154–57, 190; impatience, 148–49, 153, 155, 157, 193–94
Patterson, Orlando, 46, 87, 99, 108–9, 151, 153, 160, 163, 173
Pelikan, Jaroslav, 93
Pennington, James W. C., 75–76, 162
peregrinatio: and ambivalence, 148; and fugitivity, 64; as image system, 50; peregrinus, 41, 43, 50–51, 55, 63–64; racialization

of, 62; relation of Christians to political order, 64; and restlessness, 165; three coordinates, 9, 41–58, 63, 84, 107, 162, 176. *See also* pilgrimage (pilgrim)

Peter (apostle), 159

Pettit, Philip, 81

Philip, NourbeSe M., 66

Philippians, as Panzer text, 10, 84–87, 100, 102, 169

piety, 10, 18, 106–7, 110

pilgrimage (pilgrim): Augustine and, 33, 36, 41–45, 56–59, 73, 122, 164; and Christian citizenship, 9–10; and exile, 9, 41, 43, 47, 50–51; and fugitivity, 9–12, 48–51, 62–64, 82, 168, 205; and mastery, 65, 67, 71, 78–82, 146, 154, 162; and pluralism, 51–53, 58, 86; *totus Christus*, 71, 103. See also *peregrinatio*

Plantinga, Alvin, 125

Plato (Platonism), 42, 74, 78, 83, 96, 165, 178–79: Neoplatonism, 83, 125–26, 137

Pliny the Elder, 151–52

Plotinus, 42, 125, 135

pluralism (plurality): earthly peace in, 48, 52–55, 86; and humility, 88–91; in modernity, 43, 45, 86, 88, 182–84; and pilgrimage, 64; and race, 3, 20, 161, 184, 187; religious, 183; and slavery, 84

Porphyry, 125

pride: Christ does not want to make you proud, 71, 85, 103; and defenses of Augustine, 91–93; and dis/obedience, 105–6; and evil, 130; and the fall, 98–102, 135; and the fugitive, 28, 171; humbling of, 99; and mastery, 83, 86; and modern liberalism, 86–88; and patience, 156; and pilgrimage, 71, 103; and punishment, 135; secular, 88–91; and wealth, 111–12

prison (prisoner), 4, 14, 64, 89, 128, 155, 174, 178

property, 8, 14–15, 35, 65–66, 72, 75, 97, 146, 162, 170, 185, 200; legal, 21, 23

Prospero, 191–92, 195–97

providence: and the Christian master, 138–46; and divine sovereignty, 119, 123–24; sin and the master's house, 124–25; and time, 19, 137–47

public square, 2–3, 6, 49, 90

punishment, 29–32, 36, 59–64, 70, 89, 98–99, 118, 131–37, 142, 166–69; *fugax*, 60–63

Quintilian, 166

race (racial): and the afterlife of slavery, 13–14, 28, 38, 48, 71, 76, 85; and Augustinian Studies, 2, 9, 23, 49, 57; and Augustinian thought, 22, 35, 38–39, 61, 64, 176; and the carceral state, 11; categories of oppression, 179; and the Christian master, 15, 20, 155, 164; and COVID-19, 116; and crises of democracy, 18; domination, 111, 141; hierarchies, 3, 118; and humility, 10; and inequality, 57; and modernity, 3, 20, 44–45, 87–88, 107, 115, 161, 165, 174, 186, 197, 200; of *peregrinatio*, 62; and pluralism, 183–84; postracialism, 45; racial capitalism, 64–65, 76, 161, 183; racial slavery, 20–26, 33, 37, 117–18; racism, 18, 116, 155–56, 179–80; rejection of, 89; and religious ethics, 20; as symbol, 156, 173; "Traditions of Race Men," 188, 191; violence, 3, 19, 147

Ramelli, Ilaria L. E., 56

Rankin, John, 116

Ransby, Barbara, 81

Rawls, John, 68, 91

restlessness, 1, 28, 79, 105, 165–67, 173–74

resurrection, 149–52, 156, 204

rich man, parable of, 111–13

Rist, John, 11, 122–23, 148, 153, 158

Roberts, Neil, 9, 21, 23, 61, 81, 113, 157, 164

Robinson, Cedric, 14, 76–77, 187

Roman Catholicism, 100, 113–14, 185

Index

Rome (Roman): Augustinian critiques of, 58, 106; best citizens of, 92; Christian challenges to slavery, 71; and crucifixion, 166–72; and domination (ethics of mastery), 84–88, 111, 141–42, 163; household, 10, 16–17, 79, 99, 105, 119; jurisprudence, 60, 101, 143–46, 170; and language, 181; and public service, 92; road metaphor, 82; and "saving" enslaved people, 145; and slavery, 17–18, 27–28, 34–35, 56, 69, 96, 131, 169, 198

Rousseau, Jean-Jacques, 81

Ruddy, Deborah Wallace, 90

Ruden, Sarah, 16–18, 28, 34

sacramental optimism, 11, 173

Saint Lucia, 192

Sandoval, Alonso de, 113–14

Sarah, 29

Satan, 100–101

savage (concept), 167, 183

Schlabach, Gerald W., 90

Scott, David, 10, 120–21, 139, 146, 158, 196

Seabury, Samuel, 144–45

secularism (secular): Augustinian, 3, 52; ethical life in, 122; liberalism, 53–54, 87–88; limits of term, 164; and mastery, 155; and pilgrimage, 43, 45, 47; and pluralism, 182–83; Western, 195. *See also* pride: secular

segregation, 14, 77, 184

servants, 67, 108–10, 144

sex, 1, 8, 23, 27, 35, 76, 150–51, 168, 179–80, 200

sexism, 179–80

shame, 12–13, 23, 114, 168–69

Sharpe, Christina, 151–52

Shils, Edward, 180

Shklar, Judith, 91

silence: of the archive, 7, 28, 78, 92, 107; of bodies, 167, 170; of Christ, 76; death as, 4; and nonbeing, 20, 128–29, 133–34; silences on slavery, 20, 23, 25, 28, 123, 146, 192

sin: Augustine on, 5, 27, 84, 125; elemental realms, 35; of enslavers, 25, 156; and the fall, 101–2; and fugitivity, 72, 163; in the heavenly city, 121–23; and humility or pride, 98–99, 107, 171; and peace, 53; and providence, 124–25; and punishment, 29–34, 135; and slavery caused by sin, 123, 131–38, 145, 158, 170. *See also* evil: *privatio*

slavery (enslaved people): afterlives of, 19–21, 26, 28, 33, 37, 39, 45, 48, 57, 61, 67, 71, 76–85, 111, 118, 141, 157, 161–64, 171–76, 185, 191, 197, 201; American, 17, 57, 66, 75, 144; Atlantic, 2, 45, 75, 89, 108, 143, 145, 171, 183; auction block, 2–3, 66; "bad" slaves, 29, 31, 36–37, 45, 55, 60–61, 67, 71, 74, 80, 84, 101–35 112, 137, 145, 155; and the "break," 5, 8, 113, 174, 199; and Canaan's curse, 141; chattel, 66, 68, 72–77, 113, 131, 143, 162, 198, 200; collar, 60, 198–99; and disgust, 17–18; "ethics" of, 2, 8; and etymology, 133, 142–46; figurative, 35–36, 74–75, 96, 109, 162; as fringe, 21–24; fungibility of slave figure, 35, 116, 134, 156, 163, 169; "good" slave, 36–37, 45, 61, 67, 71–74, 80, 101–6, 145; legitimation of, 140, 145; literal, 27–30, 55, 70, 82, 96, 108, 138, 162; literary, 34, 101, 169; marronage, 43, 47, 81–82, 113, 157; metaphorical, 5, 9, 19, 26–39, 55, 67, 73, 82, 84, 96, 102, 108, 131, 164, 169–71, 201; Middle Passage, 13, 64, 89, 82, 159–60; modern, 22, 28, 61; modern life begins with, 21–26, 91, 141, 161–62; as moral dilemma, 25–26; moral dynamics in the present, 9, 28, 35, 39, 61; in the New World, 17–18, 23, 28, 32, 37, 61, 81, 124, 172–73, 192–94; and Ole Marse, 7, 104; and personhood, 76, 109, 195; plantation, 3, 6–7, 13–14, 17, 23, 28, 64, 81, 89, 109, 115, 145; revolt, 37, 73–74, 80, 115, 147; *servus vicarius*, 87, 97, 99, 135; as sign of living death,

Index

128–29; slave Christology, 36, 85, 87, 93–97, 100–104, 119; slaveholder ideology, 33, 35, 92, 139; slave morality, 85, 104; as social institution, 22, 27, 30, 67, 84; social order of, 29, 93, 100, 102, 117, 139, 165, 187, 199, 201; society, 2, 35, 57, 61, 65, 67, 73, 75–76, 99, 164, 168, 171; and the structure of reality, 134–35; subservience, 104, 153; as surrogate, 34, 151–57, 160; symbolic form, 10, 87, 167; symbolic order of, 93, 96, 102, 172; *vilicus*, 97, 106

Slavic peoples, 160

Smith, James K. A., 17–19, 23–24

souls, 28, 30, 54, 58–59, 74–75, 105, 114, 130–32, 135–35, 153–54, 165

sovereignty, 26, 59, 66, 81–82, 90, 106–9, 113, 119, 154

Spillers, Hortense, 34–35, 46, 72, 75, 116, 146, 155, 200–202

Stewart-Kroeker, Sarah, 42, 50, 63, 82

Stoicism, 30, 170

Stout, Jeffrey, 176, 179–84

Stuckey, Elma, 7

Surin, Ken, 125

Swinburne, Richard, 125

Taylor, Charles, 53

tenebrae, 12, 38, 204–5

Teubner, Jonathan, 178–85

Thurmond, D. L., 198

time: abolition's time, 10–11, 120–24; Augustinian knowledge of, 83, 90, 146; and the ethics of temporality, 146–56; "fictive" model of, 10–11, 120–21, 139; future, 10, 120, 150, 154,1 56, 167, 174; and history, 138–45; *in hoc saeculo*: 11, 121, 123; and mastery, 8; *saeculum*, 11, 31, 47–50, 56, 119, 121, 124–25, 134, 137–38, 144, 147–48, 154–57, 162, 164, 193; theological claims regarding, 165–66; time-boundedness, 90, 147–50, 178–79, 182, 186, 205; against totalization, 48–51; of transformation, 196–97

Tonstad, Linn, 94, 177, 202

tradition: Black radical, 14, 43–44, 161; *mutatis mutandis*, 19, 26, 81; traditionalist, 19–20, 39, 150, 161, 176, 179, 188, 205

transgender people, 202

translation: of *The City of God*, 143; of *Confessions*, 4–5; democratic translation, 26, 28, 36, 39, 48, 53–57, 61, 67, 81, 86, 92, 115; and naming, 161, 201; of *peregrinatio*, 41–42; Ruden, 16–19

traumas, 76, 78

Trinity, 178; *On the Trinity*, 10, 36, 54, 83–84, 87, 93–97, 100, 134

troubles, 184–85, 190–91

Trump, Donald, 2, 18, 45

Tubman, Harriet, 9, 43

Turner, Denys, 203

twilight: Augustinian, 186–88; of the creature, 178–81, 184–85; crepuscular, 178; dog and wolf expression, 7; and embeddedness, 205; and fracture, 6; ghosts at, 201; of language, 182, 196–97; of the modern, 189–94; sensibility of ambiguity, 140, 193–96; and slavery, 8; as symbol, 177; and theological method, 12; and verbing, 199, 203

Underground Railroad, 9, 43

utopia, 49, 52, 118, 148–49, 155, 158, 192–94

Valerius Maximus, 169

verbs (verbness), 7, 50, 118, 126, 197, 200–203

violence: and 1968 uprisings, 147; and Black thought, 12–14; and Christian mastery, 113–14, 152–53, 157, 185, 193; and crucifixion, 166, 172; and eschatology, 148; misnaming, 197; nonviolence, 118; and pride, 156; and race, 2–3, 19, 183; sexual, 151; state, 26, 64, 117–18; structural, 121, 141; and theology, 202; whiteness as, 12. *See also* punishment

virtue ethics, 48, 53–56

Vitoria, Francisco de, 32

Index

Vives, Juan Luis, 143–44
vulnerability, 29, 87, 111, 116–17, 120, 131, 150–56; invulnerability, 150–56, 193–94

waiting, 43, 110, 112, 123, 166–67, 191, 197, 202, 204
Walcott, Derek, 159, 190–97
Walzer, Michael, 53
Weheliye, Alexander, 19, 173
Weitham, Paul, 91
West, the (Western): Black Studies as critique of, 14; and citizenship, 43; and colonialism, 184, 200; in current age, 45; and humility, 88–89; and liberal democracy, 54; and modernity, 91, 176–77, 187–90; and secularism, 195; signs within, 173; and slave Christology, 93–94; slavery and western Christian philosophy and theology, 3, 11, 18, 21, 68–69, 164
Wetzel, James, 36–37, 47, 125, 128, 132, 178

white (whiteness): of Augustine's readership, 24, 80, 116; author's positionality, 14–15, 195; churches, 12, 14; enslaver (master), 17, 108, 114–17; as moral frame, 185; nationalism, 3; of *peregrinatio*, 62; and police, 89, 116; and power, 78, 118, 171; reformer, 13; supremacy, 3; as violence, 12
Whitefield, George, 145
Whitman, Walt, 192
Wilberforce, William, 116
Williams, Delores, 151, 164, 202
Williams, Rowan, 25, 31, 58–59, 79, 106, 124, 126, 165–66, 173
Winner, Lauren, 11
womanism, 11, 34, 72
women, 4, 11–12, 29, 89, 104, 141, 146, 167, 189, 191–92, 200, 202; figure of "the woman," 4, 189, 202
Wynter, Sylvia, 187, 190, 200

xenophobia, 179